MS0408
EVENT CODE
$ 14.50
PRICE
0C1-35
G.A. GEN ADM
SECTION/AISLE ROW/BOX SEAT
ADMISSION ONE
14.50
ADMISSION

SUNSHINE PRESENTS
OZZY OSBOURNE
MARKET SQUARE ARENA
NO CAMERAS O RECORDERS
TUE APR 8 1986 7:30 PM

GEN ADM
7APR6

CC04
A 19.50
CA 3.00
117
382 ON 73
W 22
OHL143705017
14FEB2 117

CAPITAL CENTRE
CDP
PRESENTS
AN EVENING WITH METALLI
NO OPENING ACT
WED APR 1. 1992 8PM
PORTAL 11

IV0617 GA GHT 01
EVENT CODE SECTION/BOX ROW SEAT
PRICE & ALL TAXES INCL. ADMS
CONVENIENCE CHARGE
GA
SECTION/BOX
CK 2X
GA7 61
DEL409.
21MAY98

GEN ADMISSION 20.00
ILLEGAL TO RESELL
SLAYER
DOORS AT 8:00PM
IRVING PLAZA
17 IRVING PLACE/NYC
WED JUN 17. 1998

G.A. GEN ADM A 14.50
ADMIT ONE

SUNSHINE PRESENTS
K I S S
SPECIAL GUE
MARKET

HD0706 115
EVENT CODE GATE 3
125.00
PRICE
115
SECTION/AISLE
P 21X
I 11
ROW/BOX SEAT
00M1533
A16MAY8

SUNSHINE PRESENTS
VAN HALENS'
MONSTERS OF ROCK
INDIANAPOLIS HOOSIER D
NO CAMERAS OR RBCORD
WED JUL 6 1988 1:30

APPROVED BY THE

+ special gu

Verb. Vorverka
zuzüglich örtli

min
30 min
35 min
10 min
10 min
20 min
10 min
25 min
10 min
5 min

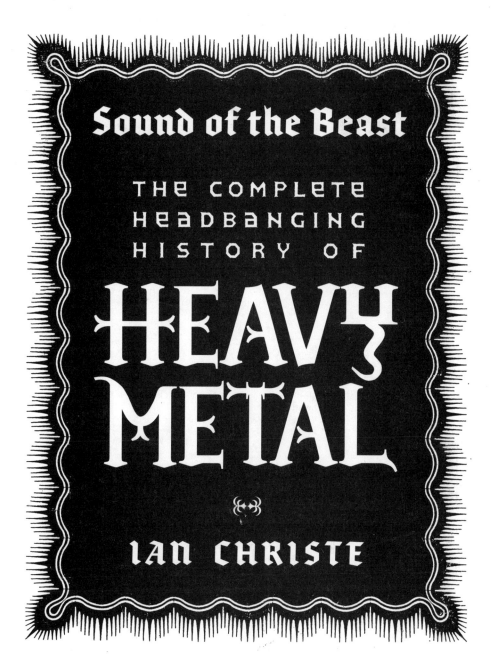

Sound of the Beast

THE COMPLETE HEADBANGING HISTORY OF

HEAVY METAL

IAN CHRISTE

HarperEntertainment

An Imprint of HarperCollins Publishers

All photographs without credits are courtesy of the author.

FIRST EDITION

Designed by Adrian Leichter

Printed on acid-free paper

Library of Congress Cataloging-in-Publication Data
Christe, Ian.
Sound of the beast: the complete headbanging history
of heavy metal / Ian Christe.—1st ed.
p. cm.
Includes index.
Discography: p.
ISBN 0-06-052362-X (hc : alk. paper)
1. Heavy metal (Music)—History and criticism. 2. Rock groups. I. Title.
ML3534.C475 2003
914.5'632047—dc21
2002068894

03 04 05 06 07 ❖/RRD 10 9 8 7 6 5 4 3 2 1

FOR THE FALLEN
AND THE FAITHFUL

❧ CONTENTS ❦

A BRIEF HEADBANGING HISTORY OF TIME

START HERE

February 13, 1970: Black Sabbath debut released

June 4, 1971: Black Sabbath goes gold in America

December 1975: Judas Priest records *Sad Wings of Destiny*

1977: First official Motörhead LP released

October 28, 1978: *Kiss Meets the Phantom of the Park* airs on NBC

December 11, 1978: Last date of Ozzy Osbourne's final tour with Black Sabbath

1980: Judas Priest's *British Steel* crowns a slew of LPs including *Iron Maiden*, Def Leppard's *On Through the Night*, Saxon's *Wheels of Steel*, and Motörhead's *Ace of Spades*

February 20, 1980: AC/DC singer Bon Scott dies

October 13, 1980: AC/DC's *Back in Black* goes platinum in U.S.

June 1981: First issue of *Kerrang!* published in London

1982: Judas Priest and Iron Maiden tour America

January 1982: Ozzy Osbourne chews the head off a bat thrown onstage in Iowa

January 1982: Venom releases *Black Metal*

March 1982: Guitarist Randy Rhoads killed in airplane crash

June 14, 1982: Metal Blade Records releases *Metal Massacre*

August 20, 1982: Elektra reissue of Mötley Crüe's *Too Fast for Love* hits *Billboard* #157

1983: David Lee Roth of Van Halen announces $1,000,000 paternity insurance policy

May 18, 1983: Judas Priest's *Screaming for Vengeance* goes platinum in U.S.

May 29, 1983: U.S. Festival '83 draws 600,000 fans for Judas Priest, Scorpions, Van Halen, and Ozzy Osbourne

April 1983: Kirk Hammett replaces Dave Mustaine as guitarist of Metallica

July 1983: Metallica releases *Kill 'Em All*

November 26, 1983: Quiet Riot's *Metal Health* hits #1 in *Billboard*

Autumn 1983: *Metal Forces* magazine launches

THE HARD ROCK DECADE: 1970s

THE NWOBHM ERA: 1978–1982

CLASSIC METAL ERA: 1983–1987

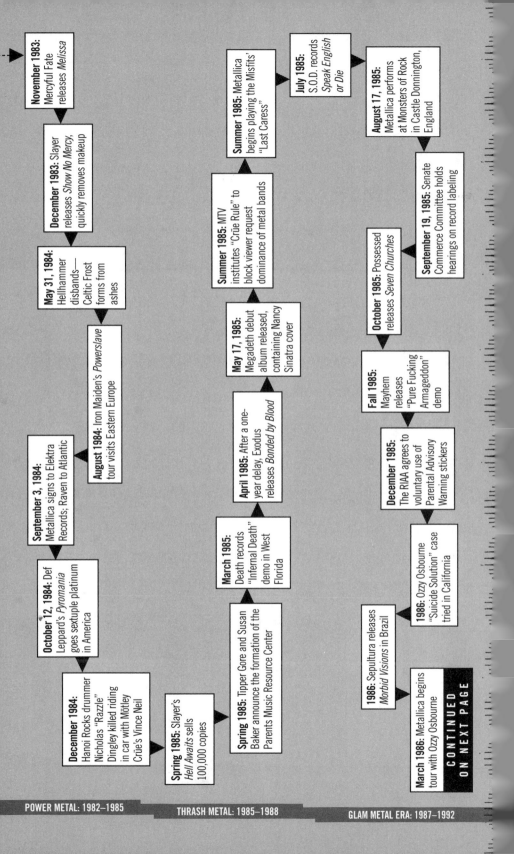

November 1983: Mercyful Fate releases *Melissa*

December 1983: Slayer releases *Show No Mercy*, quickly removes makeup

May 31, 1984: Hellhammer disbands—Celtic Frost forms from ashes

August 1984: Iron Maiden's *Powerslave* tour visits Eastern Europe

September 3, 1984: Metallica signs to Elektra Records; Raven to Atlantic

October 12, 1984: Def Leppard's *Pyromania* goes sextuple platinum in America

December 1984: Hanoi Rocks drummer Nicholas "Razzle" Dingley killed riding in car with Mötley Crüe's Vince Neil

Spring 1985: Slayer's *Hell Awaits* sells 100,000 copies

Spring 1985: Tipper Gore and Susan Baker announce the formation of the Parents Music Resource Center

March 1985: Death records "Infernal Death" demo in West Florida

April 1985: After a one-year delay, Exodus releases *Bonded by Blood*

May 17, 1985: Megadeth debut album released, containing Nancy Sinatra cover

Summer 1985: MTV institutes "Crüe Rule" to block viewer request dominance of metal bands

Summer 1985: Metallica begins playing the Misfits' "Last Caress"

July 1985: S.O.D. records *Speak English or Die*

August 17, 1985: Metallica performs at Monsters of Rock in Castle Donnington, England

September 19, 1985: Senate Commerce Committee holds hearings on record labeling

October 1985: Possessed releases *Seven Churches*

Fall 1985: Mayhem releases "Pure Fucking Armageddon" demo

December 1985: The RIAA agrees to voluntary use of Parental Advisory Warning stickers

1986: Ozzy Osbourne "Suicide Solution" case tried in California

1986: Sepultura releases *Morbid Visions* in Brazil

March 1986: Metallica begins tour with Ozzy Osbourne

CONTINUED ON NEXT PAGE

POWER METAL: 1982–1985

THRASH METAL: 1985–1988

GLAM METAL ERA: 1987–1992

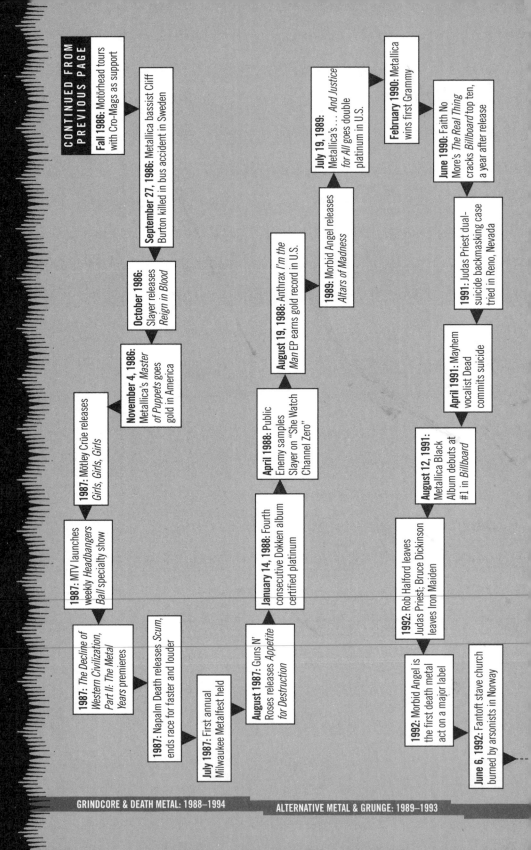

CONTINUED FROM PREVIOUS PAGE

Fall 1986: Motörhead tours with Cro-Mags as support

September 27, 1986: Metallica bassist Cliff Burton killed in bus accident in Sweden

October 1986: Slayer releases *Reign in Blood*

November 4, 1986: Metallica's *Master of Puppets* goes gold in America

1987: Mötley Crüe releases *Girls, Girls, Girls*

1987: MTV launches weekly *Headbangers Ball* specialty show

1987: *The Decline of Western Civilization, Part II: The Metal Years* premieres

1987: Napalm Death releases *Scum*, ends race for faster and louder

July 1987: First annual Milwaukee Metalfest held

August 1987: Guns N' Roses releases *Appetite for Destruction*

January 14, 1988: Fourth consecutive Dokken album certified platinum

April 1988: Public Enemy samples Slayer on "She Watch Channel Zero"

August 19, 1988: Anthrax *I'm the Man* EP earns gold record in U.S.

July 19, 1989: Metallica's *...And Justice for All* goes double platinum in U.S.

1989: Morbid Angel releases *Altars of Madness*

February 1990: Metallica wins first Grammy

June 1990: Faith No More's *The Real Thing* cracks *Billboard* top ten, a year after release

1991: Judas Priest dual-suicide backmasking case tried in Reno, Nevada

April 1991: Mayhem vocalist Dead commits suicide

August 12, 1991: Metallica Black Album debuts at #1 in *Billboard*

1992: Rob Halford leaves Judas Priest; Bruce Dickinson leaves Iron Maiden

1992: Morbid Angel is the first death metal act on a major label

June 6, 1992: Fantoft stave church burned by arsonists in Norway

GRINDCORE & DEATH METAL: 1988–1994

ALTERNATIVE METAL & GRUNGE: 1989–1993

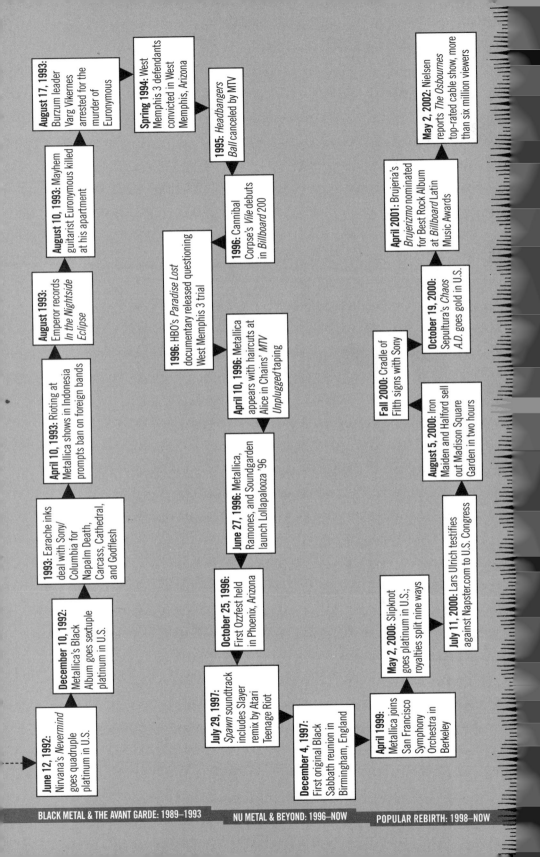

June 12, 1992: Nirvana's *Nevermind* goes quadruple platinum in U.S.

December 10, 1992: Metallica's Black Album goes sextuple platinum in U.S.

1993: Earache inks deal with Sony/Columbia for Napalm Death, Carcass, Cathedral, and Godflesh

April 10, 1993: Rioting at Metallica shows in Indonesia prompts ban on foreign bands

August 1993: Emperor records *In the Nightside Eclipse*

August 10, 1993: Mayhem guitarist Euronymous killed at his apartment

August 17, 1993: Burzum leader Varg Vikernes arrested for the murder of Euronymous

Spring 1994: West Memphis 3 defendants convicted in West Memphis, Arizona

1995: *Headbangers Ball* canceled by MTV

1996: Cannibal Corpse's *Vile* debuts in *Billboard* 200

1996: HBO's *Paradise Lost* documentary released questioning West Memphis 3 trial

April 10, 1996: Metallica appears with haircuts at Alice in Chains' *MTV Unplugged* taping

June 27, 1996: Metallica, Ramones, and Soundgarden launch Lollapalooza '96

October 25, 1996: First Ozzfest held in Phoenix, Arizona

July 29, 1997: *Spawn* soundtrack includes Slayer remix by Atari Teenage Riot

December 4, 1997: First original Black Sabbath reunion in Birmingham, England

April 1999: Metallica joins San Francisco Symphony Orchestra in Berkeley

May 2, 2000: Slipknot goes platinum in U.S.; royalties split nine ways

July 11, 2000: Lars Ulrich testifies against Napster.com to U.S. Congress

August 5, 2000: Iron Maiden and Halford sell out Madison Square Garden in two hours

Fall 2000: Cradle of Filth signs with Sony

October 19, 2000: Sepultura's *Chaos A.D.* goes gold in U.S.

April 2001: Brujeria's *Brujerizmo* nominated for Best Rock Album at *Billboard* Latin Music Awards

May 2, 2002: Nielsen reports *The Osbournes* top-rated cable show, more than six million viewers

BLACK METAL & THE AVANT GARDE: 1989–1993   NU METAL & BEYOND: 1996–NOW   POPULAR REBIRTH: 1998–NOW

Friday, February 13, 1970

In the beginning there was just a shadowy expanse of night sky and unknown. There in disquieting oblivion whirled the unanswered secrets of history, animated by forces as ancient as civilization itself—everything smoking, silvery, religious, and dark. These strong currents often lay forgotten and docile, until the opportunities of war, crisis, and anguish called forth their awful powers. They had no sound or definition of their own until trapped and subjugated by the epiphany of Black Sabbath—the wise innocents, the originators of heavy metal.

From the start Black Sabbath voiced powerful passion from beyond the perimeters of popular opinion. They were prophets bred from the downside of English society, the unemployed—people regarded as morally suspect and of negligible social worth. The four members all were born in 1948 and 1949 in Birmingham, England, a crumbling factory town surviving an age when Europe no longer prided itself on industry. Singer John Michael Osbourne, aka Ozzy, was one of six children and a convicted thief—he worked sporadically in a slaughterhouse. Guitarist Tony Iommi, the son of a candy-shop owner, was a mischievous enigma who had lopped off two right-hand fingertips in a metal-shop accident. The band's strange bassist, Terry Butler, aka Geezer, was known for an extravagant, green-colored, secondhand wardrobe. As indicated by the elegant disarray of his playing, drummer Bill Ward turned to music out of self-described frantic desperation. Coming of age in the years following World War II, the four were surrounded by the bombed-out rubble left by massive Nazi bombing raids. In the world they inherited, the only action worthwhile was to become professional misfits and adventurers.

Under the name Polka Tulk, nicked from a Birmingham rug merchant, Ozzy and company followed the path blazed by bands like the

Yardbirds, Ten Years After, and Cream, jamming endlessly and loudly on standards written by American blues artists. The mournful sound was reshaped drastically in the journey from Birmingham, Alabama, to Birmingham, England, where disarming blue notes were grotesquely warped by factory-strength amplification and the late-1960s bohemian drug scene. After switching their name to Earth, the quartet achieved greater notoriety through their blinding volume and stage show.

Then came the breakthrough—the spontaneous creation of the song "Black Sabbath." It was a pivotal new beginning for the band and fundamental to all heavy metal forever after. Here was a song based on only three tones, two of them D notes. Recounting the crisis of judgment day with fearsome suspense its narrator gasped: "What is this, that stands before me? Figure in black, which points at me. . . ." Floating on feedback drones, the dimensions of the song's horror grew and galloped into life at the climax, as doomsday ultimately consumed the unwilling protagonist. It was a grim tale worthy of Edgar Allan Poe, told through the new raven's quills of guitars, drum, and crackling microphone.

"Black Sabbath" inspired immediate awe and captivated audiences completely. The song also had an irreversible effect on the band—who in the midst of drug-tinged innocence suddenly felt their hands being drawn toward brilliance by an unseen force. Thus inspired, the ensemble soon broke free of its surroundings, departing from rock and roll to further explore the recent musical liberations of genre breakers like Miles Davis. Along with the doomy "Warning," a jam inherited from the hip blues group Aynsly Dunbar's Retaliation, "Black Sabbath" became the centerpiece of a new sound, a locus of auditory mortal dread that required the band rechristen itself Black Sabbath.

Departing from the world around him, Tony Iommi took music from the past with little concern for tradition, blazing through blues scales with his own timing and finesse. In order for him to bend guitar strings expressively without experiencing pain in his cropped fingers, the group tuned to a lower key signature. Prolonged by the timeless sustain of Iommi's masterful notes, the results brought an inspired deepness to Black Sabbath. Thus, almost by accident, from sacrifice came a devastating sound. So from his deformity came a strange beauty—and a bond to three-fingered Gypsy guitarist Django Reinhardt, one of Iommi's many unusual inspirations.

Behind Iommi's versatile guitar, Black Sabbath's rhythm section propelled its endless stream of mighty riffs with frantic breakbeats and galvanic accents. Bill Ward claimed that Black Sabbath never played "in time" but maintained unity by massive empathy—a sixth sense that encouraged the gravity of the music and drew the spectator inward. The wall of sound thus created was overpowering yet frenzied: Old films show Ward and Geezer Butler bobbing like hyperanimated marionettes in the hands of God.

Glee-stricken young ringmaster Ozzy Osbourne eased audiences into the new paradigm by clapping his hands, dancing, and nodding in charismatic contrast to the music's stony visage. Decadent and out of it, but not yet bloated or drug-addled, Ozzy pierced the heaviness behind him with his pissed-off wail. His schizophrenic vocal technique came from doubled vocals—one high and one low—spaced an octave apart. As the band tuned lower, Ozzy sang higher. Whatever rock-star swagger Ozzy possessed was swallowed by the intense purpose of the band, balanced with the too-real personal delirium of Butler's lyrics: "I tell you to enjoy life / I wish I could but it's too late."

As Black Sabbath ascended, the band trained on the same European club circuit as did the Beatles. Sabbath broke the Liverpool band's residency record at the Star Club in Hamburg, Germany, playing seven forty-five-minute spots nightly to expatriates and go-go girls in the fabled Reeperbahn red-light district. Through this grueling regimen, the quartet practiced to the brink of perfection—and became exhausted to the point of further inspiration and innovation.

Approached by Phillips Records in 1969, Sabbath recorded its landmark first album for six hundred pounds in a continuous two-day session. The tapes were mixed the next day by a studio producer who did not allow the band to interfere with his workmanship. Even given the rush job (typical recording conditions for rock bands at the time), work was completed with scant room to spare. The producer clipped an eighteen-minute guitar solo by Tony Iommi from "Warning" without consulting the band. At the urging of the record label, Sabbath cut a new version of "Evil Woman" for its first single—the song had recently been a hit for the band Crow, and the company hoped to nab a little secondhand success.

On Friday the thirteenth, February 1970, *Black Sabbath* was released by Phillips's new experimental subsidiary, Vertigo Records. The first complete heavy metal work by the first heavy metal artists, *Black Sabbath* was an addictive musical suspension of time, informed by an ominous presence that crushed the bouncy rhythms of popular rock. Along with "Black Sabbath," "Warning," and "Evil Woman," the original songs "N.I.B." and "Wicked World" floated down-tempo on immense volume and sustained feedback. Tempering the unclassifiable record, these cataclysmic events were balanced by the dreamlike tenderness of "Sleeping Village" and "Behind the Wall of Sleep."

Recalling *Children of the Damned* and other low-budget English psychological horror films, the front cover of *Black Sabbath* depicted a dilapidated English cottage overgrown with barren brush, partially obscuring the image of a pale green enchantress. The interior of the album's gatefold sleeve contained few details beyond a grim gothic poem inscribed in a giant inverted crucifix.

> *Still falls the rain, the veils of darkness shroud the*
> *blackened trees, which contorted by some unseen violence,*
> *shed their tired leaves, and bend their boughs toward a*
> *grey earth of severed bird wings. Among the grasses,*
> *poppies bleed before a gesticulating death, and young*
> *rabbits, born dead in traps, stand motionless, as though*
> *guarding the silence that surrounds and threatens to*
> *engulf all those that would listen. . . .*

Themselves strung with matching silver crosses, the members of Sabbath cultivated a creepy image—one swathed in the popular witchcraft and mysticism of the day. This won the band notoriety from self-styled Satanists and a small amount of public protest from church crusaders. Previous rock stars had enchanted pop consciousness with flowers, parades, and promises to change the world. Black Sabbath strode at the end of that procession, still preaching the need for love but warning stragglers there was no return to a naïve state of grace. While most popular contemporaries stuck to "girl bites man" territory, Sabbath sang of fatherless children and the wickedness of the world. Bill Ward later described the band's noble outsider perspective as "healthy anger."

A resonating echo from a distance of long ago, the music dramatized the conflicts of humans on earth not as current-event news stories but as mythic struggles. The entire ceremony sounded a death knell for the music known as rock and roll, which would forever after be merely the domesticated relative of heavy metal. "Black Sabbath has influenced every single band out there," says Peter Steele of Type O Negative, a band freshly inspired by Sabbath thirty years later. "They were the heaviest thing to me, and they still are. You can't get any heavier than that. I love that slow, droning, dinosaur-footsteps-through-the-woods type of sound."

Emerging like the monolith in Stanley Kubrick's *2001: A Space Odyssey,* a contemporaneous influence, Black Sabbath was as irreducible as the bottomless sea, the everlasting sky, and the mortal soul. There was no precedent—and no literal explanation of their power was needed. Their gloomy tones were a captivating siren call to a deep unsatisfied void within modern consciousness. The rumbling sludge of heavy metal was inevitable, lying in long wait to be introduced by Black Sabbath in 1970 and adored by the massive human sprawl.

Over the thirty years that followed, 100 million listeners sought refuge in the resounding cultural boom, finding a purity unmitigated by petty doubts or distractions. From Sabbath came heavy metal, which doubled in intensity and became power metal, then twisted into thrash metal. From there the music crossed paths with other forms to spawn black metal, create the unbelievable refinements of death metal, and fuse with every other sort of music, finding itself perpetually reborn. Enduring three decades of Marshall amps, guitar holocaust, and drum destruction, Black Sabbath remains the bedrock—the heavy stone slab from which all heavy metal eternally rises.

The 1970s:
Prelude to Heaviness

→ **February 13, 1970:** Black Sabbath's debut album released

→ **June 4, 1971:** *Black Sabbath* goes gold in America

→ **December 1975:** Judas Priest records *Sad Wings of Destiny*

→ **October 28, 1978:** *Kiss Meets the Phantom of the Park* airs on NBC

→ **December 11, 1978:** Last date of Ozzy Osbourne's final tour with Black Sabbath

---

Heavy metal came into being just as the previous generation's salvation, rock and roll, was in the midst of horrific disintegration. Four deaths at a free Rolling Stones concert at Altamont Raceway in December 1969 had shaken the rock community and left the youth culture disillusioned with pacifist ideals. Then, while *Black Sabbath* was marking the pop charts in April 1970, Paul McCartney effectively announced the breakup of the Beatles. Instead of comforting their audience in an uncertain world, rock giants Janis Joplin, Jimi Hendrix, and Jim Morrison all were dead of drug overdoses within a year.

Shortly after JFK, RFK, and MLK fell to the bullets of assassins, so, too, were the originators of rock and roll falling to naïve excess. Jaded and frustrated, the Love Generation that had created counter-culture left the cities in droves, returning to their homelands, heading to the hills—anything to exorcise the communal nightmares of utopia gone awry. It was the end of the 1960s and of all they represented. As the nonviolent flower children gave way to the militant Black Panther party, Kent State campus massacres, and increasingly violent street re-volts by frustrated students in Paris, Berlin, and Italy, it was out with the old hopes everywhere and in with the new pragmatism.

Black Sabbath seemed to thrive on such adversity, never pretend-ing to offer answers beyond the occasional exhortation to love thy neighbor. Though legend likes to portray the band as scraggly under-dogs, the band's debut soon took to the British Top 10 and stayed there for months. The band's maiden American tour, planned for sum-mer 1970, was canceled in light of the Manson Family murder trial. There was an extremely inhospitable climate in the United States to-ward dangerous hippies. Still, the debut record charted high in Amer-ica and sold more than a half million copies within its first year.

Vertigo Records scrambled to get more material from its dire and mysterious conscripts, inter-rupting Sabbath's nonstop touring for another recording session in September 1970. Hotly rehearsed as ever, and with intensified creative pur-pose, the band emerged after two days with the mighty *Paranoid*, its bestselling al-bum and home of signature Sabbath songs "War Pigs," "Paranoid," and "Iron Man."

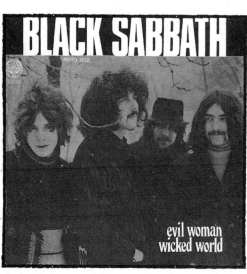

Black Sabbath's *Evil Woman* picture sleeve

While *Paranoid* retained the haunting spirit of *Black Sabbath*, the themes of the second album were less mysti-cal and more tangible. Ob-sessed with damage and loss of control, Ozzy Osbourne in plaintive voice bemoans the ills of drug addiction in "Hand of Doom," nuclear war in "Electric Funeral," and battle shock in "Iron Man." Like the mesmerizing title track of *Black Sabbath*, the soul of *Paranoid* still grew from an occult-oriented number, "Walpurgis," whose imagery powerfully summons "witches at black masses" and "sorcerers of death's construction." When recorded for *Paranoid*, however, the song was slightly rewritten as "War Pigs," a cataclysmic antiwar anthem indicting politicians for sending young and poor men off to do the bloody work of banks and nations.

Now Sabbath was becoming experienced not just as musicians but as generational spokesmen. If change was to be brought by music, Sabbath lyricist Geezer Butler saw that he would have to fight ugliness on the front lines. The new Black Sabbath songs sought peace and love—not in the flower patches of Donovan and Jefferson Airplane but in the grim reality of battlefields and human ovens. Ozzy Osbourne delivered these lyrics as if in a trance, reading messages of truth written in the sky.

Billboard magazine blithely wrote that *Paranoid* "promises to be as big as their first," and indeed the songs "Paranoid" and "Iron Man" both came close to cracking the U.S. Top 40 singles chart. It seemed that all the musical changes of the 1960s had existed solely to ease audiences into Sabbath's hard prophecies. Written allegedly in less time than it took to play, the frantic three-minute single "Paranoid" sent Sabbath's second album to number one on the British charts and number eight in America.

While the hierarchy of rock and roll imploded around them, spectators were overwhelmed by the intuition that Black Sabbath was beginning an entirely new musical era. "*Paranoid* is an anchor," says Rob Halford, singer of Judas Priest, then a local Birmingham band. "It really secures everything about the metal movement in one record. It's all there: the riffs, the vocal performance of Ozzy, the song titles, what the lyrics are about. It's just a classic defining moment."

Soon Sabbath found squatters living in their huge sonic space. Inspired acolytes, signed to one-off record deals while playing the university student-union circuit, brought early and short-lived aftershocks to the big bang. Japan's outlandish Flower Travelin' Band and South Africa's clumsy Suck went so far as to record Black Sabbath cover songs as early as 1970, when the vinyl on the original records was barely dry. Others were motivated to mimic Sabbath by the prospect of a quick buck. A 1970 album by Attila presented young Long Island crooner Billy Joel (then a rock critic and sometime psychiatric patient) dressed in Mongol warrior garb, playing a loud Hammond B3 organ to a hard rock beat, damaging ears with the songs "Amplifier Fire" and "Tear This Castle Down."

Before Black Sabbath, "heavy" had referred more to a feeling than a particular musical style, as in hippiespeak it described anything with potent mood. Jimi Hendrix and the Beatles often wrote songs that pointed toward a heavy break, a bridge between melodies that tried to resolve conflicting emotions and ideas. The "metal" in heavy metal put a steely resilience to that struggle, an unbreakable thematic strength that secured the tension and uninhibited emotion. As ordained by Black Sabbath, heavy metal was a complex maelstrom of neurosis and desire. Formed into an unbending force of deceptive simplicity, it had an omnivorous appetite for life.

As for the words themselves: Beat writer William S. Burroughs named a character in his 1964 novel *Nova Express* "Uranium Willy, the heavy metal kid." The critic Lester Bangs, an early and literate proponent of Black Sabbath, later applied the term to music. Before them, "heavy metal" was a nineteenth-century term used in warfare to describe firepower and in chemistry to designate newly discovered elements of high molecular density. When "Born to Be Wild" songwriter John Kay from Steppenwolf howled about "heavy metal thunder" in 1968, he was describing only the blare of motorcycles. Without Black Sabbath the phrase was an accident of poetry, the empty prophecy of a thousand monkeys hammering on typewriters in search of a Bible.

There were scant few stones an investigator could overturn to find precedent for how completely Black Sabbath brought and embodied a revolutionary new beginning. Another suspect in the question of heavy metal paternity, Jimi Hendrix wisely denied responsibility. Questioned by a journalist just before his death, the electric guitar visionary stepped aside, proclaiming heavy metal "the music of the future."

During the formative years Black Sabbath shared the heavy metal limelight with two other English bands, Led Zeppelin and Deep Purple. All three were foreshadowed by Cream, a short-lived, distortion-

BLACK SABBATH

Formed in Birmingham, England, in the late 1960s, Black Sabbath is the originator of heavy metal, the first loud guitar band to step outside time and explore the moody dimensions unique to the explosive new sound. The original quartet (guitarist Tony Iommi, bassist Geezer Butler, drummer Bill Ward, and singer Ozzy Osbourne) issued a slew of untouchably influential albums during the first half of the 1970s. They were two steps ahead of anyone else—louder and faster, more inventive and versatile. Above all else they had the best riffs, the huge guitar and bass lines that last a lifetime. Geezer Butler reported to *Guitar Player* many years afterward, "Lars Ulrich of Metallica said he'd never heard of Led Zeppelin when he was a kid. He was brought up on Black Sabbath albums."

Come to the Sabbath—the Essential Ozzy Albums

- ❖ *Black Sabbath* (1970)
- ❖ *Paranoid* (1970)
- ❖ *Master of Reality* (1971)
- ❖ *Vol. 4* (1972)
- ❖ *Sabbath Bloody Sabbath* (1973)
- ❖ *Sabotage* (1975)
- ❖ *Technical Ecstasy* (1976)
- ❖ *Never Say Die* (1978)

Ritchie Blackmore in Rainbow
(Roy Dressel Photography)

frenzied blues trio formed by Eric Clapton in 1966. While Black Sabbath unleashed the substance of heavy metal, Led Zeppelin and Deep Purple fleshed out the edges and gave it sex appeal. As was fashionable during a time when movie stars were joining the Church of Satan, each swathed powerful music in witchcraft. While Sabbath fended off accusations of devil worship, Zeppelin guitarist Jimmy Page lived and held court in the former estate of hedonistic English heretic Aleister Crowley. Purple's tempestuous guitarist Ritchie Blackmore habitually wore a pointed black witch's hat.

As the epitome of 1970s hard rock bands, Led Zeppelin had an enormous influence on heavy metal—the band was seminal beyond the carnal sense. Zeppelin's every gesture was grandiose, not necessarily regal but demanding kingly attention. Singer Robert Plant, guitarist Jimmy Page, bassist John Paul Jones, and drummer John Bonham stood a hundred feet high as stereotypes, longhaired hedonists whose tour exploits were immortalized in rock tomes like *Hammer of the Gods*. Fans had seen it before, mostly from the Rolling Stones, but never on such a huge scale. The thrill of it all made it metal.

Unlike popular contemporaries Grand Funk Railroad, who were content merely to pummel, Led Zeppelin shared a sense of challenge with Black Sabbath. Yet while Black Sabbath begged for revolution, Led Zeppelin was a group of musical interpreters more than originators. Zeppelin's winsome and slouching dream poem "Stairway to Heaven" had heavy moments but took a respectably reclining posture. Black Sabbath's "War Pigs," on the other hand, was all cataclysm—

searing and deeply unsatisfied. Likewise, the suburban scene on the back of the Led Zeppelin *IV* record jacket was literally a civilized version of the overgrown landscape depicted on *Black Sabbath*. There were always more bands that sounded like Led Zeppelin, because it was easier. "Stairway" might have dominated rock radio during the 1970s, but when "War Pigs" hit the jukebox, it was always something of a ceremony.

In contrast to the austere concepts of Sabbath and Zeppelin, Deep Purple was a tremendous rock and roll force that combined the propulsive wall of Jon Lord's Hammond organ, Ritchie Blackmore's moody Fender Stratocaster guitar, and Ian Gillan's unforgettable, soaring vocal wail. The band broadcast the exhilaration of fast cars in "Highway Star" and "Space Truckin'," credos for the first generation of affluent teens with access to interstate highways. These thunderous songs seemed designed to completely penetrate the tiny iron particles of 8-track tapes jammed into auto dashboards.

Though Deep Purple's "Smoke on the Water" was a bona fide metal anthem and the first basic riff of a longhaired guitarist's repertoire, the band did not consider itself heavy metal. "Never," organist Jon Lord told *Kerrang!* magazine ten years later. "We never wore studded wristbands or posed for photos with blood pouring out of our mouths. That's okay, that's for people who are into a different style of music to us." Nonetheless, Deep Purple on 1970's *In Rock* and 1972's *Machine Head* were state-of-the-art heaviness, elegant expressions of almost magical technological fury.

When the Beatles launched, their tiny amplifiers could not be heard over the screaming crowds. By the early 1970s, manufacturers like Marshall, Orange, and Sunn founded an industry that pushed the tolerances of vacuum tubes, creating vast acoustic possibilities through the deafening roar of guitars. Besides Sabbath, Zeppelin, and Purple, sheer volume itself became the extra member of the wordy Canadian hard rock act Rush, the heady Long Island group Blue Öyster Cult, the excessively dramatic London band Queen, and the imposing British virtuosos King Crimson. In this newfound universe these were the gods who defined rock excess and bombastic musical wizardry. Their careers set the standard ranked not by hit singles but in long arcs of heavily labored albums. Innovative to the point of fatigue, their fierce experiments were emulated relentlessly in the decade ahead.

Embracing a breadth of incomplete styles, many more bands played at decibel levels competing with those of nearby airports. Forgotten strains of protometal swelled arrogantly in the music of the Asterix, Titanic (from Norway), Lucifer's Friend (from England and Germany), heavy Kraut rockers Guru Guru, the haunting May Blitz (also on the Vertigo label), Master's Apprentices (from Australia), Captain Beyond (formed by members of Deep Purple and Iron Butterfly), Bang, the relatively gentle Armageddon, the morbid Texas group Bloodrock, Britain's long-running Budgie, and the Tony Iommi–produced Necromandus. After peppering the scene with powerful moments, most recordings by these obscure bands were discontinued within a few short years, but their existence enticed small audiences with possibility.

Already tucking a million album sales under its leather belt, Black Sabbath remained a daring and original entity, soon releasing two swaying party albums for catatonic souls. *Master of Reality* kicked off 1971 with the epic, unending cough of "Sweet Leaf," a love song to marijuana. Anchored in some of Tony Iommi's most concrete riffs, Sabbath drove their peace needle into the hopeful netherworld of "Children of the Grave," accelerating into the lost space mission of

Black Sabbath circa 1973
(Warner Bros.)

"Into the Void." Despite their morbidity, these were compassionate songs with gentleness as well as strength. On the ultrafragile and desolate "Solitude," Iommi even dared to reintroduce the flute—he had abandoned it years earlier for fear Sabbath would be compared to Jethro Tull.

The aptly titled *Vol. 4*, released in 1972, beamed with the light of nice acoustic melodies. Both the cocaine cry of "Snowblind" and the Santana-ish instrumental "Laguna Sunrise" reflected the breezy influence of time spent touring America and visiting California. Yet "Wheels of Confusion" and "Supernaut" were as preoccupied with insanity as anything on *Paranoid*. Geezer Butler continued giving lyrics to Ozzy that delved deep into the psyche, and the tone of the music remained intensely heavy. Extending Sabbath's popularity streak, *Vol. 4* followed *Master of Reality* into the *Billboard* Top 20 in America. The band reveled in its success, indulging in the first-time gratification of emerging rock stardom: new homes, luxury cars, girls, and drugs—judging by Ozzy's increasingly bizarre antics, not always in that order of priority.

The great rock and roll explosion volleyed small shards of heavy metal across America in the early 1970s, slipping from Woodstock, blazing from Monterey Pop, and bleeding from Altamont into giant festivals like Cal Jam—where a very stoned Black Sabbath arrived by helicopter to face 450,000 fans in 1974. It was an age of relative media scarcity, and concerts were the only way to personally experience heavy music. In this trailblazing era, being into hard rock meant putting everything into concert events—ditching school, taking the day off work, and driving as far as was necessary to experience catharsis firsthand in a live setting.

Jetting from city to city, superstar bands like Led Zeppelin brought the sound of overdriven guitars from smaller music theaters into sports stadiums. Instead of spending weeks in residency at a series of little clubs, musicians could travel across America and play for half the teen population in a few months. This meant they were constantly dislocated. Touring rock stars learned how to survive and enjoy themselves during lives spent in dressing rooms and road motels, presiding over the acid-laced creation of concert culture on a grand scale. Doing their part, fans camped out overnight for tickets, smuggled contraband pot and liquor into venues, and negotiated access to wild backstage paradise.

The power of Deep Purple dimmed in 1975, as Ritchie Blackmore quit to form the mythology-inspired band Rainbow. From Elf he recruited young singer Ronnie James Dio, who jumped into the decadence of the period. He had been a teen idol in upstate New York with Ronnie Dio and the Prophets during the 1960s, but the new brew was a long way from "Love Potion #9." "Being quite young in Rainbow,

ΉARD RΦCK

Dozens of early contemporaries of Black Sabbath contributed to the development of what would later be considered heavy metal. Some were blues-based, like Led Zeppelin and Deep Purple. Others, like King Crimson, Queen, and Rush, attempted to introduce elements of classical music. Blue Cheer and the Stooges just turned their amps to full bake and burned everything to a crisp. All were longhaired and loud, bell-bottomed and bold. Their goal was to blast ten times louder than the rock and roll explosion of the 1960s. Even after their music was forgotten, heavy metal remained indebted to the large-scale displays of bravado made during this pioneering age.

Freakography

- ❖ Alice Cooper, *Killer* (1971)
- ❖ Blue Cheer, *Vincebus Eruptum* (1967)
- ❖ Blue Öyster Cult, *Tyranny and Mutation* (1973)
- ❖ Deep Purple, *Machine Head* (1972)
- ❖ Flower Travelin' Band, *Satori* (1972)
- ❖ Hawkwind, *Hall of the Mountain Grill* (1974)
- ❖ Jimi Hendrix, *Electric Ladyland* (1968)
- ❖ King Crimson, *Starless and Bible Black* (1974)
- ❖ Led Zeppelin, *IV* (1971)
- ❖ Queen, *A Night at the Opera* (1975)
- ❖ Rush, *2112* (1976)
- ❖ The Stooges, *Raw Power* (1973)
- ❖ Thin Lizzy, *Jailbreak* (1976)
- ❖ MC5, *Kick Out the Jams* (1969)

when I had my first real chance to taste success, I saw it all for the first time," Dio says. "In the early days it was time for throwing TVs out the window. We were like, 'We can do this? Okay!' It's stupid, really, if you think about it. You were supposed to be that rock star, that's what you did. You screwed everybody all night long, and sex was wonderful. There was no AIDS—the worst that could happen is we'd catch the clap. We lived the lifestyle that Zeppelin lived, and that Sabbath lived, and that Purple lived before us."

Outside the inner sanctums the public watched the energy unleashed within rock concerts spill over into the surrounding communities and erupt into miniriots. Future heavy metal musicians, still wide-eyed grade-schoolers, filed away memories of a rumbling in the streets. Thomas Fischer, aka Tom Warrior, who later founded Celtic Frost, was a preadolescent in Switzerland. "I remember seeing Deep Purple in the early seventies," he recalls, "and seeing

Ronnie James Dio
(Roy Dressel Photography)

on the news that the concert hall was totally thrashed afterward. I remember how the parents went insane when their kids listened to that."

As the revolutionary spirit of the 1960s relaxed into a liberal attitude toward drugs, sex, and bacchanalian glory, America in the 1970s embraced easy living—a balm for the social changes of the recent past. Rock music, always a bastion of youthful rebellion, was fast becoming the desired lifestyle, and the conservative middle class did not know how to cope. Newspaper advice columnist Ann Landers counseled a distraught mother not to forsake a runaway daughter who left home to live on a tour bus with longhaired rockers. She advised suffering the shame of wayward youth, if only for the sake of the inevitable wave of bastard children—a dire perspective on young freedom.

While teens celebrating sex and drugs were scary to adults everywhere, the occult aspects of heavy rock particularly frightened the Bible Belt. "Going to Miami, going down to Baton Rouge, Louisiana, trying to get into Corpus Christi, Texas, in the seventies was not an easy task," says Sabbath drummer Bill Ward. "We had to face the mayor of the town. We were banned all the time. They were afraid of us. They really thought we were going to put a spell on you. We'd have to confront forty or fifty cops or something."

The most garish rockers responded to civic outrage by pushing the boundaries of taste and upping the fear factor. Following in the high-heeled footsteps of the 1960s act the Crazy World of Arthur Brown, the delightfully gruesome Alice Cooper developed a gory stage show based on the French Grand Guignol street theater of the 1800s, complete with costumed dwarfs and buckets of blood. By 1975, Cooper was faking his own suicide onstage nightly. "It seemed like he was not really a human being," says masked metaller Kim Bendix Peterson, aka King Diamond. "If you touched him, he would probably disappear into thin air or something. It just came across so strong."

Intensifying the efforts of Alice Cooper, an opportunistic group of New Yorkers called Kiss took their over-the-top image to the doorstep of average America. The band's silver makeup, glittery costumes, and custom-shaped guitars infused the space-age power of NASA into the hairy, leathery broth of rock, distilling two great events of the 1960s—the moon landing and the advent of loud guitars—into one spectacular escape. Released in the twelve-month period leading up to April 1975, each of the first three Kiss albums—*Kiss, Hotter Than Hell*, and *Dressed to Kill*—went gold rapidly. This led to the bloody *Alive* double live album, also released in 1975, which went platinum on the strength of loud, catchy ditties like "Cold Gin" and "Detroit Rock City." It was heavy-metal-coated rock candy, a Black Sabbath flavor of bubblegum.

Kiss went after an audience too young to understand Vietnam—its comic book–inspired stage show littered with Egyptian cat statues, crystal formations, and crumbling stone walls. It was a financial risk, taken for the sake of an unforgettable event. "When we started out, people just were baffled," says guitarist Stanley Eisen, aka Paul Stanley. "We were wearing platform boots. Our makeup was absurd. The biggest act in America at that point was John Denver. We were not cool, but we had conviction. It was a kamikaze mission. We gave ourselves no choice but to succeed. The downside could have been horrendous."

The *Destroyer* tour in 1976 was the cusp between young and hungry and larger-than-life. Despite its flamboyantly plastic presence, Kiss was still trudging through manure—an El Paso, Texas, show put the group before 10,000 border-town roughnecks in a cattle hall used regularly for livestock auctions. Across America that summer, Kiss fought the volume wars, roaring over opening acts Bob Seger and Ted Nugent, then paying a double-size electric bill for its blinding backboard of bright lights. In an age before TicketMaster, professional security squads, and metal detectors, Kiss encountered disorganized bedlam. They emerged as superstars, helping to create the professional tour circuit that would become the lifeline for heavy metal.

The makeup, blood, and fire created an indelible subdermal impression on fans, many of whom never even heard the music. Kiss shrewdly filled the widening generation gap with merchandise, creating dolls, pajamas, bubble-gum cards, a board game, a comic book published by Marvel, and a pinball machine. Already costumed superbeings, they were soon the stars of their own sci-fi movie, *Kiss Meets the Phantom of the Park*. Abandoning Dr. Seuss for "Dr. Love" soon became a rite of passage in American elementary schools. Upon reaching the other side of childhood, that huge population looked with singed retinas to heavy metal to deliver the same shock and thunder.

Black Sabbath offered listeners something more than three chords and a good show—but their audience was still left to scavenge for sounds with similar impact. By the mid-1970s, heavy metal aesthetic could be spotted, like a mythical beast, in the moody bass and complex dual guitars of Thin Lizzy, in the stagecraft of Alice Cooper, in the sizzling guitar and showy vocals of Queen, and in the thundering medieval questions of Rainbow. Then, following Sabbath out of Birmingham in 1974, Judas Priest arrived to unify and amplify these diverse highlights from hard rock's sonic palette. For the first time, heavy metal became a true genre unto itself.

With Judas Priest the chugging momentum of Deep Purple was harnessed for a threatening attack from which the histrionic peaks of Led Zeppelin were mere foothills. Nothing before matched the speed of Glenn Tipton and K. K. Downing's guitars or the high drama of Rob Halford's phenomenal voice. Judas Priest skimmed the most intense elements of the past into a cauldron and remixed perception in a magical way. "I was inventing my vocal technique as it went along, really," says Rob Halford. "I didn't really have much in terms of people that sounded cool to look around and say I wanted to sound like this or emulate that."

Judas Priest made no bones about openly proclaiming its goal: to be the world's ultimate heavy metal band. The lineage from Sabbath could have hardly been stranger. Sabbath lent the younger band its rehearsal space, and one of Judas Priest's members had briefly been involved with Earth, the band that became Black Sabbath.

Yet compared to Sabbath, Judas Priest's music was very formal, tightly organized around breaks, bridges, and dynamic peaks. As Black Sabbath coalesced according to feel instead of a steady metronome meter, Judas Priest took a heavily composed approach. The melodic, mind-expanding interplay of Tipton and Downing used twin lead guitars as carving tools to deftly cut and shape sound at high-decibel volumes. Each scorching lead guitar break was inserted in another perfect song crevice, pointing the way to new invulnerable creations. Unlike the utterly primal Black Sabbath, young players could emulate Priest without sounding like clones—the band's astonishing repertoire of musical techniques demanded further exploration.

Just as *Paranoid* had tackled politics and power struggles, on *Sad Wings of Destiny* the uncanny Rob Halford took lyrics from the extraordinary thoughts of Sun-tzu and the royal Shakespearean dramas. He ignited them with searing vocal fireworks. "I was blessed with extraordinary vocal chords that can do some bizarre things," says Halford, "and it was always a case of looking at new ways of doing things from song to song. It was all about experimentation more than anything else."

Though the "flashing senseless sabers" of "Genocide" could be seen as mere battlefield fantasy, the song was written the same year that Pol Pot was "cleansing" the prison-state of Cambodia of a million and a half ethnic minorities, many of whom were beheaded with swords. This was the mission of heavy metal: to confront the big picture—to create a connection between life and the cosmos. If there were to be love songs, they would be epics, not odes to teenage puppy love at the soda shop. Lyrical conflict would exist on a grand scale, which in the 1970s meant lashing out against despots, dictators, and antidemocratic Watergate burglars. "I always understood rock as a form of revolution of young people against the establishment," says metaller Tom Warrior of Celtic Frost. "Though nowadays, of course, it's one big commercial machine, deep within me the spirit is there. I can't deny it, because I experienced it like that when I was a kid."

Other new heavy metal bands were ruthlessly heretical, continually facing rejection. Following a space rock debut in 1972, the German hard rockers Scorpions compressed eight-minute jams into guitar-driven overdrive. Courting taboo, their 1976 album *Virgin Killer* depicted a nude fourteen-year-old girl with a shattered pane of glass over her pubescent pubic delta—and was promptly banned outright in America. The image was an exaggeration of the prevalent attitude toward sexual experimentation, and the music embraced a wild new mentality that chanted for excitement. Heavy metal audiences wanted to be shocked, and they craved the stimulation of difficult territory. "We respected other bands like Deep Purple, Led Zeppelin, but we wanted to do it differently," says Rudolph Schenker, guitarist of Scorpions. "We were a different generation."

Pigeonholed prematurely as minimalists, Black Sabbath asserted a metallic mastery on its sixth album, 1975's *Sabotage*. Following the accomplished path begun by 1973's *Sabbath Bloody Sabbath*, the LP hurtled through the looking glass with a band beset by lucid nightmares. "Hole in the Sky" and "Symptom of the Universe" were pummeling psychedelic masterpieces long overdue from the reality-altering Sabbath; yet the dominant theme of *Sabotage* was splendor in the face of cold money invaders—the cathedral-size claustrophobia of "Megalomania" and "The Writ" pushed away the lawyers and managers who had been bleeding the band dry. By this point Sabbath was experiencing the first divorces and drug breakdowns endemic to rock stars, and "Am I Going Insane," was Ozzy's great moment of clarity after allegedly spending the entirety of 1972 through 1974 on LSD. *Sabotage* was a high point for the band. Joined by the English Chamber Choir for the opulent "Supertzar," Black Sabbath proudly displayed its delusions and hoisted aloft its grandeur.

Swerving from beneath its mentor's shadow, Judas Priest modernized tremendously on 1978's *Stained Class*. Contemplating the information age, the cover depicted a metallic humanoid head being pierced by colored beams of light. Instead of crying out in protest against the powers that be, songs like "Exciter" and "Saints in Hell" spoke from the point of view of authority, wielding the merciless force of the music like a weapon. While Ozzy Osbourne's voice had remarkable emotional quality, he was not widely regarded as a gifted singer. Rob Halford, however, perfected a searing, vibrato-ridden delivery that fluttered from a banshee's wail down to an angry clenched snarl. When united with bold studio effects and the crisp guitar exchanges of Tipton and Downing, the combination of talent and technique was nothing short of state-of-the-art heavy metal genius.

Though somewhat marginalized by the press, heavy metal spoke to an unrecognized audience—and heavy acts began banding together on long concert tours in search of that support. "We really, truly created metal fans as we made album to album," says Rob Halford. "There wasn't any broad-based metal culture at the time. We would go around the UK and Europe, and eventually over to America, and people were just very slowly turning on to this brand-new style and brand-new sound. Each generation finds something that's relative musically, that they want to identify with and call their own—that's how we were connecting with our first fans."

The food of heavy metal's long life was forming. When Black Sabbath appeared from Birmingham, the sound was an aberration, emulated by many without being completely developed and expanded. After the arrival of Judas Priest, heavy metal constituted a full-fledged movement that could trace its trajectory from point A to point B. As the next wave of bands picked up the path, the cycle would take on the characteristics of an avalanche, surging onward with increasing power and momentum.

1970S PROTOMETAL

The small-fries of the late 1970s found heaviness in the unexplored crevices left in the tracks of hard rock dinosaurs. Kiss and AC/DC compressed the biggest sounds of the past into bite-size anthems. Judas Priest and Scorpions added electrifying dual guitars—an incredible new dimension that became the basis for heavy metal songwriting. Though they looked like hard rockers, these bands were the basis for something new. Their lyrics were less abstract, more tied to the life happening on the streets. As they gained momentum during the 1970s, one by one these bands left behind the lumbering gait of hard rock, crossing over completely to heavy metal.

Heavy Evidence

- AC/DC, *If You Want Blood, You've Got It* (1978)
- Judas Priest, *Sad Wings of Destiny* (1976)
- Kiss, *Double Platinum* (1978)
- Led Zeppelin, *Presence* (1976)
- New York Dolls, *New York Dolls* (1973)
- Rainbow, *Rising* (1976)
- Runaways, *Queens of Noise* (1977)
- Scorpions, *In Trance* (1975)
- Scorpions, *Tokyo Tapes* (1978)
- Robin Trower, *Live* (1976)
- UFO, *Lights Out* (1977)

Nearing the close of the 1970s, Black Sabbath's name was often openly invoked in Britain by new bands praising their influence—yet the mighty band was failing as a unit. The simmering energy of a new brood of admirers might have buoyed Sabbath's spirits, except that the band had left England for Los Angeles in 1976 to avoid paying exorbitant British income taxes. Ozzy, Iommi, Butler, and Ward were too distant to participate in the late-1970s UK music scene except on occasional visits, like absentee fathers. The insulated world they shared was beginning to crumble, as ten years of touring, personal isolation, legal woes, and heavy substance abuse took their toll.

Backed into an alcoholic corner, Ozzy Osbourne quit Black Sabbath before the recording of 1978's *Never Say Die* and was briefly re-

Never Say Die tourbook
(Collection of Omid Yamini)

placed by Savoy Brown singer Dave Walker. Ozzy returned to finish the album but soon quit Sabbath for good following a disastrous UK tour that left the band in flagging spirits. A strange New York act called the Ramones supported Sabbath's U.S. dates that year, while the Los Angeles group Van Halen—initially named Rat Salad after an instrumental on *Paranoid*—opened for Sabbath's 10th Anniversary Tour of England. The athletic performances of Van Halen upstaged the aging demons from Birmingham nightly. "They were so good," said Ozzy, "and we were at the end of our tether."

Ozzy Osbourne in 1977
(Austin [Hardrock69] Majors)

The two final Ozzy-era albums, *Never Say Die* and 1976's *Technical Ecstasy*, were the work of a fatigued band. It seemed as though on the seventh record Black Sabbath rested, and then again on the eighth. The sweeping heaviness of *Sabotage* was replaced by a casual, bluesy swing that gave listeners a breather, replacing magnificently oppressive feelings with something merely sanguine. The results reached for progress yet often resorted to therapy. Like the Beatles' *Let It Be*, it was the sound of old friends propping each other up through one last round. In fact, Bill Ward recalls singing dummy vocal tracks to guide Ozzy through his paces while recording *Never Say Die*.

When Ozzy Osbourne finally left Black Sabbath, it was more than the end of an era. His departure dissolved a personal chemistry that began when schoolyard bully Tony Iommi beat up Ozzy as a teenager and carried through eight albums that took music to a haunting, pounding new cataclysmic depth. Whether Black Sabbath would continue after Ozzy was uncertain. Whoever filled Ozzy's place—if indeed the band would even continue without him—would stand in the boots of a giant.

As when the Beatles called it a day, Ozzy split apart the Sab Four having programmed the instructional code for a new musical protocol. Even while temporarily out of commission, Black Sabbath continued to influence the younger generation from across an ocean. As it turned out, heavy metal would repeatedly prove to be best inspired from a distance—where strong impressions, memories, and images were encouraged to run amok in the imagination. Ultimately, as successive waves of bands emerged to exploit the forces Sabbath set in motion, the success and excess of all other 1970s hard rock supergroups would pale in comparison.

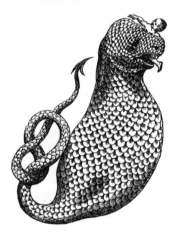

The New Wave
of British Heavy Metal

- ⇥ **1977:** First official Motörhead LP released
- ⇥ **1980:** Judas Priest's *British Steel* crowns a slew of LPs, including *Iron Maiden*, Def Leppard's *On Through the Night*, Saxon's *Wheels of Steel*, and Motörhead's *Ace of Spades*
- ⇥ **February 20, 1980:** AC/DC singer Bon Scott dies
- ⇥ **June 1981:** First issue of *Kerrang!* published in London
- ⇥ **1981:** Judas Priest and Iron Maiden tour North America

---

As Judas Priest and others ripped heavy metal away from its hard rock roots in the mid-1970s, another musical revolution called punk was doing some rock and roll housecleaning of its own. Punk countered the overprocessed, assembly-line glamour of millionaire bands like Kiss and Led Zeppelin with a simple visual violence: mismatched hair dye, safety pins worn as jewelry, and partially shaved heads. It was a hodgepodge, ragamuffin musical fashion that exaggerated and challenged cultural values, inverting the proper and championing the sick.

Like the mod and Edwardian teen scenes before it, punk was centered on the clothing boutiques of London's fashion districts—in particular the Kings Road shop founded by the Sex Pistols' manager, Malcolm McLaren. As punk rock flew the coop to New York and Los Angeles in the late 1970s, it shook up personal style and fashion, igniting social rebellion more than inciting musical revolution. Most important, punk allowed proponents the freedom to play however they wanted and to freely speak their minds. Members of the great punk bands the Sex Pistols and the Clash had played hard rock in pub bands before the liberating onset of punk. Consequently, anthems like "Anarchy in the UK" and "London Calling" were far less shocking in sound than via what they said about affairs in Great Britain.

For bands like the sardonic Fall and the austere Wire, musical simplicity was a statement. For others like X-ray Spex, it was a question of inexperience. The iconoclastic Los Angeles punk band Black Flag found this lack of interest in musical craft limiting. As guitarist Greg Ginn told *L.A. Weekly,* "I thought that if you're gonna call yourself a band and claim to play music, it's not too much to ask that you practice a couple hours, five nights a week. But a lot of people thought, 'Well, we'd rather party or hang out or this or that.' And in punk rock, there was a lot of that mentality—'Why do you need to practice so much?' It was supposed to be 'Everything's zero, and life's not worth anything, so why would you bother practicing?'"

Many of punk's buzzing barnstorms were premature stabs at playing heavy metal. For instance, London's the Damned used fast, heavy power chords in its songs, and spooky singer Dave Vanian wore pale makeup and dressed like a vampire. Like most British punks, the Damned were inspired to form by the Ramones, a Queens, New York, quartet whose 1976 UK tour inaugurated the era of faster and louder. Dressed in a uniform of blue jeans and black leather motorcycle jackets, the Ramones never hid their love for Black Sabbath. Along with a weakness for 1950s greaser bands and doo-wop, their hard-driving repertoire was derived almost entirely from the pummeling chords of "Paranoid."

Nonetheless, what little support existed for heavy metal in the music scene evaporated as major labels scrambled to sign anything wearing Mohawks and safety pins. The Sex Pistols lampooned one of their suitors with the song "EMI," teasing the moneymakers even as they shopped for a better contract. Yet within three years the feeding frenzy was over, as rude revolt was squandered on self-destruction. Sex

Pistols bassist Sid Vicious died in jail, and the band and their entourage scattered. "I think punk was important if only to show you how a crash-and-burn system operates in rock and roll," says Rob Halford of Judas Priest. "That's what it was meant to be. There were only a couple great moments that had any lasting significance."

For all its spastic gobbing in the streets, punk was continually preoccupied with the type of snobbery that was exactly what Black Sabbath had spent the better part of a decade ignoring. Consequently, status consciousness overcame tough posturing after punks tasted success. Like the Rolling Stones several years earlier, the punks bought small estates and turned to pilfering Jamaican reggae music for new ideas. "Punk has a built-in obsolescence," says Paul Stanley of Kiss, "in the fact that you're singing about being a have-not. Then success makes you a have, and the idea of being angry because you're poor is buried very quickly when your record sells. The idea is great, and the anger and emotion is great, but ultimately you have to move on, and the music's going to have to do the talking."

Wendy O. Williams and Richie Stotts of the Plasmatics
(John Michaels)

Punk did renew England's sense of musical identity and fortunately kick-started a fresh wave of rudimentary heavy metal. In 1977, the same year the label introduced the Damned, Stiff Records released the self-titled debut by Motörhead, a band whose dedication to extremes made even punk rock seem uptight. Motörhead leader Ian Kilmister, aka Lemmy, was a former roadie for the Jimi Hendrix Experience and a popular member of the LSD-fueled space rock roustabouts Hawkwind. Leveraging natural beauty—facial warts and missing teeth—with a tattoo that read BORN TO LOSE, Lemmy defied the appeal of rock-star pretty boys, far beyond even the rascally Johnny Rotten and Sid Vicious of the Sex Pistols. He was a quick-witted and charismatic endorsement for dangerous living, and became the grand lord of dirty indifference while fans copied his outlaw wardrobe of bullet belts, denim vests, cowboy shirts, and Motörhead patches.

Minding the gap between Black Sabbath and the punk explosion, Motörhead members were rude longhairs on a speed binge of hammering bass chords, distorted guitar, and rumbling drums. Steering clear of politics or mythic heroes, and singing with gravel in place of vocal cords, Lemmy trafficked in debauched songs about sex, drugs, and rock and roll. The furious initial string of Motörhead albums—*Overkill*, *Bomber*, and *Ace of Spades*—choked the English music charts, impressing on metal fans that a band could succeed commercially without sacrificing its blunt power and integrity. Black Sabbath had introduced heavy metal, Judas Priest gave it flash, and Motörhead fortified it with true grit. So equipped, heavy metal swallowed punk rock and pressed forward.

Meanwhile, the sun was setting fast on the polluted and confused British Empire. Unemployment reached 20 percent in the late 1970s, and combined with rising inflation to create a state of stagflation—a dreaded economic choke hold. Blighted by the worst conditions since World War II, the kingdom needed creative forces of all kinds. From punk came a catalyzing spark: the audacity to believe that anyone could start a rock band. "Punk created the idea of starting a record company from your garage or bedroom," says Jess Cox from new-fangled group Tygers of Pan Tang—a whirligig of riffs and hair that considered its music distinct from the past. "On a pure artist level, it didn't matter if you could play or sing—the idea was getting up onstage and making a racket." The results exhilarated a generation of teenagers dying to make their mark on vinyl.

Ozzy Osbourne confessed to singing along to Beatles songs in front of his bedroom mirror as an adolescent—likewise, John and Mark Gallagher formed Raven with one acoustic guitar, which had been a souvenir of a family trip to Spain. Novice bassist John simply

PUNK ROCK

A brief burst of enthusiasm aimed at toppling the jaded rock scene, punk rock took hold of London, New York, and then Los Angeles, replacing pseudoscientific musical wizardry with abrupt visual style. Punk had a built-in look—in fact, the Sex Pistols and the Clash could have been mistaken for bar bands if not for the orange hair and shaved heads. In California, bands like Black Flag, Germs, and X showed that all was not beach balls and sunshine. Under the regime of Governor Reagan they attacked Hollywood ideals with misfit tantrums and threats. The New York scene was brainier, save for its most storied band, the legendary minimalist pinheads the Ramones, who dressed in matching jeans and motorcycle jackets and never stopped talking about Black Sabbath.

Safety-Pin Classics
- ❖ Black Flag, *Everything Went Black* (1982)
- ❖ The Clash, *The Clash* (1979)
- ❖ The Damned, *Damned Damned Damned* (1976)
- ❖ The Fall, *Live at the Witch Trials* (1979)
- ❖ Germs, *GI* (1979)
- ❖ Plasmatics, *New Hope for the Wretched* (1980)
- ❖ Ramones, *Ramones* (1976)
- ❖ Ramones, *Rocket to Russia* (1977)
- ❖ Sex Pistols, *Never Mind the Bollocks, Here's the Sex Pistols* (1977)
- ❖ X, *Los Angeles* (1980)

tuned the instrument low when it was his turn to practice. From Radio 1 and the *Top of the Pops* television show, the brothers absorbed the glam rock thrills of Slade, Status Quo, and Sweet. Though Slade was more like catchy soccer rock than heavy metal, imitators like Raven upped the gonzo factor a thousandfold and turned the basic recipes into heavy metal staples.

When they graduated to real instruments, the first venues Raven played were semiprivate "workingmen's clubs" in Newcastle, which provided cheap beer and entertainment to fatigued dock- and factory workers. Some of these clubs hired the equivalent of Holiday Inn lounge singers. Others had off-color comedians and a few struggling rock bands. The audience sat at huge trestle tables on long wooden benches, waiting to be impressed. "You'd go before an audience that had no intention of being entertained by you and antagonize them into a reaction," recalls John Gallagher. "People were throwing pint glasses at us. We used to play shows where there'd be three sets. We'd be going nuts; then, in between sets, there'd be bingo. We'd be backstage trying not to laugh while the guy was calling out numbers."

Judas Priest also cut its teeth in the workingmen's clubs, as did emerging northern England bands like Saxon, known by the homely name Sonofabitch. Even the halfway glamorous Tygers of Pan Tang trod the boards. "The 'turn,' as they called you, played two sets of forty-five minutes between the bingo and the 'meat draw,'" recalls Tygers singer Jess Cox. "Patrons bought a raffle ticket, and the winner picked from a hat went home with a tray of cold meat! The band was expected to be utterly silent on pain of death while the bingo numbers were being called. We were expected to do a lot of cover versions, and we did tracks by the Beatles, Motörhead, Ted Nugent, and AC/DC to pad our sets. At ten P.M. the punters could dance—not before, mind, or some burly monkey in a loud jacket told them to sit down. It was a very strange experience, but a great one to hone your act for the real world."

Ten years after Black Sabbath's Star Club residency, the bohemian Hamburg clubs were closed—British bands could no longer take the ferry to Germany to earn their stripes. London bands had life a little better, with more opportunities to develop original material rather than play cover songs. By 1979 the city hosted countless neighborhood clubs where heavy music was the center of attention, including the Soundhouse, Music Machine, the Marquee, and the Bandwagon. All were stepping-stones to the hallowed Hammersmith Odeon, the 3,500-capacity West London concert capitol where Motörhead, and later Iron Maiden and Venom, recorded triumphant live albums.

Facing a void of major-label disinterest, these new British acts took matters into their own hands by forming independent specialty record labels. Small companies could survive selling a few thousand copies of their records, requiring a prolific release schedule of mini-hits. "The whole ethos of do-it-yourself record companies created the movement," says Jess Cox. "Heavy Metal Records, Ebony Records, Music For Nations, and so on. Neat Records is one big example. Neat [home of Raven] could not compete with the major labels, but then all of a sudden it was cool to be independent and small. The media supported it, so the shops stocked it, so the kids bought it."

Bands designed their own record covers, usually in black and white, compensating for simplicity with eye-grabbing logos and apocalyptic images lifted from fantasy and science-fiction comics. As word spread, established weekly British music papers like *Sounds* and *New Musical Express* began to cover the likes of Raven and Tygers of Pan Tang. They introduced readers to London front-runners Iron Maiden and Sheffield's hopefuls, Def Leppard,

Raven's first single, released in 1980

along with a whole colony of lesser-known bands still making "the turn" in regional English clubs. *Sounds* writer Geoff Barton dubbed the movement the "New Wave of British Heavy Metal," usually shortened to the conveniently written but incredibly awkward acronym NWOBHM. "The NWOBHM already existed," says John Gallagher of Raven, "but somebody from the media pointed it out and gave it that name."

The scene was ragtag, and the "New" in NWOBHM often meant inexperienced, yet there was little amateurism at play in Iron Maiden. They deftly synthesized the gothic layers of Judas Priest with the immediate danger of punk rock—a lethal and impressive combination. Clad in a black shirt with a silver spiked armband and belt, singer Paul Di'Anno, a reformed skinhead, commanded clubs with a Tom Jones swagger, coiling the microphone cable in his hand and extending his pinky finger with evident authority. Iron Maiden seemed to be playing ten times as many notes as anyone else, and its dazzling compositional approach elevated the musicianship of heavy metal for decades.

Paul Di'Anno of Iron Maiden
(EMI Records)

Though Iron Maiden was just as caustic and direct as the Sex Pistols or Motörhead, they attacked with fast unison guitar progressions instead of buzz-saw chords. Most of Maiden's songs were written by unusually aggressive bassist Steve Harris, who plucked a flurry of complex melody lines while the two guitarists hammered and pulled tricky harmonic complements. From Judas Priest, Maiden inherited finger-stepping arpeggio guitar phrases and histrionic singing, and like Priest they took pride in being a heavy metal band. An early version of Maiden had been offered a record deal in 1976 if they would just "go punk," but Harris and company held tight, relentlessly promoting their own career until the record industry was forced to take notice.

Among a flurry of seven-inch singles by peers, Iron Maiden's self-released *Soundhouse Tapes* EP hit the streets in 1979, the same year Margaret Thatcher took over as prime minister. Signaling a similar change of the musical guard, the bright riffing of "Iron Maiden," "Invasion," and "Prowler" spearheaded the NWOBHM scene. Previewing three tough spurts by a band not afraid to demonstrate musical chops, the *Tapes* were voted number one by London radio listener requests even prior to being officially released.

England embraced Iron Maiden because the band loved its country. Maiden's macabre lyrics grew from the elaborate images of "London town streets, when there's darkness and fog" envisioned by Judas Priest's 1976 song "The Ripper." From the Damned and the witchy goth-punks Siouxsie and the Banshees, Iron Maiden adopted Shakespearean stage tricks like smoke machines and haunting homemade props. Capitalizing on their surroundings, Iron Maiden's horror show evoked such typical British frights as the Hammer Films chiller features of the 1960s and the medieval torture devices on display at the Tower of London. It was merry and macabre, and all in good fun.

<hr />

In February 1980, Iron Maiden performed "Running Free" live on *Top of the Pops*, then, in May, released its self-titled *Iron Maiden* album. British heavy metal was ready for prime time—a rush of simultaneous albums appeared. Sharing the spotlight was Saxon's *Wheels of Steel*, a chrome-plated collection of solid, neck-breaking delights. Def Leppard, a group of teenagers from Sheffield, debuted with *On Through the Night*, tempering their raw exuberance with melodic Thin Lizzy–style guitars. Then Motörhead released *Ace of Spades*, the most essential of its early speed bursts, revealing the secrets of Lemmy's immortality with tales of sexual conquest and life on the road. Severing connections to the past, this impressive slate of albums brought relentless heaviness with flashes of weightless euphoria—together they formed the nucleus of the NWOBHM universe.

Heavy metal was music under pressure, with multiple layers of rhythm and melody delivering a fireworks show of high-speed sound. Accelerating the flashy ethos in heavy metal songwriting, the force of multiple guitars became a uniquely central element, encouraging more complex musical development. Even the most basic NWOBHM rogues modulated their three chords with tempo changes, guitar solos, and shifts in mood and energy. Explains Dave Mustaine, the founder of Megadeth and an early member of Metallica, "The NWOBHM brought a lot of lesser-known bands, but their musical style was much more appealing to me. It was all based on cyclical patterns of riffs."

With Black Sabbath's career temporarily on hold, Judas Priest stepped in to head this metal renaissance. They capped the deluge of 1980 with the triumphant *British Steel*, whose title and songs like "Metal Gods" explicitly name-checked the English heavy metal phenomenon. Having survived punk in London and toured briefly in America with Kiss, a wiser Judas Priest switched gears into a streamlined approach. "Living After Midnight" and "Breaking the Law" emphasized chanting choruses instead of elaborate classical constructions. "That was the big breakthrough for Priest," says Rob Halford. "It was the record that started to break down any walls of oppression in the biggest sense. Once songs like 'Living After Midnight' and 'Breaking the Law' started to hit the airwaves, then that just segued into other things."

Side by side there was no comparison between 1970s hard rock and the NWOBHM forces. The players even *looked* more aggressive after 1980—instead of flowery open shirts, bell-bottoms, and mustaches, heavy metal bands dressed in tight-fitting black leather and slick synthetic materials decorated with abstract pointed angles, lightning bolts, and shiny metal. "I remember wearing a Clash T-shirt onstage," says Jess Cox. "We also had straight trouser legs as opposed to flares. We had our hair with straight-cut fringes instead of the old center parting. I know that sounds stupid, but back in the late seventies most older rock acts had handlebar mustaches!"

Touching the larger issues instigated by punk, the NWOBHM bands also took a streetwise yet oblique approach to politics. The picture sleeve of "Sanctuary," a single from *Iron Maiden*, depicted Prime Minister Thatcher being axed in an alleyway as she attempted to tear down an Iron Maiden flyer. The British government responded to the record's popularity with an official censure, requiring that future editions place a black bar over the face of the tormented leader. For her troubles, Thatcher, who cut social programs, sold off government agencies, and fought organized labor, was later nicknamed "the Iron Maiden" by the mainstream press.

Replacing the orange Mohawks of the punk phase, heavy metal

fans adopted their own look, based largely on the tough European rockers of the 1970s (seen standing around campfires in the Who's 1973 rock opera *Quadrophenia*). These were young Germans, English, Dutch, and Italians who had survived terrorists, economic downturns, and the presence of NATO or Eastern Bloc troops during the Cold War. Like Hells Angels, they wore black leather jackets under ripped denim vests lovingly adorned with band pins and Motörhead, Thin Lizzy, or Deep Purple back patches. "My entire life I was exposed to bikers," says Tom Warrior, whose father was a motorcycle racer and racing publisher. "I found biker gangs in America, no matter how unbelievably radical they looked, the best guys ever. In Europe, especially in the early 1980s, they were more violent and involved in turf wars and prostitution and things like that. That was the fan base for Deep Purple and Motörhead. The whole heavy metal uniform is basically a clone of that."

Grasping the edges of the stage and shaking their sweaty heads in devotion to the pulsing music, these first "headbangers" clung religiously to their new classics. They gravitated into the orbits of a hundred new heavy bands—Diamond Head, Angel Witch, and Raven foremost among them. In a manic grab for attention, these groups created music that was sheer excitement—hyperactive and impossible to ignore. Raven's first two albums, *Rock Til You Drop* and *Wiped Out* charged into the 1980s with squealing vocals and guitars, crazed by the thrill of speed and sonic pyrotechnics of pure, unadulterated heavy metal. "There's no edge, no finesse, no guile to what they do," wrote *Sounds*. "Pure and simply, Raven [is] all passion."

Tying up 1980 neatly, Black Sabbath's *Paranoid* was reissued to continued acclaim. The decade-old metal archetype once again dented the UK charts—joined by Iron Maiden's debut, which rose to number four. In August 1980 *Sounds* helped promote a concert called Monsters of Rock, which brought Judas Priest, Saxon, Scorpions, Rainbow, Riot, April Wine, and 60,000 fans to the estate of Castle Donnington for the first exclusively heavy metal festival. The event plugged metal musicians in to the surging energy of a huge English audience and proved that their scene had grown well beyond its humble pub roots. Most important, when given the opportunity to show their numbers, loyal heavy metal fans responded en masse.

While new heavy metal bands were forming daily, British headbangers could uncover the latest developments only in the column margins of *Sounds* or by tracking down a copy of *Aardschok*—a magazine from Holland unfortunately written in Dutch. Following Monsters of Rock, London publishers dedicated greater portions of the English language to the new heavy metal energy. *Sounds* spun off its coverage of the NWOBHM in June 1981 into an all-metal offshoot dubbed *Kerrang!*, an onomatopoeic moniker expressing the clang of guitars, the crash of cymbals, and the snap of banging heads. Lemmy claimed that the name was copied from a Motörhead stage banner.

 Kerrang! instantly became a metal bible, hosting a stable of reassigned *Sounds* writers like Geoff Barton and Malcolm Dome who gave voice and identity to the burgeoning underworld. Like accelerated English versions of Lester Bangs and Hunter S. Thompson, they enthusiastically dove into the metal scene and regaled readers with long-winded and half-intoxicated reports of their brushes with greatness. Inside *Kerrang!*'s first issue were items on Diamond Head, Venom, Raven, and Jaguar; glorious color photos of Lemmy, Girlschool, and eccentric guitar prodigy Michael Schenker of UFO; and an investigation of the curiously British home life and rustic tea-drinking habits of Saxon. A small photo item compared the relative pudginess of Meatloaf, Simon LeBon of Duran Duran, and Iron Maiden's Paul Di'Anno.

 Kerrang! grew to be so

Kerrang! No. 1: birth of the headbanger's bible

widely read that many of the bands it championed became influential, if not always long-lived, metal icons. Among the in-house favorites was the formidable Girlschool, an all-female South London troupe heavy enough to match weaponry with Motörhead. On the 1980 *St. Valentine's Day Massacre* EP, the two sweetheart bands covered each other's songs. *Kerrang!* bestowed more space than merited by sheer musical might on Jon Mikl Thor, aka Thor, a former Mr. Teen Canada bodybuilder whose muscular sideshow included blowing up hot-water bottles like balloons and bending steel bars in his teeth. One of the tamer acts the magazine championed was Samson, whose unusual drummer, Thunderstick—an early and brief member of Iron Maiden—wore a sequined hood, never spoke, and played with a zoo cage constructed around his drums.

Motörhead/Girlschool seven-inch

The magazine had an incredible compass for talent. The cover of *Kerrang!* No. 1 pictured sweaty guitarist Angus Young of AC/DC dressed in his trademark schoolboy uniform. Inside, the magazine's list of the one hundred greatest heavy metal singles of all time was topped by AC/DC's "Whole Lotta Rosie." Though not strictly a British band, having relocated to England only in 1976 from the former penal colony of Australia, the straightforward powerhouse was a key common denominator of the NWOBHM. AC/DC survived the harsh proving grounds of Australia in the same way that Black Sabbath had trained in the blues clubs of Hamburg, Germany. At one point AC/DC's schedule called for three shows a day: high schools in the afternoons, cocktail bars in the evening, and gay dance halls at night. This relentless drive led to a slew of gritty, well-toned LPs, including *High Voltage*, *Powerage*, and *Let There Be Rock*. The band toured relentlessly, supporting Kiss, Black Sabbath, Scorpions, UFO, Alice Cooper, Aerosmith, and Rainbow, and was a fearless force onstage. Their ravenous 1979 LP *High-way to Hell*, with potent, searing guitars and a furious downbeat, was an ominous metal milestone.

Following Angus Young onto the cover of *Kerrang!* were crowd-working leather daddy Rob Halford of Judas Priest and Peter Byford, aka Biff, of Saxon—singers who defined the role of heavy metal front man with crystal-shattering vocal cords and skillful crowd management. Witnessed on Saxon's masterful 1982 live release, *The Eagle Has Landed*, Byford could easily turn a heavy metal concert into an interactive hootenanny, directed by his trademark whistling. With call-and-response patterns taken from English soccer chants, the singer pitted balcony against floor in sing-along contests. He appeared as comfortable onstage in shining white stretch pants, microphone in hand, as if he were still in his backyard sipping tea and telling war stories.

Saxon's speedy songs "Strong Arm of the Law" and "Wheels of Steel" were melodic and rousing, like breezier siblings of Motörhead numbers. Heavier Saxon tracks like "Machine Gun" relied on relentless, pounding two-guitar rhythms, laying down patterns that presaged speed metal several years later. Unusual in Saxon's repertoire was the stirring "Dallas 1 PM" from *Strong Arm of the Law*, which included original radio tapes of the John F. Kennedy assassination. More typically, Saxon's lyrics plainly voiced the outlook of an everyday head-banger—a character immortalized in "Denim and Leather," the band's great metalhead anthem: "Where were you in '79 when the dam began to burst? Did you check us out down at the local show? Were you wearing denim, wearing leather? Did you run down to the front? Did you queue for your ticket through the ice and snow?"

⟩⟨⟩⟨⟩⟨⟩⟨⟩⟨✳⟩⟨⟩⟨⟩⟨⟩⟨⟩⟨

Heavy metal had a short legacy working on its behalf by 1981, but there was no rest for the wicked. Where punk faded as a fashion statement and hard rock tottered along as nine-to-five business as usual, heavy metal offered perpetually reinvented thrills ravenously to integrate other styles into its forward push. Alongside the better-known heavy riff factories came the boogie-woogie-influenced Spider, the unabashed Sabbath copycats Witchfinder General, and the brazen Angel Witch—who synthesized the flagrant vocals of metal with the manic

NWOBHM

Though the "old wave" of British heavy metal had existed mostly in the imaginations of hard rock fans, there was something catchy about the "New Wave of British Heavy Metal" that allowed the clunky moniker to stick. Musically, the NWOBHM cut 1970s hard rock into punk-size pieces, producing a highly focused form of guitar energy. Inspired by the self-actualizing elements of punk, many of the early efforts by Iron Maiden and Diamond Head were self-released or issued by bedroom labels such as Neat and Heavy Metal Records. Fans were clustered across England and Europe, wearing black leather jackets with denim vests covered in patches and pins promoting their favorite acts. By 1980 the movement was fully realized, with hundreds of 45s in print and a handful of landmark long-players by Motörhead, Saxon, Iron Maiden, and Judas Priest. Though they were still very much London acts on the rise, these bands would dominate heavy metal for the next decade on the strength of their serious live capabilities.

Discography

- ❖ AC/DC, *Highway to Hell* (1979)
- ❖ Angel Witch, *Angel Witch* (1981)
- ❖ Def Leppard, *On Through the Night* (1980)
- ❖ Diamond Head, *Lightning to the Nations* (1980)
- ❖ Girlschool, *Hit and Run* (1981)
- ❖ Iron Maiden, *Iron Maiden* (1980)
- ❖ Iron Maiden, *Killers* (1981)
- ❖ Judas Priest, *British Steel* (1980)
- ❖ Motörhead, *Ace of Spades* (1980)
- ❖ Motörhead, *Overkill* (1979)
- ❖ Raven, *Wiped Out* (1982)
- ❖ Saxon, *Denim and Leather* (1981)
- ❖ Saxon, *Wheels of Steel* (1980)
- ❖ Various Artists, *Metal for Muthas* (1980)

rhythms of punk, espousing a peculiar anxiety over the timely topic of women's rights.

In a scene as diverse as the NWOBHM, there had to be a place where all the despised grit and filth collected. That was unlikely *Kerrang!* darling Venom, who catered to more aggressive appetites with militant Satanism and a "They want bad? We'll give them bad!" philosophy. Indebted to Kiss for inspiration and to deviant Roman emperor Caligula for execution, Venom played fast, distorted muck for the sake of speed, then sprinkled on occult imagery to scare off critics. Venom's 1981 debut, *Welcome to Hell*, and its 1982 successor, *Black Metal*, had covers encrusted with gold and silver pentagrams, goat's heads, and satanic gibberish. Bassist/singer Conrad Lant, aka Cronos; guitarist Jeff Dunn, aka Mantas; and drummer Tony Bray, aka Abaddon, were pictured wielding weapons and looking slimy as newborn devils. They made Motörhead appear civilized and the Sex Pistols seem like a friendly gang of children.

Though it was inconceivable at the time, Venom would become one of the NWOBHM's most influential bands. Their comically evil act was routinely discounted by writers and fellow musicians, but they fascinated fans. Venom could not keep a consistent tempo, their mixes were drenched in reverb and distortion to hide the ineptitude, and songs like "Poison" and "Live Like an Angel, Die Like a Devil" dissolved into howling noise by the finish. In other words, Venom was a brilliant breakthrough that threw all notions of rock's preciousness out on its ass, to be replaced by a thrilling chaotic vortex.

As Cronos told *The 7 Gates of Hell*, the mayhem started in a quaint English chapel: "We used to practice in the Methodist church in Newcastle, which we'd rent for five pounds every single Saturday. And every time Abaddon would take with him some small bits of explosives and detonate them during the rehearsals. We were rehearsing, and he was setting off these fucking pyro things! Once a neighbor called the fucking fire brigade because large red clouds of smoke were billowing out of the church. It was an ideal venue, and I believe it had a great atmosphere for writing Satan's love songs!"

There was a less-than-friendly rivalry between Venom and their Newcastle neighbors and labelmates Raven. "We don't like Raven," says Venom drummer Abaddon. "The thing is, we didn't do things the hard way. First you had to be clubbing for twenty years, and then you could have a breakthrough. We were really screwed by Neat Records. We were bringing in shitloads of money, but all of it was used to promote Raven and Tygers of Pan Tang. We like them as bands, but somehow everything went wrong." Regarded as a joke by peers, Venom weathered condescension with arrogance, opening a divide between upwardly mobile traditional heavy metal and the unholy black metal born several years later from Venom's fiery bellows.

As heavy metal culture fast became a fixture in England, the new shared goal was the conquest of a hundred cities the size of London. After the recording rush of 1980, Judas Priest, Iron Maiden, Def Leppard, and Motörhead all enlisted in a life of heavy touring abroad. NWOBHM veterans Raven hired a truck and drove south through Belgium into Europe, bringing unheard music to audiences ready for excitement. "It was real culture shock," says John Gallagher. "We'd only been to Spain when we were kids. It was amazing. People were going apeshit. They tore down a partition in the club in Milan—it was like a divider you'd see in a school lunchroom. After the show we were inundated by people wanting autographs and women who put across that they wanted to do certain things, which never happened to us before. We loved it."

Kerrang!'s competition from abroad: *Aardschok*

The international export of *Kerrang!* oriented floods of foreigners toward England, each adding individual refinements to NWOBHM formulas. Germany's Accept played to the growing metal market with a derivative approach that favored crisp, pounding rhythms. Likewise,

Japan's Loudness, New York's Riot and Manowar, and Canada's Anvil unveiled thicker riffs and niftier costumes than dubiously named Brits like Split Beaver and Bitches Sin. At the same time, London headbangers felt abandoned by a rapidly "Americanized" Def Leppard and were willing to shop for imports.

Surviving the NWOBHM required a band have persistence and luck to match its musical ability and striped trousers. "There were second-tier and third-tier bands trying to hop on the bandwagon," says John Gallagher of Raven, speaking of the likes of Brooklyn, Crucifixion, Fist, and Tytan. "All the bands were different, which you don't see too often. It wasn't so homogenized. As usual, one or two had the connections, or had a good look, or met the right people, and a lot of others fell by the wayside. We were really lucky, and we tried as hard as possible to get people interested."

The nearest miss of the NWOBHM era was Diamond Head. Its landmark *Lightning to the Nations* was recorded in 1980 and released in a plain white sleeve decorated only with the four band members' autographs. The songs were also clean and modern, jammed with a fast, antiseptic heaviness that fled the dark alleys of Iron Maiden for the gleaming skyscrapers and groceries of the unborn New Britain. Though they helped define the NWOBHM with their power chords and optimism, they became disembodied observers of their own doomed career. Diamond Head was like an ethereal ghost, damned by Led Zeppelin comparisons and incapable of discovering salvation.

In the unfinished rooms of Diamond Head's estates, however, younger musicians imagined the presence of metal beyond Judas Priest and Iron Maiden. The eager Diamond Head followers in Metallica later recorded cover versions of four of the seven songs on *Lightning to the Nations* (as well as other NWOBHM selections by Savage, Holocaust, Sweet Savage, and Blitzkreig). Says Dave Mustaine, who played in Metallica for a pivotal fourteen months before founding Megadeth, "I keep turning back to Diamond Head. When I was drinking and hanging out with [Metallica guitarist] James Hetfield, we would listen to Venom and Motörhead and Raven and Tank and Mercyful Fate and Diamond Head and Angel Witch and Witchfinder General and stuff like that."

Yet international success demanded that a band take fate into its own hands. Despite the rock-star dreams of Diamond Head's "It's Electric"—"I'm gonna be a rock and roll star, gotta groove from night to day"—history can credit the superior songcraft and work ethic of Iron Maiden for leaving records like *Lightning to the Nations* trapped in the starting gates of the British metal era. Iron Maiden fully realized the creative potential of the NWOBHM, melting together its streetwise image, horror lyric concept, and highly evolved dual-guitar musical chops—then tirelessly worked with their equally ambitious management to overcome any obstacles.

Iron Maiden's terrifying second album, *Killers*, cracked the U.S. *Billboard* chart at number sixty and sold 200,000 copies during 1981. This escalating popularity led to problems with its singer during the world tour that followed. Paul Di'Anno was a product of the clubs, but Iron Maiden was no longer a club act. The decision was made to sack Di'Anno before his behavior interfered with the band's best professional efforts. In September 1981 singer Bruce Dickinson, aka

Steve Harris, mastermind of Iron Maiden
(Todd Nakamine)

Bruce Bruce, shaved his enormous mustache and left Samson to front Iron Maiden, beginning a powerful ten-year partnership. The physical and theatrical Dickinson, a fencing enthusiast, entered just as Maiden was testing stadiums for the first time, and his larger-than-life arm movements and siren voice were designed, as in opera, to impress all the way back to the cheap seats.

Released in April 1982, Dickinson's debut with Iron Maiden, *The Number of the Beast,* was a masterfully defining moment. "After the New Wave of British Heavy Metal, that record really proved that Maiden was going to be a global force," says Rob Halford of Judas Priest. "The title's great, and it really showed a different side of metal that was coming out of the UK. It's really important for defining that British movement at the time. There are pockets in metal—like in lots of music—that are important, and this one was pretty important."

Though mocked by the *Kansas City Star* as a "humorless" novelty during 1978 U.S. appearances with Kiss, the mesmerizing Judas Priest was now selling out small coliseums in Texas and Pennsylvania, bringing Iron Maiden along for a first taste of major venues. "These were the days of really slow communication," says Rob Halford. "You just really had to go out on the road and stay on the road. All those years I was with Priest, it was literally like twenty years on the road together, with very few breaks. It was just nonstop. You had no MTV, you had no Internet, you had no street-level thing with magazines. It was just extremely primitive and in its infancy."

In response, such was the loyalty inspired by Judas Priest that impressionable new bands from abroad chose their names from every song but one on the masterful 1979 live album *Unleashed in the East*—Exciter, Running Wild, Sinner, Ripper, Green Manalishi, Victim of Changes, Genocide, and Tyrant. Only "Diamonds and Rust," a Joan Baez cover, did not inspire a namesake. For this fledgling armada of bands and hundreds yet unnamed, the first ten years of heavy metal were still just the beginning. Great Britain had conceived and created the classic heavy metal style—but in Europe, Asia, and America the future was up for grabs.

1980: The American Wasteland Awaits

- **October 13, 1980:** AC/DC's *Back in Black* goes platinum in the United States
- **January 1982:** Ozzy Osbourne chews head off a bat thrown onstage in Iowa
- **March 1982:** Guitarist Randy Rhoads killed in airplane crash
- **June 14, 1982:** Metal Blade Records releases *Metal Massacre*
- **August 20, 1982:** Elektra reissue of Mötley Crüe's *Too Fast for Love* hits Billboard at number 157

While England's heavy metal factories pressed ahead, America in 1980 was awakening from a disco dream. After dancing away the troubles of the previous decade, few American rock fans were aware of the charms of Iron Maiden, Motörhead, and Judas Priest, let alone the lesser-known Diamond Head or Angel Witch. "Disco tormented the people who were into hard rock into a corner for five years," says Ron Quintana, a San Francisco DJ and record collector. "You were like rats scurrying around underfoot—trying to find each other and tell each other about these new metal bands coming out of the woodwork."

Like heavy metal, disco had diva vocalists, and both were energetic, communal experiences. But for kids too young to trip the light fantastic, the disco nightlife was just another indulgence of the self-obsessed "me" generation. Twisted Sister, a club band popular in the suburbs around New York, rallied the dissenting vote with the majestic "Rock and Roll Saviors," whose lyrics bluntly boasted "Disco is dead!" "It was something to focus youthful hatred on," says the band's singer, Dee Snider. "Disco was so predominant that it was difficult for a rock band to find work. Disco was just completely out of control. In retrospect, it was a lifestyle issue. The music represented more than just a sound that we didn't like—it represented a certain part of the population. The disco kids were one group, and heavy metal kids were another."

There was untapped enthusiasm from many avenues in America for an ugly end to the disco daze. Audacious, reviled, and ready to ruin the twenty-first century, the Plasmatics were an apocalyptic punk rock freak show spawned from New York's seedy Times Square. They rejoiced in sound as a razor-wire barricade. Dressed onstage in shaving cream and strategic strips of black tape, singer Wendy O. Williams chain-sawed guitars in half and attacked junk cars with a sledgehammer. It was an over-the-top cartoon, celebrating the destruction of American icons for the purpose of sensationalism. "We created chaos and mayhem," says guitarist Richie Stotts. "It was dangerous sometimes, but we had a good time. Some people came after us, but they didn't get it. They were judging the band by what they thought a band should be. We didn't even say we *were* a band!"

Yet as the 1980 election of Ronald Reagan ended the free-flowing 1970s with a resounding conservative clap, punk's charge on mainstream America was already bankrupt. Like the London punk implosion, the Los Angeles scene created by X and the Germs burned out on drugs and destruction—its dangerous edge soon shaped by the music industry into the disco-influenced angles of new wave. When the sight of Germs singer Darby Crash carving his skin in the documentary *The Decline of Western Civilization* reached suburban shopping mall cineplexes, the antiauthoritarian posture stuck, but not the noxious sound. Stripped of its protest, punk music was commercialized and regurgitated as the teen movie soundtrack pabulum of Wall of Voodoo, Oingo Boingo, and the Knack. As TV teen misfit Slash from the high school sitcom *Square Pegs* protested, "I'm not punk, I'm new wave—it's a totally different head." Cue laugh track.

Beneath disco's glitter and the ruins of punk, the metal revolution gestated. "In Hollywood there was a regular swap meet in the Capitol Records parking lot," says Brian Slagel, founder of Metal Blade Records. "It was all music, and they sold anything from rare records to old 45s, and they sold a lot of bootlegs. I bought from there, and once I became friends with the people that worked at the record stores and they knew I was into metal like Kiss and AC/DC, they'd say 'Oh, you, here's a tape of another band you should check out. They're cool, too.'"

Elsewhere, heavy metal fans formed cliques within the hard rock scene. The "rats underfoot" scratched signals to one another through the classified sections of collector magazines like *Goldmine* and *Record Trader* or spotted each other at major rock events. "We saw Exodus singer Paul Baloff at all the Yesterday and Today [later called Y&T] shows," says Ron Quintana about the San Francisco scene. "That was the heaviest thing we had going. You'd see people over and over at the cool shows, and Baloff was one of them. Y&T initiated a lot of Bay Area people into hard rock, which was good."

As metalheads gathered like swarming bees, homemade cassette tapes were the pollen through which they relayed the genetic codes necessary to expand the hive. "I really got into the whole NWOBHM scene around 1979," says Brian Slagel. "I used to trade live tapes and demo tapes with people all over the world. I got into that British heavy metal because a couple friends of mine over in Europe went, 'Oh, here's a new band called Iron Maiden,' and put a couple songs on the end of a tape. Once you met one guy, he'd recommend someone else, and I just took it from there."

Across America the story was the same. A few devout believers in every area preached the word of the NWOBHM and desperately sought news of new bands and concert activity. Headbanger litanies gleaned from dog-eared copies of *Kerrang!* held the tribes together. "We'd have trivia contests all the time. We were like secret societies," says Ron Quintana. "If you met anybody from England or Europe, like when we met Lars Ulrich, we'd be quizzing them on every single band ever: 'What does Dragster sound like? Who is this Wrathchild band?' Most of them like Dragster were shit, but you'd see their name in a magazine and think they were heavy." Being a metalhead required an unusual commitment just to get new music. "Even the punks weren't reading the English papers," says Quintana, "because they had enough of a scene over here. It was the metallers who were having to look elsewhere to find anything heavy."

With no real American counterpart, the London press had the power to introduce North American bands to their home countries, like Toronto's hard-driving Anvil and New York's rough Twisted Sister. "Just because we were in *Kerrang!* a lot, we became affiliated with the NWOBHM," says Dee Snider. "Then we broke out in England, and when we came back here [to America], we were constantly being asked 'Where's your British accent?' Like Hendrix, Joan Jett, and the Stray Cats before us, we went to England to find fame and fortune and broke in reverse out of England."

Following positive coverage in *Kerrang!*, Twisted Sister's business-minded guitarist, Jay Jay French, traveled to England to land the group a European recording deal. This unconventional but necessary journey was a success, and brought a heavier British influence evidenced on 1982's *You Can't Stop Rock 'N' Roll*. "Jay came back to New York with a cassette tape of Iron Maiden's *Killers*," says Dee Snider, "and he gave it to me because bassist Mark Mendoza and I were the metalheads. I just put that thing in and said, 'Damn!' And then I also became a big fan of Saxon."

By 1980, to play anything remotely like heavy metal in Los Angeles and not be Van Halen . . . sucked. While touting the virtues of bikinis and sports cars, even the ultimate California hard rock band had its origins in Europe. Eddie Van Halen and brother Alex were immigrants from Holland, who moved to Pasadena in 1962 as Dutch-speaking elementary-schoolers. Perhaps the pair's inventive approaches to music came from the experience of moving from one culture to another—struggling through transition, they divined an entirely innovative discipline that broke from the confines of convention.

In many ways the sporty American counterpart of Led Zeppelin, Van Halen was an entity too cocky to be believed. Over their first four albums, Van Halen became the successful face of sunshine, selling the wild Hollywood lifestyle with an exuberant party-hearty attitude that did not diminish its obvious talent. The band's mascot, aerobic, lion-maned singer David Lee Roth, appropriated the unbelievable screams of Deep Purple's Ian Gillan and the horny down-home posturing of Black Oak Arkansas's Jim Dandy Mangrum. Though untouchable, they had common desires, and still ate hamburgers and drank cold beer like ordinary folks.

Van Halen was supremely exciting thanks to the brilliantly kinetic Eddie Van Halen. He made technique the guiding light of his guitar playing, and showy solos like "Eruption" took heavy metal guitar to the brink of rocket science. Instead of running blues scales up and down the neck, Van Halen attacked from all directions. "I was a big fan of Van Halen, Judas Priest, Jimi Hendrix, and Michael Schenker of UFO—players with a special feeling," says George Emmanuel, aka Trey Azagthoth, a later guitar hero from Morbid Angel. "It was extreme at that time. Eddie Van Halen came out with such flash and feeling—there was something electrifying about his sound and the way he phrased things."

The few other heavy metal bands in Los Angeles also attempted to combine more profound heavy metal with homegrown show-business flair. Diligent small-fries Quiet Riot, Snow, and Xciter mimicked the concussive anthems of Judas Priest's *British Steel* while nodding to Van Halen when showcasing their own guitar heroes. Quiet Riot featured fluid soloist Randy Rhoads, and Snow had hyperactive Carlos Cavazo, who later replaced Rhoads in Quiet Riot. Xciter displayed the haunting, melodic guitar leads of George Lynch, who later formed Dokken.

An unlikely bridge between European and American influences came in the provocative person of Ozzy Osbourne, a Los Angeles resident since moving there with Black Sabbath in 1976. After his departure from Sabbath, Ozzy rebounded from near-total self-destruction with his solo endeavor, *Blizzard of Ozz*. Penniless after a series of bad business arrangements, Ozzy was rescued through his relation-

Ozzy Osbourne: The Madman of Metal
(Jet Records)

ship with Sharon Arden, daughter of Sabbath manager Don Arden. Breaking with her father to represent the alcoholic rock star, Sharon bought out Osbourne's contract, and the pair started from scratch.

The experience of being blown away by Van Halen during his final tour with Black Sabbath seemed to impress Ozzy. On *Blizzard of Ozz* he emulated Van Halen's metallic rock with hotshot guitarist Randy Rhoads and session men Bob Daisley and Lee Kerslake. Dressing the riff-oriented Black Sabbath style in a melodic, radio-friendly California sound, Ozzy's band recorded two albums in 1980, *Blizzard of Ozz* and *Diary of a Madman*, the latter titled after a short story by Russian writer Nikolai Gogol. Many early fans of Black Sabbath were no longer listening, but there was a new generation ready for a fresh start and a liberal dose of something heavy.

Minor chords and darker metal swept over America as AC/DC's *Back in Black* reached number four in the U.S. charts in November 1980. The album was a clamorous revolt against the rock-star death by drunken asphyxiation of its longtime singer Bon Scott on February 20, 1980. Scott was a coarse, barroom diva, and after the coroner's report established the cause of his demise as "death by misadventure"—Ozzy and Randy Rhoads wrote the antialcohol song "Suicide Solution" in his honor. Instead of being quieted by the accident, AC/DC came spitting furiously out of the crypt. Without neglecting party anthems like "You Shook Me All Night Long," *Back in Black* rolled out heavy metal thunder with the ominous ringing chimes of "Hells Bells" and the slow crawl of "Rock and Roll Ain't Noise Pollution." Angus Young, the tiny lead guitarist, jabbed his riffs one breath ahead of a tight rhythm section led by his brother Malcolm—a simple wizard whose only tool was a large guitar with all controls removed except the volume knob.

Back in Black proved that heavy metal appealed to audiences in huge, previously unrecognized numbers. As it turned out, there was an entire generation of people who were sick of disco. When offered something heavier, they rushed to grasp it tightly. Also in 1981 the reissue of AC/DC's 1976 Australian album *Dirty Deeds Done Dirt Cheap* sold 5 million copies, and the late-year studio album *For Those About to Rock, We Salute You* sold 3 million. While Eddie Van Halen married sitcom star Valerie Bertinelli and entered the ranks of celebrity musicians, AC/DC singer Brian Johnson had trouble getting past security to enter his own gigs. Yet the disturbing *Back in Black* went on to sell nearly 20 million copies in America in the next two decades, besting the sales of the first four Van Halen albums with David Lee Roth combined.

With Angus Young still wearing a schoolboy uniform, squirming and shaking in an interpretive dance of boundless dementia, AC/DC became the stadium-stunning heavy metal replacement for Led Zeppelin, who had disbanded after its own rock-star death by drunken asphyxiation of drummer of John Bonham on September 25, 1980. Both bands were steeped in amplified blues and, though not especially sexy, traded on heaps of hormonally charged song material. As Led Zeppelin faded into the 1970s, AC/DC became the stepping-stone that led huge numbers of hard rock fans into heavy metal perdition.

For Americans who witnessed AC/DC live, or saw photos or a rare video of Motörhead or Saxon performing in Europe in front of thousands of fans, the good times of Van Halen could not compare. Preoccupied with finding limited-quantity records by little-known bands, Ron Quintana wrote a letter to *Kerrang!* requesting pen pals. "I wanted to network with other Americans who were into heavy metal," he says, "rather than Ted Nugent or even just the same generic Lynyrd Skynyrd hard rock that everyone was into. Writing to an English paper was the only way to get in touch with other hip Americans to trade heavy demos and bootlegs. They printed my letter in *Kerrang!* No. 4. That summer I started averaging ten to twenty letters a day, so every day would be just like Christmas. I'd get amazing packages with amazing bands that nobody had ever heard of."

Inundated with new recordings, Ron Quintana expanded his massive Xeroxed tape-trading list to include photographs and longer reviews of new records and bands. Six months after his distress signal appeared in *Kerrang!*, Quintana's list metamorphosed from a simple collector's inventory to a full-fledged fanzine, complete with live reports and editorial essays. From a long list of potential names, Quintana chose *Metal Mania*. "I was going to call my magazine *Metallica*," he says, "but Lars Ulrich liked the name better for his band, so he borrowed it."

Quintana's friend Lars Ulrich, a beginning drummer, had recently begun jamming with guitarist James Hetfield. Their new band

EARLY AMERICAN METAL

There was a homegrown hard-rock scene in Los Angeles in the 1980s, struggling against disco in the name of Van Halen. Some bands took up outlandish stage antics in order to break the monotony—most just soaked up the rays, dyed their hair blond, and tried to blend into a sea of club clones waiting for the big score. In New York nobody knew what to do with bands like Riot and Twisted Sister. Nonetheless, it mattered that these groups were competing with the English wave. For all intents and purposes Ozzy Osbourne's new band was an American entity. Along with Van Halen, Ozzy helped usher out Aerosmith, Heart, and the rest of the hard rock straphangers at the beginning of the 1980s. Soon Mötley Crüe, Ratt, and the *Metal Massacre* gang took heavy metal in a whole new direction.

Hot Rockers

- ❖ Lita Ford, *Out for Blood* (1983)
- ❖ Mötley Crüe, *Too Fast for Love* (1981)
- ❖ Ozzy Osbourne, *Blizzard of Ozz* (1980)
- ❖ Ozzy Osbourne, *Diary of a Madman* (1981)
- ❖ Quiet Riot, *II* (1979)
- ❖ Ratt, *Ratt* EP (1983)
- ❖ Riot, *Fire Down Under* (1981)
- ❖ Twisted Sister, *Under the Blade* (1982)
- ❖ Van Halen, *I* (1978)
- ❖ Van Halen, *Women and Children First* (1980)
- ❖ Various Artists, *Metal Massacre* (1982)
- ❖ Y&T, *Earthshaker* (1981)

name, "Metallica," was derived from *Encyclopedia Metallica*—the sole overview of hard rock and heavy metal then available in bookstores. It was an improvement over what Hetfield had named previous ensembles: Leather Charm and Phantom Lord. Not that it mattered much—the group's activities were limited to playing choppy Diamond Head covers in a bedroom on nights when Hetfield came over to tape LPs from Ulrich's exhaustive collection.

In August 1981 in Los Angeles, record-store clerk and radio disc jockey Brian Slagel launched the fanzine *New Heavy Metal Revue,* which covered local bands and the NWOBHM records he had been playing and importing for sale. "Slagel did a really good job

Metal Mania fanzine

with his magazine," says Ron Quintana, "but the L.A. scene was so bad that he didn't have much to work with musically." The local malaise was only occasionally punctuated by concerts, like a sold-out August 1981 appearance by influential rock/metal bridge band UFO with support act Iron Maiden before 14,000 fans at Long Beach Arena.

As Slagel's record store attracted metalheads in the region, it fostered a regular network for streams of formerly isolated metal rats. "A couple guys came in and told me about local bands," Slagel says. "Prior to that it was only Van Halen and Quiet Riot. They told me about Mötley Crüe, and Bitch, and I started going out to see them. There was finally a metal scene in L.A., and it was kind of unbelievable. We started to cover that in the fanzine, and I started to play a lot of the local bands on the radio station, too. It got bigger and bigger, and I started putting on dates at some of the clubs around here."

Soon a Los Angeles club scene developed to compare with what

Kerrang! trumpeted from London. Every Wednesday night at the Troubadour in Hollywood, Mötley Crüe and Ratt played for a one-dollar cover charge. Unlike the melodic rockers Van Halen, the new heavy metal club acts were clued in to the rapid and thundering sound of Iron Maiden. "All those bands, Ratt and Steeler and Mötley Crüe, started out really heavy," explains Slagel. "Especially Ratt—they were basically Judas Priest. They would all wear black, and they had two guys playing Flying V guitars. [Future Ozzy sideman] Jake E. Lee was in the band. Later those bands kind of evolved into the hard rock metal thing."

The very punk Mötley Crüe in particular kick-started the scene with a wild, occult-inspired stage show, as bandleader and bassist Frank Ferrano, aka Nikki Sixx, borrowed liberal amounts of blood, smoke, and fire from earlier shock rockers Alice Cooper and Kiss. As Sixx later admitted, he also inherited trappings from Sister, an early band led by Steven Duren, aka Blackie Lawless of W.A.S.P. "Our logo was a pentagram, and I used to set myself on fire," says Lawless. "When I decided that I wasn't going to do those things anymore, Nikki Sixx came to me and he asked would I mind if he did those things. I said, 'No, they're all yours,' but I cautioned him about both."

Mötley Crüe at Square One
(Coffman & Coffman Productions)

The primal version of Mötley Crüe had the monstrosity of Kiss, the dead-end energy of the Plasmatics, and the umlauts of Motörhead. The band gave English bands a run for their money, and local metalheads rallied in support. "James Hetfield got me into Mötley Crüe because he was way into them," says L.A. headbanger Katon W. DePena. "We used to go see them all the time. They were good for a total hair band."

As the popularity of heavy metal spread, Ozzy Osbourne's first two solo albums quickly went gold, despite having been initially rejected by a succession of disinterested record labels. Two incidents soon propelled the lovable singer into national infamy. First, seeking to impress his new label, CBS, Ozzy bit the head off a live dove during a 1981 meeting with executives. Then in January 1982 he chewed the head off a bat thrown onstage by a fan in Des Moines, Iowa. For that indiscretion Ozzy endured multiple rabies shots in the stomach and took Alice Cooper's throne as top rock bogeyman. Previously "acid rock" had been a playground myth, a gross-out story bragged about behind school cafeterias over furtive cigarettes. Unfounded rumors that Cooper drank a bucket of LSD-laced phlegm or that AC/DC's Angus Young impaled himself on a Gibson SG set child standards for rock mystique. With his biting antics, Ozzy Osbourne became a willing spokesman for rock-star insanity and earned the fierce loyalty of heavy metal misfits.

Parents were repelled by Ozzy's reputation, but his music after Black Sabbath was much kinder than his image. Still hoping for peace, an unfashionable sentiment in the Reagan-Thatcher era, in "Crazy Train" he commiserated "heirs of a Cold War, that's what we've become." Young teens trusted Ozzy's knowing voice in songs like "Goodbye to Romance" and "Over the Mountain," and they adored the sweet songwriting and guitar solos of Randy Rhoads, whose trademark design motif was polka dots, not pentagrams. Sadly, the crazy track of Ozzy's career was rerouted to tragedy when gifted twenty-five-year-old Rhoads died in a plane accident during the *Diary of a Madman* tour in March 1982. While attempting to buzz over the Ozzy tour bus, the pilot lost control and careened into a nearby house. The loss was devastating, and especially traumatic to Ozzy's already pummeled psyche.

There were few overnight successes in heavy metal, but bands that broke new ground were eventually paid their just rewards. Backed by steady touring, Judas Priest's *Screaming for Vengeance,* Iron Maiden's *Number of the Beast,* and Def Leppard's *High 'n' Dry* all charted in America in 1982. Along with German interlopers Scorpions, whose *Blackout* broke the *Billboard* Top 10, these marauding English bands registered just a slight tremor in the pop music scene, but their new prominence was the genesis of something great. To heavy metal's staunch supporters, there was a constant infectious sense that the music grew bigger by the day. "As we progressed into the eighties, it just exploded," says Rob Halford of Judas Priest. "Once the Americans got hold of this thing coming from Britain and took it into their own kind of style and approach, everything went global."

Energized by the upswing of activity and inspired by do-it-yourself records from the NWOBHM era, *New Heavy Metal Revue* editor Brian Slagel set about producing *Metal Massacre,* the first LP on his brand-new Metal Blade Records. "I called all the distributors that I worked with at the record store," he says, "and asked if I put together a compilation of metal bands, would they sell it?" With assurances of support on the business end, Slagel approached local bands for whom he had booked shows, including Ratt, Malice, and Steeler. He also tossed in "a couple of ringers" culled from the home-taper circuit, such as Alaska's Pandemonium and the weird Washington band Cirith Ungol.

The riotous Mötley Crüe nearly appeared on the bedroom release as well. "I booked a lot of shows for them," says Slagel. "They had a song that was all ready to be on the record, but by the time we got around to doing it, *Too Fast for Love* [the band's self-released debut] had really taken off. Their two managers came to my mom's house one day and said, 'We've got nine hundred records we pressed of this Mötley Crüe album. What do you think we should do with them?' I sent them to a distributor, and the rest is history." Pumped by exposure in a licentious *Oui* magazine photo spread (an honor afforded Motörhead the same year), Mötley Crüe's *Too Fast for Love* sold 20,000 copies in six months, leading to a deal with Elektra Records and landing the number 157 spot on the *Billboard* album chart.

To fill the last few open minutes on *Metal Massacre*, Slagel agreed to accept an entry by young metal enthusiast Lars Ulrich. "My friend John Kornarens and I met Lars in 1982 at a Michael Schenker show at the Country Club," says Slagel. "John was in the parking lot after the gig and saw this kid wearing a Saxon European tour T-shirt. We had never seen anything like that. He said he had just moved here from Denmark and he was really big into metal. The next day we all ended up at Lars's house, and we all became friends. He seemed about sixteen, I was nineteen, and John was twenty. We just used to drive around to the record stores for hours trying to find NWOBHM stuff."

Though aware of Ulrich's taste and his wide circle of contacts, Slagel was uncertain whether the young Dane actually had a band. "It was really funny. He was this crazy little kid, and he had a drum set in his room that wasn't really put together. He had been jamming with James Hetfield for a while, but there was nothing going on. When he said he was going to start a band, everyone thought, 'Yeah, sure you are, Lars.'"

James Hetfield pre–Leather Charm

The pairing of Hetfield and Ulrich represented the marriage of two great metalhead characters. James Hetfield was a middle-class loner, quietly resisting a brutal domestic grind that constantly tested his free will. He was raised with piano lessons and public school in the fading industrial Los Angeles suburb of Downey. The Hetfields were Christian Scientists, and James compared his home life to being raised in a pressure cooker. He was excused from high school health class, where his parents feared he might learn too much about his body. When Mrs. Hetfield, a former opera singer, grew sick with cancer in 1979, she refused medical care and died, leaving James without emotional support. He discovered petty theft in junior high and kept extensive lists of his pirate's booty, until—to the relief of area drugstores—he channeled his quirks into playing guitar.

Lars Ulrich, on the other hand, was a privileged scion whose sense of entitlement prevented him from embracing mundane, normal teenage pursuits. Ulrich's family left his hometown of Gentofte, Denmark, in late 1980 and relocated to Newport Beach, California, one of the most conspicuously tanned and Ferrari-laden sections of the Los Angeles sprawl. From there his father, Torben Ulrich, traveled often to compete in world-class tennis tournaments, such as the World Cup and Davis Cup, a career young Ulrich was well on his way to inheriting. The trouble was that Lars, a ranked teen player in Denmark, fell off the map entirely when pitted against California jocks.

As his sporting career ran afoul, Lars Ulrich turned his love to heavy metal—especially the heaviest possible varieties. Raised traveling frequently to international matches with his father, Ulrich thought nothing of flying to England in 1981 to catch a few shows by his idols in Diamond Head. He stalked the band and, incredibly, was invited to spend two months living with the parents of singer Sean Harris. Barely a musician himself, owning just a few mismatched pieces of a drum set, Ulrich spent days watching the band work through the less glamorous routines of rehearsing and writing songs.

Ulrich later followed Motörhead on the road in America. He recognized few boundaries when it came to absorbing not just the glory hours but the minute details of the metal bands he really loved. "That's him," says Ron Quintana, recalling the concentrated assault of his friend's fandom. Ulrich was so thoroughly consumed by heavy metal that he would make it his life—spending the next decades not only playing metal but finding new ways to beat his excitement about the music into the heads of the world.

With *Metal Massacre* offering Metallica a reason to exist, Ulrich and Hetfield found it easier to find players and form a real band. Hetfield himself had been unsure of Ulrich after an earlier meeting. In January 1982 they recruited Jamaican headbanger Lloyd Grant to play lead guitar on "Hit the Lights," a song carried over from Hetfield's previous band, Leather Charm. "James couldn't really play the lead," says Slagel, "and Lars knew Lloyd, who was a pretty good guitar player, so Lars just got him to play guitar."

Sorry as the band was, Metallica finished its recording—if only by the skin of its teeth. "Of course, they were the last band that I got the track from," Slagel says. "I think they recorded it two nights before we mastered the record." From fan to fanzine writer to fledgling record-company mogul, Slagel pressed several thousand copies of *Metal Massacre*, using money he had saved by working at Sears and borrowed from his aunt. Soon mom-and-pop metal shops in America were stocking *Metal Massacre* along with the other alluring fare imported in regular overseas relief packages.

Metal Massacre

Metallica now had a track on a record, but they had yet to play live. Grant, the only member with any developed musical ability, departed immediately. During this period the days were most often spent in a metal haze. "Back when Lloyd Grant was in the band, Metallica was really fun," says headbanger Katon DePena, who hung out at the house where James Hetfield and Metallica bassist Ron McGovney lived. "We'd go to this record store called Middle Earth and buy nothing but imports—Saxon, Motörhead, Riot, Angel Witch, Anvil, Satan, Trust, Tank, even the first Def Leppard album. Still, we all thought we could do it a little bit better and harder."

If the concert experience was akin to high mass, scattered specialty record stores were the roadside chapels of the metal world. The Record Vault in San Francisco was a hangout for the *Metal Mania* and KUSF metal gang. Back in London, the boutique Shades on St. Anne's Court was where Tom Warrior of Hellhammer discovered the first Venom single during a tourist pilgrimage. Tokyo, Japan, had The Black and Metal Kids shops. These holes in the wall catered to headbangers, stocking *Kerrang!*, spiked wristbands, intriguing UK imports, and shaped picture discs by Accept, Oz, Mercyful Fate, and Earthshaker. "Early on, the Record Exchange in Walnut Creek, California, was the heaviest store in the States, as far as I knew," says Ron Quintana. "I think I bought the first *Kerrang!* there. In fact, the first time I met Lars Ulrich, we went over and checked out that place. We freaked out those people—they didn't believe anyone knew so much about metal. We made them order all kinds of weird stuff that got the ball rolling."

By February 1982, *Kerrang!* was popular enough to warrant doubling its publishing schedule, and the editors began publishing a new issue every two weeks. *Kerrang!* became the cultural glue that kept the ragtag American metalheads inspired and united. Even a kid from Downey like James Hetfield, who had never traveled outside the country, was dropping British slang and referring to fans as punters—the *Kerrang!* term for London's front-row headbangers.

Wobbling toward something "a little bit better and harder," the embryonic Metallica went through a number of personnel changes in its first months as they found gigs opening for local talent like Roxx Regime, later known as Stryper. One of Metallica's early concerts in Costa Mesa, California, tested a five-piece configuration featuring guitarists Dave Mustaine and Brad Parker, aka Damian C. Phillips. Hetfield sang lead vocals. As bassist Ron McGovney told *Shock Waves*, the experiment ended after Phillips quickly proved wrong for the job. "While James, Lars, and I were getting dressed to go onstage, we heard this guitar solo, so we looked over the railing of the dressing room and saw Brad onstage by himself just blazing away on his guitar! That was Metallica's first and last gig with Damian C. Phillips."

Phillips later resurfaced in the lipstick-laden glam band Odin, but despite such missteps the bright green "go" switch was engaged for Metallica. The band's lineup hardened around Lars Ulrich, James Hetfield, Ron McGovney, and Dave Mustaine. In one year Ulrich had graduated from extraordinary fan to drummer of a fledgling heavy metal force, and bootlegs of Metallica concerts began to circulate up the West Coast and even across the waters to Europe. Soon after the June 1982 release of *Metal Massacre*, Lars Ulrich reported losing his virginity at a party at Dave Mustaine's house.

For Brian Slagel the *Metal Massacre* gambit was a different kind of success. The entire first pressing of 4,500 copies sold out in one week, as fans rallied around a record featuring a dozen nearly unknown regional bands. Slagel had correctly guessed the taste of the emerging hard-edged heavy metal audience, even underestimating its scope. His picks were certainly the cream of the unharvested crop. Most of them—Ratt, Ron Keel and Yngwie Malmsteen's band Steeler,

Malice, Black 'N Blue, even the homely Metallica—eventually signed major-label deals. (For this reason Ratt and Steeler were removed from subsequent pressings of *Metal Massacre;* a more experienced Metallica also slipped in a newer version of "Hit the Lights" recorded with Mustaine.)

At this stage the do-it-yourself metal fanatics did not expect to make money, and Slagel was ill equipped to finance and manage the scene's growth. "All the distributors called asking for more, but I didn't have any money and didn't know what to do," he says. "We had a meeting with a guy who was managing the Dixie Dregs, and he had a label deal with RCA. We never got paid, and it was a complete nightmare. I didn't know what the heck I was doing. I was just some twenty-one-year-old kid who thought it was great."

Slagel set about replicating his success with the 1982 compilation *Metal Massacre II,* again joining California bands Warlord, Savage Grace, and Trauma with far-flung acts like Hawaii's Aloha, featuring future Megadeth guitarist Marty Friedman. He hoped to lead the record with a track by the mystical Danish troupe Mercyful Fate but lost touch with them after a management shake-up. Instead he turned to leather-clad locals Armored Saint, who cruised into position with the rousing "Lesson Well Learned."

Progressing just as quickly, in July 1982 Metallica recorded "No Life 'Til Leather," a demo tape featuring the songs "Hit the Lights," "Mechanix," "Motorbreath," "Seek & Destroy," "Metal Militia," "Jump in the Fire," and "Phantom Lord." The sound was bright and brash, with energy that overcame traditional concepts of tunefulness. Hetfield's voice was high and whiny, and Dave Mustaine's guitar solos were charged and frantic. The cuts resonated like a faster, heavier, younger American version of what the Brits had been doing in Diamond Head. While not yet arriving at the flowing force that would become their trademark, the tape proved that Metallica had learned to play, and it garnered the acclaim of fans who wanted to hear the NWOBHM taken one step further.

"No Life 'Til Leather" paved Metallica's way out of town, leading to its first appearance in San Francisco on September 18, 1982. At a

"No Life 'Til Leather" demo case

show to promote *Metal Massacre*, the band that had been quietly doing its own thing in Los Angeles suddenly encountered tape traders who had already previewed the Metallica cassette. "It was supposed to be Metallica, Bitch, and Cirith Ungol," says Brian Slagel, "but Cirith Ungol dropped out at the last minute. When Metallica came out, it was like magic. The crowd was going wild, and the band just sort of freaked out. They had a few fans in L.A., but nothing like this. It was unbelievable. I knew at that point they should leave L.A."

Compared to the music-industry feeder trough that was Los Angeles, San Francisco was a cultural island and creative paradise. The city offered a more urban environment, with a higher density of clubs, record stores, and radio stations staffed by friends eager to push each other to heavier heights. As NWOBHM bands had unraveled the frayed ends of British hard rock, bands like Trauma and Exodus gleefully presided over the extinction of Bay Area wimp rockers Starship and Journey. Says Jeff Hanneman of Slayer, "When we first heard Exodus, I was surprised there was a band that kinda sounded like us, playing the same style of music. I was stoked the first time we played in Frisco that somebody actually played something similar to our style."

In hindsight it was unlikely that the denim-jacketed and pimply Metallica would have found such acceptance in Los Angeles, where show business would always rate higher than musical might. The most extreme example was W.A.S.P., whose blaring shock rock came with an elaborate stage show that included torture instruments, skulls on poles, and more fire, smoke, and lights than Halloween in the Munsters' front parlor. "Before we became successful, my dad had a construction company," explains bandleader Blackie Lawless, "so when I came to California, I worked for a special-effects company and built fog machines and pyro. A lot of that went into the show. Because I had firsthand information, I knew what was and wasn't possible. Especially the exploding codpiece and stuff like that."

Without makeup or exploding codpieces, Metallica's appearance was anti-image. Sticking with leather jackets, denim vests, T-shirts, and the occasional spiked or studded belt, Metallica looked like the headbangers in the front row of every Iron Maiden and Judas Priest show. Their pins and patches held together the classic image of the metal fan, not the flashy rock star. There was finally a hopping heavy metal scene in L.A.—Mötley Crüe, Ratt, Quiet Riot, and Dokken all landed major recording deals by the end of 1982. The irony was that total metal boosters Metallica did not fit in to the new environment.

The deciding factor in Metallica's leaving Los Angeles was a desire to replace Ron McGovney with the wiry and forceful bassist Cliff Burton: A 1970s throwback with long straight hair and flared bell-bottom jeans, Burton played in Trauma, a San Francisco band that appeared on *Metal Massacre II.* "Trauma was pretty generic hard rock," says Ron Quintana, "with a weird-looking bass player [Burton] who was really good. They wore matching outfits, and they had the Judas Priest guitar-swinging moves. The couple guitarists and the singer wore custom-made lightning bolts on their leathers. Cliff always looked the same, like he just walked in off of Haight Street, but the other three guys looked alike. We thought they were cool, because at least they weren't pop-glam crap."

Burton liked the no-nonsense, aggressive approach of Metallica. After significant cajoling over a period of months, he agreed to leave Trauma to join Metallica on December 28, 1982, stipulating that he would not have to uproot from family and friends in the Bay Area. Six weeks later the mountain happily moved to Mohammed. Ulrich, Hetfield, and Mustaine hauled their gear north, stashing Marshall amps and cassette-tape collections at a soon-to-be greatly punished house in El Cerrito, California—immediately decorated with posters of Michael Schenker, UFO, and Motörhead alongside banners promoting various brands of cheap beer.

It was bold for a band as ambitious as Metallica to abandon the Los Angeles music industry, but San Francisco clearly had the fans, and Metallica invested in its relationship with them. As the chorus heralding America's newfound infatuation with heavy metal swelled in the background, Metallica concentrated on its audience and its craft. The promoters and music-business lawyers could find them later.

Heavy Metal America:
Highways & Video Waves

> ➤ **May 18, 1983:** Judas Priest *Screaming for Vengeance* goes platinum in the United States
>
> ➤ **May 29, 1983:** U.S. Festival '83 draws 600,000 fans for Judas Priest, Scorpions, Van Halen, and Ozzy Osbourne
>
> ➤ **November 26, 1983:** Quiet Riot's *Metal Health* hits #1 in *Billboard*
>
> ➤ **October 12, 1984:** Def Leppard's *Pyromania* goes sextuple platinum in the United States

---

No longer the exclusive domain of die-hard devotees by 1983, heavy metal was airlifted into America and popularized through larger and more frequent concert tours. Fans whose idea of excitement was rearranged by AC/DC were completely swept off their feet by Judas Priest, Iron Maiden, Black Sabbath, and other British invaders. Video would soon offer immense exposure, but the groundwork was established over years spent on the road cultivating a growing and immensely loyal audience base.

Rare appearances by Iron Maiden and Judas Priest on the radio and covers of American rock magazines were nowhere near commensurate with their status in the hearts of headbangers. "Some people buy songs," notes Iron Maiden manager Rod Smallwood, "and some people buy bands." In April 1983, after years on the margins of the music industry, Judas Priest was awarded its first U.S. platinum album for *Screaming for Vengeance*. Iron Maiden's *Number of the Beast* and *Piece of Mind* also both went gold the same year. Positive signs indicated that Def Leppard's *Pyromania* would soon follow suit. The top British heavy metal bands were finally enjoying success on their own terms in America, the largest and most lucrative market in the world.

For American teenagers, heavy metal became the soundtrack to a cultural revolution that included cable television and the first home computers and arcade video games. While Judas Priest sang of high-tech satellites in "Electric Eye," fans were plugging in to a new portable personal cassette player called the Sony Walkman, then blasting aliens in attention-addling electronic amusements like Vanguard, Robotron, Asteroids, Battlezone, and Defender. Saving the universe one quarter at a time to a backdrop of high-energy music, a nation of adrenaline addicts found hope in the future. As the games later grew faster and more intricate, so would heavy metal.

The country was also demonstrating an appetite for adventure scenarios and alternate realities. The popular Dungeons & Dragons role-playing game brought to life the quests of fantasy literature like the *Lord of the Rings* trilogy by J.R.R. Tolkien—another son of Birmingham, England. In the layered escapist universe of D&D, players assumed the roles of various social and ethnic beings like elves, warriors, magic users, and bardic musicians. The plots of the games generally involved killing monsters and collecting treasure while pursuing some greater heroic goal. Much of heavy metal took place on similar turf, a realm of dark towers and impenetrable wilderness populated by battles and adversity. "You've gotta write about heavy subjects; the metallers freak out over it," Dan Beehler of Exciter told Canada's *The New Music* television show. "It's better than something like 'I was walking down the street, da da,' you know? The medieval days were heavy; it was certain death for most people. That's what metal's all about—it's a fight."

Black Sabbath rejoined the metal campaign with a formidable new front man in Ronnie James Dio. He reverently refurbished and reinvented the band's stately doom with grandiose concepts. Staying with Sabbath for two studio albums, *Heaven and Hell* and *Mob Rules*, Dio found a fertile fantasy framework for the big Sabbath themes of madness and desolation—his "Children of the Sea" bemoaned environmental decline through the eyes of a dying ocean planet.

Since his early 1970s band Elf, Dio had written quintessential fantasy lyrics. In Rainbow those included "Man on the Silver Mountain" and the parable "Stargazer"—about a wizard who cripples civilization by attempting to build a stone tower to the stars. "I grew up reading Sir Walter Scott and Arthurian tales," says Dio. "Then I got really interested in science fiction, which also seemed to cloak characters in words and costumes that were very medieval. These were people, I realized, that were telling me the future. You read an Arthur Clarke book, or Isaac Asimov, and when they told you something's going to happen in ten years, they were right. They were just so brilliant, and they allowed me to use my imagination. When I became a songwriter, I thought what better thing to do than do what no one else is doing—to tell fantasy tales. Smartest thing I ever did."

After leaving Sabbath and launching a solo career, Dio simplified his stories substantially for a younger heavy metal audience. The 1983 debut *Holy Diver* by his band, Dio, reduced lush moral landscapes to simple good-versus-evil conflicts, using the lyrical duality of "Rainbow in the Dark" and "Holy Diver" to raise questions about deceit and hypocrisy in romance and religion. In the sharp contrasts of Dio's imagery, there was always a built-in contradiction that fed adolescent revolt: a black side to every white light and a hidden secret behind every loud proclamation of truth. In a similar way, Dio's music balanced torrents of rage with brief acoustic interludes.

Even as Judas Priest and Iron Maiden mounted their twentieth-century westward expansion into America, the lyrical messages remained much pricklier than commercial radio fodder. Iron Maiden's screeching "Run to the Hills" from *Number of the Beast* decried the European conquest of a wild and free America: "White man came across the sea / Brought us pain and misery." The exact theme was treated by Judas Priest on *Stained Class* in 1978, where "Savage" chastised European colonists, "You poisoned my tribe with civilized progress / Baptizing our blood with disease / You christened our bodies with sadness and suffering / Saying then that your god is well pleased."

These finger-pointing history lessons were not typical rock topics, but audiences appeared to appreciate the forceful fables. "I was never a tits-and-ass lyricist," says Rob Halford. "I could never write 'The Thong Song,' but I could write 'Breakin' the Law.' At the end of the day, music is about having a fuckin' good time, but if you can put in something a bit more than that, it's just more satisfying. I'm not a guy with a message by any standards, but I'd like to feel that the things that I write about are important issues that not only affect me but affect everybody else."

While radio stuck to the feathered-hair light rock of Journey, Foreigner, and Asia, heavy metal bands ignored playlists and thrived in a separate sphere, the concert hall. Now a national draw, Ronnie James Dio acted out the dramas of his modern madrigals on the spacious stages of sports arenas. "I began getting big stages together soon after I saw the first Alice Cooper concert," says Dio. "I saw the first show where they hung him. The next show I saw with Alice, they electrocuted him. At the next one they chopped his head off. I was so impressed as a member of the audience that I was getting much more than I bargained for. I wasn't getting just music, I was getting this kind of Disneyland."

This visual flair and flash matched the scale of coliseum venues, and heavy metal acts connected like a winning team at the box office. First touring America with Judas Priest in 1981, Iron Maiden had already played in sold-out 8,000-seat venues. During the summer of 1983, Maiden returned as a headliner with the enormous *Piece of Mind* show, complete with World War II films and mock brain surgery on an eight-foot-high zombie. Two NWOBHM veterans came in tow: Fastway, formed by ex-members of Motörhead and UFO; and Saxon, whose new *Power & the Glory* LP was a million-selling career pinnacle. The laws of physics applied nothing but upward motion to Iron Maiden—the band's subsequent *Powerslave* tour in 1985 advanced to a whopping twenty-five countries, accompanied by a mammoth Egyptian-themed set worthy of Broadway, requiring a rig

CLASSIC HEAVY METAL

This is the definition of heavy metal with a capital HM—bands that were the cream of the NWOBHM, along with whoever else could carry a tune the size of Mount Olympus. Bold statements were delivered via massive, rolling waves of tour buses hauling ass across America to take over the lives of teenagers. They had computers, they had video games, and they had stacks of exploding cassette tapes in their Walkman tape players blasting futuristic sounds at warp speeds. While AC/DC and Black Sabbath remained primal, dark, and brilliant, Def Leppard, Iron Maiden, and Judas Priest turned twin-guitar harmonies into rocket science, creating a gigantic new vocabulary for heavy metal. The songs were about real-life scary things, and the players were strictly business, tossing aside their fringed leather jackets for sharp, fitted, synthetic costumes decorated with metal spikes and studs. Somewhere underneath it all were a few rock riffs, but by 1984 heavy metal was past the point of departure.

Bang Your Head

- ❖ AC/DC, *Back in Black* (1981)
- ❖ AC/DC, *For Those About to Rock, We Salute You* (1981)
- ❖ Black Sabbath, *Heaven and Hell* (1980)
- ❖ Black Sabbath, *Mob Rules* (1981)
- ❖ Def Leppard, *High 'n' Dry* (1982)
- ❖ Dio, *Holy Diver* (1983)
- ❖ Iron Maiden, *Number of the Beast* (1982)
- ❖ Iron Maiden, *Piece of Mind* (1983)
- ❖ Judas Priest, *Screaming for Vengeance* (1982)
- ❖ Judas Priest, *Defenders of the Faith* (1984)
- ❖ Queensryche, *Queensryche* EP (1983)
- ❖ Saxon, *Power & the Glory* (1983)
- ❖ Scorpions, *Blackout* (1982)

of over seven hundred lights.

At the height of popularity during his *Sacred Heart* tour in 1986, Ronnie James Dio created a castle stage set. The band began each night with Dio's image projected onto a giant crystal ball floating over the crowd. Toward the end of the show, Dio battled a dragon with a glowing laser sword. This production required six semi trucks, a fleet of buses, and a small army of fifty crew members—including four laser technicians and a

Bruce Dickinson and Eddie of Iron Maiden
(Todd Nakamine)

dragon handler—all of which undertook a two-year expedition around the globe. "It became quite a traveling circus," says Dio. "It was just giving something more to the kids. We gave them a dragon, we gave them a fantasy for two hours, and we gave them a chance to escape. We thought that was important."

Working with elaborate set pieces was expensive, and travel was exhausting, but radio promotion was also costly, and free airplay remained scarce for heavy music. Touring bands soaked up the cost of their lights and lasers with extensive merchandising, like tour programs, scarves, and the ever-present official black concert T-shirts with tour dates printed on the back. Compared to revenue from record sales, bands took home a larger percentage of these profits—and the authentic aura of concert artifacts gave fans a kind of heavy metal costume. As Larry Lalonde of Possessed remembers junior high in suburban California, "I had to have my Iron Maiden shirt on the first day of school in seventh grade."

Lavishly printed tour T-shirts were fantastic promotion, ushering the imagery of heavy metal out of record stores and onto the streets. The leader in product design, by 1982 Iron Maiden was already one of the top three merchandising acts in America. That same year Long Island graphic-arts student Carlton Ridenhour, aka Chuck D, formed the influential rap group Public Enemy. He recalls being struck by

Maiden's artwork. "Public Enemy's whole thing of building concept records actually came off of myself and producer Hank Shocklee just being amazed at groups like Iron Maiden being able to run a series of concepts on their album covers and how they relied on graphics."

The Iron Maiden logo was itself designed by bassist Steve Harris, a trained draftsman, and it headlined hundreds of LPs, singles, and T-shirts. Almost all were simultaneously adorned with paintings of Maiden's widely recognized mascot, "Eddie" (an affectionate term for "headbanger"), the creation of artist Derek Riggs. "Eddie was designed about one and a half years before I met Iron Maiden, before they even had a recording contract," says Riggs. "It was during the English punk movement of the late seventies and early eighties. I was experimenting with putting symbolism into pictures so that they could be read like a narrative. I was thinking about the philosophy of the time and the idea that the youth of the day was being wasted by society. I took this 'wasted youth' idea and personified it as Eddie."

A bouquet of Eddies: Iron Maiden's alter ego
(Castle Records)

This ghoulish icon of decay first stared from lidless eyes on the cover of 1980's *Iron Maiden*, appearing as a teen slasher standing under electric streetlamps. "He was initially designed as a punk album cover, so his hair was short, orange, and went straight up in the air," Riggs says. "The image itself was taken from a photograph I had of a dried and decaying head which had been stuck onto a tank and used as propaganda in both the Second World War and the Vietnam War. I took this image and dressed it in a T-shirt and then placed it into a city environment because I wanted it to live in the street—just around the corner, not a million miles away. The band asked me to give it a bit more hair to make it fit with the heavy metal scene a bit better, and this picture became Iron Maiden's first cover."

Eddie evolved over dozens of appearances into an all-purpose mascot, an immortal beacon of good luck for the long-lived Iron Maiden. Later paintings took him off the street and into the action of songs as a flag-waving English redcoat for "The Trooper," a dog-fighting World War II pilot for "Aces High," and an Egyptian sphinxlike edifice for "Powerslave." The iconic force of Eddie inspired a battalion of heavy metal mascots, not limited to Y&T's spaceman, Voivod's the Voivod, S.O.D.'s Sargeant D. Sacred Reich's gas-masked mutant, Flotsam & Jetsam's Flossie the sea monster, and Megadeth's Vic Rattlehead. Indeed, a band alter ego was one of the few tricks that Metallica did not later adopt from Iron Maiden's resourceful path.

As Iron Maiden later replaced its brief heavy metal blasts with ornate, tumultuous instrumentals, its album covers depicted settings that looked like the psychedelic dreamscapes of 1970s art rock. Eddie's reassuring presence doubtlessly helped Iron Maiden sell this long-winding transformation to listeners. As merchandise sales and the proliferation of imitations attested, Eddie became part of the folk fabric—like an undead Mickey Mouse. "Someone in England made a huge cutout Eddie out of wood," says creator Derek Riggs, "and put it above their house so it loomed over the rooftop with its arm outstretched. It was Eddie from the *Number of the Beast* album and stood about fifty feet tall. I have also seen him on people's car bonnets, arm tattoos, a fairground haunted house ride, and there was a Spanish rock band who just copied the *Number of the Beast* cover and used it on their album. They got in a lot of trouble from Maiden."

Accompanying the T-shirts passed down directly from the bands, a few other general-purpose adornments prepared fans for the metal adventure. "You gotta have a spiked belt—it's a spirit thing," says lanky metal bassist Dan Lilker. "I guess around 1982 I started seeing lots of pictures of Iron Maiden, Priest, and Venom. I went to Butterfly, on West Eighth Street [in New York], and for what seemed like the princely sum of thirty-five dollars bought a spiked belt. Boy, was I proud of it. You never wanted to tuck your shirt in, but I was almost tempted—just to show it off."

While heavy metal prospered slightly on the periphery of the public eye, heavy metal garb and gear were an expedient means for metalheads to identify other true believers. For instance, Celtic Frost hailed from the outskirts of Zurich, Switzerland. "Those were a bunch of really small farm villages," says founder Tom Warrior. "You basically knew the teenagers from the other villages. There were only so many heavy metal fans, so we stuck out like sore thumbs. There was an instant bond, because we were standing alone against thousands of people laughing at us."

Musicians endorsed the lively heavy metal vision by dressing in aggressive accoutrements. A living temple of spikes and leather, Judas Priest singer Rob Halford expanded his burgeoning heavy metal image in 1978 to include a whip, which he liked to crack on the shoulders of fans in the front row—once costing the band a censure from Britain's *Top of the Pops* television show. As Priest's popularity soared, Halford's tough-guy image blossomed to full fruition in nightly onstage motorcycle rides. His wardrobe was often copied and wildly exaggerated—not only by adulatory metal extremists like Venom and Exciter. Struggling to compete in the new era, many 1970s rockers began to don black leather in order to cash in on metal chic. Ted Nugent, famous for dressing only in a loincloth, appeared in black leather on his 1981 solo album, *Nugent*. Even Thin Lizzy, the aging idols of Iron Maiden and Motörhead, dressed in matching studded black leather gauntlets in a 1983 publicity photo.

Outsiders found the choice of garments strange, intriguing, or even threatening. For most heavy metal fans, the gear's significance began and ended with powerful music, but it was an aggressive layer of protective clothing in the battle against complacency. Eugene Klein, aka Gene Simmons—the fire-breathing demon of Kiss, wore leather and spikes in the early 1970s and claims to have been oblivious to the gear's history in sex bondage. "We lived in New York, but in some ways we were very sheltered," he says. "When we decided to wear studs on leather, whether it was on a crotch or on a guitar strap, we thought it looked cool. We never picked up on the underground S&M thing."

Weird guitar shapes were also instrumental in heavy metal's visual lexicon. The Gibson Flying V symbolized the ultramodern styles of players like Michael Schenker, K. K. Downing of Judas Priest, and later Kirk Hammett and James Hetfield of Metallica. Though its spacecraft shape seemed very timely, the Flying V dated to 1947, when, in response to taunts from rival Leo Fender that his guitar designs were stale, Gibson president Ted McCarty crafted the unconventional instrument along with the equally metal-ready Gibson Explorer. Though middle-aged by 1983, the angular axes became weapons of choice for heavy metal, aerodynamic props for a new range of choreographed onstage moves, like magic wands for unlocking the power of a mighty wall of Marshall amps.

In the lower-budget echelon, struggling new bands had similar fanciful ideas but could sometimes barely afford more than a bag of makeup to create a show. Seeking to establish a name as the ultimate band for die-hard heavy metal fans, the ultrametal quartet Manowar crafted Conan-like togs from animal fur. Already renowned for smashing into each other like crazy onstage, Raven took to wearing lacrosse pads. They earned the tag "athletic rock" after drummer Rob "Wacko" Hunter started wearing a hockey helmet in 1982, protecting his head while he used it to smash cymbals. "We were in New York, and Rob went into a store and saw the ice-hockey helmet," says Raven's John Gallagher. "He was putting a character together. It was like worldwide wrestling, but he looked more like something from Tron than anything else."

The Los Angeles venue the Country Club—located in a Reseda strip mall and previously used as a set for the punk episode of the cop show *CHiPs*—often presented Metal Blade Records discoveries like Armored Saint and the kinky female-fronted Bitch. Even at the semipro level they knew the importance and power of heavy metal imagery—Armored Saint performed in convincing home-

John Bush of Armored Saint
(Todd Nakamine)

made battle regalia, while Bitch singer Betsy dressed in a dominatrix costume and wielded a bullwhip. Their attempts at pageantry clashed with the realities of a shoestring operation. "It was a pain in the ass to put all that stuff on," says Armored Saint singer John Bush. "Our wardrobe case used to smell so bad. It was worse in the winter. You'd have to put on this huge thing, and it was cold, and still wet, and it smelled. I look back and laugh, but at the time it was cool. Like when you're a little boy and you have a bad haircut."

ᘒ ✦✦✦✦✦✦✦✦✦✦✦ ᘐ

The extent of heavy metal's ascendancy became dramatically apparent the final scorching weekend of May 1983 at the U.S. Festival, a televised four-day outdoor music fest in San Bernardino, California, altruistically funded by Apple Computer inventor Steve Wozniak. Crowds nearing 300,000 on Saturday watched new wavers INXS, Flock of Seagulls, Men at Work, and the Clash, and a similar multitude assembled Monday for performances by U2, the Pretenders, and David Bowie. These were the darlings of radio, the industry-endorsed outgrowths of punk—yet it was the heavy metal lineup on Sunday that drew an unexpected teeming throng of more than 600,000, turning heads and stealing thunder from traditional rock fare.

Apple inventor Steve Wozniak with the Van Halens
(Dan Sokol)

Beginning at noon on Sunday, the club band Quiet Riot played, followed by little-known Mötley Crüe, clad in black leather and studs in the sweltering heat. Early afternoon brought Ozzy Osbourne in an ornate, feathered witch doctor's headdress, playing a mix of Black Sabbath and solo-era hits with the help of new guitarist Jake E. Lee. Then came the unrelenting Judas Priest, whose singer took the stage by driving a motorcycle through a wall of Marshall guitar amps. "That day was a highlight," says Rob Halford. "That was like the climax of the sensational tour that Priest had for *Screaming for Vengeance* beginning in 1981. The album had gone platinum, and the U.S. Festival was just an absolutely incredible moment. To finish with that particular show at the end of that record and touring cycle was just a real validating moment. Of course, it created more stress. We were like, 'Oh, God, now we have to top this!'"

After a cooling-off period courtesy of the Canadian power trio Triumph, a squadron of four German fighter airplanes flew over the undiminished crowd at nightfall, introducing Scorpions. A seasoned touring band with eight albums behind them, Scorpions delivered a long, powerful set, culminating in a five-minute orgy of ecstatic noise and guitar feedback. Headliners Van Halen brought the day and their hardest era to a close with metallic luster, untarnished by the slurred delivery of singer David Lee Roth.

A two-hour *U.S. Festival Special* ran on Showtime throughout the summer, beaming images of heavy metal crusaders in action through the emerging medium of cable television. Cable was a technological innovation that would soon prove as essential an ally to heavy metal as had the cassette tape. Taking notice, music-video outlets like the USA Network's *Radio 1990* and *Night Flight* and Canada's *Much Music* began airing clips from bands like Def Leppard, Scorpions, and Krokus. As television bent to acknowledge the success of heavy metal touring acts, it seemed that a victory had been won over the likes of Adam and the Ants and Duran Duran—made-for-TV bands from England's "new romantic" movement whom metalheads had fingered as avowed foes.

While radio continued to steer clear of all but the tamest ballads, in 1983 a new all-music television channel called MTV began investing more wisely in the rising popularity of heavy metal in America. Initially the cable channel had emulated the programming strategies of commercial radio, from which it also culled its on-air hosts. In order to avoid being usurped by a powerful radio network, MTV now needed to branch into new territory. The novelty of new wave videos by Flock of Seagulls and Devo had gathered much-needed early attention for the channel, but advertisers were growing restless. To build an empire safe from imitation and hostile takeovers, the company needed to progress to something flashier and at the same time more bankable.

Heavy metal was perfect: a platinum-selling new music genre complete with attention-getting stage sets, vivid album art, and bright costumes. "MTV came on board, and they were looking for bands that had visual value," recalls Twisted Sister singer Dee Snider. "I think one of the reasons they embraced heavy metal, and were very involved in that resurgence, is because heavy metal and hard rock had always been visually driven. To us it was natural. We were already dressing up and doing a stage show—just stick a camera in front of us and we were ready to go."

Primping and snarling, heavy metal bands made glamorous and outrageous pinups. Even as former members Peter Gabriel and Phil Collins of 1970s progressive rock band Genesis were reinvented as solo video stars, heavy metal fought to replace rock and roll clichés with fresh sounds and fun antagonism. "There were bands that died a death with the birth of MTV, like Supertramp and Joe Jackson," recalls Dee Snider. "I remember .38 Special had a lot of platinum records and hit singles, but they were just like blah to look at, whereas the metal bands were able to give them a show."

Powered by videos for "Photograph," "Foolin'" and "Rock of Ages," the most visible heavy metal act of the summer of 1983 was NWOBHM prodigy Def Leppard, who had become more cute than lethal. Blocked from topping the *Billboard* chart by the unprecedented thirty-seven-week run at number one of Michael Jackson's *Thriller*, by year's end the group nonetheless burned through nearly 4 million copies of their third album, *Pyromania*.

Los Angeles club veterans Quiet Riot finally knocked over Jackson at the close of 1983, and in November their *Metal Health* went to number one. Though a little hackneyed, Quiet Riot was an undeniable influence on things to come—*Metal Health*'s "Slick Black Cadillac" was covered by James Hetfield and Ron McGovney in their pre-Metallica band. As outgoing Quiet Riot singer Kevin DuBrow told *Kerrang!*, "I believe we've now sold over two million albums and the single should go top ten this week. What is really exciting is that it will be the first time that a true heavy metal single has made the U.S.

Metal health nuts: Quiet Riot
(Deborah Laws/Metalflakes.com)

top ten!" Indeed, if heavy metal was heard only underground three years prior, its virtues were now shouted out in aerobics classes across the country; the chart-topping "Metal Health" urging, "Bang your head! Metal health will drive you mad!"

Following Quiet Riot's day in the sun, a succession of heavier video stars from Southern California brought metal to the masses. First came Mötley Crüe, whose fist-pounding 1983 breakthrough, *Shout at the Devil*, was heavy metal burlesque, resplendent with pentagrams, fire, and black leather. Then Ratt, whose videos for "Round and Round" and "Wanted Man" pushed its 1984 debut, *Out of the Cellar*, to number seven in the United States, was soon selling 3 million copies. Also in 1984, Twisted Sister's *Stay Hungry* went double platinum on the strength of medium-defining music videos for "We're Not Gonna Take It" and "I Wanna Rock."

Appearances on MTV clearly had a huge effect on promoting bands, doubling or tripling sales possible by touring alone—yet, curiously, very few bands grew heavier after being on MTV. Following *Pyromania*, NWOBHM veterans Def Leppard transformed into something unrecognizably bland. They were not alone. Via the machinations of success, most bands in Los Angeles seemed to become overdressed balladeers. Ratt had begun in clubs wearing black leather and imitating British metal, but by its second album the band sounded much more like Gary Numan, an edgy but emotionless video rock contemporary. Only the guitars and haircuts kept a metal sheen, as producers coaxed the bands out of the live element and increasingly toward commercial compromise.

Dedicated touring and MTV videos represented two markedly different career strategies, one emphasizing music and the other stressing image. Initially both were aspects of a heavy metal superstar's career. "It's fair to say that even Judas Priest was influenced by the opportunities that existed only in America through radio and through TV," says Rob Halford. "If you look and sound a certain way, it can open up to a potentially bigger audience. The way that Priest handled that is first and foremost we said that we would never be a sellout band. We were never in this for the money. There's a way of handling it and developing it while still remaining true to the beliefs of what your music is about, while hoping that you're making something that can reach more people. It's a fine balance, really."

A slew of successful tours united credible metal heroes with MTV metallers. Black Sabbath recruited former Deep Purple singer Ian Gillan in 1983 for their last surge of power before a long malaise and toured with MTV upstarts Quiet Riot. Likewise, Ozzy Osbourne teamed with the hungry young opening act Mötley Crüe, and Iron Maiden traveled extensively in 1984 with Twisted Sister. If the head-liners suffered in record sales compared to their mass-marketed open-ers, they still saved in video promotion costs and partially recouped in T-shirt sales. To the benefit of everyone involved, fans accepted all heavy metal equally during this first innocent burst of popularity.

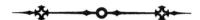

Even as heavy metal rapidly reaped commercial rewards, rock and roll flunkies were utterly unprepared. *The New Rolling Stone Record Guide*, a consumer guide released in 1983, summarized Judas Priest's first nine albums in an insulting twenty words, including "grunting" and "vulgar." The music magazine of record totally failed to recognize that the rules had changed. "Dull-witted and flatulent as ever" wrote *Rolling Stone* of Black Sabbath's *Mob Rules*. "Dio's lyrics are unin-spired and clichéd." Of Iron Maiden's breakthrough the magazine wrote, "The *Number of the Beast* blusters along aimlessly, proving again that bad music is hell." Def Leppard, Saxon, and the NWOBHM movement were utterly ignored. Among the crucial bands only Motör-head was reviewed favorably. Due credit was given to Lemmy's lyrics, inasmuch as they reminded the writer of the Clash—who were by this point an irrelevant Casbah-rocking force only in frat rock.

Though the aging American rock music press denigrated Judas Priest and dismissed Black Sabbath's entire discography with conde-scending one-star reviews, it was music and energy that drove progress, not the dictates of Beatles-generation critics. The new cov-eted audience consisted of the children of Baby Boomers. This was a different generation from the one that needed folk songs from James Taylor and Carly Simon to negotiate painful relationships in the 1970s. Heavy metal fans themselves were often products of divorce, looking for direction in larger-than-life expressions of humanity.

Soon the less prestigious teen rock magazines *Circus* and *Hit Parader* responded to readers alienated by *Rolling Stone*. *Circus* had

VIDEΦ ⅯETAL

Heavy metal was a complete package of screaming licks and fantastic imagery, and in 1983 the struggling cable network MTV picked up on the heavy metal look in a major way. Of the early heavy metal bands that went platinum in the 1980s, many relied on the strength of their videos.

Videography

❖ Def Leppard, *Pyromania* (1983)
"Rock of Ages," "Photograph," "Foolin'," "Rock Rock 'Til You Drop"

❖ Dokken, *Tooth and Nail* (1984)
"Tooth and Nail," "Alone Again"

❖ Mötley Crüe, *Shout at the Devil* (1983)
"Looks That Kill," "Too Young to Fall in Love"

❖ Quiet Riot, *Metal Health* (1983)
"Metal Health," "Cum On Feel the Noize"

❖ Ratt, *Out of the Cellar* (1984)
"Round and Round," "Wanted Man"

❖ Scorpions, *Love at First Sting* (1984)
"Rock You Like a Hurricane," "Still Loving You"

❖ Twisted Sister, *Stay Hungry* (1984)
"I Wanna Rock," "We're Not Gonna Take It," "The Price"

struggled through several permutations, including *Circus Weekly*—a 1970s precursor to *Teen People* that ran profiles on stars like Miss Piggy and Clint Eastwood. *Hit Parader* was a provocateur of pubescent passions dating back to teen idols Elvis and Fabian. These magazines added larger portions of metal coverage slowly, until the Pat Benatar interviews, Robert Plant pinups, and REO Speedwagon song lyrics were eventually phased out completely.

The two magazines, later joined by *Rip*, poured Mötley Crüe, Scorpions, and Iron Maiden in supersizes through American 7-Elevens, supermarkets, and drugstores. Gratefully, the editorial agenda was beholden to the loyalties of heavy metal fans, not the short-term needs of record companies. "*Circus* was all based on reader polls," says Ben Liemer, then managing editor. "All the publicists would ask, 'What do I have to do to get on the cover of your magazine?' I'd always say, 'There's not a damn thing you can do until your name shows up in that little box'—the one that said, 'Please write to us and tell us what five acts you'd like us to cover more.' We would always do whatever the readers wanted."

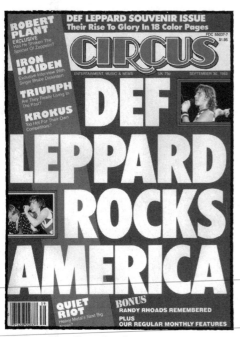

Heavy metal headlines: *Circus* in 1983

Packed with sweaty live photos, metal fan magazines acted as at-home extensions of the concert experience, publishing tour dates and news items about massive stage shows still in development. Though the homogenizing effect of MTV on the music was troubling, twenty-four hours of videos daily represented only the tip of the metal iceberg. "There was never enough metal on MTV to satisfy the metalheads anyway," says Liemer. "They would always be playing Michael Jackson and cheesy Norwegian pop bands."

With monthly circulation around 450,000 for *Circus* and 250,000 for *Hit Parader*, the metal glossies provided a heavy metal lifeline that overwhelmed the still-influential but more specialized import *Kerrang!* The key was not investigating a wide spread of heavy metal bands but providing incessant repetition of the most powerful. "We were not as open to covering new bands as you'd think," says Liemer. "They had to work their way up in popularity. I remember Dokken was selling records in markets in 1983 where there was no airplay, and there was no MTV, and their label, Elektra. attributed it to magazines like *Circus* and *Hit Parader* covering them month after month. We definitely had an effect out there, and people gave us gold and platinum records because of that."

With well-attended tours, cable television, and monthly national magazines, heavy metal fans were no longer invisible—they were a booming subculture with an increasingly public face and loads of forward momentum. To metal fans who had watched metal rise from the Capitol Records parking lot to national exposure, anything seemed possible. Says Blackie Lawless of W.A.S.P., an eventual MTV star whose 1984 debut single, "Animal (F**k Like a Beast)," was deemed too offensive by its label for American release, "It's surprising. You might have thought we might have been a little too much for MTV, but they were young, they were mavericks, and they were willing to take chances."

Still, MTV support for harder-hitting bands was limited to an occasional clip or concert special. Iron Maiden and Judas Priest kept up their rigorous touring schedules, playing music directly to the fans most nights of the year. MTV was capable of fueling a fad, but for a young band like Metallica—lacking the teen-idol looks of Ratt and striving for a sound as profound as possible—the kind of success it envisioned would come from a different channel. With heavy metal's popularity at an all-time high, the next wave of headbangers would soon push its newfound clout in its own way, whether the rest of world was ready or not.

Fevered Fans:
Metallica & Power Metal

➤ **April 1983:** Kirk Hammett replaces Dave
  Mustaine as guitarist of Metallica
➤ **July 1983:** Metallica releases *Kill 'Em All*
➤ **Autumn 1983:** *Metal Forces* magazine
  launches
➤ **November 1983:** Mercyful Fate releases
  Melissa

As heavy metal mushroomed into a major national trend, the do-it-yourself sector had less difficulty lifting itself up by its bootstraps. "Two years ago, when we started, people said we had to play punk or new wave," said Dan Beehler of the Ottawa, Canada, group Exciter in a 1983 television interview. "Where's punk today? I think metal has been there since the late sixties, only it was underground. In the past year metal has gotten bigger than it's ever been. A lot of people think heavy metal is mindless, because there are no harmonies, but I would just describe it as total energy."

Even as mighty *Kerrang!* continued to dispense the latest holy word of metal from London, new voices from the wilderness threatened its dominance and authority. Besides the mainstream *Circus* and *Hit Parader* in America, every European country now had its own luscious heavy metal magazine, as France's *Enfer*, Germany's *Metal Hammer*, and Holland's long-running *Aardschok* each offered a glossy color perspective on heavy happenings. The influence of tape trading grew stronger when the London-based streetwise *Metal Forces* launched in 1983. It focused on music rather than the local social scene and cast an open web to snare articles on NWOBHM relics, unsigned Hollywood glam acts, and demo cassettes by extreme underground demons.

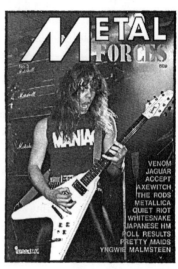

Metal Forces No. 3

In the United States, *Metal Mania* and *New Heavy Metal Revue* were joined by dozens of self-produced metal fanzines, including *Whiplash, Headbanger, Midwest Metal Militia,* and *Powerthrash.* The king of these one-man operations was New Yorker Bob Muldowney, who began publishing *Kick Ass Monthly* in 1981. He focused on metal not as a regional movement but as a proud ideology to be harvested wherever it flourished. This self-proclaimed "Journalistic Poser Holocaust" rarely lived up to its monthly schedule, yet *Kick Ass* became a dominant critical voice thanks to Muldowney's vehement and tireless editorializing. "Why do commercial metal bands feel that, to be successful, one's music must be weak, lame, and about as exciting as toast?" began a May 1984 diatribe against Quiet Riot and Mötley Crüe. "To me, *Kick Ass Monthly* was the bible," says Roadrunner Records' A&R director Monte Conner. "I used to worship that guy. He was the original tell-it-like-is master of brutality."

At the same time, former *New Heavy Metal Revue* editor Brian Slagel developed Metal Blade Records into a full-time operation that was unseasoned yet professional. From a tiny room in his mother's house Slagel oversaw recording sessions, designed album covers, and called radio stations and record stores to promote his few releases. With a growing reputation after its *Metal Massacre* appearance, Metal Blade discovery Metallica seemed ready to record to a full-length album. They already had a snazzy title: *Metal Up Your Ass.* "Of course I expected to release the first Metallica LP," says Slagel. "But they came to me and asked for eight thousand dollars to put out a record. I didn't have that kind of money, and I didn't know where to get it. It was like, 'Sorry, guys.' They had a vision of what they wanted to do, and they needed a little bit more money, so they just kind of moved on."

Metallica found other options. As their "No Life 'Til Leather" demo garnered a reputation, the band was wooed by another shoe-string operation, Megaforce Records in Old Bridge, New Jersey. Pro-prietor Johnny Z, aka Johnny Z, had started like Slagel by booking metal shows, bringing Raven from England and Anvil from Canada to play for New York crowds amped by reading about them in *Ker-rang!* He sold metal goods at his record store, Rock & Roll Heaven, located in the inauspicious Route 18 Flea Market in Jersey. Zazula had no money either, so he first attempted to broker a deal for Metal-lica with several New York–based major labels. After being laughed out of a succession of meetings, Zazula and his wife, Marsha, bor-rowed the recording budget. "Marsha and I put ourselves in a lot of debt to make that album," he told *Kerrang!* "We really took a chance with our lives. We didn't want to start a record company at all, but we ended up putting the record out on our own because of the lack of interest elsewhere."

Not fully comprehending the modest size of Zazula's offer, in April 1983 Metallica drove a small van thirty-five hundred miles cross-country from San Francisco to New York. Unable to afford a ho-tel, the band of twenty-year-olds on their first trip to the Big Apple slept under U-Haul blankets in the Music Building in Jamaica, Queens. They practiced in a rehearsal space down the hall from Anthrax—a local teenage band in awe of Metallica's "No Life 'Til Leather." Barely old enough to buy cigarettes, the members of An-thrax were graduating from 1970s hard-rock-influenced originals like "Satan's Wheels" to a faster sound resembling Iron Maiden's. Dan Lilker played bass in Anthrax and remembers looking after his West Coast comrades. "We would take them down to the market and every-thing," he says. "We'd go down to their room and drink some beers. Cliff smoked herb, and I did, like typical bass players. They were kids a long way from home who were real excited about this. They had come over on a wing and a prayer. They were broke. They just trusted Johnny Z to put them in the studio and make sure they ate."

In the throes of this adventure, where beer often took the place of food, the last thing Dave Mustaine expected was to be ousted from Metallica for his drinking. Regardless, escalating tension and a drunken run-in with death on the road from California turned his three bandmates against the unruly guitarist. "It was really tough for me, because I didn't get a warning," says Mustaine. He came to terms with his anger years later—and then only to a limited degree. "They didn't say, 'Dave, you're drinking too much.' The truth of the matter is that I imbibed the same amount that they did, but my reaction to alcohol was violent, and it made them happy. I knew I was a real heavy drinker, but I didn't really realize that my drinking was going to cost me my job."

Unlike expelled bassist Ron McGovney (who realized he was fired as the band gradually tossed his shoes and clothes from the van after meeting Cliff Burton), Mustaine's ejection from Metallica was harsh, abrupt, and by all reports unexpected. "It was really hard for me to listen to their music for the longest time," says Mustaine. "In retrospect, knowing our plan—which was to rule the world—would I have hesitated if it had been anyone else in the band doing the same thing, to tell them to get the fuck out? No. Would I have given them a warning? I don't know. I might have."

Despite hanging out with Metallica every day, Dan Lilker and Anthrax "couldn't tell at all" that the change was coming. "[Anthrax guitarist] Scott Ian and I came out of rehearsal," Lilker says, "and we saw Cliff Burton and James Hetfield in the lobby. They had just come back from a trip to the deli. They said, 'We threw Dave out this morning.' Scott went, 'Bullshit!' and Cliff looked at him and said, 'Bullshit, bullshit'—and we all know two negatives equal a positive."

Banished from the band he helped build, Dave Mustaine left on a long, lonely Greyhound bus trip from Manhattan's Port Authority to Los Angeles. The very next night, in flew twenty-year-old Exodus guitarist Kirk Hammett to replace him. Exodus had opened for Metallica previously, but the two San Francisco bands were not yet well-acquainted. Still, Metallica's road manager pushed Exodus's demo tape on Metallica, impressing them with Hammett's flashy, "European" style of playing.

A Catholic-school boy who switched to public school in junior high, Hammett had a giggly personality and dedication to guitar. Though Cliff Burton dressed the part of a hippie, it was Hammett who actually grew up within the city of San Francisco, and he recalls having his face painted with flowers as a preschooler at a peace-and-love street fair. Says Les Claypool of Primus, who met Hammett in El Sobrante, California, "I was in algebra in ninth grade with Kirk, and Mr. Kelly was our teacher. First of all, he didn't like Kirk. Every day he'd get on Kirk's case, because Kirk was just like, 'Hey, man,' a Cheech and Chong burnout kinda guy. Mr. Kelly would bend a paper clip into a loop, then stick it in his ear and pull out balls of wax with it. Kirk and I would just sit there and watch."

In contrast to the arrogant and outgoing Mustaine, Hammett was a shy thrasher—"this little kid from SF," according to Dan Lilker. He played his first show with Metallica during the summer of 1983 at the Showplace in Dover, New Jersey, with Anthrax supporting. "Kirk definitely looked nervous," Lilker recalls. "He was looking at James the whole time, to make sure he was playing everything right—while still doing his headbanging, just with his head turned to one side."

Adapting to the circumstances, Hammett gelled quickly with Metallica, picking up many of Mustaine's guitar solos and adding a few of his own. After only four weeks of practice, the new lineup hiked north in May 1983 to the secluded metal stronghold of Rochester, New York, to record its debut album at the now-defunct Music America studios. Manowar's Joey DeMaio lived in the area and recommended the space for its upstairs ballroom, a suitably dramatic location for Lars Ulrich to record his drums. The material Metallica put to tape was essentially identical to "No Life 'Til Leather"—but what a difference a year made in the performance.

Released in July 1983, Metallica's *Kill 'Em All* was undeniable— steeped deeply in the fresh traditions of metal, it determinedly improved and expanded the field. The lyrics showed a band obsessed with the metal universe. The opening song, "Hit the Lights," piled on guitar solos, drum fills, and excitement in a wild exhortation to the live-concert experience. Then came the drug-riffing frenzy of "Motor-

Metallica's first official photo
(Megaforce Records)

breath," the hot fervor of "Jump in the Fire," the emotional overdrive of "No Remorse," all barreling toward the helmeted legions of "Metal Militia." In the compulsive ode to headbanging, "Whiplash," the band boasted—or prophesied—"Hotel rooms and motorways, life out here is raw / But we will never stop, we will never quit, cause we are Metallica."

The glories of metal were praised on nearly every song. With songwriter Dave Mustaine gone, the sexual double entendre of "Mechanix" from the demo tape was rewritten to create "Four Horse-men," a forceful doomsday scenario played out against the relentless unison riffing of Hetfield and Hammett. The lyrics were cribbed from the biblical book of Revelation, and harked back to the cataclysms of early Black Sabbath and Judas Priest. Even so, there was little doubt that the four horsemen in question were in fact Metallica, sweeping the land clean of anything but the heaviest, most powerful metal.

Making his recording debut with Metallica, Cliff Burton pulled the hyperactive band back down to earth with his bass playing, applying torque with his emphasis on moody counterpoint. Burton's emotional soliloquy, "Anesthesia (Pulling Teeth)" was *Kill 'Em All*'s wild card, capturing the controlled flailing of an uninhibited madman, a cool statement in a universe overpopulated by wanky Van Halen–inspired guitar solos. For three and a half minutes Burton the contrarian emphasized not so much the bass notes themselves as the long, ragged, wa-wa-pedal-inflected spaces between them.

Employing gruff vocals, prominent bass lines, and unwavering rhythm guitar, *Kill 'Em All* replaced the high, whiny notes of early-1980s metal with dense, brooding tones that carried the massive and unstoppable load of Black Sabbath minus the melancholia. The chugging thunk of Hetfield and Hammett's twin Gibson Flying V guitars was hypnotic and explosive, with frequent tempo changes fused together by Hammett's finger-racing guitar flash. Soon much imitated were the trademark muted guitar riffs, a startling rhythmic element at the forefront of Metallica's sound, generated by holding the meat of the picking hand over the base of the strings, producing a compressed mechanical chunking sound instead of a ringing cry.

What's more, *Kill 'Em All* blazed faster than anyone short of Motörhead, whose influence was felt in the galloping rhythms and thunderous drums. *Kill 'Em All* might have been the first record fast enough that when fans played it to the point of skipping, a full chorus could be captured in a single revolution of the vinyl. Observes Katon DePena, whose band Hirax was one of the quickest of the 1980s, "It's cool to play fast, but you've got to be able to write a riff, and that's what made Metallica incredible."

Skirting the speed frontier, Metallica was almost forced to speed up to find a niche. Due to the long-term relationships between heavy metal bands and their fans, Judas Priest and Iron Maiden were only growing more popular with age—not disappearing into obscurity like so many out-of-work one-hit radio wonders. The only choice for new metal bands was to expand on the furious firmament. Says metal visionary Tom Warrior of hearing Metallica in his native Switzerland, "I couldn't believe when the British metal wave triggered the American metal wave, how the American bands blew everything away. They had a much more clinical approach to heaviness. Whereas the British bands had this publike aura around them, the Americans just sounded like heavy machines."

Lacking a strong lead vocalist, Metallica emphasized its groove, a basic shift in the way heavy music was organized. In the world of flamboyant singers, Hetfield's gruff, laid-back chanting obscured stealthy melodic hooks behind killer guitars and cagey drumming. Vocals were no longer leading the way, a distinction that eventually became a point of departure for Metallica from other heavy metal acts at that time. "I really have a lot of respect for James," says Katon W. DePena. "With 'No Life 'Til Leather' I remember thinking that if James would just sing like James, instead of trying to sound like Vince Neil, then it would be good. When *Kill 'Em All* came out, that's exactly what he did."

Yet even after the release of their debut, Metallica remained unsure of Hetfield as a singer. Though growing more comfortable with the role, he was singing only because no one else wanted the job. The band still considered enlisting a conventional lead vocalist and front man, confining Hetfield to rhythm guitar. "Shit like that affects your performance when you have to change a song arrangement around in the middle of it all," Lars Ulrich told *Kick Ass Monthly,* "especially when you don't have a front man who, during technical problems, could just stand and rap with the crowd for five minutes. That's one of the reasons we are looking for a front man that we're probably never gonna find, because there's nobody crazy enough to fit in with what we're doing."

As late as 1984 there was still one likely candidate. "There's only been one guy—it's not really a secret anymore," said Ulrich in *Kick Ass,* "—that we have really been keen on getting for the band, and that's the front man for Armored Saint, John Bush. They're like kids that have grown up together, and I think he'd be very insecure about leaving the situation he's in. He's got the fuckin' best voice. No matter what band he's in—in like five years, he's only nineteen now, he is gonna be one of the biggest singers and front men. He's gonna be up there with Dio."

John Bush recalls being courted by Metallica, a process that included frequent pressure from both Ulrich and Johnny Z. "When they were still contemplating the singer thing, Armored Saint had just started," Bush says. "We were cool, and I guess they thought I was hip, and they kept bugging me to join the band. I just didn't know them. I was like, 'Who's this band?' All the guys in Armored

Saint and I had grown up together, so I wasn't going to quit my buddies' band. I never regret it—it would have changed everything. I was not meant to be in Metallica. That's just the way it is."

To differentiate their approach, young bands like Metallica began to call their music "power metal." There was not a tremendous stylistic difference between established acts like Dio and up-and-comers like Armored Saint and Manowar, but these power metal acts buttressed every aspect of their operations to double the impact of the riffs and the imagery. It might have been taken for granted that those thorny exteriors would soften with increased commercial success. In 1983, however, Metallica revealed new codes and tricks that streamlined and oversaturated the sound, creating magnetic metal-hearted music that was less subject to commercial change.

Metallica's *Kill 'Em All* sold a surprising 17,000 copies within two weeks of its release, mostly through the distribution networks that serviced mom-and-pop record stores. Many headbangers had been clearing room in their record collections for something more intense than Iron Maiden. As Exciter's Dan Beehler told Canadian television, "The kids in Europe today have had their fill of Priest and Sabbath, and they seem to be going towards the Venom, and picking up on Exciter, Metallica, and Anvil—the younger metal. They seem to be really getting into metal at wicked speeds, as heavy as possible."

The NWOBHM revelations of 1980 had become articles of faith to young fans, and times were ripe for progress. Following the success of *Kill 'Em All*, Megaforce cultivated a powerhouse roster that showcased this new kind of metal not oriented toward radio or MTV. As if on a mission, the label scooped up Manowar, Exciter, Anthrax, and Raven. Each released one breakthrough album after another. There was nothing homogeneous to the sound, yet the warrior anthems of Manowar and the accelerated scramble of Raven shared an attention-grabbing desire for something new.

Still woefully inexperienced, yet developing quickly, Anthrax on *Fistful of Metal* sped up in direct response to Metallica, relying more heavily on rhythm guitar and a double-bass drum set. After

New York thrashers Anthrax in 1983 with tall singer Neil Turbin

they began playing power metal, the intricate British-style song craft had to be matched by thunderous speed, which became possible with the addition of Charlie Benante, an aggressively fast drummer. "He definitely pushed us to take songs like 'Panic,' which were good molten metal songs," says bassist Dan Lilker, "and speed them up enough so they had a desperate, panicky edge to them." These were children of the 1970s—Anthrax recorded the Alice Cooper song "I'm 18" for *Fistful of Metal* one day after its youngest member had turned nineteen.

In contrast to the charming yet untested Anthrax, the well-seasoned Danish band Mercyful Fate played elaborately agile compositions that even outclassed the scrubby banging of Metallica. Unfortunately, they were stranded in Denmark, far from a metal hotbed. Things changed after Dutch entrepreneur Cees Wessels's Roadrunner Records began licensing American products by Metal Blade, Megaforce, and others for sale in Europe. Earlier, anyone seeking to capitalize on Europe's fanatical love of metal had to pack a suitcase and travel to each country seeking a sales outlet. As Roadrunner became a central licensing point for the Continent, Wessel and his affiliated labels from across the Atlantic thrived. Music for Nations soon began doing similar deals in England.

While importing Metallica records to Europe, Roadrunner signed and then licensed Mercyful Fate's *Melissa* to Megaforce. *Melissa* arrived at a truly magical moment—the juncture of classic heavy metal, power metal, and the furtive black metal movement—

yet resisted falling wholly into any of those styles. Led by the versatile and often bewildering vocals of King Diamond, the Danish quintet used archaic guitar scales and catchy, galloping rhythm riffs to summon a dark suite of smoky songs about the supernatural. Each track on *Melissa*—including "Evil," "Curse of the Pharaohs," and "Satan's Fall"—beckoned listeners to otherworldly destinations via black horse-drawn carriage, casting an unrivaled mystical emotional spell.

The unusual singer King Diamond topped Mercyful Fate's sound with a style that rose and fell from echoing falsetto to anguished growl. "It seemed like it was songs recorded today that could have been written a long time ago," says Diamond of *Melissa*. "It had a lot to do with the sound, of course, but always having that unique songwriting. I haven't heard another band sounding like that. Even the simplest passages were written from the heart, and people can tell Mercyful Fate from a few notes." As the singer commented in a 1983 interview, "I want people to go home thinking, 'Well, I saw it and I heard it, but I don't know how they did it.'"

Melissa remained a cult favorite, equally esteemed by early thrashers Dave Mustaine and Dan Lilker, the members of Norwegian black metal band Emperor, and platinum-selling hitmakers Slipknot. "*Melissa* was really incredible," recalls a captivated Trey Azagthoth of Morbid Angel. "It's quite special. The way the songs were structured was unorthodox. They had guitar parts that were so weird. It wasn't just a band playing—they were like musicians for a ceremony, and the singer was like a high priest narrating the story. I picked up on it the same way Black Sabbath was very ceremonial."

With such artistic successes Megaforce also had its share of errors. Confident that the Seattle group Metal Church would sign to his unstoppable label, Johnny Z prematurely printed an advertisement promoting them along with Metallica and Mercyful Fate. "No offense to Johnny Z," says Metal Church vocalist David Wayne, "but our attorney said that contract was full of mud, and we sent it back. Johnny called our lawyer some names, and we ended up producing the album ourselves." Undeterred, Johnny Z sought to bridge an era by signing Blue Cheer, the legendary late-1960s sludge power trio whose cover of "Summertime Blues" was allegedly promotion for a brand of LSD. Their roots metal return, *The Beast Is Back*, took a short trip to nowhere. Power metalheads were firmly oriented toward the future.

PØWER METAL

When young bands started doubling the already brain-bending attributes of heavy metal, adding steroid tonnage to the most explosive moments, they created power metal. The term was used broadly to describe everything from the wall of sound of Exciter to the doomy black cries of Mercyful Fate, ultimately defining a sound with twice the crunch of classic heavy metal. Two times the speed, two times the spikes—power metal had double everything. Accept, Jag Panzer, and Warlock took dual-guitar leads, histrionic vocals, and pounding drums to a powerful place—without radically rearranging the rules of Judas Priest and Iron Maiden. Likewise they pushed heavy metal's image: Metallica wore black spandex and bullet belts, Anthrax dressed in matching animal prints, Manowar donned real fur outfits, and King Diamond of Mercyful Fate put on ghostly face paint. Their music protected the inner core of metal from MTV video compromise and paved the way for thrash metal soon afterward.

Fists Held High

- ❖ Accept, *Restless and Wild* (1983)
- ❖ Anthrax, *Fistful of Metal* (1984)
- ❖ Anvil, *Metal on Metal* (1982)
- ❖ Exciter, *Violence and Force* (1984)
- ❖ Jag Panzer, *Ample Destruction* (1984)
- ❖ Manowar, *Hail to England* (1984)
- ❖ Mercyful Fate, *Don't Break the Oath* (1984)
- ❖ Metallica, *Kill 'Em All* (1983)
- ❖ Raven, *All for One* (1983)
- ❖ Savatage, *Sirens* (1983)
- ❖ Thrust, *Fist Held High* (1984)
- ❖ Warlock, *Burning the Witches* (1984)
- ❖ Warlord, *Deliver Us* (1983)

The promise of Megaforce's progenies remained a drastic contrast to their impoverished realities. Offered four days of recording time by a tiny Dutch label prior to signing with Roadrunner, Mercyful Fate took its show on the road. "The studio was in Holland in an attic of a school—it looked like a military field hospital," says King Diamond. "That's where we worked. Then we played three or four shows in Holland. Our car was full of equipment on the roof, and inside we were sitting with amps on our laps. We had to drive eighteen or nineteen hours down there. When we arrived, I couldn't stand up—our legs were dead, our arms were dead, and it was really crazy. The wheels on the van were pointing outwards. Our friends thought we weren't even going to make the border."

By the time Mercyful Fate reached America in 1984, the band's stature as a live act was creeping up on its ceremonial ambitions. King Diamond was singing into a cross-shaped microphone stand fashioned from human bones, and the members of Metallica were waiting in San Francisco among the throng. "Slayer kind of sounded like Venom, and for a while Metallica kinda sounded like a revved-up Motörhead," recalls Ron Quintana. "Neither one was like Mercyful Fate, who were shockingly good and sounded much more advanced when we finally heard them."

Even then circumstances remained dire. "Our first American tour with Motörhead, we shared one bus, and it was just no money," says King Diamond. "It was constantly a problem to get money for gas to get to the next city. We got three dollars per day, and you had to decide whether to get a pack of cigarettes

Kill 'Em All for One 1983 tour shirt

or a burger. We had to borrow money from suspicious people to make the next city and pay it back later. We didn't look at it as a problem, because we didn't know any better. Then later on, when you hit the world on different terms, you really appreciate success. If we were still touring like that, I would be dead by now."

Despite these hardships there was immense desire among the new independent bands to reenact the legendary touring regimes of Iron Maiden and live the conquest that Judas Priest and Black Sabbath had before them. Even as Metallica struggled with unreliable equipment, the band was embarking on a heavy metal dream—performing unprecedented music to growing audiences of die-hard fans. While Iron Maiden and Dio piloted their fleets of semi trucks filled with lighting trusses and laser technicians across America's highways, Metallica was willing to ride along the side roads.

In 1983 Johnny Z organized the first American tour for his prize act, Raven, whose sizzling *All for One* LP he had licensed from Neat Records. In search of a support act, he presented his wild card. "Johnny Z wanted to bring us over to tour America," says Raven's John Gallagher. "He says, 'We've got this young band, they're the biggest thing in California.' I thought, 'What? Bigger than Y&T?' He put this tape on of a band going '*RRRRRRR!*' I thought, 'What the hell is this?' Of course it was Metallica."

While power metal bands found it easy to rate equal billing with heavy metal stars in fanzines, it remained difficult to tour comfortably without major-label backing. The so-called *Kill 'Em All for One* tour was booked by phone by Zazula himself, and it led Raven, Metallica, and the tour crew across the country with few amenities. Seventeen people lived for weeks in a simple Winnebago camper designed for a vacationing family of four. "By the third date we had the tour manager up against the wall," says John Gallagher, "saying, 'Get some beds we can sleep on or we'll kill you.' We were living on ten dollars per diem. It was completely guerrilla warfare."

In larger cities the bill fared well. In Chicago, James Hetfield nicked a bit of showmanship from Saxon, trying to engage the crowds in a rough shout-along of "Metal up your ass!" As a stage chant, Metallica's rejected album title worked well—fans lined up across the front of the stage shaking their fists and waving their dirty hair in appreciation of this coarse young band. A few copies of *Kill*

'Em All tossed into the crowd by Hetfield were ripped to shreds like raw meat in the fangs of starving wolves. Other dates were less encouraging. "We woke up in Arkansas in an outdoor amphitheater," recalls John Gallagher, "in a natural bowl with a little stage surrounded by totem poles. There were trucks outside selling catfish. People from there couldn't understand any of us foreigners. We arrived with our little gear to play to 1,000 people in a club, and they put us in a 10,000-seat arena. There were two forklifts holding up a little light truss, and maybe 300 people there. Talk about embarrassing."

Above all, the two bands shared wide-eyed charm. "James made the music, and Lars gave it the push," says John Gallagher. "We were a couple years older and had played a lot more. They were just real happy to be out on the road. You could tell Lars was the wheeler-dealer. Lars didn't know one end of a drum set from the other. He needed to change the bottom head on the snare drum, and he didn't know how to take the snares off, so he just cut them off with pliers. It didn't matter."

While far from measuring its success in platinum albums, power metal was pushed forward quickly by the support of fans. Looking back to do-it-yourself demo tapes like "No Life 'Til Leather," the Metallica cassette that by now had been duplicated thousands of times, young metal fans spawned their own wild new bands and promoted and distributed them through letters and fanzines. Where Brian Slagel had had barely enough bands to fill the first *Metal Massacre* sampler, now dozens of groups were deluging him with their music every week.

The credit due to the rabid audience base could not be underestimated. Tape trading was a unique distribution and promotion system that scaled to fit the success of the artist, encouraging creativity while fueling minitrends. Crazed bands like Overkill, Hirax, and Voivod sold thousands of demo tapes through an accumulation of fanzine praise, tape-trader ads, and thanks-list appearances on other bands' records and tapes. Afterward they moved on to recording deals with guaranteed, if limited, sales results.

Like the NWOBHM, the power metal bands were self-sufficient inventors addicted to innovation. Instead of centering on one city like London, they were geographically dispersed. As a wide network developed around fanzines and small-time record labels, public awareness of power metal lifted the underground scene to a new level of possibility. Larger numbers of fans were beginning to look beyond MTV. "We had no idea it was going to be some monster," says Dan Lilker of Anthrax. "It was very exciting, and we hoped it was going to do well. It was a crucial time for that shit in America."

Across the country the antics and the music were getting wilder and weirder. Florida's Nasty Savage revived the Plasmatics' show-stopping stunt of smashing a television set, with the improvement of dropping it onto singer Nasty Ronnie's armored chest. The band Medieval resembled a twisted Metallica from suburban Michigan. Their "All Knobs to the Right" demo showcased sludgy thrash by members who had all adopted the cryptic stage name "Ambuist." Then came Agent Steel from Los Angeles, fronted by self-proclaimed outer-space alien John Cyriis. A wide-eyed screamer with a small Afro and a bullet belt, he convinced his stalwart sidemen to toss out their leathers in favor of matching orange jumpsuits. The underground metal scene nurtured these visions, then connected the dots around the perimeter to define a movement.

Though the imagery could be overwhelmingly macho, it was important to notice that metal's power was as appealing to young women as it was men. Well before *Xena: The Warrior Princess* proved this,

Mayhemic penbanger:
Nasty Ronnie of Nasty Savage writes

there were many women who wanted to play with swords instead of Barbie dolls. "Being a girl? It didn't mean anything to me," says "Metal" Maria Ferraro, who bought her Motörhead records from Johnny Z's garage before becoming the first Megaforce Records employee. "I never felt like being a girl kept me from doing anything, or I was never looked at in a different way. I felt almost empowered because I was involved in all of this, and a lot of girls weren't."

And in an era of falsetto screams, the higher natural range of women made them stunning vocalists for power metal bands in search of high-end piercing wails. The voices of Betsy Weiss of early Metal Blade act Bitch, Nicole Lee of Znowhite, Dorothy Pesch of Germany's Warlock, "Kate" of the Belgian group Acid, Dawn Crosby of Detente, Ann Boleyn of Hellion, Debbie Gunn of Sacramento's Sentinel Beast, the French thrash band Witches, the Swedish band Ice Age, Lynda "Tam" Simpson of Sacrilege UK, and Lori Bravo of Nuclear Death all ran the gamut from glissando to guttural. Following pioneers Girlschool, these musicians faced discrimination in the record business, but fought through frequent chauvinism with the help of metal's self-sufficient message. In this formative time period, the metal scene was a progressive force, and far less sexist than rock music as whole.

Nonetheless, the music business was still overwhelmed by heavy metal. As late as September 1984, when anyone with a pulse could feel the tremors of Metallica, *Musician* stumbled through a special heavy metal issue highlighting leather-jacketed teenyboppers Billy Idol and Joan Jett, praising second-tier bands Fastway and Krokus, and unctuously declaring sacred Iron Maiden the worst heavy metal band going. It seemed the editors were trying to measure metric tons with a yardstick, and were completely incapable of facing the changes erupting around them.

Yet if Johnny Z had succeeded in finding a deal for Metallica instead of releasing their albums independently, the trajectory of heavy metal would have been altered drastically. The music industry at the time of *Kill 'Em All* did scramble to sign heavy metal acts. In its estimation this often meant "metallized" versions of 1970s hard rock bands like Y&T, Rainbow, and even Michael Bolton. Even with brash bands like Tygers of Pan Tang and the Swiss group Krokus, no sooner would a label ink a deal than it would try guiding the music into radio-friendly territory, thus stripping away the heavy grit that appealed to fans in the first place. Fortunately, Metallica's music was barely recognized by A&R executives as anything but amateurish noise, unfit for public consumption.

Thankfully, it was not until Megaforce's subsequent success that major record companies began to pay full attention to the metal underground. When that time came, the harder bands were already trading on a large national and international loyalty built via fanzines and skin-of-their-teeth tours, as increasing numbers of fans learned to bypass the big names and head straight for the strong stuff. Making it on their own meant clout when dealing with the music industry—and gave ambitious bands like Metallica time to hone their sonic attack and thrive on their own impetuous terms.

Slayer: Kings of Black Metal Devils

- ➺ **January 1982:** Venom releases *Black Metal*
- ➺ **December 1983:** Slayer releases *Show No Mercy*, quickly removes makeup
- ➺ **May 31, 1984:** Hellhammer disbands— Celtic Frost forms from ashes
- ➺ **October 1985:** Possessed releases *Seven Churches*
- ➺ **Spring 1985:** Slayer's *Hell Awaits* sells 100,000 copies

---

Still operating under the very nose of the entertainment business in Los Angeles, Brian Slagel's homegrown Metal Blade Records by 1984 was selling tens of thousands of albums by bands whose quirks seemed to preclude any future jump to a major label. For an expanding number of hard-core metallers, the underground was reason enough to exist. This darker music was the dense honey in the center of heavy metal's buzzing hive, and its rewards were still thought more personal than commercial. "The day the first *Metal Massacre* record came out," says Slagel, "somebody told me 'You're going to look back on this day when this metal thing gets really big.' And we were like, 'Yeah, right.'"

Like its precursors, *Metal Massacre III* launched a number of bullet-belted careers, none more impressive than that of Los Angeles crew Slayer. Destined to become one of the most respected and awe-inspiring elements in metal's formidable front, Slayer was still raw when Brian Slagel caught them opening for Bitch at the Woodstock in Anaheim. "I went because Bitch were friends of mine, and Slayer was amazing," says Slagel. "They played eight or nine songs, and most of them were covers, including an amazing version of 'Phantom of the Opera' by Iron Maiden. I went backstage and talked to the kid who was managing them and asked them to be on the next *Metal Massacre* record."

Formed in Huntington Beach in 1982, Slayer existed not just outside the ranks of local glam bands headed for MTV but even on the fringe of the power metal clique revolving around Metallica. For one thing, Slayer was nonplussed by the NWOBHM. "We'd see other bands wearing T-shirts and check it out," recalls guitarist Kerry King. "I remember going to a record store to see what was up. We'd listen to it, but we didn't dig it. I remember Metallica played Diamond Head's 'Am I Evil?' live way before they recorded it. I figured out who it was, but when I heard the original, it was crap, boring."

After losing Metallica to Johnny Z due to lack of resources, Brian Slagel was barely in a better position to retain Slayer, yet he persisted, "We kept in touch, and they kept getting better and better," he says. "They were awesome, so we wanted to do a full-length album. At that point we still had no money. We could only do the album if they paid for the recording, which they eventually ended up doing."

The result was *Show No Mercy*, released in December 1983, a devastating collection of primitive brilliance that changed things drastically for Metal Blade. Ultrasatanic anthems like "The Antichrist," "Die by the Sword," and "Black Magic" sounded like malicious, hurried versions of Iron Maiden's *Killers*—except at Slayer's hectic tempo, the intricate instrumental breaks were reduced to a few seconds in their hasty entirety. In place of operatic vocals, singer/bassist Tom Araya let loose hellish screams. Lead guitarists Kerry King and Jeff Hanneman adjusted the unison melodic riffs of Iron Maiden to a minor key or plainly played them out of key. King in particular favored lead breaks that were flashy, fractured, and made full use of the whammy bar and extra frets on his B. C. Rich Mockingbird guitar. "Kerry's solos were pretty out there," assesses Hanneman.

This was metal holocaust with no hope of prettiness or polish. Slayer played the wild chugging of Metallica with a careless, wild-eyed edge instead of a relentless groove, and they lavished *Show No Mercy* with Satanism and hymns to evil circumstances. The aim was not exactly world domination, but rather total destruction. "I think what we did was take what metal was, injected some punk into it, and just went from there," says Kerry King. Heavy metal fans had long been obsessed with discovering the flashiest players and the heaviest bands—*Show No Mercy*, like its more polished rival *Kill 'Em All*, broke the scales of both measures. Suddenly, young bands were tossing away twin guitar harmonies in favor of a new standard: Who played fastest? Dan Lilker had recently left Anthrax and formed Nuclear Assault, and he recalls first hearing *Show No Mercy:* "Of course, one of our instincts was 'Oh, God, now there's another really fast band out there, we have to speed up!' There was a sense of competition."

Between Metallica and Slayer especially, that competitive spirit sometimes led to acrimony. In an early interview with *Kick Ass Monthly*, Lars Ulrich was unusually caustic about his fellow travelers. "It pisses me off, especially with Slayer," he said. "[In October 1982] we were headlining and they were our opening act. They played all covers: Judas Priest, Deep Purple, Iron Maiden, and Def Leppard. Slayer was all covers. When they played with us, that was the night that they said, 'Holy fuck! We've gotta be fast metal, too!' So it's obvious where their influences come from."

If Diamond Head was not exactly Slayer's speed, one relic from the British era clearly had an effect: NWOBHM rejects Venom. Long after giving up its Iron Maiden and Judas Priest covers, Slayer kept Venom's "Witching Hour" in its live repertoire—a measure of Venom's explosive influence on all things dark and dirty. Likewise, Metallica was thrilled to embark across Europe with Venom on the brief Seven Dates of Hell tour, beginning in Switzerland in February 1984. Venom's influence on the young metal fanatics was blatant. "You know James Hetfield of Metallica?" drummer Abaddon told two Swedish journalists. "I would swear that he suddenly started to walk like Cronos [Venom's singer, a bodybuilder who swaggered with arms swinging like a caveman.]"

Unquestionably the most extreme band of its time, Venom peaked in 1984 with *At War with Satan,* an album featuring a 17-minute track by the same name. Indulging every excess of its considerably crazy career, Venom raunched through the complete saga of hell's minions assaulting heaven. In the irony-laden story line, demons invade heaven and toss out the angels, who then regroup in hell and return tainted with wrath to disrupt and destroy the demonic victory party. Taking up an entire album side with this deranged concept was commercial blasphemy from a band with little hope of radio airplay.

Rather than slog their way across America like Mercyful Fate or Raven, Venom was satisfied to rarely stray from Britain, cashing in its chips in a sensational over-the-top semiannual stage extravaganza of lights, flames, and smoke. Pushing the extremes of album design as well, *At War with Satan* came packaged in a deluxe, gold-embossed, leathery gatefold sleeve, including glossy poster and inserts promoting scarves, badges, and other Venom-wear. If the band could not make an impact on the airwaves, it was surely going to make itself known sitting against the record player.

For the seriously music-minded, enchantment with a band as prone to overkill as Venom was an obligatory yet passing phase. "After I was asked to leave Metallica," recalls Dave Mustaine, "I was listening to Mercyful Fate and Diamond Head, but I wasn't really listening to Venom. I liked the fact that it was disturbing, but the playing was nowhere near as good as the shock factor." Nonetheless, the anarchic and bizarre band encouraged a veritable legion of imitators.

Hellhammer, a band from Nurensdorf, a farm village of 3,000 on the outskirts of Zurich, Switzerland, was one of the earliest to revisit Venom's chaotic satanic din—after lowering the musical bar considerably. "Since we weren't good enough yet to create something of our own, what we really did was copy the flying shit out of Venom," says Tom Warrior, who then used the name Satanic Slaughter. "The song titles, the riffs, down to our ludicrous stage names—everything was copied from Venom. We thought Venom was the heaviest band, and we wanted to be heavier. Everybody thought we were a new heavy band, but in reality we were just a miserable photocopy."

Hellhammer was possibly the most extreme example of imagination overpowering ability in a quest to reach ever-weirder heights. Still, such Xerox art was vastly entertaining on its own terms. The marrow-curdling shrieking that introduced "Triumph of Death" on its *Apocalyptic Raids* EP was a textbook case of the less-is-more school of dramatic metal—staging two-note guitar riffs with Klaus Kinski–esque vocal howls and dungeon production values. Writer Bernard Doe scoffed at Hellhammer in a *Metal Forces* review. "All I can say is this band are sure suckers for punishment," he wrote, comparing "The Third of the Storms (Evoked Damnation)" to "Metallica's 'Whiplash' being played by a bunch of three-year-olds."

Instead of it squashing his low-budget visions, the hammering Tom Warrior took from the press taught him the value of any kind of publicity. "That Hellhammer had a limited musical quality—that we needed to work like insane-os—was clear to us way before *Metal Forces* wrote about us," he says. "We were just playing at our limits. We didn't have any formal training, and we had to find out everything for ourselves. We received a number of really bad reviews, and those created such publicity that the band was talked about immediately by everybody, because everybody wanted to hear why a band got such extreme reviews. A lot of teenagers were looking for the same thing we were, the same kind of musical rebellion, and they just dug into the demo. Whether the reviews were bad or not, we were an instant insider tip."

Not quite ready for Metal Blade and Megaforce, the rawer underground bands became staples of the growing tape-trading domain. In Italy there was Bulldozer, with its slavish Venom-esque dirges. Germany produced Sodom, Destruction, and Tormentor. Greece offered Rotting Christ. Canada spawned Slaughter and Sacrifice. Brazil proffered Sepultura, Vulcano, and the senselessly dedicated Sarcofago, whose members wore primitive black-and-white "corpse paint" on their faces to symbolize a battlelike defiance of the church. Naming their style after a Venom album, these were the first black metal bands, the self-obsessed product of the metal subculture, with no overarching message or critique of society beyond the mere fact of their hostile existence.

Sometimes the power of the music mattered less than a creepy atmosphere and a convincing aura of secrecy. Such was the case with Sweden's Bathory, whose guitars sounded like sewing machines and whose drums seemed to be built of wet cardboard. The band's first album, 1984's *Bathory*, depicted the image of an eerie goat, and the second, 1985's *The Return*, simply offered a picture of the moon receding behind clouds. The minimal images conjured a huge mystique, as the crude lack of bearings set imaginations afire. "Ninety-nine percent of everything was in the heads of people," says Bathory bandleader Quorthon. "After some time we realized people were drawn to the band because of the mysterious aspect. It wasn't something we created. We would just have a shitty picture in a fanzine, and people would buy the fantasy. It's the force of ignorance. When you tell somebody the true story, you are ruining their idea of something. In reality Bathory was a combination of the influence of Kate Bush,

with a friend playing drums and patching up a little bit of the drums with a computer snare. People don't want that—it's like losing Santa Claus. Every time I talk about it, I kill a small part of me and the band."

Even Venom, the long-maligned originators of dirty black metal—whose entire career King Diamond called "a publicity stunt"—was not proud of its proliferate progeny. "We're not really influenced by what's going on these days," Venom singer Cronos told *Metal Forces* in 1985. "Bathory—that guy Quorthon is a dick. I mean, he's doing what we were doing on *Welcome to Hell*. It's ridiculous!" Only one year after *At War with Satan*, though, Venom had already been replaced by a hundred younger bands striving to be wilder

Quorthon of Sweden's Bathory
(New Renaissance)

and more outrageous. As promotional materials from Noise Records promised, "Hellhammer makes Venom sound like the Bee Gees!"

In many ways these bands were still pantomiming in front of the bedroom mirror with counterparts around the world acting as a reflection. When young black metal bands did play live, their skills were ridiculously limited. For example, Mayhem, the force that introduced black metal to Norway, formed in the autumn of 1984 playing Venom and Metallica covers. The band rehearsed in a barn and allegedly finished its first show by crushing a bass guitar and showing their asses. It was crude entertainment, yet infinitely more fun than merely watching the canned careers of more skilled and self-important musicians.

Wherever heavy metal was in danger of becoming too clean, black metal soon took hold. Bathory represented the antithesis of the pretentious Swedish cult guitarist Yngwie Malmsteen, a tedious virtuoso. Malmsteen possessed all the qualities of metal heroes Ritchie Blackmore and Eddie Van Halen but flashed his fingers on a Stratocaster guitar like a casino dealer shuffling cards—too precise, especially in an era when the best music tended to lack precision. He embodied a sterile, egocentric strain of metal that collapsed on itself when left too long in the sun. As much as Hellhammer represented ideas in place of skill, it was infinitely preferable to technique without soul.

At the time of *Show No Mercy*, Slayer still leaned heavily on image and shock value. In contrast to Metallica's blue jeans, Slayer wore studded leather chokers and spiked armbands. The members applied thick black eye makeup before performing, during a period immortalized by the photos adorning the first album. "All the metal bands like Mötley Crüe and Pandemonium were wearing makeup, but it was girly," explains Jeff Hanneman. "We wanted to look like men, so we looked like football players!"

Playing in San Francisco with Exodus, Laaz Rocket, and "thrash with class" act Savage Grace, Slayer received a roaring welcome, as had Metallica—but Bay Area bangers giggled at the band's contrived presentation. Tom Araya recalls taking a bit of advice from the fans and throwing away his greasepaint. Present at the show, Ron Quintana agrees. "They were kind of laughed at. People up here told them to take off the makeup, and, surprisingly, the makeup didn't last. I don't think they ever wore it again."

Musically as well, Slayer ascended from the swirling dark pit, remaining the technically advanced high priests of Venom-inspired

EARLY BLACK METAL

Initially considered bad power metal by the fanzine writers of the mid-1980s, the first leather-bedecked and upside-down-crossed black metal bands received the kind of dismissive reception previously reserved for punk rock. Still, coverage continued, due to the popularity and extremity of the bands, and soon there were little tributes to Venom running wild everywhere. The imitation of satanic extremes soon developed into something deeper in Slayer, Bathory, Possessed, and Celtic Frost, seeding a dedicated cult that had no interest in the flashy colors and need for attention of regular heavy metal. The speed was grueling, and raw, primitive emotion burned from the heart. As their minions grew into the millions, black metal became an underground fixture, forming the spiritual basis and direct musical inspiration for death metal.

Satan's Love Songs
- ❖ Bathory, *Under the Sign of the Black Mark* (1987)
- ❖ Destruction, *Sentence of Death* (1984)
- ❖ Hellhammer, *Apocalyptic Raids* (1984)
- ❖ Morbid Angel, *Abominations of Desolation* (1986)
- ❖ NME, *Unholy Death* (1985)
- ❖ Possessed, *Seven Churches* (1985)
- ❖ Sepultura, *Morbid Visions* (1988)
- ❖ Slayer, *Hell Awaits* (1985)
- ❖ Slayer, *Show No Mercy* (1984)
- ❖ Sodom, *Obsessed by Cruelty* (1986)
- ❖ Venom, *Black Metal* (1982)
- ❖ Venom, *Welcome to Hell* (1981)

devil's metal. On the *Haunting the Chapel* EP, with its unbelievably fast "Chemical Warfare," Slayer crested to a point that left the standards of power metal behind. While playing so fast that individual notes were hardly discernible, guitarists King and Hanneman sketched out rough approximations of melodies from the horrific side of Iron Maiden and Judas Priest. Whenever the two guitarists veered

Slayer live in 1985
(Todd Nakamine)

out of time and control, drummer Dave Lombardo pounded order through the center.

In early 1985 Slayer revealed *Hell Awaits,* displaying newfound mastery of this increasing speed. As whirlpools of controlled chaos consumed tracks like "Kill Again," the music took on an advanced and sinister character. Both

"Hell Awaits" and "At Dawn They Sleep" were epic narratives with tempo changes, instrumental breaks, and swarming passages—it was clear the rules were fresh and provisional. Though production remained muddy, the technical skill of the twin guitarists was vastly improved. Tom Araya's vocal range still modulated between growls and energetic screams, never losing its musical quality. What's more, "In Praise of Death" and "Hardening of the Arteries" were as fast as anything Slayer ever played. It was advanced study from a band that had clearly graduated since *Show No Mercy,* and the band fed from these basic creative fountains for many years after. The landmark *Reign in Blood* later stripped Slayer down to its most effective form, but *Hell Awaits* proved that greatness did not need to be so precise.

Unlike the playful Hellhammer and Bathory, Slayer had serious aspirations. Yet perhaps because Metallica had a head start with melody, Slayer continued its push to become extremely fast and heavy. It pursued that path long after Metallica had professed a lack of interest in pure speed. As a result Slayer cultivated a narrower but more intensely dedicated audience. *Hell Awaits* quickly sold 100,000 copies, a major hit by any independent-label standards and the first great success for Metal Blade. "The Slayer stuff started to explode just after Armored Saint had been signed to a major label," Brian Slagel recalls. "That's pretty much when Metal Blade became a real thing."

Metal Blade had now established a cycle of testing new talent on its compilation series then signing the popular bands to longer recording deals. From 1984's *Metal Massacre V* the label kept Fates Warning, Omen, and Voivod—and lost Metal Church and Overkill to higher bidders. Metal Blade also began licensing the best and earliest of the European power metal and black metal bands, like the highly vaunted debut mini-LPs from Sodom, Destruction, and the perversely appealing Hellhammer.

For Exciter, whose 1983 LP *Heavy Metal Maniac* stood alongside Metallica's *Kill 'Em All* at the very forefront of power metal, the dawn of the rawer black metal genre was reason to worry. "All these fifteen-year-old kids all of a sudden came out putting albums out, going ten thousand miles an hour, putting Satanic lyrics on, and they sell like a hundred thousand copies," complained singer/drummer Dan Beehler to *Kick Ass Monthly*. "You can only take that garbage so far. Some bands do speed well, like Metallica, and they're successful as a result, but you can't take some of these little kids out of a basement, throw them onstage in front of five thousand people, and expect 'em to be good."

Though Tom Warrior retained no illusions about the short-lived Hellhammer, he defends the unique qualities of the underbelly. "No matter how low the technical level of some of the harder music is—and many times it sure is," he says, "it is nearly impossible to play convincingly to audiences if one doesn't live, breathe, and understand it, if it isn't rooted in one's very blood. Because hard music lives so much from primitive instincts of power—from guts—it is hard for an outsider to really master it mentally and physically, no matter how talented and willing that outsider might be."

Emerging as carriers of a new strain of innovative metal, Warrior and Martin Ain launched Celtic Frost after they stopped chasing Venom into satanic metal perdition. They disbanded their flamboyantly disgraced act Hellhammer, and—as Warrior puts it, "learned how to really play guitar." According to Warrior the group chose its two-word name in homage to Cirith Ungol, a fantasy-inspired band from *Metal Massacre*. On songs like "Dawn of Meggido" and "Tears

Tom Warrior of Celtic Frost
(Jean-François "Big" Lavallée/Metal K.O. Productions)

in a Prophet's Dream," Warrior, bassist Ain, and drummer Reed St. Mark were as powerful as Slayer without leaning on the tried-and-true formula of pentagrams and devil horns.

There was a huge difference between Celtic Frost and Hellhammer. Steeped in total heaviness, the crushing Frost relied on curious influences from outside the realm of metal, like the weird noises and otherworldly impulses Warrior first found in Brian Eno's 1970s band Roxy Music. In the 1980s heavy metal had become the premiere outlet for strange and interesting sounds. As drummer Away of Voivod told *Kick Ass Monthly*, "There is a band for which I've got real respect, Celtic Frost. Their lyrics are original and intelligent, and when you're listening to them, you know that those guys have real strange minds."

In 1985 Celtic Frost released *Morbid Tales*, a multithudding suite of formidable power riffs, and then in 1986 produced its genre-busting epic *To Mega Therion*—Greek for "the big beast." With a thick guitar sound best described as groaning, the record had elements of Metallica and Slayer as performed by an agile granite monster, lumbering but deftly sure of its choreography. "*To Mega Therion* was basically an expression of my own immaturity and male urgings," recalls Tom Warrior. "That's why it has such a Conan-like fantasy touch to it. It's made for people in puberty, definitely. That's certainly the roots of heavy metal. That whole sense of revolution and wanting to be powerful is definitely a puberty thing. Fans don't have to be offended by that. Everybody goes through it. That's why heavy metal is so powerful."

For the cover of *To Mega Therion*, Swiss painter H. R. Giger lent his struggling countrymen free use of *Satan I*, a 1977 painting of a tentacle-sprouting demon armed with a slingshot made from the outstretched arms of a crucified Christ. Though they lived fifteen minutes from the Oscar-winning *Alien* artist, Celtic Frost approached

Giger by mail in true tape-trader style, submitting a lengthy explanatory package. "On Mother's Day of 1984, the phone!" writes Tom Warrior. "It's H. R. Giger in person! He's not only a total gentleman but astonishes us by wasting little time before delving into the possibilities of how to make the cooperation work, including the large-format presentation of artwork." As the taut tendrils of *To Mega Therion* reached beyond the colored pencil skulls of *Metal Massacre V,* it marked a change from amateurish fandom to real artistry.

While Metallica eyed the mainstream, Slayer, Celtic Frost, and Bathory rapidly changed the rules of the underground. Separated by talent and geography but united by international money orders and tape trading, one impulse all the stamp-licking, black metal spawn shared was a fetish for all things outrageously satanic, including pentagrams, inverted crosses, and the ever-present emblem of a goat's head. Says guitarist Trey Azagthoth of Morbid Angel, a band formed during the heady days of 1984, "Back then there was a big thing about attacking Christianity. I was raised Christian, and I was kind of brainwashed, and I hated those beliefs. I can understand, now that I've studied psychology and I know the importance of religion, how people get conditioned to beliefs and develop perceptive filters."

Virulent new players joined Slayer on the cutting edge, playing with skill to match their guts. In junior high, outside San Francisco, Larry Lalonde and Jeff Becerra played UFO songs in Blizzard. They wore sleeveless American-flag shirts and grew hair to their shoulders, the farthest their mothers would permit. Upon reaching high school the pair were recruited by Mike Torrao and Mike Sus for the less-wholesome Possessed. "Their singer had shot himself in the head," says Becerra, "and they didn't have a bass player. I wanted to go heavier anyway. I was more into being heavy as far as drinking beer, going out with as many girls as I could, and playing as fast and heavy as I could, like Motörhead. I asked Mike what the name of the band was, and he said 'Possessed.' I said it sounded kinda satanic, and he said, 'Well, it is!' That was kinda scary."

Still, Possessed soon found a manager in a girlfriend's mother—fifty-something Bay Area dealmaker Debbie Abono. An anomalous

DEMOS OF DOOM

Many of the giant, influential recordings of the black metal genre never appeared on vinyl at all but were shared internationally by tens of thousands of underground tape traders. By the time these bands landed record deals, they were already household names—at least in the basement.

Demo-Tape Trader Top Ten

- ❖ Death, "Infernal Death" (1985)
- ❖ Hellhammer, "Triumph of Death" (1983)
- ❖ Messiah, "Infernal Thrashing" (1984)
- ❖ Slaughter, "Surrender or Die" (1984)
- ❖ Morbid Angel, "Thy Kingdom Come" (1985)
- ❖ Nasty Savage, "Wage of Mayhem" (1984)
- ❖ Necrophagia, "Death Is Fun" (1985)
- ❖ Repulsion, "Horrified (1986)
- ❖ Voivod, "Morgoth Invasion" (1984)
- ❖ Voor, "Evil Metal" (1984)

presence in the scene, Abono became responsible for this group of thrill-seeking satanist teenagers who drank like greedy fish and still made it to school in the morning. "We didn't really do much as far as touring," recalls guitarist Larry Lalonde, although the group traveled to Europe and Canada. "We recorded the albums on Easter vacation, so I never missed any school."

The first Possessed album, *Seven Churches*, channeled all the destructive madness of these sixteen-year-old American teens upward into a byzantine fest of chaos, speed, and Satanism. Though it was unbelievable that four high-schoolers could craft such masterful madness, Possessed in late 1985 pushed Slayer's sound so far into evil darkness that it became something new. Vocalist Jeff Becerra recalls the physical strain of performing such frantic music. "It's fucking aerobics. *Seven Churches* was the worst album to do on tour. We were in trouble. There were times, playing that stuff in clubs without air-conditioning, when I felt like Muhammad Ali. I couldn't do anything. I didn't know if I was going to vomit or pass out. It was like a jogger's high."

Seven Churches was not the primitive roar of Venom, Bathory, or Hellhammer either—as musicians, the members of Possessed were just as much into guitar wizardry as they were lyrical witchcraft. The battle between technique and raw energy made the record a brilliant, timeless blast—it towered like a spontaneous cathedral, making the fast, violent, hardcore punk records of its day sound like ugly Soviet concrete boxes. Along with *Hell Awaits* and demo tapes by the Florida band Death, *Seven Churches* laid the groundwork for what eventually became death metal—the ultimate confluence of black metal's satanic madness and well-practiced traditional metal musicianship. "Possessed [was] different from all the other bands who were coming out at that time," Chuck Schuldiner of Death later told *Metal Maniacs*. "They weren't pure noise, and they attempted to incorporate a lot of different musical ideas into their songwriting, not just rehash the same thing. They were into progressing as a band, which paved the way for other groups to expand their sound and do different things."

The nominal allegiance to the devil stood strong, acting as a marker against mainstream acceptance. To some degree, black-magic-inspired lyrics even led followers into a larger social and moral debate.

King Diamond's fascination with the occult surfaced long before Venom or Slayer in pre–Mercyful Fate bands like Brats and Black Rose. "There's some meaning behind it," he says. "Back when we were struggling in Denmark, we had a priest on our case. He was doing the best to ban even our demo tapes from being played on the radio. They set up a two-way thing where we could both talk on the air. He said the obvious things [about *Nuns Have No Fun*, a mini-album depicting the crucifixion of a nude witch], and I said 'This is a drawing of the religion you stand for. They did this for real to millions of people!'"

Call black metal's dress code and arcane semantics an addictive power fantasy for rejects, but it required a special rarefied sensibility for fans to don shirts depicting giant blazing pentagrams and memorize long lyrical lines of barely audible blasphemy. Constant shout-outs to Satan were distracting and distressing to the unassimilated ear, but, like most youth ideologies, mock devil worship merely expressed the desire to smash societal restraints and carve a space for unfettered fun. Or, in the words of Possessed's Larry Lalonde, "If you believe in all of this Satan stuff, you have to be stupid!"

The PMRC's Antimetal Panic

While Slayer provoked the profane in its underworld, headbangers appeared in public everywhere, milling around strip malls with long, unkempt (and often kempt) hair and sporting T-shirts that bore the frequently frightful names and imagery of bands like Ratt, Def Leppard, Iron Maiden, and Venom. America's authority figures were starting to feel greatly antagonized—there remained a large group of people to whom "deaf leopard" sounded like a bestial atrocity. In the eyes of the older generation, the highly visible and seemingly universal appeal of heavy metal was an invasion of something horribly wrong.

After MTV brought the rock arena into the home, the entertaining hedonism that Ann Landers feared in the 1970s could no longer be contained solely in concert halls. Rebellion was now a fixture in American living rooms. Credit for the channel's popularity was shared by acts touting metal madness, like the carnally obsessed Scorpions, the hairy cross-dressers Twisted Sister, and the lipstick satanists Mötley Crüe. Twisted Sister, for instance, was a gang of big, hairy New Yorkers who dressed in exaggerated and ironic female drag. They were led by Dee Snider, a gruesome figure *Kerrang!* compared to Bette Midler for his garish makeup and long, curling tresses. The band's immensely popular MTV hit "We're Not Gonna Take It" depicted the big-city monsters stomping through a suburban neighborhood—a perfect cartoon of how the cable medium itself was snaking through the tidy lawns of the American Midwest.

Anti–AC/DC pamphlet from Germany

A cultural war was brewing, and heavy metal became the punching bag. Even when not explicitly urging a revolt in the streets, the attitudes of heavy metal made a visible threat to public order. Although metal was not the only music to upset moral crusaders, with its obvious taunts the movement served as a fantastic scapegoat. For the same extra-musical reasons that Iron Maiden's *Number of the Beast* piqued the interest of teenagers, it appalled excitable adults. Soon a veritable bouquet of reactionary forces strung together an unexpectedly successful attack on heavy metal's social power.

Responding to what some saw as a crisis of extreme music, the Parents' Music Resource Center political-advocacy group, or PMRC, formed in 1984 at the impetus of Susan Baker, Tipper Gore, and several other wives of ranking members of Congress. The group advanced the theory that rising suicide and rape statistics among teenagers could be blamed on lewd rock lyrics. "They had raised the drinking age," notes Dee Snider of Twisted Sister, "and there were certain magazines [*Playboy* and *Penthouse*] that weren't being carried by 7-Eleven. There was clearly a conservative grip on things, and the audience was too caught up in partying to react."

Though the Washington Wives were often portrayed as a cackling group of middle-aged busybodies, Susan Baker and Tipper Gore were among the most politically effective women in the country in 1984. Both had worked for decades alongside ambitious spouses. Baker's Republican husband, James, was secretary of the treasury, and later secretary of state. Gore's husband, Al, a Democratic senator representing Tennessee, sat on the Senate Commerce Committee. He became vice president of the United States in 1992 and famously missed being elected president in 2000 by a quirk in the electoral system. The entire list of PMRC co-chairs included the wives of 10 percent of the Senate—their demeanor was soft, but their influence was frightening.

The PMRC progressed quickly in Reagan-era Washington. Its wonderfully simple explanation for existing problems cost nothing and blamed a segment of the populace that was not particularly politically active—or even of voting age. Furthermore, to oppose the PMRC worldview, in the eyes of conservatives, was to advocate moral degeneracy of the worst kind. "That's pretty much the way the PMRC

parents' music resource center

300 Metropolitan Square
655 Fifteenth Street, N.W.
Washington, D.C. 20005

Dear Friend,

Just as we explained on the Phil Donahue show, the Parents' Music Resource Center needs your support. Not for the sake of the Center, but for the young people of America, perhaps your children.

Today's young people are surrounded by music, rock music. It is so pervasive that we almost forget it's even there. But make no mistake, it is there, too much of it drumming more and more destructive messages into the minds of our children.

The average teenager listens to rock music four to six hours daily! That's more hours of rock music than hours of classroom instruction. Unfortunately, in much of that music the message is negative, even harmful.

Because too many of today's rock artists -- through radio, records, television videos, videocassettes -- advocate aggressive and hostile rebellion, the abuse of drugs and alcohol, irresponsible sexuality, sexual perversions, violence and involvement in the occult.

PMRC fund-raising letter

worked," said James Hetfield of Metallica to journalist K. J. Doughton. "They'd look for bad shit and find it. Because you're gonna find what you're looking for, even if it ain't there to someone else, or ain't there at all."

Less democratic governments had long addressed the threat of rock music with severe sanctions. In 1975 several Black Sabbath songs were banned by the South Korean Federation of Cultural Organizations, which pegged the music as "subversive and antiwar." Korean radio stations, all government owned, ceased playing heavy metal, and longhaired youths were given haircuts on the spot by scissors-wielding policemen. The PMRC and its friends might have welcomed a similar cleansing in America, but such constitutional concepts as freedom of speech required less obvious tactics.

On September 19, 1985, the Senate Commerce Committee convened hearings at the insistence of Mrs. Baker and Mrs. Gore to advance their belief that record albums should be rated and restricted in the same manner as movies. As Tipper Gore told the mostly Republican panel, "We're asking the recording industry to voluntarily assist parents who are concerned by placing a warning label on music products inappropriate for younger children due to explicit sexual or violent content." Meanwhile, religious protesters outside the congressional offices waved placards for the TV cameras reading ROCK MUSIC DESTROYS KIDS and WE'VE HAD ENOUGH.

This was not an invitation to a dialogue—it was a setup. Still, Twisted Sister was among those targeted for indecency, so the band's charismatic singer, Dee Snider, went to Washington along with the brainy rocker Frank Zappa and the wholesome singer/songwriter John Denver. "They contacted my management," Snider says, "and wanted to know if I would come and testify, figuring, 'Let's get the most recognizable character in metal at the time and put him up there as the poster boy for censorship.' They were caught off guard, because they didn't know I spoke English fluently."

To illustrate their outrage, the PMRC presented oversize album covers and recited offensive lyrics, mostly out of context. To stoke the impulses of the press, the organization tabulated a list of the most shocking artists of the day, a haphazard collection including Madonna, Def Leppard, Wendy O. Williams, W.A.S.P., Mötley Crüe, and the Mentors. Most of the artists were chosen for overt sexuality, but there was also particular attention paid to songs dealing with the occult. Most of them had never reached, or were ever intended to reach, such a large mass-media audience. "I guess the worst thing that ever happened to us was kind of good," notes King Diamond. "The PMRC put Mercyful Fate on their Filthy Fifteen list. I think from us they picked 'Into the Coven' or something, but they could have picked any song!"

Dee Snider responded to questions before the conference committee appropriately dressed in a sleeveless black T-shirt with long frizzled blond hair erupting from his head. Under examination by Senator Gore, Snider suggested that parents, not government, should take responsibility for the music their children bring into the house. When Gore asked Snider if such monitoring was reasonable, the singer quipped, "Being a parent isn't a reasonable thing, it's a hard thing. I'm a parent, and I know."

After delivering a statement scorning senators for wasting the country's time, Frank Zappa proposed simply that rock lyrics be printed on the outside of record jackets. Zappa told reporters on Capitol Hill, "You know what worries me about what's happening here today? This is government as entertainment. These people have plenty to do besides talking about whether or not somebody's little Johnny gets to see the Blackie Lawless cover with the buzz-saw blade between his legs."

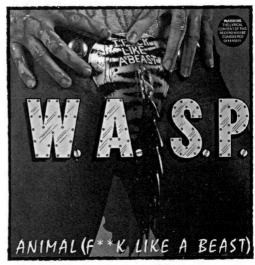

"We Are Sexual Perverts"

Indeed, for shock rockers like Lawless, outraged parishioners were all part of the show. Says Lawless of W.A.S.P.'s first tour of England, "You've got the local clergy and all the Catholic Church following us everywhere, buying tickets and bringing people to the shows. They're bringing a hundred people in at a time, and they're down in the middle of the room praying while we're up onstage. It was quite a surrealistic thing."

Nonetheless, fear-mongering remained a growth sector during the Reagan administration, as the PMRC hearings empowered a job class of self-proclaimed occult experts—bizarre modern-day witch-hunters who lectured at PTA meetings, encouraged letter-writing campaigns, and wormed their way into TV news segments with alarming regularity. The gravy train extended to a greedy procession of born-again comedians, retired police officers, and evangelical ministers such as Bob Larson, author of a series of books attacking rock music. In the self-published 1983 book *Rock*, for example, Larson fed the terror of the ignorant with far-fetched warnings concerning Black Sabbath's supposed use of astral projection and chicken-blood rituals.

The saber rattling continued following the PMRC hearings, yet King Diamond believes that the Moral Majority learned to intentionally pick weak targets. "If these organizations want to get on your case, they check up on you. If you're reasonably bright and you can substantiate what you're saying, they don't want to pick a fight with you."

Yet even the evangelical Christian metal act Stryper was not spared the fervor of the self-righteous. The band voluntarily recalled its 1986 album, *To Hell with the Devil*, due to controversy over the New Testament–inspired cover artwork. "We got a lot of flak from Christian people who thought we put a pentagram on it just for the sake of putting a pentagram on it," says Stryper's singer, Michael Sweet. "One of the angels had ripped a necklace off of Satan's neck and cast it away, and that's the pentagram. People just misinterpreted that, so just to avoid controversy and avoid potential problems, we came out with a plain black cover with just the Stryper logo on it."

To most musicians the puzzling panic in Washington merely seemed like a collection of irate parents banging on the bedroom door. Ultimately the PMRC inquisitors were not righteous enough and the accused not sufficiently wicked to mandate any government action. "After all was said and done, more was said than done," says Blackie Lawless. So it appeared, yet the crusade against metalheads was far from over.

Despite a winning performance in Washington by Dee Snider, the leading recording-industry trade group bowed to PMRC pressure of

"PØRN RØCK"

This nonexistent genre has the rare distinction of being compiled by legislators, rather than musicians. Some of the bands were sensational pop stars, others, like W.A.S.P., were obscure scum-mongers who might have lived out their careers in relative obscurity without the benefit of this media blitz. The goal was to educate parents, but the outcome was welcome meddling with the sales of heavy metal records. Even the LPs that perished on protest bonfires were paid for. Worst of all, however, the PMRC lent legitimacy to the idea that singing about devils and monsters is a form of witchcraft, a crazy red herring that put metal musicians on the defensive—and sometimes the offensive—for decades.

Tipper Gore's Hit Parade—the "Filthy Fifteen"

(Proposed ratings: X—Sexual Content, D/A—Drugs/Alcohol, V—Violence, O—Occult)

- ❖ AC/DC, "Let Me Put My Love into You"   X
- ❖ Black Sabbath, "Trashed"   D/A
- ❖ Cyndi Lauper, "She Bop"   X
- ❖ Def Leppard, "High 'n' Dry"   D/A
- ❖ Judas Priest, "Eat Me Alive"   X
- ❖ Madonna, "Dress You Up"   X
- ❖ Mary Jane Girls, "My House"   X
- ❖ Mercyful Fate, "Into the Coven"   O
- ❖ Mötley Crüe, "Bastard"   V
- ❖ Prince, "Darling Nikki"   X
- ❖ Sheena Easton, "Sugar Walls"   X
- ❖ Twisted Sister, "We're Not Gonna Take It"   V
- ❖ Vanity, "Strap on Robby Baby"   X
- ❖ Venom, "Possessed"   O
- ❖ W.A.S.P., "(Animal) F**k Like a Beast"   X

its own accord. While representing the music industry during the PMRC hearings, the Recording Industry Association of America, or RIAA, was also lobbying for the right to collect a tax on blank recording media. In political terms some concession made business sense. "I saw it as a great opportunity to carry the flag for heavy metal," says Dee Snider of his adventure on Capitol Hill, "figuring everyone would follow me into battle. The other bands laid low, and the audience was apathetic. I was sorely mistaken and very disappointed when I saw the industry cave before we even spoke."

In December 1985 the RIAA agreed to voluntarily sticker potentially offensive releases, ultimately leading to implementation of the standardized black-and-white Parental Advisory Warning labels in 1990. Though supporters argued that such notification did not suppress freedom of expression, superstores like Wal-Mart promptly initiated a litmus test policy, refusing to carry "dirty" records with parental-advisory stickers. Thus began the first marketwide censorship of rock music in America. The RIAA's controversial decision to sticker was quietly followed by the Audio Home Recording Act in 1992, which enacted a sliding tax on digital recording hardware like DAT players and a 3 percent tax on blank recording media payable to an affiliate of the RIAA.

Dee Snider's Teenage Survival Guide, published in 1987

Aside from the Home Recording Act, the Senate was also hotly debating cable regulation in the 1980s, which led to scrutiny of music videos. Dee Snider believes that MTV deep-sixed Twisted Sister's patently inoffensive "Be Chrool to Your Scuel" clip as a conciliatory gesture to the congressional powers. "The parents thought we were the evil villains," Snider adds, "but the kids knew we were one of the least offensive bands out there. They were willing to sacrifice our band so they could continue to listen to Mötley Crüe.

And the mothers and fathers thought they'd accomplished something."

The business of saving America's children thus complete, the PMRC embarked on increasingly bizarre endeavors during the late 1980s. A few years after the hearings the group established a pay-per-minute telephone hot line that dispersed advice on Satanism and hosted a voice-mail menu of lyrical transgressions organized by specific performers. They also sold cassettes of "clean" music by the composer of *The Towering Inferno* theme—extremely ironic, considering that the PMRC had vilified Def Leppard for depicting a burning building on its *Pyromania* album cover.

Even as heavy metal examined the problems of society, sensationalistic voices declared loudly that heavy metal itself was the problem. Many legislators were embarrassed by their roles in the PMRC hearings, but the outcome validated a long-running assault against heavy metal. The appearance of the stickers, an apparent admission of guilt, fed a financial boon for groups like the Moral Majority, a coalition of activist religious fundamentalists led by televangelist Jerry Falwell. Lewd rock lyrics became the clarion call of Falwell's masterful fundraising operation, scaring up millions of dollars earmarked for political operations such as reversing the legality of abortion, opposing "forced busing," and replacing the theory of evolution in the schools with biblical creationism.

The parental-warning stickers marked the start of a long cat-and-mouse game between the record industry and moral watchdogs, creating a cynical symbiosis with which it was always easy to find bands willing to play along for publicity value. Though the vanguard of metal attempted to stay above the smears, the taint of misunderstanding would continue to plague the music. "The conservatives are still there, but they're just quieter," adds Dee Snider fifteen years later. "The censorship is everywhere, but it is more insidious. Big chain stores are doing most of the dirty work themselves."

⊰ VIII ⊱

Rattleheads:
The Mental Metal Reaction

→ **September 3, 1984:** Metallica signs
to Elektra Records, Raven to Atlantic,
Anthrax to Island

→ **April 1985:** After a one-year delay,
Exodus releases *Bonded by Blood*

→ **May 17, 1985:** Megadeth debut album
released, featuring Nancy Sinatra cover

→ **August 17, 1985:** Metallica performs at
Monsters of Rock in Castle Donnington,
England

Needless to say, as far as heavy metal was concerned, none of the presumptions of the PMRC and its allies had any basis in reality—least of all allegations of Black Sabbath practicing astral projection. The PMRC and its by-product businesses had taken on metal as the junk culture they saw presented on MTV, full of fake blood and exploding codpieces. All the while, a smarter new breed of bands was on the verge of making its commercial impact. Continuing the lyrical seriousness of classic heavy metal, the increasingly popular power metal bands were grazing on profound subjects, tackling the big themes of nuclear war, crime and punishment, and social injustice.

Previously Metallica had not shied from the demonic tendencies of heavy metal. Though the demo version of "Jump in the Fire" was a sexual boast, just before recording *Kill 'Em All*, the band changed the lyrics to the more brimstone-scented "Down in the depths of my fiery home—the summons bell will chime." Furthermore, in a nice display of music-company opportunism by the group's British label, Music for Nations, the UK release of this catchy single depicted a horned orange demon emerging from a wall of flames. While writing its second album in 1984, though the PMRC was still merely a proposal, Metallica was already eager to put distance between itself and devilish gimmicks.

A world advanced from its precursor, Metallica made *Ride the Lightning* with producer Flemming Rasmussen at Sweet Silence Studio in Lars Ulrich's homeland, Denmark, a natural choice for a band that identified so closely with its European roots. Bereft of odes to headbanging, *Ride the Lightning* abandoned the metal vacuum of *Kill 'Em All* for more difficult and insightful lyrical themes. Thwarting accusations that the band had slowed down, the album opened with a brief acoustic intro interrupted by the megaton blast of "Fight Fire with Fire," a stunning admonition against nuclear war, specifically the Cold War–era defense strategy of mutually assured destruction.

Elsewhere on *Ride the Lightning*, the title track tackled capital punishment, and the introspective "Fade to Black" offered a plea against suicide. On the pounding "For Whom the Bell Tolls," James Hetfield paraphrased writer Ernest Hemingway to summon a powerful battleground scene witnessed through the eyes of a young soldier. For the first time, Kirk Hammett poured his fluid guitar style into the songwriting, as well as injecting a few bits of repertoire. Relaying the Old Testament story of a vengeful God sending plagues to Egypt to punish the pharaohs, "Creeping Death" took its entire hypnotic bridge from "Dying by His Hand," an old Exodus number.

An instrumental, initially named "When Hell Freezes Over," underwent great internal scrutiny. "There's only one thing that I'm kind of against with that title," Lars Ulrich told *Kick Ass Monthly*. "There's one word in there, it's spelled H-E-L-L, which we try to stay away from as much as possible, because we don't want to be associated with any kind of Satanism or that shit. We think that 'When Hell Freezes Over' is probably non-satanic enough for us to live with, since there's no lyrics saying 'I wanna suck Satan's dick' or anything like that." The moody instrumental retained its icy overtones but appeared on *Light-*

ning with the H. P. Lovecraft–inspired name "The Call of Ktulu."

Far from being satanic overlords, Metallica was even a little spooked by the occult proclivities of some of its contemporaries. Rasmussen's recording studio was located next to Mercyful Fate's rehearsal hall—while in Denmark, Metallica relied on them for practice space and equipment loans. "James mentioned that they wrote some of the music for *Ride the Lightning* in our rehearsal room," recalls King Diamond. "My book full of new lyrics was there, and he and Lars wanted to look at them, but they were kind of scared. They thought I was gonna put a curse on them, but they looked anyway. Then they heard us coming, so they quickly closed the book. They were so scared when I came in that I would know—and then I walked straight over to the book and looked in it. Years later James said it freaked them out so bad. I had no idea."

Metal had crashed through commercial barriers and made great musical advances thus far in the 1980s. After the PMRC attacked this prominence, metalheads stepped into a cultural war that had been escalating since the 1950s. In the days of Elvis Presley many of the same fundamentalist preachers had begun burning rock and roll records—even though Congress at the time was more concerned with communists than Satanists. Now Metallica stood up to the challenge of social responsibility. If the improving quality of the music was not enough to keep opponents at bay, then at least the quarrel would be over the merits of the message. Most important, if national leaders were going to busy themselves with policing rock music, then it became the job of metal musicians to talk to young people about issues of substance.

⊳⊳⊳⊳⊳◉⊲⊲⊲⊲⊲

As it turned out, this is exactly what the fans wanted to hear. Emerging from its metal cocoon, Metallica faced a world of bright prospects. The growing heavy metal world was clearing a path for aggressive new faces, breaking the bottleneck created by British metal giants and MTV sensations. The independent bands pledged they would never sell their souls to MTV in order to make friends with the marketplace. Yet as large numbers of substance-hungry listeners arrived, the music of independent labels was finally attracting the mainstream music business through sheer force of numbers.

Following a tour of Europe in support of Twisted Sister, Metallica joined Raven and Anthrax for an electrifying show at New York's Roseland Ballroom on September 3, 1984. Though the crowd was rife with talent scouts, some were still a little unclear on the concept: Raven's John Gallagher recalls a drunken Elektra employee backstage praising Metallica's set, though the band had yet to hit the stage. No matter, there was raging good cheer aplenty during the heady night for all three bands and their shared label, Megaforce. After the swirling sweat and hair cleared in the large dance hall, label head Jon Zazula handed off his three prize catches to new major-label homes: Metallica went to Elektra Records, and Raven to Atlantic Records. Anthrax was soon signed to Island Records. The metal underground had met its moneymakers.

1984 Metallica Metal Militia fan club newsletter

The following day Zazula was shocked when Lars Ulrich called to announce that Metallica was also splitting with Megaforce's sister company, Crazed Management, in favor of Q Prime Management, in a deal partially brokered by *Kerrang!* writer Xavier Russell over a pay phone. Q Prime partners Cliff Burnstein and Peter Mensch had previously worked for the hard-won success of AC/DC, and their canny instinct for exploiting metal talent also guided Def Leppard's video-driven ascent from Sheffield bar band to pop metal whipping boys. With Metallica seizing the chance to realize its aspirations, Zazula had little choice but to reluctantly agree to release his rising star.

Thus far Metallica operated by its own rules, and even the band was startled by how well its back-alley approach worked. After the release of *Ride the Lightning*, Metallica tasted critical respect that transcended the taunts of born-again bigots. However, not every song on *Lightning* was a praiseworthy artistic triumph. In fact, the band later admitted that the oddly mundane "Escape" was a contrived and fruitless attempt to write a radio-friendly tune. It was a concession that would soon prove unnecessary—though still justifiable during a time when even Judas Priest was employing professional songwriting help (*Screaming for Vengeance*'s "Take These Chains" and *Defenders of the Faith*'s "Some Heads Are Gonna Roll") in hopes of achieving a radio hit.

Instead Metallica was gaining significant college-radio airplay for "Am I Evil?," an eight-minute anthem found only in the import section of metal specialty stores. Following the custom of releasing non-album material that had proven immensely successful for Iron Maiden, Metallica's UK label, Music for Nations, produced a limited *Creeping Death* EP that gave fans something extra without taxing the band's creative wellspring. On the A-side was *Ride the Lightning*'s "Creeping Death," while the B-side, subtitled "Garage Days Revisited," presented cover versions of Diamond Head's "Am I Evil?" and Blitzkrieg's "Blitzkrieg." With stampeding unison riffing by Hammett, Hetfield, and Burton, the peculiarities of these two overlooked NWOBHM standards made powerful sense to young audiences who might have never heard the originals.

Even as an import, mom-and-pop stores were able to get out 40,000 copies of the EP. Thousands of fans took up the quest, begging rides from their friends to out-of-the-way strip malls where metal hideouts were found. With a cover song full of weird, Oedipal lyrical turns—"My mother was a witch. She was burned alive"—resolving in a fatalistic chant—"Am I evil? Yes I am. I am man."—Metallica found its version of a hit single. "Am I Evil?" became a Metallica trademark, performed thousands of times in the hard-gigging years ahead and tacked on to a successful Elektra Records reissue of *Kill 'Em All*. On the other hand, the band's more overt attempt at radio play, "Escape," was barely ever mentioned or played again.

Riding the buzz of *Lightning*, Metallica joined friends and fellow Q Prime clients Armored Saint for a North American tour starting in late 1984. Though ostensibly a three-part package bill with W.A.S.P.—the latest and wildest band to crawl out of the Los Angeles clubs onto MTV—the days of underground bands coexisting with MTV groups

were coming to an end. Dubbed by *Kick Ass Monthly*'s Bob Muldowney the "Two Out of Three Ain't Bad" tour, the winter dates were
legendary for the harsh treatment W.A.S.P. received at the hands of
rabid Metallica fans. Due to a paperwork gaffe by his immigration
lawyer, Lars Ulrich missed the first date in Boston. When Metallica
picked up in Nova Scotia, they found that fans had already decided to
play favorites.

There was a profound difference between the music-obsessed
Metallica and the headline-grabbing W.A.S.P., who threw raw meat
into the audience and tortured a scantily clad "virgin" onstage. "I have
a lot of fond memories," insists W.A.S.P.'s Blackie Lawless. "You had
two bands that were young, enthusiastic, and had the same kind of
take-no-prisoners attitude. It was like two boxers standing in middle of
the ring staring each other down before it starts, but not only doing it
to each other but to the audience, too. I've never been in the same situation. Even when we played with Kiss in 1986—they were already past
their heyday, and as far as we were concerned, outdoing them wasn't
really a feather in our cap."

The scope of the metal showdown varied wildly, playing to 400
fans in San Diego one night and 4,400 in Hollywood the next. While
the venues were not sold out every single night, the tour successfully
pushed *Ride the Lightning*—still the property of the metal indie
Megaforce—to number one hundred on the *Billboard* album chart.
By the time they got to Phoenix, where Flotsam & Jetsam bassist Jason Newsted viewed Metallica live for the first time, the tour had become a celebration on wheels. Metallica, the champions of underground metal, were officially on the high road to national popularity.
"It was a great time," John Bush of Armored Saint says. "Metal was
raging, and all three bands were doing well." As Metallica thrashed
W.A.S.P.'s tired blood and guts on a nightly basis, its early decision to
move away from Los Angeles was vindicated. Now Metallica's allies
were everywhere traces of metal could be found.

Ride the Lightning was one example of how the do-it-yourself
approach could work for power metal in a big way. Florida's Savatage
signed to Atlantic Records after rousing headbanger approval with its
pounding 1983 independent album, *Sirens*. With the help of *Kerrang!*,
the Seattle act Queensryche sold 25,000 copies of its self-titled 1983 debut EP on 206 Records before signing to EMI Records six months later.

After rejecting Jon Zazula's offer, Metal Church sold 72,000 copies of its self-released debut album, then parlayed that success into a long-term deal with Elektra. When it came to supporting new talent, big record labels lagged far behind what fans had already discovered.

Without an established niche and a bankable fan base, however, signing to a major label could be painful. As a long line of Los Angeles locals went to major labels, the lesser-known Armored Saint signed with Chrysalis in 1984. Unfortunately, Armored Saint occupied a middle ground between Judas Priest and Metallica. It was hard enough for fans to classify them—let alone a record company looking for the next Ratt. "I think they weren't completely aware of what we were," says vocalist John Bush. "We never really fit in with the image bands in L.A. We always sounded like we were from Birmingham, England."

Armored Saint instantly regretted the label's decision to hire former Kiss producer Michael James Jackson for its debut. "*March of the Saint* was just way too polished," says John Bush. "We were this live, crazy band, and they made us sound like a refined group. That's never what we were about." Consequently the group turned its critically acclaimed 1985 follow-up, *Delirious Nomad*, into "a complete rebellion against refinement, and against Chrysalis." The record salvaged the band's credibility but left its career on the rocks. Too late the band learned that its strength was in its quirks.

Likewise, signing to Atlantic Records in 1984 brought the beginning of bad times for Raven. "We wanted to write songs with stronger hooks," says John Gallagher. "That became *Stay Hard*, which was maybe a little more commercial, but Atlantic played up our crazy image." Toning down its over-the-top music made Raven sound surprisingly conventional. With a plethora of power metal now available, metal fans deserted Raven for fresh pastures. "Back then we were kind of alienated from our fans—you only met them at the show," Gallagher says. "That could never happen now. We only heard people telling us we were great. We never heard any of the negative."

※※※※※※※※※※※※※※※※

While his former bandmates caught widespread accolades, shunned Metallica guitarist Dave Mustaine resurfaced in 1985 with his stunningly mature new band—originally named Fallen Angel in sardonic reference to his fall from grace. Dubbed Megadeth—a name that summoned images of deadly nuclear warheads instead of dark devilry—the band's early lineup featured a whirlwind of rhythm guitarists. Slayer's highly recognizable Kerry King, wearing a gauntlet of six-inch nails, made sporadic appearances in the band's inconsistent roster. "[King's tenure] was a day or two here or there randomly for a long period of time," says Mustaine. "When we first met Kerry he was very innocent. He was not a drug user or a drinker or anything like that. He was very much into black metal. I showed him my particular rhythm style, which I know he was very intrigued by. He was really fun to be around."

Megadeth was Mustaine's return in a blaze of glory. After being ousted from Metallica, he

Dave Mustaine in Megadeth
(Todd Nakamine)

had returned straight to his hometown of Los Angeles without even stopping by the El Cerrito house to retrieve his personal possessions. He became devoted to plotting his vindication. "I was still very angry about my getting asked to leave Metallica," says Mustaine, "and I wanted to outmetal them." Despite touches of high-speed jazz fusion, Megadeth was powerfully toned, with a wild edge that at its best offered greater possibility than the strict, bludgeoning fury of Metallica. The Megadeth debut, *Killing Is My Business . . . And Business Is Good*, "was a very aggressively heavy album," says Mustaine. "I wouldn't redo it now. I think that I wasted a lot of great riffs in those songs. You could probably make a dozen songs out of two or three of those songs, because each one has five or more riffs in it."

Along with bassist Dave Ellefson, *Killing Is My Business* featured drummer Gar Samuelson and lead guitarist Chris Poland, who worked repairing instruments for Slayer on the side. Mustaine and Ellefson were die-hard thrashers, but Samuelson and Poland had few preconceptions of how to play metal. They delivered something quirky, layered with unusual chord combinations, and brilliant. "Gar was very jazz-influenced, and so was Chris," says Mustaine, "and that probably had a lot to do with it." Songs were almost arbitrarily contrary, designed to defy expectation. They included the antioccult warning "Looking Down the Cross," a hectic cover of Nancy Sinatra's "These Boots Are Made for Walkin'," and "The Mechanix," the early Mustaine-penned Metallica song that appeared on *Kill 'Em All* as "The Four Horsemen"—here presented at twice the speed.

Yet even as Mustaine attempted to forcibly "outmetal" Metallica, the troubled guitarist was not alone. Kirk Hammett's former band, Exodus, relied on a heavy violence metaphor to express its claws-extended ascent. On *Bonded by Blood,* the band's much-anticipated 1985 debut, songs like "A Lesson in Violence" expressed the metal struggle as a literal street fight. "Bonded by Blood" saw the union of headbangers as a blood pact, with singer Paul Baloff shrieking, "Bang your head against the stage and metal takes its price/Bonded by blood." The gleeful thuggery of the lyrics cheered the metallic war of "Deliver Us to Evil," another charming ode to destruction. Relating the attack to world affairs, the exotic "And Then There Were None" cast Exodus as a ragged coastal tribe, ready for one push of a red button to send them into a primitive, radioactive wasteland.

The return of Dave Mustaine

Thrashers who had previewed Exodus only via Metallica's recycled "Dying by His Hand" riff rejoiced to discover more of the same. From somewhere between the chugging E-string rhythms of *Kill 'Em*

All and the more sculpted terrain of *Ride the Lightning,* Exodus unleashed a huge terrain of syncopated headbanger thrills, designed for maximum physical reaction from denim- and leather-clad bodies. As *Bonded by Blood* put a premium on its lock-step rhythmic groove, the hefty guitars of Gary Holt and Rick Hunolt were supported and embellished by the enduring voice of Baloff, who sounded like a gleeful victim of unspeakable pain. Like their comrades in the equally violent Slayer, Exodus jettisoned the intricacies of Iron Maiden and went for the jugular.

Unlike the punk rockers they admired, who were content merely to sing of anarchy and destruction, Exodus lived in a zone of complete mayhem, surrounded by broken glass. Instantly a major influence on headbangers everywhere, the band followed Metallica to the forefront of the San Francisco Bay Area thrash metal scene, which also spawned Death Angel, Legacy (later called Testament), Possessed, Forbidden Evil, Defiance, Heathen, Violence, Hexx, Mordred, and dozens more during the remainder of the decade. As perfected in the Bay Area, the entire thrash metal paradigm took the larger-than-life sound and energy of heavy metal to a new intensity, while remaining exceedingly down-to-earth in attitude.

If Metallica initially appeared underdressed for the heavy metal party, it was now joined by acres of blue-jean-clad comrades whose only nod to haberdashery was an army-surplus bullet belt around the waist. Since 1982 Armored Saint had been attired head to toe in studded leather armor—a guise that began to feel clean unwieldy formality. "We thought it was cool, but that was never the main reason for the band," says singer John Bush. "We always were way more serious about our music. It helped us

A lesson in violence: Bay Area gig flyer

look a little different than everybody else. It was funny when Metallica came along and became huge, and they were just wearing jeans and T-shirts. We thought, 'Whoa, this ain't gonna work anymore.'"

As the influence of Slayer pressured other bands to play deathly fast, *Ride the Lightning* urged confrontational subject matter that went well beyond escapism. As countless new bands formed, they no longer emulated the soaring, operatic vocal styles of Iron Maiden and Judas Priest. They stuck to a gruff, Lemmy-derived bark like James Hetfield, or a menacing, polysyllabic litany like Tom Araya—who soon excised the screams from his vocabulary. The hallmarks of power metal were revealed as merely a transitional phase between heavy metal and something entirely new: thrash metal. Thrash metal released the pounding gait of power metal into a full gallop, a hectic, breakneck, roller coaster of heavy, rapid sixteenth notes, odd timing shifts, and all-out fury. Instead of "wimping out" over time, the groups were just getting heavier.

Power metal bands like Anvil, still dressing in red leather bondage outfits and playing guitar solos with phallus-shaped vibrators, felt the chance for mass popularity slipping through their fingers. They had paid their dues and paved the way for Metallica, but were lost now in the wake of dozens of faster bands. There had been an instant years earlier when Lars Ulrich bragged that his band would someday be bigger than Anvil, and already that moment seemed laughable. "Remember Anvil?" asks Dan Lilker of Nuclear Assault. "When thrash got big and bands like Metallica and Anthrax started taking over and playing faster, those guys seemed pretty bitter about it. I remember reading an interview with Anvil, and they were saying, 'All those bands do is play fast, and there's no talent to it, there's no song structure.' It wasn't true, it was just frustration."

For one major hotbed of thrash mastery, West Germany, it took a little convincing for fans and bands to drop the dress code. Headbangers from the struggling nation were historically ravenous, known for drinking themselves into oblivion and seen diving from the tops of bus shelters before AC/DC concerts. They bore their devotion to metal openly, decking themselves to the nines in metal garb. "Their fashion I always thought was really funny, and I'm saying that in a fond way," says Dan Lilker. "They've got to have the striped pants and

THRASH METAL

By 1985 power metal was no longer fast enough to contain the tempo of the underground. A new generation of thrash metal bands seemingly overnight switched to riffing in Metallica-style triplets. While power metal was heavy metal on steroids, thrash metal's repeated fluttering notes lifted effortlessly into flight. This music was constantly in motion, an intricate flood of enormous sound. Stage costumes and other showbiz trappings went out the door as 'bangers tucked their heads down and concentrated on music and more serious lyrics. Casual observers also called this speed metal; purists would point out that thrash metal relies more on long, wrenching rhythmic breaks, while speed metal, as played by Agent Steel and Destruction, is a cleaner and more musically intricate subcategory, still loyal to the dueling melodies of classic metal.

Titans of Thrash

- ❖ Anthrax, *Spreading the Disease* (1985)
- ❖ Artillery, *Fear of Tomorrow* (1985)
- ❖ Carnivore, *Carnivore* (1985)
- ❖ Death Angel, *The Ultraviolence* (1987)
- ❖ Exodus, *Bonded by Blood* (1985)
- ❖ Holy Terror, *Terror and Submission* (1987)
- ❖ Megadeth, *Killing Is My Business . . . And Business Is Good* (1985)
- ❖ Metal Church, *Metal Church* (1984)
- ❖ Metallica, *Master of Puppets* (1986)
- ❖ Metallica, *Ride the Lightning* (1984)
- ❖ Nuclear Assault, *Game Over* (1986)
- ❖ Slayer, *Reign in Blood* (1986)
- ❖ Testament, *The New Order* (1988)
- ❖ Voivod, *Killing Technology* (1988)
- ❖ Whiplash, *Power & Pain* (1985)

the whole uniform—it's great. You've never seen so many bracelets flying around, and the bands were all great shit."

Scorpions put Germany on the hard rock map in the 1970s, but
after 1981's supercharged *Blackout*, the band expended its energy on
a series of hugely successful, ballad-laden, made-for-MTV albums like
Love at First Sting. German metal in the early 1980s was anchored by
Accept, who cracked NWOBHM codes with the finely crafted records
Breaker, Restless & Wild, and *Balls to the Wall*. By the mid-1980s a
phalanx of German troops, including Running Wild, Warlock,
Deathrow, Living Death, and Grave Digger took their marching orders
from Judas Priest and Iron Maiden's twin-guitar harmonies. Still, the
country's metal quotient undoubtedly reached full, glorious satura-
tion with speed metal and the unchained creations of Destruction,
Sodom, and Kreator.

Ascending early from Venom-influenced black metal, the Syke,
Germany, trio called Destruction debuted on the 1984 *Sentence of
Death* EP, festooned with no less an arsenal than seven and a half bullet belts, three upside-down crosses, twelve spiked wristbands, three
leather gloves, a half tube of black lipstick, and at least two studded
collars. Though their over-the-top approach raised suspicions, the
band thrashed violently and skillfully enough to disarm skeptics who
accused them of exploiting the black metal fad. With a weightless feel
and an occasional punk sneer, Destruction further proved its might
with two masterful long-players, 1985's *Infernal Overkill* and 1986's
Eternal Devastation.

As its music grew faster and more careful, Destruction had a
great hand in creating speed metal—the intricate Maiden-meets-
Metallica subset of thrash metal that emphasized rhythmic tricks
without losing the dual-guitar craft of Judas Priest. There was little in-
trinsic difference between speed metal and thrash metal. With the sudden boom of fast, raging bands, however, it sometimes helped to distinguish between the throbbing, rhythm-heavy thrash metal and something a bit cleaner and more melodic—dubbed speed metal.

Much heavier on their feet than Destruction, the bluntly named
Sodom had a rougher time climbing out of the Venom cesspool. Their
ultracrude *In the Sign of Evil* EP offered elementary tracks like
"Blasphemer," featuring a nursery-rhyme melody and nonfluent
lyrics: "I read Satanic Bible with fucking grown / masturbate to kill

myself." Sodom bettered themselves significantly with the wild, ugly garage metal of *Obsessed by Cruelty*. By *Persecution Mania* in 1987, they had evolved into a Teutonic invasion force, well suited to the saturation-strike sound systems of the rapidly growing outdoor European metal festivals. To that end, *Persecution Mania*'s "Bombenhagel" was especially noteworthy, where the band cast aside its heavily accented English in favor of guttural German—an emotional moment for many a fist-waving Rheinland metal patriot.

Sodom: Die Metallköpfe
(SPV)

The most accomplished and long-lived of the German thrash metal bands was the Essen group Kreator, who, though exceedingly young, had formed under the name Tormentor in 1982. Kreator exchanged members with Sodom frequently, as both bands struggled to tour across Europe without rest. Led by gurgling vocalist/guitarist Mille Petrozza, the band threshed melodic guitar arpeggios with a speedy undertow of syncopated riffs on *Endless Pain, Pleasure to Kill,* and the impressive *Terrible Certainty.* Coloring the speed and evil intentions of Slayer with Metallica's sense of tunefulness and social conscience, songs like "Toxic Trace" and "Storming with Menace" were a skilled and determined metallic assault on existing notions of music.

Once the province of the steel lords of England, by 1985 heavy metal had become a giant terrifying red ball, bouncing across the Atlantic and back, transplanting ideas between distant nations and leaving huge crushed craters in its wake. The thrash metal underground was literally a worldwide web, united by postal communications, international touring, and even computers—in 1986 the MetalliBashers dial-up BBS bulletin board began offering metal news, Overkill interviews, Megadeth lyrics, and chemical-weapon recipes for download, over 300-baud modems.

As Metallica's influence made itself known in Western Europe, so did the fever spread to the hallowed birthplace of heavy metal, Great Britain. Yet after giving the world so many of the original soldiers, the musicians of merry old England never really grasped the fundamental thrash ethic—that a riff could be an end unto itself. British bands were still chasing Iron Maiden and Saxon down the path of pomp and glory, while thrash metal's instinct needed be go-for-the-throat. Searching in desperation for "Britain's answer to Metallica," *Kerrang!* and *Metal Forces* offered such worn redcoat cloth as Wolfpack, Onslaught, Acid Reign, and Xentrix. All made the fatal mistake of equating thrash with playing standard metal at higher speeds, inconclusively fumbling at attempts to combine majesty with street appeal. The goofy Xentrix remake of the *Ghostbusters* theme song certainly marked the low point of a craze for thrash metal cover songs.

Anxious to prove itself a worthy successor rather than a mere band of snotty foreign upstarts, Metallica joined the Monsters of Rock festival on August 17, 1985, at Castle Donnington. Though Europe now offered countless metal events throughout the summer, England's Donnington bash remained the original. Festival organizers scheduled Metallica on the bill beneath Bon Jovi and ZZ Top but above Ratt. Metallica was far short of the glam band's platinum popularity in America, but pop metal was a lesser factor in England, where music videos were broadcast only weekly. Live onstage, Metallica certainly had the advantage, winning over English fans with typical insouciance. "If you came here to see spandex, eye makeup, and the words 'oh, baby' in every fuckin' song, this ain't the fuckin' band," James Hetfield told a crowd of 70,000.

Donnington was a prestigious annual gathering spot, even as its once-green fields were trampled to a muddy brown by the throng of drunken maniacs. Though fans persisted in pelting Metallica with

GERMAN SPEED METAL

The German bands had the true grit of thrash metal but retained a precise melodic edge that showed devotion to the unique traits of heavy metal songwriting. Add on a gonzo sense of dress and an undying pool of prometal energy, and these bands cemented the country's status as a haven for headbangers.

Kein Schlaf Bis Deutschland

- ❖ Assassin, *Interstellar Experience* (1988)
- ❖ Celtic Frost [Swiss-German], *To Mega Therion* (1986)
- ❖ Coroner [Swiss-German], *No More Color* (1989)
- ❖ Deathrow, *Raging Steel* (1987)
- ❖ Destruction, *Infernal Overkill* (1985)
- ❖ Kreator, *Terrible Certainty* (1988)
- ❖ Living Death, *Vengeance of Hell* (1984)
- ❖ Running Wild, *Gates to Purgatory* (1985)
- ❖ Sodom, *Persecution Mania* (1987)

fruit and other projectiles, by the end of their set the band understood they had passed a hazing ritual—a trial by friendly fire. Cliff Burton calmly chewed a pear thrown from the crowd that became embedded in his bass amp. "British audiences are strange," mused Lars Ulrich to *Metal Forces*. "Once you've convinced yourself that just because you're being bombarded by two-liter bottles full of piss, mud, and ham sandwiches doesn't mean that they don't like you, and you've learnt to play your instrument while ducking and running away from things, then yeah, it was great fun."

The tastemakers of England enthusiastically claimed Metallica

Snake of Voivod, live in Montreal
(Jean-François "Big" Lavallée/Metal K.O. Productions)

as rightful heirs to Iron Maiden, Judas Priest, Motörhead, and Black Sabbath. Further acknowledging the popularity of the underground, *Kerrang!* spawned *Mega Metal Kerrang!* in 1985, specifically to focus on the post-Maiden tones of Metallica, Slayer, and Kreator—bringing the full-color treatment to the thrash metal scene that most fanzines had lacked. In a country without MTV, such print media still held powerful sway, and the bands they endorsed would someday inherit the kingdom.

Thrash metal was experiencing many defining moments, developing an identity separate from heavy metal. In November 1985 nearly 7,000 raging metalheads converged on freezing Montreal, Canada, for the World War III weekend festival with Celtic Frost, Possessed, Destruction, Nasty Savage, and hometown heroes Voivod. It was a dream bill of the most intense and intriguing bands from far-flung locales like Switzerland, San Francisco, Germany, and Florida. "It was an extremely exciting time," recalls Tom Warrior of Celtic Frost. "The whole injection of fresh power into this music was really exciting. It was really a sense of a brotherhood among a lot of bands. I look back now and think everybody was really naïve. I just liked the revolutionary character of the whole thing. That a bunch of idiots went out into the world and made this a household music, and it worked."

Full Speed Ahead: Thrash Metal Attacks!

➤ **Summer 1985:** MTV institutes "Crüe Rule" to block viewer-request dominance by metal bands

➤ **March 1986:** Metallica begins tour with Ozzy Osbourne

➤ **September 27, 1986:** Metallica bassist Cliff Burton killed in bus accident in Sweden

➤ **October 1986:** Slayer releases *Reign in Blood*

➤ **November 4, 1986:** Metallica's *Master of Puppets* goes gold in the United States

---

Honed by touring and high on the *Billboard*-charting success of the Elektra Records reissue of *Ride the Lightning*, Metallica headed home on August 31, 1985, to play the Day on the Green festival in Oakland, California. They shared the stage with former Bay Area hard rock champions Y&T, the Scorpions, and two fellow alumni of the first *Metal Massacre:* Ratt and Yngwie Malmsteen's Rising Force. Even as Metallica tackled the world, it was exhilarating to face a sold-out hometown crowd of 60,000. While the groups played their usual set of raging songs, not just friends and family but an entire stadium of newcomers applauded the heavy metal band that still shunned radio ballads and MTV videos.

In a city famous for its unconventional folk heroes, the story of Metallica was hot news. On New Year's Eve 1985 they headlined a thrash metal marathon at the San Francisco Civic Center with Exodus, Metal Church, Megadeth, and several thousand thrashers in attendance. Arms and limbs flailing, acting out their every curious, destructive impulse, the thrashers were more like punk rockers than leather-clad heavy metal clubgoers. Their venue-crushing antics and the backstage mayhem of Metallica themselves were actually a constant source of distress to legendary Bay Area concert promoter Bill Graham. The rock-era hippie icon resented playing the role of disciplinarian every time the giddy Metallica felt like destroying a dressing room or breaking a few mirrors.

New Year's thrash summit, 1985 flyer

Metallica finally released its first new record for Elektra, *Master of Puppets*, on February 21, 1986. As Appalachian fiddle songs emulated crying birds, the Delta blues adopted locomotive rhythms, and Judas Priest captured the scream of Concorde jets, Metallica's motions in 1986 represented the sound of collapsing buildings, volcanoes erupting, and huge ships run aground without stopping. It was a highly finessed maelstrom. Expanding the grand plans of Black Sabbath with blinding flashes of lightning and subaquatic detonations, Metallica was so fast it seemed to be happening in several places at once. They had atom-splitting power—fitting for a band preoccupied with nuclear war.

The first Metallica album to feature no songwriting by Dave Mustaine, *Master of Puppets* concentrated on improving rather than relentlessly reinventing the band's sound. The product of five months back in Denmark with Flemming Rasmussen, the songs mimicked the dynamics of *Ride the Lightning* almost exactly, but in richer, more impressive form. Both albums opened with furious bashers—"Fight Fire" and "Battery"—then segued into the moody, anthemic title tracks, followed with powerful, slow ballads—"Fade to Black" and "Welcome Home (Sanitarium)." Even as *Ride the Lightning*

Danish thrashers Artillery with
Metallica producer Flemming Rasmussen
(Roadrunner Records)

closed with the extended instrumental "The Call of Ktulu," *Master of Puppets* placed the epic bass suite "Orion" one step from the end.

The horror stories of writer H. P. Lovecraft, first explored by Metallica in "The Call of Ktulu," were revisited in "The Thing That Should Not Be," an ultraheavy, lurching number that rumbled like a colossal mountain on wheels. "It's about huge things marching around!" Cliff Burton exclaimed to *Metal Mania*. "Huge fuckers so big they compete with buildings in size!" Addressing the hypocrisy on both sides of the PMRC's metal-morality debates, James Hetfield hissed in "Leper Messiah": "Circus comes to town / you play the lead clown" and "Send me money, send me green / heaven you will meet / make a contribution and you'll get the better seat."

Capping the momentum of *Lightning*, major-label Metallica was still brasher than all rivals—yet refined enough to challenge the heavyweights of heavy metal. Regardless of the album's stunning and studied breakthroughs, the nonmetal press remained incapable of understanding *Master of Puppets*. Scribbled one mercifully unnamed *Billboard* reviewer, "Danish hard rock quartet again impresses with well-crafted arrangements and solid technique; material is usual run-of-the-mill metal, with hyper-speed guitars in the fore." On the verge of becoming a household name, Metallica still did not merit a fact-check.

By 1986, America was in the full throes of an amazing rage to thrash, and the music business inevitably responded. Slayer was wooed from Metal Blade by rap impresario Rick Rubin for his label Def Jam, also home to LL Cool J and Run-DMC. This created a stir among music cognoscenti, who wondered not only how the most evil band on the planet would fare on a major label but also how they could mesh with their rap music labelmates. Soon Exodus and Megadeth both left the indie Combat for Capitol Records. Even the half-rotten deviled eggs in Venom joined the parade, inking the first direct artist contract with mail-order music consolidator K-Tel, of late-night television renown.

Together Metallica, Slayer, Megadeth, and Anthrax comprised the "Big Four" of thrash metal. Anthrax had already jumped into the big time, releasing *Spreading the Disease* on Island Records in 1985. Compared with the ferocity of its peers, the attitude of Anthrax was downright festive. After cutting its teeth on Megaforce and touring with Raven, the good-natured Anthrax continually sought ways to differentiate itself from its old friends in Metallica. The group crafted a commercial formula that combined crunching speed guitars with the smooth, soaring voice of Joey Belladonna, whom guitarist Dan Spitz compared to Journey singer Steve Perry. Avoiding heavy metal clichés and downplaying rock-star behavior, *Spreading the Disease* invited friendly thrashers, traditional heavy metallers, and hardcore punk fans alike to join its high-energy party.

Yet even as the Big Four signed to major labels and cultivated an audience of hundreds of thousands with mass distribution, advertising, and marketing, they took pains to keep core fans involved in their careers. Fully aware of their tape-trading roots, these bands were careful not to alienate their constituent base, and so they maintained contact with the fanzines

Dave Mustaine reaches out

and specialty radio stations that had supported them from the start. To promote Megadeth's first major-label outing, *Peace Sells But Who's Buying?*, Dave Mustaine wrote letters to radio hosts and fanzine editors listed in the back of *Kick Ass Monthly* and *Metal Forces*.

As they were tapped in to the stars of tomorrow, networks of tape traders became viable business alliances, offering young thrashers a third path to prosperity besides MTV and touring. Dutch label Road-runner opened its American office in November 1986 with two employees. Finding talent was simple—all the company had to do was open up a copy of *Metal Forces* and read the demo reviews. Along with former Mercyful Fate front man King Diamond, Roadrunner signed contracts with two bands well known to tape traders: New York's Carnivore and New Jersey's Whiplash. "All the cool bands were coming out of the U.S.," says Roadrunner's A&R director Monte Conner. "That's where all the happening signings were."

Once *Master of Puppets* hit the Kmarts, a little piece of underground metal jumped into the carts of every family shopping for a jumbo carton of laundry detergent. As the band hoped, Metallica's album sales began closing the gap between true heaviness and the MTV video metal scene. "We started covering Metallica around the end of *Ride the Lightning*," says Ben Liemer, editor of *Circus*, a fan magazine that claimed a circulation of 480,000 in the late 1980s. "During *Master of Puppets* it must have been twenty-eight straight months we had a Metallica story. I'm not kidding. That's what the kids wanted."

Continuing the time-tested touring gambit, Metallica secured the coveted opening slot on Ozzy Osbourne's *Ultimate Sin* tour, beginning in March 1986 and continuing across the entirety of America during the sweltering summer months. Metallica clearly hoped to follow Mötley Crüe, whose *Shout at the Devil* broke nationally during a 1984 touring stint with the madman of rock. Everyone respected Ozzy. The Americanized former Black Sabbath singer had a reputation for recruiting the next big thing as an opening act, as much as he did for scooping up hotshot young guitarists—Randy Rhoads from Quiet Riot, Brad Gillis from Night Ranger, and Jake E. Lee from Ratt.

Like most of his heavy metal contemporaries, Ozzy delivered on a promise to bring ever bigger and more grandiose stages to his audience. *The Ultimate Sin* tour had the singer descending from the rafters while nestled in the lap of an enormous golden Buddha. Yet alone among his peers Ozzy clung to the viewpoint that the concert experience should be a mind-altering communal event with the vaguest threat of becoming a riot. To that end Metallica was a perfect match for Ozzy, and audiences agreed. Hovering in the *Billboard* Top 30 since its release, during the Ozzy tour *Master of Puppets* became Metallica's first gold record, with sales of more than half a million copies and counting.

With image-oriented metal in regular rotation, MTV still mistakenly retained a wait-and-see approach to Metallica and the other Big Four bands. In contrast, Mötley Crüe spent the summer of 1985 cresting on the success of its "Home Sweet Home" video, a weepy lament about life on the road. Voted number one for weeks on end by callers, the video's success eventually led MTV to institute a "Crüe Rule," which stated that no video could be the viewer favorite for longer than three months.

As the network was reticent to add more metal, there was pressure on the existing roster of hot rocking video stars to airbrush away any outrageous hues. As Mötley Crüe covered moldy teen standard "Smokin' in the Boys Room" and Twisted Sister covered "Leader of the Pack," the video medium was systematically processing metal's scary stalwarts into a repulsive form of rock nostalgia. Instead of fighting parents and the PMRC, video metal bands were entertaining them. The rewards of the mass audience were just too seductive. Even Judas Priest appeared uncharacteristically neutered in 1986 on its synthesizer-heavy *Turbo*, accompanied by a small fleet of stylized videos that depict the band's adventures in a motorcyle-laden future world.

Worries of overexposure led MTV to consider cutting back on heavy metal in 1985. Instead Dee Snider helped initiate the *Heavy Metal Mania* specialty show. "I had the idea that they should at least give the viewers a metal show that they could focus the audience with," he says, "because they'll always tune in. I was trying to get some bands in there who had no videos, like Metallica. I would show little clips of them and try to get away from the mainstream. I re-member Motörhead gave me an *Ace of Spades* jacket to wear. The only other way I could get them on was to use their music in the credit roll, because [Motörhead's] 'Killed by Death' didn't pass MTV's muster."

Metallica certainly had the budget to produce a video for *Master of Puppets*, but their managers advised against it. The band's com-mercial aspirations and integrity were now balanced by the voices of experience. "Cliff Burnstein thinks that Metallica is gonna be big, but doing it in our own way," Lars Ulrich explained to *Kick Ass Monthly*. "The way we're gonna be big, hopefully in four or five years, is gonna be quite a different way than any other band has done it, except maybe Iron Maiden. It's gonna be a sort of thing where you don't have to follow any trends or get airplay, you don't need to make videos, you just sort of do it through a really good street buzz. Keeping a down-to-earth thing going with kids, doing what you wanna do."

After five years with Metallica, Ulrich had experi-enced enough steady growth in his band to develop a bold and almost prophetic vision of success. "With the new man-agement behind us, what we're doing could be the next big thing," he told *Kick Ass*. "Most of the bands coming today are trendy. What Metal-lica is doing is timeless. The public will change for us in a few years, instead of us chang-ing for them." Or, as James Hetfield summarized his

Kerry King of Slayer
(Jonathan Munro)

blunt approach to breaking Metallica into the mainstream, "If it don't fit, force it. If it breaks, it was defective and needed to be replaced anyway."

Metallica's rise was watched closely by old rivals who kept the competition lively. A year into the ringing success of *Master of Puppets*, Slayer struck back loudly with *Reign in Blood*, the album that would define its career. Still unrepentantly and mercilessly demonic, Slayer humbled its many black metal imitators while appealing to an extreme segment of society far beyond metal tape traders. Appearing on a record label known mainly for rap music, freakishly fast songs like "Criminally Insane" and "Angel of Death" attracted many fans who had previously shunned pentagram metal like the plague.

With new label chief and producer Rick Rubin, the band fused the dynamic peaks and lulls of *Hell Awaits* into a constant panicked frenzy of violent metal. Shepherded by the Nazis and Satans of Tom Araya's frantically fast storytelling, *Reign in Blood* was a permanently metabolism-altering experience. It was the first time that Slayer's sharp speed—increasingly influenced by hardcore punk—was not dampened by muffled, dime-store production values. When fans and critics complained that the LP clocked in at a scarce thirty minutes, guitarist Jeff Hanneman retorted that the ten songs featured just as many verses, choruses, and solos as on any Judas Priest record—metal was just faster now.

When James Hetfield cracked his arm skateboarding in Indiana during the summer 1986 tour with Ozzy, the remedy was simple—the band called on guitar technician John Marshall to handle rhythm guitar, and a new touring contract stipulated that Hetfield would stay away from skate ramps in the future. While the band was playing the best music of its career to a steadily expanding roar of approval, a few broken bones were just a chuckle to the Metallica juggernaut.

The next collision, however, was devastating. On a frozen stretch of Swedish highway the night of September 27, 1986, the Metallica tour bus flipped after sliding over a long patch of hidden ice. Cliff Burton was killed. "He just got thrown out the window, and boom, the bus landed on him," Lars Ulrich told VH1. "By all accounts, he never woke up." Furious and distraught, James Hetfield tracked backward along the highway in pajamas, looking for the treacherous ice, for somewhere to place wrathful blame. As the obscure NWOBHM band

Aragorn had weirdly prophesied five years earlier on a Neat Records seven-inch: "Black ice / It's a killer."

Cliff was a wild twenty-four-year-old lamb, seemingly anointed against calamity. Dying young was something that happened to 1960s-era rock stars, obsolete figures of careless excess. Even with his bell-bottoms, Cliff was not that kind of a throwback. He was vibrant and vociferous, a crucial ally in chaotic situations. His loss was the sacrifice of an innocent, a nightmarish fairy-tale scene complete with Cliff's legs sticking out from beneath the tour bus like the Wicked Witch of the West's. As Ozzy Osbourne had lost guitarist Randy Rhoads in a plane accident and AC/DC its singer Bon Scott to drinking, Metallica now had its own metallic martyr.

The entire heavy metal scene was collectively thrown into disbelieving grief. Testament singer Chuck Billy described to *Sounds of Death* how the bassist's demise put the cash register success of thrash metal in perspective. "The representatives from Megaforce flew out to come see us play, and when they got to our rehearsal studio they were all bummed out. They told us they had been up all night long because they had just gotten word at two in the morning that Cliff Burton had died. We didn't even feel like playing but we went ahead anyway and did a few songs without much emotion. When we were done, they said, 'Okay, you've got a deal,' but it was a really weird vibe."

Jason Newsted of Flotsam & Jetsam recalls weeping at home in Arizona, his tears wetting the open newspaper. "I think Cliff was the real key guy to Metallica for a long time," says John Bush of Armored Saint. "He kept it real. Not that the other guys didn't, but he kept it extremely real. Just his look and his attitude. His whole persona was cool. It was pretty devastating when he passed away." To commemorate the comrade they had once fed and housed at the Queens Music Building, Anthrax bought a page in *Kerrang!* reading, BELL-BOTTOMS RULE!! LAUGH IT UP, WE MISS YOU.

Burton was cremated, and his ashes were spread throughout favorite spots in the wilds of Northern California. At his memorial service on October 7, 1986, "Orion," Burton's lengthy instrumental composition from *Master of Puppets*, was played at the site of a simple stone marker. THANK YOU FOR YOUR BEAUTIFUL MUSIC, read the epitaph.

Where the departure of previous members had always brought a new beginning for Metallica, the death of Cliff Burton was the tragic end of the ambitious young era of the group. "I just recall our tour manager saying, 'Okay, let's get the band together and take them back to the hotel,'" James Hetfield told writer K. J. Doughton. "The only thing I could think was, 'The band? No way! There ain't no band. The band is not "the band" right now. It's just three guys.'"

The Hollywood Glambangers

- **1983:** David Lee Roth of Van Halen announces $1 million paternity insurance policy
- **December 1984:** Hanoi Rocks drummer Nicholas "Razzle" Dingley killed riding in car with Mötley Crüe's Vince Neil
- **1987:** MTV launches weekly *Headbangers Ball* specialty show
- **1987:** *The Decline of Western Civilization, Part II: The Metal Years* premieres
- **August 1987:** Guns N' Roses releases *Appetite for Destruction*
- **January 14, 1988:** Fourth consecutive Dokken album certified platinum

Back in hazy Los Angeles, hair had grown dangerously high. The Hollywood clubs bounced new wave bands out on their skinny ties after Quiet Riot sold 4 million albums in 1984. Soon after, Mötley Crüe and Ratt each quickly sold their first 2 million each. In the wake of MTV's timely discovery of heavy metal, the City of Angels sent out a national casting call for multiplatinum blonds and abusers of hair products of all kinds. By the time David Lee Roth left Van Halen for Las Vegas in 1985, the original hard rock hedonist of L.A. was barely missed— there was a surplus of contenders to take his place at the orgy.

A fabled rock and roll wonderland of triumphs and terrors, the stretch of West Hollywood known as the Sunset Strip hosted the most infamous heavy metal hangouts: in 1987 the Roxy, the Troubadour, Whisky-A-Go-Go, and the Rainbow Bar & Grill. In the mid-1960s and 1970s these clubs were spawning ground for the legendary likes of Love, the Doors, and the Runaways—all star-crossed bands whose stories ended in the gritty glory of jail, death, or rehab. In the metal era the Strip—the Great White Way of L.A.—was carpeted wall to wall with shaggy manes, its corners pasted thick with hand-printed posters advertising the misspelled names of a new generation.

To anyone with rock-star dreams, the smog of secondhand cigarette smoke and hair spray was an enchanting mist. "It was like arriving in an oasis in the desert," says Dee Snider, who took his first trip with Twisted Sister to Los Angeles in 1983. "We'd been fighting this battle since I joined in 1976, and we pull into town at ten o'clock in the morning and Iron Maiden is playing on the radio. We heard our songs, and everywhere you looked, it was just heavy metal heaven."

Smack in the middle of the revelry was Mötley Crüe, who claimed a centrally located party house above the Strip. Heavy metal poster kids in America since their 1984 tour with Ozzy Osbourne, the decadent Crüe brought shades of symbolic satanic rebellion into the living room. As Armored Saint singer John Bush says of *Shout at the Devil*, "It's probably not one of my favorite records, but it had a huge impact on the scene. It had an image thing that you couldn't deny. Just the impact of opening up the cover [to see Mötley Crüe in doomsday drag, surrounded by flames]—the flamboyance of that was something you had to acknowledge, because it was that powerful."

Several platinum albums later, the Crüe's gaudy makeup had smeared across the city in a Max Factor nightmare of rouge, lipstick, and false beauty marks. One-upping the competition was sometimes a matter of practicing to the point of perfect musical chops—as was the case with Dokken, whose unusual guitar chords showed uncommon melodic force. More often young lookers in the crowd won attention by increasing the limits of the glamour and adding another swatch of leopard-print spandex to the singer's microphone stand. Dirtbag rockers dyed, bleached, and teased their hair into synthetic floral displays, then spent their last pennies on platform boots, vinyl pants, ripped T-shirts, and extra-strength mascara.

One after another, bands from the Los Angeles clubs took heavy metal riffs and imagery to the MTV bank. Quiet Riot's *Metal Health* sold 4 million, and its follow-up, *Condition Critical*, sold another million. Ratt's first two albums, *Out of the Cellar* and *Invasion of Your Privacy*, each sold 2 million copies, and its third sold 1 million. Great White sold 1 million copies of its debut album, *Once Bitten*, and 2 million of the next, *Twice Shy*. The hook-savvy Dokken had a total of four million-selling platinum releases. As of 1987, Mötley Crüe's *Shout at the Devil*, *Theatre of Pain*, and *Girls, Girls, Girls* had all sold more than 2 million copies each, with no sign of relenting.

Under their androgynous exteriors Ratt and Dokken were cold and calculating songwriters, crooning sweet nothings from anesthetized hearts—jaded seducers whose lyrics openly admitted they were in it for the money. As a consequence there was ruthlessness to the glam metal bands that sounded shocking as they took over the Top 40 singles chart. Where British heavy metal dealt mostly with tragic romance when it talked about love at all, sex was a major theme of glam metal. Frosty-haired male pinups played into little girls' bedroom fantasies, then treated the young maidens like dirt. Winger's cradle-robber hit "Seventeen" gladly boasted, "Daddy says she's too young / but she's old enough for me." Though the music was bright and soft, the effect was icy, a product of pop in the 1980s.

If image was a crucial selling point, the ultimate sellout was the power ballad—usually a maudlin, pseudo-acoustic love song complete with weepy guitar solo and lovelorn sing-along chorus. After the phenomenal popularity of Mötley Crüe's "Home Sweet Home" doubled the band's audience size, power ballads warped Hollywood metal in a major way. Newer bands like Poison and Danger Danger skipped the hip-grinding, knife-flashing threat of early Mötley Crüe entirely and headed straight for the guaranteed gold of good-time radio fodder. "Those bands, in their style and approach, that's what I call tits-and-ass metal," comments Rob Halford of Judas Priest. "Nothing wrong with that—I wouldn't expect anything else to come out of Hollywood."

Back on the Strip the local culture turned rock-video values into reality, as young women worked as go-go dancers to buy groceries for their boyfriends—many of them future rock stars who dressed like strippers themselves. These hair rockers clung to traditional male sexual roles while shunning the responsibilities. "That's how a lot of bands made it in the early days, at least in L.A.," says Ben Liemer, editor of *Circus*, a primary source of glam metal pinups. "There were enough women that wanted to hang out with rock stars, knowing that they could be the next big thing. The bands were more accessible at the clubs, and it was easier to get into the dressing room there. You can't believe it—those guys just got over. Women would buy them clothes, take them out to dinner, and buy them drinks and drugs."

In odd but obvious ways, glam metal in the 1980s was a testing ground for changing gender roles—often cultivating the seed of the 1960s sexual revolution through the strange television landscape of the 1970s. While fertilizing metal's choke hold on pop culture, MTV consolidated the signals into something that would sell soft drinks. In the surreal metal music videos stereotypical sitcom plots were winning out over challenging content. The narratives of concept videos by Poison and Warrant showed insecure young males gaining supernatural power over women and portrayed conflict between teens and the older generation like a 1980s version of *Happy Days*.

In contrast, even while playing to the generation gap, L.A. thrashers Megadeth came to MTV with "Peace Sells . . . But Who's Buying?"—a snide indictment of military-industrial doublespeak such as "peacekeeping missiles." In that video a disapproving father enters the TV room and barks to his metalhead son, "Turn this off, I want to watch the news!" The longhaired resister quickly flips the channel back to Megadeth's vision of tanks rolling across the sand. "This *is* the news," he asserts in defiance.

Both were breeds of heavy metal, but their intentions were intensely different. "You had the bands like Metallica that just would go out in a T-shirt and jeans and play loud, heavy, tight, tight, hard rock," says Michael Sweet of Stryper about the local scene. "And then you had the glam thing going that started to take off, with the big hair and the makeup and the shiny clothes. Not to be mean, but those guys weren't masters at their instruments. It was more of a show."

The flecks of true grit in the glam metal reality fell from the ratty hair of Hanoi Rocks. A *Kerrang!* favorite that was also universally admired by Hollywood bands, Hanoi was an extremely passionate and supremely image-conscious Finnish act that released five diverse albums in its five years. While saxophone-wielding singer Matti Fagerholm, aka Michael Monroe, pushed an ultrafeminine urchin image, the band seared with a ragtag pastiche of high-energy moves nabbed from the Ramones, the Clash, Sweet, David Bowie, and Iggy Pop. As the hungry band became more confident between 1981's poppy *Hanoi Rocks, Bangkok Shocks, Saigon Shakes* and 1984's rugged *Two Steps from the Move,* the eclectic sound flirted with heavy metal.

Mike Monroe of Hanoi Rocks, Virrat, Finland, January 1982 *(Raimo Autio)*

Hanoi Rocks was a group of strange pioneers, overcoming secondhand style with genuine passion for wild music and the rock way of life. Monroe pushed the limits of androgyny to extremes at a time before it was safe. "We went to do press at our label," he told journalist Martin Popoff, "and when I went to the men's room, all the men had to leave because they were too intimidated [by my jewelry and makeup]. That was weird. I was going, 'What the hell is this?' So the label was not even prepared to deal with a band like that. We were way ahead of our time in that sense, and years later all these bands have copied us. Poison, for example. They were not a good rock band at all but they got huge, and after that, CBS was again looking for bands like Hanoi."

Tragically, Hanoi Rocks was destroyed in 1984 during its first trip to L.A. While partying with Mötley Crüe, drummer Nicholas Dingley, aka Razzle, was killed in a car accident during a run to the liquor store with Mötley Crüe singer Vincent Neil Wharton, aka Vince Neil. Occurring in mid-December, Razzle's passing spooked fans of Hanoi's prophetic anthem "Dead by Christmas." For driving the car, which also maimed two passengers in an oncoming vehicle, Neil was ordered by the court to pay a $2.6 million fine, serve thirty days in jail, and perform two hundred hours of community service. "I deserved to be punished more than that," he later told VH1. Hanoi officially disbanded in May 1985, while the Crüe adopted Hanoi Rocks' gypsy image on the 1985 album *Theatre of Pain.*

With simple needs and money rolling in, the party continued unabated. Dressed in fishnet gloves and wielding neon guitars, a third and fourth generation of Hollywood metallers appeared on the scene. Many were sleazy bar bands that lacked the heart of British metal or even the originality of Ratt. "Mötley Crüe definitely spawned it," says Los Angeles native Katon DePena. "We knew they were Hollywood guys, so it made sense that they dressed in [drag] costume. It was just funny. After Poison came, that's when everything started flooding. You saw so many pretty bands coming down."

Strained of all dangerous details, the feminine-looking Poison sold 7 million records in America during the 1980s, totaling more than 11 million by 1991. These refugees from Mechanicsburg, Pennsylvania, were third-generation heirs to Van Halen's legacy of outrageousness with one-tenth the musical muscle. "Poison was just about having a good time," says *Circus* editor Ben Liemer. "There wasn't a reflective bone in their body. 'Every Rose Has Its Thorn' was about as reflective and as contemplative and as soulful as they could manage. Priest and Maiden were very proud of the fact that they were good. I don't think Poison or Mötley Crüe worried about that too much, at least until later."

From the Sunset Strip it was a quick cruise to the Hollywood film studios, so along with a slew of monster and horror movies marketed to heavy metal teens came a number of films that used heavy metal as source material. Of particular local interest, *The Decline of Western Civilization, Part II: The Metal Years*, the sequel to a punk documentary shot in 1979, examined the gilded age of glam metal in Los Angeles. Unable to contact luminaries like Ronnie James Dio, whom director Penelope Spheeris called the "godfather of it all," the film worked within its environment, revealing the specific hopes and heartbreaks of struggling rock stars on Sunset Boulevard.

Glamorous staged interviews with superstars Kiss, Aerosmith, and Ozzy Osbourne offset a harrowing segment starring W.A.S.P. guitarist Chris Holmes, floating in a backyard swimming pool littered with empty vodka bottles while his mother watched with grief. In contrast, giggly glam supergroup Poison looked and acted like grateful lottery winners. Playing the role of naysayer, only Dave Mustaine of Megadeth punctured the mystique of the star machine, telling would-be MTV idols not to quit their day jobs. The Megadeth performance closing the movie raged in comparison to live performances by hair-

GLAM METAL

Sprouting from a crack in the sidewalk of Hollywood, California, glam metal was the product of heavy metal energy, MTV glitz, and a remnant of hard rock leer. Though Guns N' Roses, Poison, and even David Lee Roth came from the Midwest, somehow every cross-dressing lite metal act with a pink guitar seemed to land in Los Angeles during the late 1980s, where they found girlfriends to support them until they were blessed by the inevitable light of stardom. Unfortunately for the Finnish band Hanoi Rocks—the spiritual forerunners of Poison, Guns N' Roses, and later Mötley Crüe—its date with Hollywood turned to tragedy when drummer Razzle was killed in a drunk driving incident. Undeterred, the glam machine purred decadently onward until the end of the decade, when poser dreams were squashed between grunge and the unstoppable assault of Metallica. For better or worse, the mile-high hair, women's lingerie, and thick rouge defined heavy metal attire in the popular memory.

Guilty Pleasures

- ❖ Cinderella, *Night Songs* (1986)
- ❖ Dokken, *Tooth and Nail* (1987)
- ❖ Faster Pussycat, *Faster Pussycat* (1987)
- ❖ Guns N' Roses, *Appetite for Destruction* (1987)
- ❖ Hanoi Rocks, *Back to Mystery City* (1984)
- ❖ Mötley Crüe, *Girls, Girls, Girls* (1987)
- ❖ Nitro, *O.F.R.* (1989)
- ❖ Ozzy Osbourne, *The Ultimate Sin* (1986)
- ❖ Poison, *Look What the Cat Dragged In* (1987)
- ❖ Ratt, *Dancing Undercover* (1986)
- ❖ Stryper, *To Hell with the Devil* (1986)
- ❖ Warrant, *Cherry Pie* (1990)
- ❖ W.A.S.P., *W.A.S.P.* (1984)

spray hazards Faster Pussycat, Lizzy Borden, Seduce, London, and Odin. Not surprisingly, Megadeth's career was one of the few that lasted longer than a can of Aqua Net.

As a portrait of heavy metal in 1988, the picture might have been incomplete. "I don't doubt that it's a good movie, but they should have picked underground bands instead of a bunch of glam bands," grumbles Blaine Cook of the Accüsed. Yet the night the film premiered, a crowd of ticket holders and empty-handed loiterers grew large enough to shut down Hollywood Boulevard, drawing a small army of motorcycle cops to barricade the theater. A giant lens peering into the strange local metal phenomenon, the movie was a sensation. "As far as limiting it to what was going on in Hollywood at the time," says Blackie Lawless of W.A.S.P., "the movie was probably pretty accurate."

Glancing at glam metal's dominance of the *Billboard* charts in the late 1980s, it seemed any band with a blond singer, a hotshot guitarist, a power ballad, and a wardrobe case could score—if its video was played on MTV. The metal rush incited countless runaway teenagers to flee their Nebraska farms and seek fame and fortune in California. Luckless rockers slugging it out in bars from Queens to Miami migrated west and placed "Bassist Seeks Band" advertisements in the local music papers. Merciless club promoters charged this endless supply of would-be stars up to five hundred dollars a night to perform under infamous "pay-to-play" arrangements—and there was never a shortage of emerging talent to take the bait.

As the hair teased higher and out of control, the Hollywood dream machines created their own clueless rendition of heavy metal. Easy as it was for music studios to manufacture the Monkees or create a punk band with a package of safety pins, the culture industry applied Max Factor to white-bread-and-water rock pretenders like Winger, Vain, and Bullet Boys, then waited to see if heads would bang. Bang they did, however lightly. After Vixen was discovered performing in a garage in the low-budget beach comedy *Hardbodies*, EMI Records gave the all-female band of midwestern transplants a glam makeover (ironically, to look more "girlish"), sent them on tour with Scorpions, and promptly scored a gold album for the self-titled *Vixen*.

Glam metal was so entrenched in Hollywood that it spawned its own headbanger trade school, Musicians Institute, encompassing the

Guitar Institute of Technology (GIT), and its offshoots the Bass Institute of Technology (BIT), Percussion Institute of Technology (PIT), and Vocal Institute of Technology (VIT). Instead of slaving away in solitude like Eddie Van Halen or Randy Rhoads, young hotshots copied licks from a chalkboard, studied flashy stage tricks, and for final exams played showcase gigs to label scouts in the GIT auditorium. The small campus became a magnet for fledgling players, a frizzed-out networking center for up-and-coming lords of the whammy bar.

If the problem in Los Angeles in 1981 was lack of metal, the drawback to the city's music scene in 1987 was the overwhelming success of heavy metal of the most disposable type. Established bands like Kiss and Whitesnake permed their hair, opened powder compacts, and played power ballads to feed the diet metal market. At least Ozzy Osbourne's frosted hair spray could be attributed to not-quite-temporary insanity—longtime fans took to calling him the "Mad Housewife," with all due respect. Y&T had been Northern California's hard rock hope in the late 1970s, but by 1986 they were just another group of hair salesmen. "They were a good, tight band," says *Metal Mania* publisher Ron Quintana, "until MTV came along and they went glam like a lot of bands."

Even God got into the act. Labelmates of Slayer and Poison on the indie Enigma, the Orange County "white metal" staples Stryper drew platinum sales from power ballads with ambiguous Christian content. Stryper shrewdly appealed to skeptical parents by preaching a pro-God message but did not sacrifice metal flair. Throwing free Bibles adorned with Stryper stickers into concert audiences, they claimed that their gaudy black-and-yellow jumpsuits referred to "stripes" left on the hide of Jesus by the whip of Pontius Pilate. "I

"Mad Housewife"–era Ozzy Osbourne
(Deborah Laws/Metalflakes.com)

think in the very beginning it was mainly Christians that were buying Stryper records and going to Stryper shows," says singer Michael Sweet. "But when we broke in *Soldiers Under Command* and especially *To Hell with the Devil,* when you walked into a Stryper show, you felt like you were at a typical rock and roll show. People were drunk, you could smell pot in the air—all that stuff was going on. I think after a while it would set in, what we were talking about. There'd

Jon Bon Jovi
(Deborah Lynn Laws)

be a shocked look on certain faces, in a good way: 'Aw, man, these guys are Christians!'"

A notable exception to the Hollywood rule, New Jersey singer John Bongiovi, aka Jon Bon Jovi, spoke of good times without decadence and disorder. The frosted-hair prince of power ballads banked four platinum albums in the 1980s via hits like "Bad Medicine," "You Give Love a Bad Name," and the road-weary "Wanted Dead or Alive." Raised in the music business, Bon Jovi also discovered the Philadelphia bar band Cinderella, a heavily AC/DC–influenced act whose *Night Songs* and *Long Cold Winter* each sold 2 million copies. Bon Jovi later played wily mentor to another Garden State metal act, Skid Row, in exchange for a publishing interest in power anthems like "Youth Gone Wild"—a financial arrangement that burst into a public feud between the two groups.

Back at ground zero, in every way except megastardom the Hollywood glam craze reached its unreal summit with Nitro. Nitro was a pickup group formed by vocalist Jim Gillette—whose stage gimmick was shattering a crystal glass with his voice—and Michael Angelo—who upped the gonzo factor by playing an X-shaped guitar with four functional necks. Gillette and Angelo also peddled metal-technique instruction tapes in the back pages of *Hit Parader,* and the pair's songwriting sounded like a juiced-up draftsman's jumble of Ratt, Accept, and Mötley Crüe riffs, overloaded with guitar solos and drum fills.

If Mötley Crüe was the pinnacle of quick-fix rock and roll, Nitro became the further distilled epitome, an abstraction on top of a derivation, firing delusion up oversize nostrils with silver pistols. Nitro's load-blowing *O.F.R.* ("Out-Fucking-Rageous") was incredibly bugged-out treble noise from a bunch of prodigies with skyscraper hair and a knack for electronic wizardry. Their half-minute falsetto wails and tightly strung guitar squiggles respected hit formulas, yet the kamikaze results were too octane-laden for mainstream use. Their music did feature prominently in *Suburban Commando*, a comedy starring the wrestler Hulk Hogan—a match that could only have happened in the late 1980s cultural climate that spawned *Max Headroom* and *Alf,* extreme in its plastic pathology.

Nitro, the highest and the fastest
(Rampage Records)

As MTV bands partied on in crash pads cluttered with royalty statements, others paused to reflect on the meaning of their accomplishments. "I really wanted to make metal mainstream, and for all the right reasons," wrote Dee Snider. "I loved this underdog so much that I felt that we deserved to be in the fucking elevators. We deserved to be on in the restaurants, and at halftime in football games.

What I didn't realize is that if I had succeeded—which some bands did later on, Bon Jovi, Warrant, and Winger—once it got into the mainstream, it was over. It was always the underdog image that kept it alive."

Even as the heavy metal bandwagon primped to the point of implosion, a surly new savior grabbed the reins. Ultimately the most successful band to come from Hollywood during the teased-hair era, Guns N' Roses were semihomeless scavengers at the time of their breakthrough, *Appetite for Destruction*. They tried every trick in the metal book. Appealing to the underground, their self-released 1985 *Live?!*@ Like a Suicide* EP, which had already sold 10,000 copies, was quietly re-pressed by Geffen Records in early 1987 to cultivate credible support for the band's official debut. Meanwhile, the members were fine actors who played MTV like virtuosos. *Appetite*'s first video, "Welcome to the Jungle," portrayed singer William Bailey, aka Axl Rose, as a greenhorn stepping off a Greyhound bus from Nowheresville, immediately confronting a TV image of himself as rock and roll predator.

Breathing a second wind into glam metal, *Appetite* allied the desperation of Sunset Strip with the riffs of AC/DC and the aloof punk anger of the Sex Pistols, while interpreting thrash metal energy for conventional rock audiences. While marketers formulated metal into tidy boxes, the runaway success of Guns N' Roses proved that kids listened to a much wider range of styles than record-store categories would suggest. The reborn street preachers of eclectic sleaze, they added a tinge of Megadeth's knowing nastiness to the gypsy promises of Hanoi Rocks—the forerunning Finnish urchins whose entire back catalog Axl Rose himself rereleased in 1991.

Unlike the party rock of Poison, Guns N' Roses spat out scathing social commentary from the perspective of Rose, a self-obsessed narcissist and top-notch rock star. As their real-life drugs, sex, and violence made *National Enquirer* headlines, the band wove its exploits into the self-referential story lines of a stream of MTV videos. At the same time, the band toured with Iron Maiden and proved a vehement force onstage, where previous graduates of the L.A. clubs had disappointed. A scheme was hatched in 1988 that Aerosmith, the godfathers of rock for gravel road grope sessions, would tour with Guns N' Roses. Never mind the antidrug lectures from clean and sober Aerosmith, now seeking a piece of the power-ballad cash cow with tunes like "Angel." Guns N' Roses went to number one on July 23, the second week of the tour, and a *Rolling Stone* writer sent to interview Aerosmith came home with a cover story instead on the strange new heroes of Hollywood.

Guns N' Roses recharged and almost single-handedly sustained the Sunset Strip sleaze system for several years. Axl Rose eventually brought about the destruction of the band, but his angry outbursts were intensely believable to fans who understood how he felt. As Rose lashed out at memories of his

Guns N' Roses guitarist Slash
(Deborah Laws/Metalflakes.com)

parents, school officials, and other childhood oppressors back in Lafayette, Indiana, the American listening audience rewarded his lack of self-control by scooping up 15 million copies of *Appetite for Destruction*. With this meteoric number, Guns N' Roses set the target for which all other metal would aim in the coming decade.

Down to its sprawling topography, the unique nature of Los Angeles sustained the heavy metal runaways of Middle America like no other city. "I think the reason L.A. was such a hotbed for metal in the 1980s is because L.A. is the biggest suburban city in the world," says Twisted Sister's Dee Snider. "It's a city, so it had the clout of New York, but the way it's laid out has a real suburban feel to it. It's the perfect breeding ground for heavy metal. Something to do with sitting in your car, driving around, listening to tapes."

In 1987, glam metal found a spiritual home apart from the Sunset Strip when MTV launched its successful *Headbangers Ball* program—a weekly special of exclusively heavy metal videos. The new show dropped former metalhead-in-residence Dee Snider after he requested a paycheck. "We did *Heavy Metal Mania* monthly for about a year and a half," he says. "Then I asked for some money, and

ꟽETAL ꟽOVIES

With half the metalhead population of America migrating to Hollywood during the late 1980s, it was inevitable that wild-eyed, raving heavy metal would influence the video revolution.

Straight to Video, Straight to Hell

❖ *Over the Edge* **(1979)** Matt Dillon's screen debut, a late-1970s look at the great wasteland of California's tract-house paradise. Sort of the first of a trilogy, along with *River's Edge* and *Gummo*.

❖ *Kiss Meets the Phantom of the Park* **(1978)** Kiss versus Kiss = Kiss wins either way.

❖ *Heavy Metal* **(1981)** Animated fantasy film featuring one minute of Black Sabbath in surround sound.

❖ *This Is Spinal Tap* **(1984)** A heavy metal mockumentary that lampoons rock excess but almost doesn't go far enough.

❖ *The Dungeonmaster* **(1985)** Strange cable classic about computers and role-playing games, starring W.A.S.P.

❖ *Trick or Treat* **(1986)** Skippy from *Family Ties* is possessed by the spirit of a devil-worshipping dead heavy metal star.

❖ *River's Edge* **(1986)** When a group of New Jersey teens discovers their friend is not only not a virgin but dead, Crispin Glover goes apeshit (with help from Dennis Hopper and Slayer songs).

❖ *Heavy Metal Parking Lot* (1986) Headbanger verité from Washington, D.C., the capital of unself-conscious behavior.

❖ *Rock and Roll Nightmare* (1987) A Canadian heavy metal act discovers a demon while recording in a barn. Starring Thor.

❖ *Decline of Western Civilization Part II: The Metal Years* (1988) An inside look at where hair was highest: Sunset Strip. Compelling arguments for why Metallica moved away from Los Angeles.

❖ *Black Roses* (1988) A film with a message: Heavy metal bands are demons sent to destroy the lives of teenagers. Not based on fact, but starring real-life metal drummer Carmine Appice from Ozzy Osbourne's band.

❖ *Airheads* (1993) A low-expectation Adam Sandler comedy whose creators were looking into their cultural viewfinder upside down. "It was a real eye-opener as to why Hollywood movies suck, and why they cost so much," says cult movie expert Rob Zombie, who cameos with White Zombie in the film. "I said, 'You can do whatever you want with your movie, but I don't want to be embarrassed. Get real kids in here, and we'll play a real show—you can film that. They forgot to get any real kids, so I show up and there are all these extras wearing wigs, totally dressed up like 1982, S*hout at the Devil.* There were literally like sixty-year-old guys wearing these fake blond wigs."

❖ *Gummo* (1997) Chair wrestling, improvised slap fights, albino sex kittens, and a sound track featuring Brujeria, Burzum, and Bathory. Morally ambiguous chain yanking at its best.

they said, 'Oh, well, this is publicity for you.' I said, 'You've got to be fucking kidding me. I can't walk out my frigging front door without a bodyguard—the whole world knows what I look like!"

As *Headbangers Ball* grew into a Saturday night institution, a succession of willing victims hosted the show. From the comfort of their living rooms, viewers made great sport of bashing two hopeless VJs in particular: straight arrow Adam Curry and well-connected Sunset Strip club owner Riki Rachtman. "I thought [Rachtman] was very disinterested in what he was doing," singer Bobby Ellsworth of Overkill told *Metal Dreams*. "I thought he couldn't give a flying fuck who was sitting next to him. Maybe he and I just didn't hit it off, but I've really had no interesting conversation with this guy after meeting four times. He hasn't heard one song on the record and he's gonna talk it up like it's the best thing since canned beer. It was one of the more painful things to do."

Changing MTV's approach, *Headbangers Ball* at least nodded to the emerging thrash metal genre by occasionally squeezing one or two clips into a three-hour episode. "MTV was a joke," says Megaforce Records' Maria Ferraro of getting Overkill and Testament played. "There was no outlet except *Headbangers Ball*, and even that was political. It was hard. It wasn't payola, it was getting a video to them that somebody liked, and the stars being aligned properly so they'd say, 'Okay, I guess I'll do it.'" Jumping through those hoops could pay off handsomely—after MTV briefly embraced Testament's *Practice What You Preach*, sales of the LP zoomed to 285,000 copies.

In the heart of Hollywood, however, the music industry shunted heavier metal bands away from the epicenter of popularity. Most gigs on Sunset Strip were still glam showcases, where bars were essentially hired out as audition rooms for A&R scouts. "That was kind of a sad thing," says Katon W. DePena of Hirax—depicted on the group's second album leaping out of a garbage dumpster. "We didn't really care about it, but we knew it wasn't going to help our scene at all. In fact, it made it worse for us, because at our shows there was more movement on the dance floor, and a lot of those club owners didn't like it."

Hard-core headbangers hit back against the light of heart. Shortly after arriving in Los Angeles and signing to Metal Blade, Chicago transplant Thrust released *Fist Held High*, containing the call to arms "Posers Will Die!" The anthem decried club lizards on "rock-star trips," who appeared at every show but preferred chatting at the bar to headbanging. Witness to similar wars in the punk scene, the band Sonic Youth captured the us-versus-them attitude nicely with a song titled "Non Metal Dude Wearing Metal Tee."

In a world where the most precious commodity was the fleeting sound of a sacred band, the trivial became the battleground. "Our singer's ex-girlfriend was a really good cartoonist," says Exodus guitarist Gary Holt, "and she drew up these comics that showed us knifing and beating up Mötley Crüe clones. We were constantly drinking and chain-sawing and jackhammering people to death. They were just for our own amusement, and then it spread off to our fans in the local club scene."

Fueling the skirmishes, Exodus singer Paul Baloff rallied crowds with tall tales of throwing glam rockers through windows and cutting off their primped hair. "Baloff was probably the most unforgiving," Gary Holt recalls. "After Baloff was long out of Exodus, King Diamond played in San Francisco, and Paul's band, Piranha, was playing an after-show party. Paul had these hedge clippers he called his 'helicopter trout,' and he was sitting there snipping the hair off some King Diamond roadie who had a nice poser hairdo. The dude was just sitting there trying to lightly brush Paul away like he was a little insect or something, and Paul was cutting chunks until the dude's hair was totally rearranged!"

New wave, punk, and disco all had previously served as foils to heavy metal. Now that America had gone metal, the musical family was splitting into self-righteous factions. When the innocent-looking Stryper traveled to a Dutch metal festival in 1985, the glam Christians found themselves walking into a lion's den. "We were playing with Raven and Testament, just all these dark speed metal bands," says singer Michael Sweet. "Everyone there just absolutely hated us. They were actually chanting 'F-U-C-K Stryper, F-U-C-K Stryper.' We came out to hear what they were saying, and we couldn't believe it. We wanted to go home. We were like little boys—our knees were shaking. We changed our whole set list, and did all our heavy songs, and didn't hold back, and told them Jesus is the way. After about five songs we won them over, but it was crazy. There was an upside-down cross with Stryper on it that they lit on fire. They had a picture of my brother's head on a woman's body—not a complete nudie picture, but you know the type of thing. We were dodging stuff they threw at us. It was scary."

Yet as Stryper brought a few souls to the church, so did MTV bands indoctrinate new believers to heavy metal. Even Metallica's James Hetfield had begun headbanger life as a major Mötley Crüe fan.

Over the long run, the so-called posers made metal visible to the public eye, and their popularity benefited the nocturnal world of the underground. "When we played our heavy music in Europe," recalls Tom Warrior of Celtic Frost, "all we had at our shows were drunken males in leather jackets. I don't mean that as a disrespect, it's just a fact that ninety-five percent of the audience were males who just came to headbang their puberty out of their bodies. In America, with the same music, we had females and adults at our shows, and it was a completely different aura. It was like heaven."

Until the day thrash metal usurped glam on a massive scale, Poison and Mötley Crüe remained the first point of access for new fans. As Chuck Klosterman wrote in his metal memoir, *Fargo Rock City*, "Hair metal was a wormhole for every Midwestern kid who was too naïve to understand why he wasn't happy."

Outside Los Angeles, *Headbangers Ball* fueled a hilarious age of guilty pleasures, igniting the excesses of heavy metal across America as never before. Where *Decline II* played into the conventions of Tinseltown, photographing its subjects in soft studio sets, the crude video *Heavy Metal Parking Lot* documented the less glamorous customs of an arena parking lot outside a Judas Priest show in Washington, D.C. Directed by Jeff Krulik and John Heyn, the 1986 film revealed suburban teens from Maryland and Virginia drinking bourbon as they transfigured from mundane reality to concert-hall ecstasy. "We are not juvenile delinquents, although we act like that," explained one frenetic tailgater. "We try to be civilized, but we can't!"

Wild and crazy: *Heavy Metal Parking Lot* (John Heyn/Jeff Krulik)

In *Heavy Metal Parking Lot* the unfiltered reality was laid bare. The camera captured an argument over the merits of opening act Dokken, a vanload of happy Latinos in Iron Maiden and Metallica shirts, and a kid in matching zebra-striped tank top and stretch pants delivering a drunken soliloquy against punk ("It belongs on Mars") and Madonna ("She's a dick"). "In 1986 nobody had cameras." says Krulik. "We lucked out. We didn't particularly target Judas Priest, but they were at their peak, and they were headlining at the Cap Center on a spring day. They're like the Rolling Stones or the Beatles of heavy metal. Their music will stand the test of time."

At the soaring level of heavy metal's success in 1987, the fan base was essentially the average American consumer: the same people that drank Pepsi, shopped at Kmart, ate at Burger King, visited Disneyland, and otherwise kept the American economy afloat. In all its silly valor, *Heavy Metal Parking Lot* immortalized teenagers using heavy metal to break free. Underneath the makeup and spandex the professional partygoers in Mötley Crüe were not so different in motivation. "We all came of age going through this kind of experience," says director Krulik of his creation. "That's what makes it, very happily so, a cultural touchstone. Someone mentions Metallica, who weren't huge back then, and they are now enormous stars. It's evergreen. We didn't know what we had until almost ten years later."

XI

United Forces:
Metal and Hardcore Punk

➤ **July 1985:** S.O.D. records *Speak English or Die*

➤ **Summer 1985:** Metallica begins playing the Misfits' "Last Caress"

➤ **Fall 1986:** Motörhead tours with Cro-Mags

➤ **1987:** Napalm Death releases *Scum*; ends race for faster and louder

---

On the opposite side of the looking glass from the hair metal headbangers were the hardcore punks—virulently anti-establishment characters whose sound and culture grew from punk rock building blocks during the 1980s. Beginning with Black Flag in Los Angeles, the Misfits in New Jersey, and Bad Brains in Washington, D.C., a surging, angry wall of sound moved inward from the coasts through a string of regional teenage bands, meeting halfway in the American Midwest. Michigan was the heart of hardcore country and birthplace in 1967 of punk's founding fathers, the Stooges. There, Die Kreuzen, Negative Approach, and the Necros from neighboring Dayton, Ohio, tore apart church basements, VFW halls, and any place an unsuspecting landlord could be convinced to allow a show.

Early-1980s do-it-yourself releases like Black Flag's *Damaged* and Die Kreuzen's *Cows & Beer* featured cheap, distorted guitars tearing over frantic rock drumming, and they expressed extreme dissatisfaction with adolescent norms in Middle America.

Die Kreuzen, Columbus Church, Indiana, 1981
(Scott Colburn)

These records were vinyl nonconformist manifestos—sold cheaply for gas money as bands toured an ever-shifting circuit of small college towns and fledgling urban punk scenes. The best records by the Misfits and Negative Approach were out of print by the time word of the groups could spread nationally. The meager yet vast infrastructure of hardcore simply demanded a constant wave of very similar-sounding bands coughing out intensely personal anthems about schoolyard betrayal, mental confusion, and antigovernment rebellion.

In the mid-1980s a second rash of hardcore groups—known, like guerrilla cells, by initials such as GBH, SNFU, and MDC—began playing more intense hardcore that sounded like a stripped-down amateur take on speed metal. On this bleeding edge lived two high-speed masters: Texas's Dirty Rotten Imbeciles, aka D.R.I., and North Carolina's Corrosion of Conformity, aka C.O.C. Crossing over a new frontier of frenzy, D.R.I.'s 1983 *Dirty Rotten* LP fought a personal war of agitated chords and heart-attack drumbeats. Only four of twenty-two tracks were more than a minute long. "That first D.R.I. album? C'mon! That's a record that you can't throw shit at," gushes Katon W. DePena of Hirax. "Nothing's better for that time. We'd go to see them or play with them, and there'd be a set list that had like fifty-something songs on it!"

Consequently, bands like Hirax from the powerful thrash metal end of heavy metal began to speed up, grabbing elements from the blur of hardcore punk. After lightly brushing against each other during the birthing days of Motörhead and the Damned, heavy metal fans and punks had been like warring tribes—sometimes literally doing battle in the streets of London. Earlier in the 1980s Def Leppard's Joe Elliott was the voice of many metallers, calling punk "gutter music." Coming from the singer of a band that shellacked its NWOBHM roots with multiplatinum MTV metal sales, however, such epithets by the late 1980s started to sound like ringing endorsements.

Katon DePena of Hirax
(Courtesy of Katon DePena)

Besides the blistering music, the hysteric paranoia of hardcore lyrics also appealed to the newly cauterized sense of civic consciousness in PMRC-persecuted metalheads. Embroiled in epic censorship struggles of its own over its 1985 *Frankenchrist* LP, the left-wing Dead Kennedys in particular inspired Metallica and Megadeth to replace their traditional metal mythology with lyrics that directly attacked more earthly Satans. "I really liked the Dead Kennedys because of what Jello Biafra was saying," says Dave Mustaine of Megadeth. "A lot of the other stuff people were singing about just seemed like drivel."

The horror film–inspired Misfits became legendary after succumbing to massive internal entropy and disbanding in 1984. Though he dressed in blue denim like a mellow 1970s acid rocker, it was wired fiend Cliff Burton who force-fed the Misfits to his bandmates in Metallica by monopolizing the tape deck in the tour bus with a ninety-minute bootleg tape of greatest hits labeled "Misfits." Metallica played the first of several Misfits covers, "Last Caress," in stadiums with Ozzy Osbourne. "They couldn't play 'Green Hell' because Lars couldn't play the thrash beats!" recalls former Misfits singer Glenn Danzig. Both songs became Metallica live standards, and the renewed interest in his music soon brought Danzig to the attention of Rick Rubin, who signed the singer on the condition that he disband his current adventurous band, Samhain, and concentrate on developing as a solo act.

As Metallica and Megadeth jumped the fence and embraced the glam-killing properties of hardcore, the long-lasting divisions between metalheads and punks were erased. The growing respect was mutual, once hardcore punks understood that the heavy metal that flowed from the veins of Motörhead and Black Sabbath was not the same as the cheesy aerosol music they saw on MTV. "People don't recognize Sabbath for the power of what they had," C.O.C. guitarist Woody Weatherman told *Metal Maniacs*. "'War Pigs' and 'Children of the Grave' did more to make me think than a lot of punk rock songs. They just laid it on the line, just totally told how it is."

The power lines of punk and metal fused together completely in the catalyzing Stormtroopers of Death, a hardcore side-project formed in April 1985 by members of Anthrax. Combining a sense of humor cultivated by repeated viewing of *Caddyshack* with a crunching guitar, S.O.D. was a metalhead's dream of how hardcore should sound. The lineup brought bassist Dan Lilker—ousted a few years earlier from Anthrax by former singer Neil Turbin—back together with Anthrax guitarist Scott Ian and drummer Charlie Benante. "Scott still wanted to play with me in some manner," Lilker says. "He wasn't happy about me leaving the band."

Unlike the inspired amateurism of midwestern teenage hardcore, the Stormtroopers of Death were top-notch professional musicians ripping into short bursts of hardcore punk— akin to installing a turbo racing engine in a go-cart. Their short spurts of ripping thrash were ordered into action by the loud vocals of Billy Milano, formerly bassist of the Psychos. With a knack for pushing people's buttons, Milano was equal parts comedian and New Jersey thug who considered himself an artist. "I do write poetry," says Milano. "A couple years ago I had a whole bunch of poems circulating. It's not real poetry, it's more like art, with words instead of pictures."

Speak English or Die sprinkled personal jokes among extreme responses. "Chromatic Death" advocated human annihilation

Billy Milano of S.O.D.

HARDCORE PUNK

After punk's heyday in the late 1970s, a younger generation was inspired to continue shocking attacks against the status quo through underground gigs and records. Any kid with a white T-shirt and a Magic Marker could join the club, banging out adolescent uncertainty in a room filled with peers equally addicted to brazen power and nonconformity. British hardcore bands like GBH and especially Discharge were more preoccupied with global politics. American hardcore was a succession of scene revolts, chastising uncool behavior with a litany of antisocial anthems. Alone in the crowd, the Misfits wore ghoulish makeup and retained a heavy metal fascination with skulls and crossbones. Many of these bands were essentially heavy metal bands minus the commercial expectations.

Skinheads, Brains, and Guts

- Agnostic Front, *Victim in Pain* (1984)
- Bad Brains, *I Against I* (1986)
- Black Flag, *Damaged* (1981)
- Black Flag, *My War* (1982)
- Circle Jerks, *Group Sex* (1981)
- D.I., *Team Goon* (1981)
- Die Kreuzen, *Die Kreuzen* (1984)
- Discharge, *See Nothing, Hear Nothing, Say Nothing* (1984)
- GBH, *City Baby Attacked by Rats* (1982)
- Minor Threat, *Out of Step* (1983)
- Misfits, *Walk Among Us* (1982)
- Negative Approach, *Tied Down* (1983)
- Suicidal Tendencies, *Suicidal Tendencies* (1983)

as a measure of environmental cleanup, and "Speak English or Die" and "Fuck the Middle East" stirred up controversy in the conscientious punk scene. Forced to defend themselves against charges of Nazism and nationalism, the members noted that Lilker and Ian were both Jewish, and Milano and Benante descendants of recent Italian immigrants. Besides the self-explanatory "Kill Yourself," an example of their unforgiving humor was "The Ballad of Jimi Hendrix," set to the opening strains of the late guitarist's "Purple Haze." After eight seconds the song ended abruptly with the disrespectful punch line "You're dead!"

At the same time, S.O.D.'s "United Forces" urged collaboration between the punk and metal troops: "It doesn't matter how you wear your hair / It's what's inside your head." Indeed, fans accustomed to Iron Maiden and even Metallica's ten-minute strolls through the park found S.O.D.'s eight-second songs hilarious. There was a refreshing carelessness to the operation that contrasted with how life in heavy metal was growing so altogether serious. The Dead Kennedys stickers on Slayer's guitars and Metallica's GBH and Discharge T-shirts had advertised this alliance for a few years already—now the cat was out of the bag.

Released by Megaforce Records, *Speak English or Die* rose in popularity until S.O.D. rivaled its members' regular jobs in the more established Anthrax. After its unauthorized tribute to horror hero "Freddy Kreuger" found its way into the offices of New Line Cinema, S.O.D. was approached by the studio to write music for a sequel to the popular *Nightmare on Elm Street*. In anticipation the band posed for publicity photos with actor Robert Englund in full Kreuger costume. "That's kind of why S.O.D. was cut short back then," recalls Lilker. "Other people in Anthrax were getting angry about it. You gotta remember, it was supposed to be this project like, 'Oh, they're just going to get it out of their system,' and then, boom, it got fucking huge." By 1999 *Speak English or Die* had sold more than a million copies worldwide.

The crossover had begun. By late 1985 the Los Angeles hardcore bands Suicidal Tendencies and Circle Jerks were tempering their speed assault with slower, heavier riffs in order to lure the huge metal audience. The critical British band Discharge did the same, and soon concert promoters like Goldenvoice in Los Angeles and Rock Hotel in

Crossover in effect: Anthrax and Possessed meet D.R.I. and C.O.C.

New York were cultivating a unified scene with giant spectaculars that put Motörhead and the hardcore punk Cro-Mags together on the same bill. By way of contrast there were almost no examples still to be found of thrash metal bands ever playing shows with MTV glam metal groups.

As metal infected the hardcore scene, the spiky-haired English Dogs threw down their protest anthems in favor of medieval-themed hymns on the aptly titled *Metalmorphosis*. Likewise, one of the most brilliantly spastic hardcore groups, the Bad Brains—a group of self-styled Rastafarians from suburban Maryland—fought the problems of human wickedness with the intensity of hardcore, the religious soul of reggae, and the sharp instrumental skills of metal on their powerful *I Against I*. Hosts of bands, including the Hare Krishna hardcore group Cro-Mags and the dreadlocked C.O.C., took inspiration from the same forward-reaching spirit—discovering discordant music and creating a heterogeneous new social scene.

Remaining at the forefront of metal-hardcore fusion in New York, S.O.D.'s Dan Lilker joined with John Connelly to form the quirky Nuclear Assault. Wholly dedicated to cross-genre impurities, the quartet gigged at Sunday afternoon matinees at punk club CBGB with Agnostic Front, then played heavy metal strongholds like L'Amour with thrash troopers Overkill. "Believe me, there were more shiny satin jackets and metal jewelry in L'Amour than you could shake a stick at," says Lilker. "You could practically be blinded in there. We straddled that divide. One day we'd be playing hardcore shows with crazed skinheads jumping right over you, and a couple days later we'd play at L'Amour and there would be some girls in the front poking their elbows at each other trying to get your attention."

Leading the crossover band Carnivore in the mid-1980s, towering singer Peter Steele, aka Petrus T. Steele, found that merging the tribes was not always easy. "There was a clear distinction between black metal, and speed metal, and punk, and hardcore, and rap," Steele says. "There was almost no crossover. Nuclear Assault and S.O.D. were just starting to cross over, and we wanted to be one of those bands. I liked the heaviness of metal, but I liked the violence and the excitement at hardcore shows, and I wanted to incorporate both. We had a lot of trouble, because metal kids saw Carnivore as outdated and image-heavy, and the hardcore kids didn't accept us because we had long hair."

Indeed, for punks still living a Sid Vicious fantasy, accusing a band of having "gone metal" was a wounding insult. When Kirk Hammett of Metallica joined the Crumbsuckers onstage at CBGB, the audience spit at him and bruised his ego with shouts of "rock star," leading to Hammett's clobbering a heckler with his guitar. Ultimately the punk scene remained as much a testing ground for attitudes as for music—and metal fans saw the obnoxiousness as part of the appeal.

Resentment of heavy metal interlopers increased in the late 1980s after do-it-yourself punk labels were suddenly forced to compete with new hardcore-oriented spinoffs of business-savvy metal indies. Combat spawned CombatCore, Roadrunner formed Hawker, and Metal Blade dallied with Death Records. The very fact that these companies were organized and making money made them morally suspect in the eyes of some punks. "People give you flak automatically because you're on Combat Records," says Blaine Cook of the Accüsed, sole punks on the label among bullet-belted thrashers Megadeth, Agent Steel, and Possessed. "Combat's just another independent label, but I guess there's an attitude that goes along with heavy metal, and [punks] feel it carries over to the business aspect."

Like it or not, metal rejuvenated the urgency of the hardcore punk scene at a crucial hour. While the originators of hardcore punk—Necros, Redd Kross, Negative Approach, Minor Threat, and Black Flag—disbanded and grew their hair, young hardcore acts like Attitude Adjustment and Underdog suddenly sprang from a fountain of Exodus riffs. Also, many headbangers took hardcore's revolutionary promise at face value—during a time when most punks were dangerously close to losing their faith in nihilism. "In some of the younger scenes they just got done watching *Sid and Nancy* and *The Decline of Western Civilization*," says Blaine Cook of the Accüsed, describing two punk exploitation movies. "They still think that's what it is to be a punk rocker, but it's eight to ten years later now. It's becoming a costume, like the new resurgence of hippies who still think it's 1967, wearing tie-dyed shirts and listening to the Grateful Dead. There's supposed to be more to the hardcore scene than just the fashion and the music aspect, y'know? There's supposed to be a set of ideals and attitudes that go beyond the trashing of the clubs and the violence and the swastikas and the Mohawks and the shock value. In my opinion that grew old a long time ago. If you're going to shock somebody, do it with your intelligence, not your three-foot-high green Mohawk."

In the late 1980s the territories were merging to become one and the same. Younger fans embraced thrash metal and hardcore punk to the benefit of both breeds of rejected music. The value differences between hardcore and metal were often based on stereotypes that did not necessarily hold true: bald heads versus long hair, "straight-edge" tee-totaling versus alcoholic abandon, and self-produced basement shows versus concert halls. At the end of the day pentagrams looked well enough like anarchy symbols.

As metal encountered punk music, fashion, politics, and ethics, a broader sense of identity developed. Metalheads realized there was more to life than hating posers and pushing for world domination, and started thinking of their scene in terms of a culture separate from the mind-controlling mass-media empire that never understood them anyway. The resulting underground pride influenced the development of metal in the next decade. As Euronymous of the black metal band Mayhem described the heavy music subculture in Norway to *Morbid Mag* in 1987, "More and more people seem to become active in the scene, which I think is good. One thing which also is good is that punks and thrashers now start uniting. But I think that more girls should get into the scene!"

As advertised by the Anthrax videos "Madhouse" and "Indians," the Megadeth clip "Wake Up Dead," and various MTV specials, the influence of hardcore punk also brought slam dancing and stage diving into the densely packed and more professional metal environment.

The original Black Sabbath *(Warner Bros.)*

► **Michael Schenker, Flying V wunderkind** *(Tim Falke)*

▲ **Eddie Van Halen**
(Austin [Hardrock69] Majors)

► **U.S. Festival '83** *(Dan Sokol)*

Nikki Sixx of Mötley Crüe
(Deborah Laws/Metalflakes.com)

▲ Iron Maiden's *Powerslave* stage *(Todd Nakamine)*

► **King Diamond
of Mercyful Fate**
(Todd Nakamine)

▼ **Mantas and Cronos of Venom** *(Todd Nakamine)*

Slayer at Fender's Ballroom
(Todd Nakamine)

▲ Paul Baloff and Gary Holt of Exodus *(Todd Nakamine)*

◀ Thrashers! Raging the front row—Katon W. DePena, center
(Todd Nakamine)

▲ Rob Halford
(Deborah Laws/Metalflakes.com)

► Metallica (with John Marshall)
in Oslo, Norway, September 25, 1986
(Vidar Sandnes)

▲ Dave Mustaine in Megadeth *(Jonathan Munro)*

▲ **Out there: Voivod live in 1986**
(Jean-François "Big" Lavallée/Metal K.O. Productions)

▼ **Glenn Danzig** *(Christy Lee Davis)*

Lars Ulrich, Lord of Drums
(Deborah Laws/Metalflakes.com)

1990s-era Napalm Death in Berlin
(Earache publicity photo)

James Hetfield in motion *(Deborah Laws/Metalflakes.com)*

▲ **Morbid Angel live** *(Harry Maat, The Dark Arts)*

▼ **Abbath and Demonaz of Immortal** *(Osmose Productions)*

▲ Samoth, Ihsahn, and Trym of Emperor in 1999 *(Morten Andersen)*

▼ Four of nine Slipknot members raging at Ozzfest *(Samantha Nickerson)*

Symphony and Metallica in Berlin
(Filip Malinowski)

The return of Ozzy Osbourne
(Deborah Laws/Metalflakes.com)

Heavy metal godfather: Lemmy of Motörhead
(Deborah Laws/Metalflakes.com)

METALCORE

In the mid-1980s thrash metal bands like Metallica and Slayer began openly admiring the fast, hardcore punk of DRI, GBH, and SNFU—to name a few initials. With two subcultures running neck and neck in speed and energy, something had to give. Hardcore already drew significantly, if secretly, from heavy metal dating back to Motörhead. In the late 1980s, the underground became a hodgepodge of metallic guitar, socially conscious lyrics, and crunching speed rhythms. Unlike their brethren in the black metal underground, these bands dismissed leather and spikes in favor of typical American teen wear: goofy T-shirts, shorts, and sweat socks. They didn't take themselves too seriously, but their contributions were crucial. Too dirty and noisy to be heavy metal, too technically adept to be punk, these bands hung on the periphery, reveling in freedom.

Crossover Dreams

- The Accüsed, *Return of Martha Splatterhead* (1985)
- Corrosion of Conformity, *Animosity* (1985)
- Cro-Mags, *The Age of Quarrel* (1986)
- Cryptic Slaughter, *Convicted* (1986)
- Dirty Rotten Imbeciles, *Dealing with It* (1985)
- Dr. Know, *Plug In Jesus* (1984)
- Excel, *Split Image* (1987)
- Hirax, *Hate, Fear and Power* (1987)
- Prong, *Force Fed* (1987)
- Samhain, *November Coming Fire* (1986)
- S.O.D., *Speak English or Die* (1985)
- Wehrmacht, *Shark Attack* (1987)

Aggressive music demanded violent physical responses that sent bodies colliding into one another—even the most frantic headbanging was no longer enough. As guitarist Gary Holt recalls an especially chaotic Exodus event, "One guy left in an ambulance because he hit headfirst after stage diving, and a couple guys got broken noses. It was pretty out of hand, and we weren't even playing! We were just lip-synching for the video shoot!"

Concert-hall violence had been a rock and roll hazard since fans rioted after performances by Deep Purple and Black Sabbath in the early 1970s. Now, with the increasing popularity of hardcore, slam dancing—or "moshing," as it was dubbed by the S.O.D. song "Milano Mosh"—spread from underground club shows to large-scale arena venues. Security guards struggled to interpret the difference between

Crowd surfing at an Anthrax show
(Dean Sternberg)

dancing and fighting. "I go into a concert situation and see people going absolutely insane moshing and slamming," says Dave Mustaine of Megadeth. "We were one of the bands that started that in America. It started off with pogo-ing and doing the worm in the punk scene, and then when the metal scene came along, the people wanted to dance like that, but they didn't know what pogo-ing and doing the worm was, so they invented slam dancing."

In the song "Caught in a Mosh," Anthrax glorified the slam pit as a metaphor for life struggles. Yet as onstage interlopers stomped on guitar cables and jostled musicians during intricate guitar solos, the experience was not universally appreciated. "We were sick and tired of the ultrahardcore fans in Europe," says Tom Warrior of these excursions. "They would be so violent in the front row that the other fans couldn't enjoy the show anymore. It had nothing to do with music anymore. It was just antisocial. We became so frustrated that we intentionally altered our music to be more intellectual and more melodic in order to scare those fans away, because they were making it impossible for the large majority of fans to enjoy our shows."

One of the most aggressive and punk-inspired metal bands, Slayer had problems playing in its home city of Los Angeles due to the destruction of property that inevitably followed its packed performances. "We were playing with Slayer at the Olympic, and a guy hit me in the throat with his shoe," says David Wayne of Metal Church. "The blow just about paralyzed my vocal cords. It made me so mad that I put my mike down, and as soon as I saw the other shoe, I dove over a six-foot photo pit and went down with my hands around this guy's throat. His little buddies proceeded to kick the tar out of me. I'm laying down there with all these feet on top of my head, with guys putting boots in my ribs, thinking, 'You dumb asshole, your anger got the best of you, now you're gonna die on the ground in front of your own show.'"

When even Judas Priest and AC/DC began depicting stage divers and body surfing in their MTV videos, it was clear that the mosh had been brought mainstream. The age-old practice of headbanging seemed innocent in comparison to flailing limbs, bodies smashing into each other, and a crush of thousands of fans pressing against the stage. Bands in the metal arena learned that rough crowds came with the territory—it was understood that metalheads would risk life and limb in order to

NOTICE: STAGE DIVING

WELCOME TO BOGART'S AND TONIGHT'S CONCERT

WE HAVE AND WE WANT TO CONTINUE TO BRING THE BEST HARDCORE BANDS IN THE WORLD TO BOGART'S. BUT WE NEED YOUR COOPERATION AND UNDERSTANDING.

STAGE DIVING PRESENTS TOO GREAT A RISK TO THE DIVER, THE AUDIENCE, AND THE CLUB ITSELF, TO ALLOW IT.

THEREFORE, WE DO NOT PERMIT STAGE DIVING AT ANY TIME.

PLEASE UNDERSTAND THAT BOGART'S CAN NOT AND WILL NOT TOLERATE STAGE DIVING OR ANY OTHER BEHAVIOR OR ACT THAT MAY BE POTENTIALLY HARMFUL OR A VIOLATION OF ANY LAW OR ORDINANCE.

SO IF YOU GET ON THE STAGE TONIGHT, OR DO SOMETHING YOU SHOULDN'T, BE PREPARED TO BE EJECTED AND TO LOSE THE BUCKS IT COST YOU TO GET IN.

IT'S JUST NOT WORTH IT.

HEY, HAVE A GOOD TIME TONIGHT...AND ENJOY THE BANDS. BUT JUST BE COOL.

THANK YOU FOR YOUR COOPERATION... UNDERSTANDING...SUPPORT...AND YOUR PATRONAGE.

BOGART'S

Metal club flyer banning stage diving

experience something real. "There comes a point where you have to feel like someone gives a shit that you're actually playing," notes Rob Zombie of White Zombie. "It's so much cooler to play where kids are going nuts, and every show looks like it ends in a riot. Security guards get nailed, kids get hurt, things are broke, and there's total damage. It becomes this insane, fun event. Watching Slayer is like going to a riot. Your blood's pumping."

If the majority of bands circulating in the tape-trading underground in 1985 wanted to be Metallica, in 1987 most new names played a cross-pollinated S.O.D.–style hybrid called metalcore, or simply crossover. In these groups shaved heads mingled with long hair, as punk drummers and singers wrestled musically with metal guitarists. As with any deceptively simple idea, S.O.D. inspired countless imitators. Among the fastest, with the sickest senses of humor, were Intense Mutilation, Sore Throat, and R.C.—all of whom pushed the songs-per-minute barrier into double digits. The cruel Anal Cunt, or A.C., was a project band like S.O.D., founded by bassist Seth Putnam from the Boston thrash group Executioner. A.C.'s ultimate statement was an 88-song seven-inch single, later topped by their own 5,643-song seven-inch—roughly ten untitled song blurts per second.

A preeminent forerunner of this synthesis was the Accüsed, from Seattle, Washington, a smaller city where hardcore metal fans and punks teamed together out of necessity. *The Return of Martha Splatterhead* featured guitar riffs and rough, plowing bass that were sickeningly catchy and combined the dark hardcore of Discharge and the

Grindcore godfathers Blaine Cook (l) and Tommy Niemeyer (r) of the Accüsed
(Courtesy of Blaine Cook)

black metal of Venom. The atrocities of their gory, comic graphics rang the same alarms as did the Misfits, but the songs were delivered faster, with greater caustic, metallic finesse. Jerking onstage like an out-of-control marionette, vocalist Blaine Cook coughed out his vocal scrapings in an expressive off-balance screech, the most extreme delivery since that of Motörhead's Lemmy. The obvious painfulness of the style was impressive. "My throat's fucked up," says Cook. "I don't have polyps or anything, but there's scar tissue."

Several years older than his bandmates, Cook had already released an album with the Fartz on the punk label Alternative Tentacles before meeting his precocious future bandmates Tommy, Chewy, and Dana in 1983. "They came down from Seattle to Portland," he says, "where the Fartz were playing with Poison Idea. They were like thirteen or fourteen. Chewy didn't even own a bass, or an amp, or a cabinet. Even when he was expelled from the band, he was playing out of borrowed equipment using a cheap copy bass that he had to tune up after every song."

The Accüsed were leaders on a club circuit that ran between Los Angeles, San Francisco, Portland, and Seattle of young bands bursting with speed and chaotic energy. In the music of Mace, Hirax, Wehrmacht, and Cryptic Slaughter, the fastest hardcore punk was swirling together with underground metal and blowing away the limits of both forms. These metalcore bands wrote reckless, socially aware anthems like Excel's monstrous "Insecurity" and Wehrmacht's "Balance of Opinion"—emulating hardcore yet peeling off Iron Maiden riffs as fast as humanly possible. "We just liked bands that were fast and heavy, and we liked punk," says Katon W. DePena of Hirax, who inherited its drummer from D.R.I. "We were the only band that played with D.R.I. and C.O.C., and then Celtic Frost and Venom. We were doing shit that nobody else was doing, and we didn't care. I never took myself that seriously."

While the graduates of the original *Metal Massacre* were now collecting gold and platinum albums, the rules of the underground had changed, veering away from the elaborate constructions of its heavy metal roots toward something resembling total obliteration. Endorsing this new breed, Metal Blade Records tapped Hirax, Dark Angel, and Possessed for *Metal Massacre VI* and Cryptic Slaughter for *Metal Massacre VII*. Yet the honors were not as necessary. In this age of widespread tape trading, the bands were already renowned for their demos and live tapes by the time Brian Slagel's albums could be manufactured and distributed to stores. In 1987 everyone with access to a cassette-tape dubbing machine was already a metal insider.

Following the preparatory steps of the metalcore bands came a new wave of bands calling their music grindcore, who raised the bar to the highest limits. As it stapled notice of discontent across the heads of the speechless metal underground, grindcore made all previous music sound quaint. If traditional heavy metal bands were feeling the heat from Metallica, Slayer, Megadeth, and Anthrax, the likes of England's Napalm Death were ready to completely bury the old guard deep in the bitter ground.

The latest turbulent and astonishing band from Birmingham, now a rebuilt city with one of the most racially diverse populations in Britain, Napalm Death consisted of a rotating multitude of members. Almost none of them were even born when Black Sabbath or Judas Priest first walked their city's streets. "People presume that just because we've got long hair we're into Judas Priest and Iron Maiden," says vocalist Jeff Walker of the decimating Carcass, who shared a guitarist with Napalm Death. "That really isn't the influence at all. [Grindcore] is the result of growing up in a time when bands like that were pop music, and we went for things that were more underground and obscure, be it hardcore punk or extreme death metal or whatever."

The bedroom label Earache Records, formed to license albums by the Accüsed in the UK, marketed dozens of groups under the enticing and all-encompassing grindcore banner. The sound was a dense spattering of black metal, hardcore, and thrash metal accelerated nearly to the point of atom-splitting self-destruction. Thrash metal had simplified arrangements to squeeze maximum power into the riffs. In grindcore there was almost no song structure—only a blurry, sustained outpouring of the ultimate speed and ferocity. It replayed all the heaviest music of the previous ten years on fast forward.

Even a metal scene that had endured all manner of speed, gimmicks, and noise was not too callused for the first Napalm Death album, *Scum*. Released in 1987 by Earache, *Scum* was the culmination of a ten-year race for harder and faster, and nothing could sensibly have been more of either. Drummer and band spokesman Mick Harris used a two-string guitar and a distortion box to write shatteringly fast political hot flashes, twenty-eight of which fit onto the LP. Though unpolished, it was the most radical debut since Metallica's *Kill 'Em All*, pulsing with thick, slamming cacophony in its full-bore posteverything onslaught.

After skipping the development of thrash metal, England was returning to the fore. Repeat appearances by Napalm Death and likeminded blasters Doom and Extreme Noise Terror on the influential John Peel BBC radio show earned grindcore the billing of sadistic savior of British rock. "The hardcore stuff was like a renaissance for us of punk music," says Nick Bullen, bassist and founding member of Napalm Death. "Between 1978 and 1984 there were six years of other music: industrial, electronic, reggae, psychedelic, and anything we came across. That was our second wind to go back to something like Napalm Death."

Plans for a mixed slate of grindcore bands to wreak havoc on *Top of the Pops* television show were nixed by the BBC, yet Extreme Noise Terror eventually had its chance at media terrorism when invited by the KLF to help destroy the BRIT television awards show in February 1992. Never a hit in America, the KLF were a bunch of conceptual pop tricksters who won the hearts of their home country with stunts like recording country singer Tammy Wynette in a rap context. Performing at the prestigious BRIT awards, Extreme Noise Terror blasted the KLF hit "3 A.M. Eternal" into oblivion while the KLF sprayed the audience with machine guns preloaded with blanks. When the KLF were awarded "Best British Group" honors later that night, a messenger announced that the band had left the premises and retired from music, the saviors of pop appropriately opting to implode in the roaring spray of a blasting grindcore drumbeat.

One year after *Scum*, Napalm Death released *From Enslavement to Obliteration* and shook expectations by introducing into grindcore the ultraheavy influence of the New York art band the Swans. As fast as *Scum* had been, the opening salvo of *From Enslavement*'s "Evolved as One" opened the doors with slow, painful fury—an industrial furnace built for incinerating the fat and the false. Even after downshift-

GRINDCORE

At its inception grindcore was a superfast faction of the intense underground sound of metalcore, the crossover of punk and metal. The key to grindcore was the blast beat, a pulverizing, mechanical strobing of the snare drum, punctuated by hasty rolls around the drum set. Bands like Napalm Death and Doom took the tortured vocals of the Accüsed and played misshapen guitar licks a million miles a minute. Though death metal already existed, grindcore set new standards for the genre, adding more intelligent lyrics along with music that was not necessarily evil, but totally decimating. After missing the boat with thrash metal, Great Britain finally reclaimed its pioneering role in metal, offering the intriguing array of brutal bands showcased on the Earache label.

Faster Than You'll Ever Be

- Bolt Thrower, *BBC Peel Sessions* (1988)
- Brutal Truth, *Extreme Conditions Demand Extreme Responses* (1992)
- Carcass, *Symphonies of Sickness* (1989)
- Doom, *BBC Peel Sessions* (1989)
- Extreme Noise Terror, *Holocaust in Your Head* (1989)
- Napalm Death, *Scum* (1987)
- Napalm Death, *From Enslavement to Obliteration* (1988)
- Sore Throat, *Unhindered by Talent* (1989)

ing to a snail's pace, Napalm Death could still instantly return to vaporization speed. *From Enslavement* slipped a full twenty-two tracks onto the vinyl, each alarmingly titled like block-print newspaper headlines: "Cock-Rock Alienation," "Uncertainty Blurs the Vision," and "Mentally Murdered."

Miraculously, Napalm Death survived to further a full slate of creative inventions, though the band remained a revolving door of volatile personalities. Each side of *Scum* featured a different band roster, the result of short attention spans and impatience. "We were a bit younger, and we didn't know how to discuss things," recalls bassist Shane Embury, who remained with the group after working on *From Enslavement to Obliteration*. "Back then we were so isolated as members we weren't friends in the rational sense. Something would spark up an argument, not even over a musical thing, and someone would get up and leave the band rather than work it out."

Discharged members of Napalm Death went on to form bands fitting every category and description of extreme expression. Guitarist Justin Broadrick spawned Godflesh, Head of David, and Loop, all among the first heavy acts to use drum machines and ambient song structures. Guitarist Bill Steer returned to Carcass, where grindcore reconnected with metal virtuosity. Vocalist Lee Dorrian slowed things down to a gravestone's creep with his doom metal band Cathedral, and drummer Mick Harris helped along an early version of Extreme Noise Terror before launching the electronic-dub group Scorn. As the blast patterns emanating from this roster of surprises indicated, Napalm Death had effectively ended the race for harder and faster. The coming years would instead require heavy metal to become better and brighter.

XII

And Platinum for "One"... Metal Matures

- ➤ **July 1987:** First annual Milwaukee Metalfest held
- ➤ **April 1988:** Public Enemy samples Slayer on "She Watch Channel Zero"
- ➤ **August 19, 1988:** Anthrax *I'm the Man* EP earns gold record in the United States
- ➤ **July 19, 1989:** Metallica's . . . *And Justice for All* goes double platinum in the United States
- ➤ **June 1990:** Faith No More's *The Real Thing* cracks *Billboard* Top 10, a year after release

---

While dallying with hardcore, Metallica's first priority was still to rule the metal world—now an enormous, thriving realm. Cliff Burton and James Hetfield had sometimes ventilated through Spastik Children, a goof-off stupor-group that would play "London Dungeon" by the Misfits repeatedly during a performance. The band carried on sporadically after the passing of Burton, playing an engagement at the birthday party of old friend Ron Quintana. "Those shows all became fiascoes," says Quintana, "because the club owners would leak that Metallica was playing a special show, but they wouldn't say it was Spastik Children. That would always create friction, because all those guys wanted to do was get up there and play really badly on the wrong instruments and annoy people. They eventually got tired of people yelling, 'Play "Ride the Lightning"!' At that point forget it—Metallica was just too big."

Heavy metal was experiencing a golden age, and Metallica was poised to join the multiplatinum ranks of Ratt and Mötley Crüe when the death of Cliff Burton stopped them in their tracks. Still recovering from the loss of their bassist, Metallica returned to its unused rehearsal space in late October 1986, soon after the bus accident in Sweden. Hundreds of applicants plugged in to Cliff Burton's abandoned bass gear and auditioned in vain for a band loath to replace a dear friend. Among the parade was Kirk Hammett's pal from algebra class, Les Claypool, who was rejected on the grounds that he played too well. Others were shown the door based on looks alone, seconds after entering the room.

On the recommendation of Brian Slagel, Lars Ulrich eventually hired Jason Newsted—the letter writer, songwriter, and source of energy behind Phoenix, Arizona–based Flotsam & Jetsam, a graduate of *Metal Massacre VII*. In him Metallica found not a fully equivalent replacement for Cliff Burton but a reverent substitute. Among his primary qualifications: Metallica was his favorite band. Something of a latecomer to Diamond Head and the other NWOBHM groups, Newsted grew up listening to Kiss and Motown records, and he professed an affinity for jazz fusion. Yet the disciplined zeal he developed in Flotsam prepared him perfectly to jump aboard the Metallica juggernaut.

Metallica debuted the new member at a surprise-appearance opening for Metal Church on November 8, 1986, at the Country Club in Reseda, California. Those in

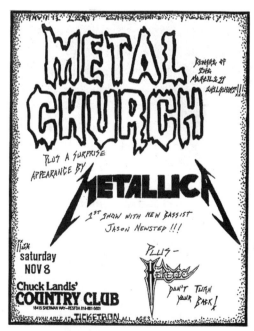

Underground flyer for Jason Newsted's first Metallica show

attendance could be excused for thinking that the band had grabbed a fan from the audience, strapped a bass on him, and ordered him to thrash—after turning his volume down so low he could do little harm. That was not far from the truth.

Hetfield, Ulrich, and Hammett had been in awe of their former bassist, but Newsted they ran ragged. The band spent the end of 1986 in Japan, where an intense and by most accounts permanent period of hazing began. Whenever one of them missed Cliff Burton, something bad happened to Newsted. They took his drinks and clothing, they told foreign hosts he was gay, and they assaulted his hotel room in the wee hours of the morning. Newsted responded with his own weird behavior: packing away sandwiches from the backstage buffet each night in case he was asked to leave unexpectedly the next morning. Complaining to AP that there were no Denny's diners on the road in Europe, he sounded a little lost in a band that had a Danish drummer and who worshipped old-world heavy metal.

Metallica canceled a scheduled appearance on *Saturday Night Live* in March 1987 because James Hetfield again broke his arm skateboarding, further forestalling arrival on the main stage of American life. Instead Metallica recruited opening act Metal Church and completed the remainder of the transatlantic tour of Europe, America, and Canada that had been halted by the bus accident the previous October. The bill sold thousands of tickets each night—during the months of delay, thrash metal's upsurge had wildly accelerated. "It was the time of my life," recalls Metal Church singer David Wayne. "Every night we were in an arena. The worst we played was like huge theaters. It was mind-boggling. It just blows you away to see that many screaming metal fans. Heavy metal was at its peak, and it was sweet, brother."

Soon *The $5.98 E.P., Garage Days Re-Revisited* presented Jason the new kid and several other changes to the masses. Released on August 21, 1987, the album was smartly titled after its retail price. This prevented record stores from selling the EP as a full-price new Metallica album, for which there was now substantial demand. All tracks on the record were cover versions of Metallica's favorite songs, continuing the practice begun when "Am I Evil?" and "Blitzkrieg" appeared on the import *Creeping Death*.

The $5.98 E.P. surprised the public with music by cult acts

Budgie, Killing Joke, Diamond Head, the Misfits, and Holocaust—associations that clearly set Metallica apart from hair metal superstars Mötley Crüe, who had just recorded Elvis Presley's "Jailhouse Rock." Diamond Head and Holocaust were classic NWOBHM bands, but obscurities in America: Budgie was an early-1970s English pub band with a heavy shot of Black Sabbath in its beer. Killing Joke helped define the evocative and macabre postpunk movement in Britain. By clear design none of these groups had anything to do with prevailing metal trends—the eclectic selections on *Garage Days* simply explained Metallica's heritage to fans and peeked into the band's current frame of mind.

As for the reject pile, Metallica had decided against material by other hardcore bands such as Discharge, as well as more songs by Diamond Head and the NWOBHM doom group Witchfinder General—though similiar selections trickled out continually on limited-release B-sides and imports. Cliff Burton had often half sarcastically mentioned a desire to play Lynyrd Skynyrd's "Free Bird," a generic rock anthem that would certainly have called for a raging Metallica overhaul. The band declined, though, to perform that familiar encore for their departed bassist.

Crossing into new commercial territory with a flurry of chart activity, the low-budget release *The $5.98 E.P., Garage Days Re-Revisited* immediately cracked the *Billboard* Hot 30, just as *Master of Puppets* was ending its seventy-two-week run on the album charts. In December 1987 *The $5.98 E.P.* was certified gold, proving that an unassuming and casual approach would keep fans by Metallica's side as the band became more dangerously popular. January 1988 brought the Elektra reissue of *Kill 'Em All*. Now widely promoted, the band's debut LP took its own place in *Billboard* five years after it was first released as a hastily financed independent dark horse.

In December 1987 Metallica released *Cliff 'Em All*, a video collection of camcorder bootlegs and television appearances highlighted by several eye-opening free-form bass solos by Burton. In do-it-yourself fashion the footage was gathered mostly on the cheap from underground videotape traders. Nonetheless, the tape went platinum, with Burton's share of the royalties going to his parents, Jan and Ray Burton. As a measure of its wide appeal, the band was surprised to receive a number of letters from kids upset to see Burton smoking weed on *Cliff 'Em All*. The message was clear: The quartet was no longer playing only to its peers—now there was a younger generation expecting to look up to Metallica as role models.

Regrouped emotionally and refitted for action, the members of Metallica found that in absentia their popularity had grown exponentially. Not quite yet a household name, the band was on the brink of the kind of success enjoyed by former foils like Quiet Riot and Ratt—Los Angeles glam bands now several albums into their careers, still selling multiplatinum but clearly running out of time. Rising above the now vast and rich heavy metal underground, Metallica was on the verge of destroying a host of heavy metal clichés with a distinguished, grand-scale rebuttal, crowning the heavy metal 1980s with a master's thesis on heaviness.

With the greatest expectations, Metallica imported Danish engineer Flemming Rasmussen to a Los Angeles studio in January 1988 to record its first studio album in almost two years. Working from rough tapes of guitar riffs, the team spent the winter months twiddling knobs, intent on the meticulous work of outdoing its fantastic three-album rise. Revealing commercial desires, the band first tried recording with Guns N' Roses producer Mike Clink—but reverted to Rasmussen after bristling under the suggestions of a "golden-eared" studio professional with no experience in the trenches of real metal. Guided well by its management team at Q Prime, Metallica seemed to be succeeding beyond conventional advice. If the band's next effort went platinum with no radio, no MTV, and no gimmicks, Metallica would not be just a gritty alternative to glam metal—they would be its replacement.

The fourth Metallica album was finished by early summer, but its release was delayed until after a blockbuster twenty-six-date summer American stadium tour with Van Halen, Scorpions, Dokken, and Kingdom Come, dubbed "Monsters of Rock." If Metallica's fifty-five-minute sets had put Ozzy Osbourne through his paces every night of the six-month *Ultimate Sin* journey in 1986, it was par for the course—the crowd only loved Ozzy more for offering the extra value of a great opener. The story was different in 1988, as Metallica absolutely stole the show. What was supposed to be a powerhouse bill combining the best of heavy metal transformed into a passing of the baton from heavyweights and lightweights alike to Metallica, the band in a class of its own.

The massive events grossed more than $1 million in ticket sales nightly, yet Van Halen was routinely facing vacant seats at the end of the night after satisfied fans left early. "It's just a simple fact of life on this tour," notes Lars Ulrich. In fact, more fans went home from Monsters of Rock with Metallica T-shirts than those of any other band, and rumors estimated Metallica sales above those of all four other acts combined. After the Ozzy tour *Master of Puppets* became Metallica's first gold record—during the Monsters tour it was bumped up to platinum. Said Van Halen singer Sammy Hagar to *Hit Parader:* "They'll be the new kings of rock, just you wait and see."

Finally, at the end of August 1988, the weighty double album *. . . And Justice for All* shipped to colossal response. Elongating the thrasher-era Metallica sound to its limit, the record bore more riffing force and less catchy songwriting than anything from the band since the never-ending side two of *Kill 'Em All.* If *The $5.98 E.P.* hinted at the band's expanded range of musical influences, *Justice* unveiled a strict continuation of Metallica's most basic tenets over an hour of long, brainy multipart epics. The songs shunned the guitar solos and catchy choruses of good-time heavy metal, yet instead of simple punk-influenced songwriting, the album steadfastly labored to maintain the band's precious integrity with drawn-out and strenuous song structures.

The new album suffered from the loss of a major musical dimension, Cliff Burton, who would likely have explored the thrash metal of *Master of Puppets* more deeply rather than simply extending its playing time. Furthermore, *Justice* appeared to have been produced under duress—the impaired mix obscured the bass entirely and inordinately favored the overproduced clack of Lars Ulrich's drums. The trademark rhythm guitars were buried, and headbangers had to reach for their tone controls at home in order to retrieve the gentle balance between subtlety and power. Yet in intensifying and laying bare its rhythmic riffing, Metallica conquered critics with musical gravity. "The band's breakneck tempos and staggering chops would impress even the most elitist jazz-fusion aficionado," gushed *Rolling Stone.* Not that the rock magazine of record had developed a curious new appreciation for thrash metal—two weeks earlier it dismissed Slayer's masterfully mixed pace of *South of Heaven* as "genuinely offensive Satanic drivel."

As hoped, the subject matter of *Justice* was exceedingly serious, displaying an enlightened social outlook gleaned from hardcore punk. "Blackened" cursed the blighting of the natural environment, while ". . . And Justice for All" decried the failure of the judicial system. The somewhat tender and religious "To Live Is to Die" used riffs and lyrics written by Cliff Burton. "Dyer's Eve" revealed the lapsed Christian Scientist in James Hetfield, the song tingling with pain from a family in which discipline always trumped emotion. "Probably about half our fans actually think about it; the rest just like the heaviness of the music," Jason Newsted told AP of Metallica's lauded lyrics. "When the chorus comes around, they know the words, that's about it. The other half really looks into it, and gets their heavy, heavy interpretations. They tend to overanalyze. I like it better when they get involved with what the song is actually about, but as long as they are happy listening to the music, that's my main concern."

Nearly every major U.S. newspaper rushed to recognize this intelligent "new" alloy of heavy metal called thrash metal. Headlines found the metal front lines as the *New York Times* noted Metallica's HEAVY METAL, WEIGHTY WORDS. The *Washington Post* gauged METALLICA'S PLATINUM OVERDRIVE; THE BAND AND ITS HIGH-DECIBEL DEPARTURE FROM THE HEAVY METAL MIND-SET. Most dramatically, former hometown paper the *Los Angeles Times* cooed over METALLICA AND POETRY OF THE POWER CHORD; THE NEW METAL IS SOUL MUSIC FOR SUBURBAN WHITE BOYS.

Sonic shortcomings and adamant heft notwithstanding, the unrelenting *Justice* immediately became the first Metallica record to enter the *Billboard* Top 10. Nearly eight years after its birth, Metallica had suddenly arrived at mainstream cool, becoming a behemoth among birds of a lighter feather. "It says that we can still do what we want, and people like it," a bewildered Newsted told AP. "I can't really fathom it. It's a weird thing to look at *Billboard* and see it amongst Whitney Houston and INXS." Propelled quickly past longlooming milestones, *Justice* was simultaneously certified gold and platinum on Halloween 1988, only nine weeks after its release. The

ambitious double album went on to sell 7 million copies and counting, one of the most ardent and unsympathetic musical successes
ever recorded.

As Metallica thrashed toward respectability with teeth bared, the
band's compatriots were finding their own visions of maturity. Holy
Terror and Testament had begun injecting sophisticated melodic
twists into Bay Area–style thrash metal after *Master of Puppets*. Now
Slayer, whose *Reign in Blood* staked the heart of the high-speed extreme the previous year, returned in 1987 with *South of Heaven*, daring to play slowly. Rather than pursue the sweltering Napalm Death
grindcore brigade into sheer rapid-fire oblivion, *South of Heaven*
paced the band's terrific twin-guitar riffing down to the more percepti-
ble speeds of its Judas Priest roots. With that shift Slayer produced a
durable and multifaceted masterpiece on par with Priest's *Sad Wings
of Destiny* and earned a like share of respectability.

The masters of thrash metal absorbed the lessons of hardcore
punk and moved onward and upward, while the underground shot off
toward sonic oblivion and destinations unknown. At the peak of heavy
metal's most successful hour, there was room in the commercial arena
for creative music expressed in elegant and well-considered ways. The
metal scene had already proved it could produce bands that were exponentially more punishing, but the most brilliant of contemporary
metal was coming now from the synthesis of tradition with radical new
influences. As Tony Iommi once said of Black Sabbath, "We thought
it would kill the band if we weren't allowed to grow up within it."

In the late 1980s, heady metal efforts by Celtic Frost and Voivod
brought eclecticism, experimentation, and astounding elements of
maturity. Always ravenous for progress, Celtic Frost had taken vast
strides in three brief years since forming from the rubble of Hellhammer. For 1987's *Into the Pandemonium* the band spent four wintry
months in a Berlin studio recording with classical musicians and opera
singers. Joining graveyard thrash with choirs, Latin percussion, and
synthesizers, the Swiss trio intrigued fans and terrified their business
partners. "Our label, Noise Records, was an upstart company that
wanted to have the heaviest band in the world," says Tom Warrior.

"When we told them we were going to do a really avant-garde album, they didn't know what the hell that meant. It was the time of Exodus, Metallica, Slayer, and Anthrax, and the company expected that."

Instead *Into the Pandemonium* introduced drum machines and samplers on "One (In Their Pride)," a protoindustrial track that nodded to Belgium's Front 242. "The dance track threw me for a little while, and I'm probably not the only one," says Nuclear Assault bassist Dan Lilker. "But I think by then some of the stuff that Frost had been doing on *To Mega Therion* with female vocals and orchestration got people ready for some of the avant-garde stuff." Indeed— as Metallica proved with platinum sales of an album loaded with eight-minute epics—the metal market was affording bands unprecedented leeway.

Subverting the craze for thrash metal overhauls instigated by Metallica's *$5.98 E.P.*, Celtic Frost offered an unlikely rendition of the new wave hit "Mexican Radio" by Wall of Voodoo. When Noise Records representatives finally made it to the studio to listen to the work-in-progress, all they heard was the sound of their own financial ruin. "Instead of taking the risk, they tried to force us to change," says Warrior, "but the album had already cost too much, and it was impossible to change anything. At the time nobody knew if that would sell, but nowadays, of course, *Pandemonium* is the key album of the band."

Equals to Celtic Frost in staunch individuality, their Noise Records labelmates Voivod made the transition sublimely from subterranean noise-mongers to post–thrash metal sophisticates. First appearing alongside Hellhammer on *Metal Massacre V,* the band went from noisy Motörhead worship on their 1984 debut, *War and Pain*, to a clean yet heavy, polyrhythmic science-fiction slam four years later. From its icy stronghold in Montreal, the French-speaking band brilliantly indicted humanity's technology-driven alienation and fear of the unfamiliar. The fourth album, 1988's *Dimension Hatross*, represented the progressive pinnacle of their evolution, as booming drums battered mind-expanding layers of extended guitar chords within a heavy mechanical system. Their meticulous music emulated the cacophony of a landscape of competing factories, yet its human spirit was overwhelming.

Epitomizing metal's search for enhanced sensory experience,

Voivod dwelled deep within the alternate universe summoned by its music. Drummer Michael Langevin, aka Away, was a talented visual artist influenced by the French illustrators of *Métal Hurlant* magazine. Away himself created every Voivod album cover and experimented with early computer animation in videos for *Dimension Hatross*. "We were always talking about different things," says Voivod vocalist Denis Belanger, aka Snake, "reading books that give us ideas and reading science-fiction magazines like *Omni*. We tried to mix fiction with reality in the Voivod concept, and then those three things move in and out of each other. Music is for feeling different than normal life, and that's what I expect."

The generation that grew up with heavy metal was now entering college, and was ready for innovative sounds and ideas. As major label MCA Records tapped Voivod in 1989, the band's fifth LP, *Nothingface*, featured a more conventional sound and a minor hit with a cover of Pink Floyd's "Astronomy Domine." Turned on its side, the familiar song attracted new listeners to Voivod's strange inventions. As Pink Floyd brought new possibility to rock and roll music twenty years earlier, so Voivod injected giant brains into metal—while still charged with ample energy to raise the hairs of the average thrasher. As with prior Voivod albums, *Nothingface* touched on the big themes of civilization's being anointed and ultimately tainted by technology. The songs "Pre-Ignition" and "Missing Sequences" described a mythical kind of metal poisoning in robots while alluding to the real-life epidemic of aluminum-related Alzheimer's disease along the St. Lawrence Seaway coursing through Montreal.

Even the glam scene was showing signs of sophistication, sprouting bands like Tesla and Extreme to counterbalance its chain saw–wielding novelty acts like Jackyl. In 1985, a less welcoming time for complex metal, arguments over commercial direction had split apart Mercyful Fate, one of the creative treasures of the early 1980s. Only a few years later guitarist Hank Shermann's mainstream direction had already proved self-defeating—while vocalist King Diamond charted in *Billboard* by continuing the gothic horror of Mercyful Fate. Drawing from classic heavy metal ghost stories, King Diamond also nodded to thrash metal by dealing with social issues, which he dubbed "life philosophy"—the mysteries of human relations. His 1987 album, *Abigail*, was an eighteenth-century horror tale fraught with contemporary relevance. "It deals with what you'd call bastard children, children born out of marriage," he says. "Children who are looked down upon because they don't have both mom and dad. Like when Vice President Quayle had this brilliant comment that all children should have a mom and a dad."

King Diamond sang of witches with the understanding that in many parts of Europe in the 1800s "witches" were merely unmarried women. "That story of *Abigail* was inspired by what happened to my own mama," he explains. "My real grandmother—the bitch, she really was—she was a servant in a professor's house in Denmark, and the professor's son got her pregnant. It was like scandal, scandal—she must have the child somewhere else. My mother was raised by a nice family, but later on she got in contact with my grandmother and went to a different part of Denmark to take care of her when she got ill. One day the neighbor came over, and my mom overheard a conversation: 'Who is that nice lady who is staying with you these days?' My grandmother said, 'Oh, it's just an old friend.' She didn't even admit or recognize that she had a daughter. There's a lot of deep stuff behind every song we do, and to raise these questions affects everyone."

Soon, not only the Big Four bands—Metallica, Slayer, Megadeth, and Anthrax—but also second-rung ringers like Exodus, King Diamond, Metal Church, and Testament were populating the *Billboard* charts and increasingly in need of professional support. As the entire thrash metal scene graduated to the big leagues, MTV finally set aside a half-hour segment of *Headbangers Ball* for those bands, and corporate magazines like *Creem Thrash Metal* were launched to publicize the bands to a national audience. Suddenly, independent labels like Metal Blade and Megaforce coped with album sales surging into the hundreds of thousands.

For many years specialty metal companies had been family operations. Now these entrepreneurs went legit, forming alliances with major labels as they retained contractual ties to graduating bands. "Johnny Z was like a metal trader on the stock market, and Marsha Zazula worked for Mattel," says former Megaforce Records publicist Maria Ferraro. "They knew nothing about the music business. We learned everything from the bottom up, and that's the best way. Using your wits and your taste instead of just throwing the big money around."

The success of Metallica indicated that the future was not in Hollywood glam metal—major labels would now be forced to court underground tastemakers instead of tinkering with formulas. Consequently the independent operators who were big fish in the underground pond found themselves fending off sharks from the mainstream music industry. They were holding hot tickets, and their assets looked attractive to scavengers. "In the late eighties and early nineties, when metal was really huge," Brian Slagel of Metal Blade recalls, "the majors were spending so much money it was hard to compete with them. We had fifteen or twenty different employees move on to majors. It was almost the same as with a band, where you find them, develop them, and they become some big thing."

From college radio, fanzine editors, and bedroom labels, an entire cottage industry developed. The CMJ Music Marathon, a struggling yearly conference allowing college radio programmers a glimpse into the music industry and its expense accounts, added a metal marathon tailored to the two hundred American radio stations with metal specialty shows. The promotions firm Concrete Marketing, founded to hype metal records to stores and radio, soon launched the Foundations Forum—an annual metal trade show in Los Angeles. The business of selling metal had its own tricks. Unlike pop music, whose audience did not mind being told what to think, heavy metal fans were incredibly keyed to musical affairs and thus much harder to influence. Savvy labels such as Roadrunner and Combat experimented with cracking the codes of the underground through street-marketing techniques—like circulating advance tracks from upcoming releases on cassettes designed to look like demo tapes.

In the performance realm thrash metal soon gained its own annual concert festival in America, when Milwaukee Metalfest emerged in answer to yearly European outings like Holland's earthquaking Aardschok fest and England's mammoth Monsters of Rock at Castle Donnington. Organized by the same concert promoter who brought Raven and Metallica to the Midwest in 1983, the first Milwaukee Metalfest in 1987 featured King Diamond along with Nuclear Assault, Hallow's Eve, At War, Sacrifice, Trouble, Death Angel, Death,

Zoetrope, and Kublai Khan, a band featuring ex–Megadeth guitarist Greg Handevidt. It was a dream lineup—though many other unconfirmed bands publicized before the show were only a pipe dream. "Because of the size of the hall, it was any thrash band's nightmare," adds Dan Lilker of Nuclear Assault. "If you played any faster than a power metal band, it was a total washout. There was a bunch of gear up there all day that everyone had been hammering away on. But we saw people and friends from all around the world. We'd always heard about festivals in Europe, like at Dynamo, but we didn't have them here. Obviously it was a different thing culturally—in Europe people aren't as spoiled. They'll sleep in a dirty pit in the mud for three days."

Large and frequent tours had been the backbone of heavy metal, insulating Judas Priest, Iron Maiden, and Dio against the demands of commercial radio. Now the regimen of touring tested Anthrax, Megadeth, Slayer, and Metallica. They had risen through the ranks of tape trading and were now in some cases headlining their own stadium tours and dealing with seasoned crews in established venues. As Nuclear Assault found itself sharing a record label with R.E.M., Dan Lilker remembers the shift—from punk clubs to showcase gigs for music-industry lifers with ponytails and satin jackets. "We dealt with that whole polished thing, but we just giggled a little bit and took it with a grain of salt," he says. "It just made it interesting, meeting people like that."

Having savored its resistance long enough, Metallica finally filmed its first video for MTV during the first week of December 1988—late in the game, considering that the album had already gone platinum. The seven-and-a-half-minute "One" was a far cry from typical fare by Mötley Crüe or Poison, which relied on strippers, scarves, and shaving-cream fights for visual interest. A long, grim effort by a band powerful enough to dictate its terms, "One" combined stark black-and-white band footage with scenes from Dalton Trumbo's 1971 film *Johnny Got His Gun*. Thus continued the antiwar theme of *Ride the Lightning*'s "For Whom the Bell Tolls" and *Master of Puppets*' "Disposable Heroes"—and the critical acclaim.

However tasteful and poignant its first rock video, Metallica had entered the entertainment mainstream. Inevitable reactionary responses followed in metal circles, the first notes of a backlash. "People overestimate Metallica because they're Metallica," said S.O.D. singer Billy Milano. "The whole thing is, Sabbath had that sound fourteen years ago. Twelve years ago they were rocking out heavier than anything today. You can't even get heavier than Sabbath. Sabbath was the rudimentary of everything."

Unquestionably Metallica was a bona fide sensation, but flak from the punters only compelled them to stay grounded—to resist the temptation to let success go to their heads. After all, what would Cliff Burton think? As he said in an interview segment from the *Cliff 'Em All* video—itself now multiplatinum—"We're not trying to be something big and fancy. It's just us, doing what we do. Let's keep it that way."

Yet while bullet belts and flying hair once provided enough visual excitement, Metallica was now challenged with the logistical problems of entertaining hundreds of thousands of new fans as a headlining stadium act. "We don't need fifty-feet-tall dragons to sell our tickets," Lars Ulrich insisted to *Kerrang!*, but soon James Hetfield adopted Glenn Danzig's black jeans, wrist gauntlets, and sleeveless black shirts as the band streamlined its anti-image to meet arena-size expectations. Though many show-business traditions went against the band's ethic, Metallica soon developed a large-scale stage set. Befitting the group's op-ed page–inspired lyrics, the stage included a towering faux marble statue representing *Justice*, which crumbled in ruins at the end of each night, leaving audiences to contemplate the decaying state of America's judicial institutions.

With wider recognition King Diamond's budget also finally grew to meet his aspirations. His 1988 *Them* tour saw the mystic metaler dragging a Broadway-like stage show to theaters across America. Incorporating an actress to play the dual role of scantily clad heroine Missy and her hobbling grandma, the ghostly production traveled with a two-story haunted house set, a wheelchair, a teapot, and many pounds of pyrotechnics. All of this entertaining hoopla was topped off by a ten-minute medley of Mercyful Fate songs—a strange treatment of sacrosanct metal classics later aped by Metallica. If thrash metal someday engendered a Las Vegas casino show, King Diamond would be the fake-blood-drinking emcee—wearing his black top hat and waving his trademark bone cross mic stand, like a showman's cane.

❧ ✦✦✦✦✦✦✦ ❧

The timing of songs about economic inequality and the justice system could not be better, as thrash metal continued to appeal to an America that was ready to face sober reality. As recession and covert wars came alive after ten years of relative prosperity, the country started to demand music that faced troubled times with strong emotion and spirit. Even the masters of fantasy were turning to lyrics that smacked of social realism. "I couldn't tell people 'go have a dream, it'll come true,'" says Ronnie James Dio, "because dreams weren't coming true for anybody."

The social message of Metallica's . . . *And Justice for All* was mirrored in another critically acclaimed 1988 album, Public Enemy's rap music masterpiece, *It Takes a Nation of Millions to Hold Us Back*. Vocalists Chuck D and William Drayton, aka Flavor Flav, depicted their own bleak impression of American justice, with the band staring defiantly from behind prison bars on the album cover. Public Enemy even name-checked Anthrax in songs with heavy-sounding titles like "Bring the Noise" and "Black Steel in the Hour of Chaos."

Produced by the innovative Bomb Squad, the music of Public Enemy showcased a nearly orchestral level of layered digital samples, including a bite borrowed from "Angel of Death" by their Def Jam labelmates Slayer. "The particular style of *It Takes a Nation of Millions* came from what [Def Jam founder] Rick Rubin had already done with Run-DMC," says Chuck D. "We just upped the ante into even crazier music. We liked aggressive shit, and we could rock over anything. The Slayer sample in 'She Watch Channel Zero' put a forceful theme to it. My voice with its power and also Flavor's voice with its power on the treble side were able to cut through the noise. We were never afraid of any sound or any type of music."

Debuting in 1988 with *Straight Outta Compton*, the rap group NWA could be considered the Slayer to Public Enemy's Metallica, advocating aggression instead of circumspection. Like Slayer, their albums required PMRC–approved parental-advisory labels, though NWA willingly recorded clean versions for wider sales. At least one

NWA lyric reacted to a ban on the band by commercial black radio and MTV with familiar Metallica-style defiance: "Fuck crossover to them, let them cross over to us." In heavy metal vernacular: The posers must die.

Like Metallica and its Megaforce Records colleagues, NWA first climbed to platinum sales via independent albums popularized through word of mouth. This harder-edged rap music was a reality check that paralleled the resistant stance of heavy metal in many ways, boasting angry lyrical content and prompting fearful response from the powers in control. "Megaforce was built on metal," says Chuck D. "It would be defiant, and it would be against the status quo, and it would be, 'Fuck that and fuck this.' [Indie rap labels] Def Jam and Ruthless built themselves off different ideals, but they were similar. Independence, defiance . . . machoism. It's like, 'I ain't gonna bow down and do things the way everybody else does. We're going to make our own mark.' I dug that rebelliousness."

As heavy metal was frequently dismissed on the basis of its fluffy MTV personalities, rap music was widely mocked on the basis of Top 40 offerings by lightweights like MC Hammer and the Van Halen–sampling Tone Loc. Yet across these stereotypes the heavy metal and hip-hop scenes had long been eyeballing each other with curiosity and admiration. *Wheels of Steel* was the title of a Saxon album way before becoming common parlance for a pair of DJ turntables, and the hardest early mixes by Grandmaster Flash and DJ Afrika Bambaata were built on a foundation of essential breakbeats from Black Sabbath and AC/DC records. The 1987 Boogie Down Productions anthem "Dope Beat" consisted of leader KRS-One rapping over the familiar intro riff juggled from two copies of AC/DC's "Back in Black." As samplers became prevalent, rapper Ice-T based the title track to his 1987 debut, *Rhyme Pays*, on Black Sabbath's "War Pigs" and later created "Midnight" on the ominous foundation of "Black Sabbath" itself. The influential Jungle Brothers based a track from their second LP on Bill Ward's crisp drum break from "Behind the Wall of Sleep" on *Black Sabbath*.

Perhaps the worst aspect of rap music was that in the 1990s its enormous success began to lure talented African-American musicians away from heavy metal. Though stereotyped as "white music," heavy metal itself was a voice from outside the dominant culture, and in its world race distinctions would always be secondary to talent. The original drummer of Judas Priest, Chris Campbell, was a black Englishman. Thin Lizzy's revered leader, Phil Lynott, was as black as he was Irish. Metallica's first lead guitarist, Lloyd Grant, the only band member who could play the guitar solo for "Hit the Lights" on *Metal Massacre*, was Jamaican. Needless to say, the race of performers was only one aspect of the equation—never especially relevant to the metal spirit.

The multiracial influence on metal's development was remarkably diverse, if not entirely color blind—even guitarist Slash of the proud rednecks Guns N' Roses had an African-American mother. Two black musicians from Chicago helped found that city's thrash metal scene: towering seven-foot guitarist Ian Tafoya of Znowhite, and denim-bedecked bassist Calvin Humphrey of Zoetrope. In Cleveland, Ohio, a revered all-black power metal band crushed posers under the tongue-in-cheek name Black Death.

Underground legend Katon W. DePena of Hirax—a one-man letter-writing hurricane—kept his unusual soaring vocal attack as Hirax developed from power metal to metalcore style. When asked about his unique voice, he cited the 1950s soul singer Sam Cooke as a primary inspiration. On the commercial front there was L.A.'s Sound Barrier, and later the platinum-selling New York group Living Colour. The technical shred-master Tony MacAlpine was among the elite members of the 1980s guitar-god pantheon, inspired by the fretboard voice of Jimi Hendrix.

<hr/>

Naturally, metal musicians in the United States began to explore rap music—taking creative risks alongside foreign bands Voivod and Celtic Frost. Once again, Anthrax arrived at this critical juncture. Anthrax could never seem to resist a new diversion—besides dabbling with punk in S.O.D., the band loved to show off outside interests like skateboarding and comic books. Amid the band's pile of gold albums, the sole platinum success was *I'm the Man*, a 1988 novelty EP of metal-injected rapping that followed a lower-profile collaboration with R&B rappers UTFO. Anthrax was aware of the surrounding musical climate "almost sometimes to their disadvantage," says later singer

HARDCORE RAP

Coming at heavy metal from a different angle, hardcore rap acts in New York and Los Angeles were building tough records from scraps found on Black Sabbath and AC/DC slabs. Rappers were initially toastmasters, who entertained crowds at street parties in the late 1970s while DJs spun records together to form new songs. By the late 1980s the approaches of the MCs and the DJs had become much more sophisticated, turning to digital-sampling technology and opening up a new world for recording. Public Enemy sampled Slayer, and The Geto Boys soon introduced murderous lyrics lifted from the same splatter movies as death metal.

Sounds of the Streets

❖ Boogie Down Productions, *Criminal Minded* (1987)
❖ The Geto Boys, *The Geto Boys* (1990)
❖ Grandmaster Flash and the Furious Five, *The Message* (1982)
❖ Ice Cube, *AmeriKKKa's Most Wanted* (1990)
❖ Ice-T, *Power* (1988)
❖ Kool Moe Dee, *Kool Moe Dee* (1986)
❖ NWA, *Straight Outta Compton* (1988)
❖ Onyx, *Bacdafucup* (1993)
❖ Public Enemy, *It Takes a Nation of Millions to Hold Us Back* (1988)
❖ Schoolly D, *The Adventures of Schoolly D* (1987)

John Bush. "They were rapping, and they did [the Native American protest song] 'Indians,' which merged two different types of music together when that wasn't a trendy thing to do. They're always ahead of popular thinking—that's what happens with people who are overly intelligent."

But the brainiest union of thrash metal and rap influences was San Francisco's Faith No More, featuring a black front man, a gay keyboard player, and a gun-toting guitarist who had grown up with Cliff Burton. Faith No More's sarcastic 1987 college radio hit, "We Care a Lot," was an oddity that dared bridge the gap between S.O.D. and lighter funk music. The strange synthesizer-based band benefited tremendously from the patronage of local allies Metallica, who trumpeted the band's unorthodox appeal at every opportunity. One critic joked that James Hetfield sporting a band's shirt on stage—or, in Faith No More's case, on the back cover of *The $5.98 E.P.*—was worth 100,000 record sales.

Tiring of a regime of speed and violence, other San Francisco thrashers adapted mosh music to make it suitable for less violent forms of dancing. Exodus released a cover of War's funky "Low Rider," and some Exodus members dabbled in drum-machine jams with Jason Newsted. As Tres Gringos, they prepared a never-released side-project record called *Funk You*. With the syncopated rhythmic orientation of thrash metal, the transition was surprisingly easy. Leaving progressive thrashers Blind Illusion, bassist Les Claypool recruited Possessed guitarist Larry Lalonde for the party band Primus, a vehicle for Claypool's vast repertoire of quirky cartoon voices and banjo-style bass playing. Though he had been deemed too proficient to join Metallica, Claypool now found an eager audience as he quick-fired popcorn bass riffs in a Slayer-like flurry.

Soon the eclectic mingling of aggression and grooves became a trend, as the likes of Limbomaniacs and Mind Funk issued less welcome adventures in funk metal. Formed and named in the mid-1980s after a King Arthur character, the lightweight thrash act Mordred later rerecorded Rick James's "Super Freak," adding turntable effects and scratching by Aaron Vaughn, aka DJ Pause. Though seemingly incongruous, his tough rapper garb—Chess King black leather jacket, skullcap, and heavy gold jewelry—was not that different from the leather and spikes of a hardcore headbanger. Regardless, the outcome was painfully undercooked, lampooning the clichés of rap and metal instead of forging the two into anything worthwhile.

Early missteps aside, the convergence of rap and metal was a likely eventuality. If approximately 20 million metal records and 8 million rap albums were sold in 1989, many were landing on the same record players. No matter how major-label marketing departments tried to slice up the demographics, listeners were not living in a vacuum, nor were they limiting their musical choices. The coming decade would see a vast development of groove-oriented metal in America, culminating with immense mainstream popularity in the late 1990s. At the close of the decade, however, Faith No More was enough to demonstrate that many thrashers had outgrown their denim and leather jackets and were changing into something new.

While enjoying multiplatinum sales of its thrash opus . . . *And Justice for All*, Metallica widened the focus of contemporary metal, bringing on the road innovative metal hybrids like Faith No More, the Cult, Queensryche, and Soundgarden. Save for Queensryche—the Seattle band whose brainy exploits were already a far cry from its black leather origins—these were bands from entirely outside the metal pecking order, largely unknown to the underground. None played metal in the spiked-wristband sense of the term. "Some people think heaviness is distortion, loud volume, or kicking drums," Soundgarden's Kim Thayil told *Sheet Metal*. "They all may have a place in warranting a heavy sound, but above all it's got to be mind-bending."

Soon *Kerrang!* felt it needed a new mandate befitting the changing times, and countless pages once dedicated to Saxon and Iron Maiden were revamped

The real thing: Faith No More in 1989
(Concrete)

FUNK METAL

The syncopated rhythms of thrash metal mixed well with the layered drum rhythms of hardcore rap music. For anyone inspired to overlay the two, the pair was a match made in heaven. In the rush to recombine the differing styles, however, funk metal often became a slipshod fallback for bands tired of copying Metallica. Primus, whose complex songwriting advanced over several humor-laced albums, survived the brief trend. Faith No More leaned more heavily on its rock side over time. The glad-handing Mind Funk, Limbomaniacs, and Mordred all bit the dust. But ten years later MTV viewers would learn that those who do not learn from history are doomed to tune down and repeat it.

Dancing Fools

❖ Anthrax, *I'm the Man* (1987)
❖ Faith No More, *Introduce Yourself* (1987)
❖ Fishbone, *Truth & Soul* (1988)
❖ Infectious Grooves, *The Plague That Makes Your Booty Move* (1991)
❖ Limbomaniacs, *Stinky Grooves* (1990)
❖ Mind Funk, *Mind Funk* (1991)
❖ Mordred, *Fools Game* (1989)
❖ Primus, *Frizzle Fry* (1990)
❖ Red Hot Chili Peppers, *The Uplift Mofo Party Plan* (1987)
❖ 24-7 Spyz, *Gumbo Millennium* (1990)

and surrendered to Metallica, Faith No More, and occasionally Napalm Death, the pulse of the underground. As the introduction of new singer Mike Patton in 1989 ushered in a more streamlined sound, Faith No More's *The Real Thing* became a sleeper hit, sneaking up on *Billboard* one year after its release. Wrote *Kerrang!*, "It was finally the album to smash down the walls after a decade of generally average banality. Faith No More had made Metal something great again."

Faith No More was certainly opening the windows and airing out the castle, but its panoramic perspective was founded on ten years of amazing, fist-waving advances. *Kerrang!* did a disservice to its heritage by throwing the baby out with the well-used bathwater. "*Kerrang!* in the early days was important, because it focused only on heavy metal music," says Ronnie James Dio. "They embraced Dio rapidly, and we were on the cover quite a few times. Then they decided we'd had enough success. Eventually *Kerrang!* became *Kerrap!* to a lot of people. I know the feelings Iron Maiden have about them. I don't think they'll play in England at all, just because of the British press. I think the good writers went away, and the guys who had been making the tea became the writers."

These new realities were scary. Dio's tour for *Sacred Heart* was voted Best Stage Production in the mid-1980s by the concert-industry magazine *Pollstar*, but in the age of Metallica's insouciant thrashing, the singer found his legendary dramatic flair mocked by uppity metal magazines. "As the media is wont to do, especially the British press, they tore us right down," Dio says. "We got so soured on hearing them complain about our dragon that we said, 'Fine, just think of all the money we can save.' So Maiden stopped presenting big stages, we stopped doing it, Priest stopped doing it—just because I think we felt really slighted that we were trying to give so much more and the press just kept castigating us so much."

Unruly press notwithstanding, any band was destined for early retirement when it took its popularity for granted in an increasingly volatile and competitive musical form. "A lot of people were very successful during the 1980s, like Judas Priest and Iron Maiden and Motörhead," notes Dave Mustaine of Megadeth, "and a lot of them, sadly, have fallen by the wayside, because for whatever reason they weren't really willing to modernize their music."

Even bands with ears closer to the ground fell out of step with the pace of change. Raven stuck it out in America for the entirety of the 1980s without experiencing massive success. After being groomed into oblivion and eventually dropped from Atlantic Records, they regrouped on the indie Combat Records, eager to relive early NWOBHM glories with a small company. "Initially it sounded great," recalls John Gallagher. "We really wanted to push the hard-end stuff. The people at Combat were saying, 'Yeah, Raven [was] commercial, but they're back.' But we got caught in between the pop metal bands and the hardcore thrash like Slayer, and it was miserable."

At the close of the 1980s the towers of traditional heavy metal were crumbling. Returning to Europe, Metallica outsold Iron Maiden in Belgium threefold. "The day there ain't no Iron Maiden to spearhead British music is the day heavy metal takes a swift downward pitch in this green and pleasant land of ours," wrote Howard Johnson in *Kerrang!* in 1989. Yet as Margaret Thatcher was deposed in 1990, so waned Iron Maiden's breed of dissent. Longtime singer Bruce Dickinson left the band in 1992 to spend time with his family. In semiretirement he recorded an election-year novelty single with Rowan Atkinson, aka Mr. Bean, and authored two comic novels, *The Adventures of Lord Iffy Boatrace* and *The Missionary Position: The Further Adventures of Lord Iffy*—detailing the exploits of a cross-dressing English nobleman.

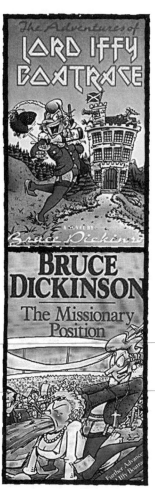

Paper maiden:
Bruce Dickinson's books

Though sales remained steady, by 1989 the guitar solos, crowd sing-alongs, and stage pageantry of traditional British heavy metal lost its glory in comparison to the vibrant colors of a brave new world. After years at battle the pivotal British band Saxon took a two-year hiatus, to be replaced at the front lines by young reinforcements. "Our record company and management wanted us to adapt even more to the American market," notes Saxon vocalist Biff Byford tartly, "but you can't sell Coca-Cola to the Americans." Their decade-plus careers had outlasted disco and punk, but now heavy metal's old guard was being put out to pasture.

⊱⊱⊱⊱⊱⊱❋⊰⊰⊰⊰⊰⊰

For the next generation, the 1990s beckoned with hints of creative renewal and no signs of weakening in the unprecedented base of support. At the close of Metallica's marathon 140-city 1989 tour of North America, the band's numbers were incredible—grossing more than $21 million, it ranked seventh in the annual *Pollstar* tally of box-office receipts, behind blockbusters like the Rolling Stones, The Who, and the Grateful Dead. Metallica had risen to the very top of heavy metal and was mobilizing for the next big step toward world domination.

At the 1989 Grammy Awards, where the band performed live to fanatic applause, Metallica was nominated in the brand-new Best Metal Performance category alongside Jane's Addiction, Iggy Pop, AC/DC, and Jethro Tull. The new category was a nod to heavy metal's huge popularity, yet after a decade of platinum albums by metal acts, the music business still fostered metal's outsider status by flubbing even the most basic attempts at recognition. Groans were audible in the theater and disbelief echoed across the country, as presenter Lita Ford opened the envelope to reveal that the winners were Jethro Tull—aging deliverers of fanciful flutes and concept records. Metallica's sales figures got it in the door, but the music industry's concept of heavy metal still dated to a time before even Black Sabbath existed.

Ten years after *Metal Massacre*, Metallica remained an underdog, albeit on a huge scale. From the dais of the 1989 MTV Video Awards, fellow musician Duff McKagen of Guns N' Roses acknowledged the greater significance of "One" even as he took home the Best Video prize for "Sweet Child O' Mine." Red-faced by the public reaction to their Jethro Tull gaffe, the thousands of recording engineers, lawyers, accountants, and show-business cronies comprising the Recording Academy took the next opportunity and voted "One" a Grammy for Best Metal Performance in February 1990. Metallica was finally graced with the laurels of legitimacy. To fans it was expected that the clueless establishment would hand out trophies to dinosaurs.

With a Grammy now in Metallica's hands, however, the days of one-star reviews for heavy metal bands were finally over.

Welcomed even where Judas Priest and Iron Maiden were not, Metallica took metal to a new level of respectability. Heavy metal could no longer be purely an outsider's paradise, a game of secret record stores and tape trader's treasure stashes. Heavy metal held the popular majority, and Metallica had become ambassador to the world outside the heavy metal parking lot. *Justice* had already sold more than 2 million copies in two years, and nearly every fan of heavy metal was now a Metallica loyalist. With the *New York Times* lauding its "fast, adrenaline-charged music," Metallica sought new sacred cattle to scorch.

XIII

Transforming the 1990s: The Black Album & Beyond

➤ **February 1990:** Metallica wins first Grammy

➤ **August 12, 1991:** Metallica Black Album debuts at #1 in *Billboard*

➤ **1992:** Rob Halford leaves Judas Priest, Bruce Dickinson leaves Iron Maiden

➤ **June 12, 1992:** Nirvana's *Nevermind* goes quadruple platinum in the United States

➤ **December 10, 1992:** Metallica Black Album goes sextuple platinum in the United States

Returning to the recording studio in the fall of 1990, Metallica departed drastically from the arc of its first four albums. As was evident from demo versions of new songs by Lars Ulrich and James Hetfield, the band had taken up the strenuous task of translating its innovative speed guitars and fluttering drums to the universal language of rock and roll. The pressure on the duo and their bandmates was great to broaden their appeal—but Metallica would lose everything if it sacrificed its identity.

Now accustomed to touring large arenas, what Metallica discovered about stadium acoustics was that fans could react well to the slow crunch of "For Whom the Bell Tolls" but were paralyzed by the fast-pinning spears of "Blackened." With that in mind the band crafted a thick sound befitting universal popularity—one that would carry to the back rows of big venues and punch through the speakers of tiny transistor radios. The product of these labors, *Metallica*, the Black Album, would eventually make the band a household name 50 million times over. It would turn America into a nation of headbangers—housewives, sailors, software programmers, major-league ballplayers, and all.

In creating the Black Album, the band compromised itself in carefully considered ways. Metallica had recorded . . . *And Justice for All* under its own authority, but was persuaded this time to hire Canadian producer Bob Rock, a hitmaker for Mötley Crüe and Bon Jovi. Rock had also previously recorded hardcore punks like the Subhumans around his native Vancouver, British Columbia. While *Justice* revealed the band's weakness for excess, Rock forced Metallica into an editing discipline to match their ambition, urging that they pare down songs to something—as James Hetfield noted—"quite a bit more simple."

As was obvious from the six-note opening call of "Enter Sandman," the entire rhythm structure was a departure from the signature thrashing that had been the band's bread and butter. Compared to the anthems of *Master of Puppets*, the new tracks were slightly slower in tempo and had half as many monster riffs per song. Instead of employing constant chugging, muted E-strings, Hammett and Hetfield let their guitar strings ring out clearly, emphasizing obvious, attention-grabbing melodic hooks while retaining the reliable NWOBHM formula of three riffs and a variation.

The two Metallica guitarists had played pretty acoustic song intros since *Ride the Lightning*. Now such moments extended to comprise whole songs, like "Nothing Else Matters," whose haunting landscape rang reminiscent of Iron Maiden's "Remember Tomorrow" and "Children of the Damned." Though song structures were simpler on the Black Album, the arrangements were not sparse. The Hammett and Hetfield guitar arsenal—twin Gibson Flying Vs already jettisoned in favor of more finessed ESP and Ibanez instruments—was augmented on "Nothing Else Matters" by twelve-string guitar, sitar, synthesizer, and the orchestral flourishes of conductor Michael Kamen, layered in lush and cinematic sound.

The more thrash metal bombast was cleared away, the more emotional heft was required of the group. One of the album's truest steps forward, "The Unforgiven" incorporated the epic western influence of Ennio Morricone's movie sound tracks, allowing James Hetfield to explore a newfound cowboy persona. While recording *Metallica*, Hetfield lost his voice and was instructed by a vocal coach on how to better manage this valuable asset. His distinctive gruff style had become one of the most recognizable and important ingredients in the Metallica sound—a far cry from the guitarist who sang only because no one else would take the job. Previous Metalli-ballads "Fade to Black" and "One" were already established tearjerkers for hardened hearts. Now a slew of more controlled and expressive tracks followed suit.

Instead of firing broadsides at monolithic targets, Metallica discovered that protest music could speak to the soul of the individual, especially those left to flounder by the culture at large. "Being a hardcore Metallica fan," says Shawn Crahan of the band Slipknot, "I totally respect the Black Album for the fact that Bob Rock made them search inside themselves and reach different demons that they were uncomfortable with. When you're going through your success, you need to evolve. I personally am a fan of when Hetfield reached deep inside. I really feel that. I think more people need to reinvent themselves for the bands that they love, instead of blaming it all on the musician."

On his third outing with the band, Jason Newsted came into his own. The impaired mix of . . . *And Justice for All* had rendered his bass inaudible, earning him the reputation of a greenhorn overwhelmed by headstrong and sometimes physically intimidating bandmates. Where Cliff Burton's bass had been a cool, black presence lurking beneath "Orion" and "The Call of Ktulu," Newsted's sound was impatiently aggressive, based on a forthright picking attack. While powerful, especially on "My Friend of Misery," his sole songwriting contribution, Newsted's notes usually stood in with the dominant riffs of the song—further streamlining the sound.

The genetic code of heaviness prevailed, yet a division emerged between fans who accepted the "Rock" influences and others upset that the band did not progress by continuing to push heavy metal further into new realms. After all, Metallica had not risen to multiplatinum sales on the strength of its smoothness—in clarifying their aims, the band cleansed itself of turmoil. As Toronto critic Martin Popoff unmercifully called the changes in his mixed review of the Black Album, "Bob Rock brings out the hidden Canadian mediocrity in a band over-correcting on their criminally complicated predecessor."

For the first time the underground's loyalty to Metallica was tested, and it emerged supportive within limits. "The record was a lot better than . . . *And Justice for All*, which I found very meandering and unsure of itself," says longtime ally Dan Lilker. "I was convinced those songs on *Justice* were too long and wandering, and there were riffs thrown in just for the sake of expanding the length. The Black record I really liked—it was a return to more direct songs. In my opinion it's the last good heavy record they have, but they can tell me to fuck off."

Willing to market its new sound with all available powers the band debuted an MTV video for "Enter Sandman" two weeks before the album's release. Reviewers gushed, but the approval of the press barely mattered. Metallica had become the rare kind of powerhouse celebrity that carved its own musical trends, bending the shape of the cultural curve to fit its trajectory. AC/DC's *Back in Black* LP charged the metal sound of the 1980s with the dark blues of "Hells Bells" and "You Shook Me All Night Long." Now Metallica's very similar-looking CD jolted the 1990s with the straight-ahead muscularity of "Nothing Else Matters" and "Enter Sandman." Released on August 12, 1991, *Metallica* entered the *Billboard* chart at number one and went double platinum two weeks later.

Much had changed during the year that Metallica spent in the recording studio. Video footage released from their soundproof interment showed Lars Ulrich malevolently tossing darts at a pinup poster of Kip Winger, whose light metal act, Winger, won a gold album in 1990. By the time *Metallica* was released the next year that bubblegum band had lost its flavor, and Winger was well on its way to breaking up in early 1993.

In a quick and savage reversal of fortune, MTV's hair metal had fallen flat, and as a result the overnight careers of bands like Warrant and Nelson dangled limply. The 1991 number-one *Billboard* debut of Skid Row's *Slave to the Grind* was the last gasp of the kind of heavy metal that spent too much time admiring itself in the mirror—inspiring a better-late-than-never *Rolling Stone* cover with singer Sebastian Bach posing beside the banner HEAVY METAL NATION. American heavy metal fans now sought the substance and realism that they found in James Hetfield's patented scowl. The colorful rebellion and fist-pumping schoolyard cheers of Twisted Sister and Quiet Riot suddenly seemed quaint.

Bye-bye to the bad boys of glam
(Deborah Laws/Metalflakes.com)

Nowhere was this shift more evident than in Los Angeles, as the powder-puff party went to wreckage overnight. "When we hit 1990 and 1991, music was changing, and it was difficult for bands like Stryper—especially for Stryper—to make that crossover," says Michael Sweet, singer of one of the most image-heavy L.A. bands. "We attempted that with *Against the Law*, and I think musically we achieved it, but I think as far as our persona and the way we came across, we failed. We went from being these happy guys who smiled and were filled with joy and peace to these guys who were trying to look tough and mean and bad. It just didn't work. After that, I just kind of saw all the signs."

Limiting its airplay of sleaze-minded Hollywood bands as awareness of AIDS and safe sex reached a public pinnacle, MTV's uneasy relationship with metal turned predatory. The network's animated series *Beavis & Butt-head* characterized metal fans as chortling dopes in search of cheap thrills.

Any perception of an overall heavy metal weakening, however, was the creation of television executives. After courting mainstream status throughout every phase of its rebellion, the underground was finally charging aboveground. Trading on the benefits of Metallica's major breakthrough, the remaining Big Four bands of thrash metal—Megadeth, Slayer, and Anthrax—embarked on the nationwide Clash of the Titans trek in 1991. Complete with loud, caustic jostling among rivals, the tour peaked during a sold-out night at New York's Madison Square Garden on June 28, proclaiming the arrival of a new heavy metal regime.

Following the success of the comic rap music detour, *I'm the Man*, Anthrax took a more serious stab at putting guitars to a beat in 1991, when it covered "Bring the Noise" by Public Enemy. "I mentioned Anthrax in the original 'Bring the Noise,'" notes Public Enemy leader Chuck D, "which they always thought was a compliment that came out of a gracious nowhere. So they repaid the favor, and to me it really was the beginning of rap music and rock really being on the same plane. In 1991 the fact that a thrash metal group was covering a rap record was a whole new thing. People considered rap records a novelty and not real shit. Step two was doing the video, and step three was being able to cut it live, which we did very well."

The high point of the genre-breaking tour by Anthrax and Public Enemy was a sold-out hometown show before 15,000 fans in New York. "I don't think Aerosmith respected Run-DMC enough to go around and perform 'Walk this Way' together live in 1986," says Chuck D. "So I decided in 1991 to pick up the gauntlet. Even with Anthrax thrashing their guitars through the number—when we got down live, I cut through that motherfucker like a buzz saw. George Clinton said, 'Damn, you're one of the few people I know that can bust a Marshall amp in the ass.'"

Appearing on the late-night *Arsenio Hall Show* in July 1992, Megadeth also highlighted a banner year with *Countdown to Extinction*, which topped out at number two in *Billboard*. Driven by the furor of leader Dave Mustaine, now a twelve-stepper in addiction recovery, the CD was a mellifluous and solid heavy metal vessel whose thrash metal roots came out in fast virtuoso breaks. Songs like "Foreclosure of a Dream," which dealt with the mortgage forfeiture of bassist Dave Ellefson's family farm in Minnesota, illustrated a dissatisfaction similar to Metallica's in more verbose prose, topped off with a sound bite from the reviled George Bush "read my lips—no new taxes" speech.

Heavy metal's issues were now in harmony with the country's concerns, and thrash metal's social criticism found its way out of the record stores. During the 1992 election season, Dave Mustaine reported on the Democratic National Convention for MTV. "I went with a guy from MTV News and a guy from [voting advocacy group] Rock the Vote," he says. "We went into the DNC, and we cornered people. I think it was being held at Madison Square Garden. We talked with Nebraska senator Bob Kerrey and the other candidates."

In a new role as celebrity activist for election-law reform, Mustaine joined a coalition pushing for simplified access to voter registration. The so-called Motor Voter legislation was credited with doubling the election-day turnout of young voters over the next ten years. "I met Gore and Clinton when the Motor Voter bill was signed," Mustaine says. "That's probably one of my greatest accomplishments. Yeah, great, so I'm a heavy metal superstar, but I helped make a law here. That's something where my kids can look back and say their dad helped do something good for this country."

At the close of 1992, with the dust still settling after a tumultuous year, the powerhouse lineup of Megadeth, Anthrax, Motörhead, and Soundgarden challenged Metallica—now widely regarded favorites—for the Best Metal Performance with Vocal Grammy. Jethro Tull had vanished in a puff of smoke, leaving an array of more worthy headbangers to compete for bragging rights. Not hip to the movement, ceremony emcee Whoopi Goldberg weakly imitated the frantic drumming posture of Lars Ulrich after Metallica's performance of "Enter Sandman." Nobody laughed with her—at that moment the world sided with Metallica. The Black Album took the prize.

As *Metallica* broke into the pop world with obvious excitement, debate followed over whether heavy metal at the Grammys was a bad thing. The outcome depended on how far a person enjoyed seeing heavy metal leap into the mainstream. "I love all the early stuff by Metallica," says Rob Halford of Judas Priest. "Everything was going great for me until the Black Album, but because of what it represented, I'll have to applaud that one as well. I just love the adventure that Metallica created. They were metal freaks."

As heavy metal became commonplace, it formed the backbone of the complex musical landscape of the early 1990s. True heavy metal was not pop music—its virtues were not always apparent on first listen—but it was now a commercial monolith nonetheless, and the basis for limitless new directions in pop. With the new decade, it was wise not only for failing glam metal bands like Stryper but also for musicians of all shades to darken their style with something heavier.

The buzzword became "alternative metal," as bands everywhere grew long hair, neglected their razors, and leaned into metal-issue stacks of Marshall guitar amps. "[Our] new stuff is pretty damn heavy, that's for sure," singer Black Francis of definitive college-rock band the Pixies told *Melody Maker* in 1991. "We watch MTV and see those bands like Nelson and Warrant and think surely it's possible to do a better job with that kind of music."

British new wavers Depeche Mode showed off a denim and leather image, and postpunk group the Cult rocked radio with metal-influenced hits like "Love Removal Machine." The 1970s funk-inspired Red Hot Chili Peppers repaid the attention of metal fans by speeding up and adding grittier guitar solos. The Chicago duo Ministry was a dramatic example of heavy metal hegemony: the former disco synth act that signed with Anthrax's agency, Crazed Management, grew beards, ran drum machines through distortion pedals, and loaded samplers with powerhouse guitar sounds.

Once engaged with the outside world, heavy metal began to change in reaction to its many strange reflections. Pioneers like Chrome and Suicide for years had played electronic music that resembled heavy metal. Now Faith No More and Type O Negative finally embraced the most spurned of instruments—the electronic synthesizer—threatening the dominance of the hallmark Judas Priest–style dueling guitars with new technology. "I was aware of Kraftwerk for probably fucking ten years," says Håvard Ellefsen, aka Mortiis, who began a career as a heavy keyboard act in 1993. "But during the eighties, when you're into heavy metal and in your early teens, you can't properly be allowed to enjoy metal and synthesized music at the same time, because your pals would beat you up! That's just the unwritten rule, which was fucking stupid."

In truth, most traditional heavy metal bands employed keyboard players—at least in the privacy of the recording studio. Deep Purple's music was based on the heavy electric ivories of Jon Lord, and Black Sabbath also used keyboard players extensively. On 1974's *Sabbath Bloody Sabbath*, Rick Wakeman of Yes was a credited guest, and Ozzy Osbourne himself played synthesizer on "Who Are You?" Yet ever since Iron Maiden battled Duran Duran and the new romantics on the London music charts, keyboards had symbolized simpering wimpdom, a fate worse than disco. Though new waver Thomas Dolby added a blatant keyboard overdub to the radio mix of Def Leppard's "Bringing on the Heartbreak," he was credited under a pseudonym to safeguard the band's reputation.

As a consequence, keyboard players were rarely seen amid the garish productions of 1980s metal concerts. Although he joined in 1979 and performed on every album beginning with *Heaven and Hell*, Black Sabbath's longtime organist, Geoff Nicholls, was still positioned offstage during live performances. Dio's loyal keyboardist, Claude Schnell, integral to set staples like "Rainbow in the Dark," waited until 1984 for a place in the onstage castle. "He paid his dues," says Ronnie James Dio. "He was willing to be behind the stage, to do what he had to do. It didn't make him happy, but I told him, 'Stick with this and there's going to be a time when you're going to have your own spot.' Eventually that happened. It had to. I don't see how you can take another musician and just stick him in a hole somewhere."

In the 1990s, digital sampling and a more adventurous musical climate allowed keyboards a greater piece of the limelight. The Swiss trio Young Gods used a strange configuration of live drummer and singer buttressed by a sampler-wielding keyboard maniac who banged his head crazily while triggering samples of electric guitar. After leaving his thrash metal band, Carnivore, behind in the 1980s and enrolling in the New York Police Academy, Peter T. Steele returned in 1991 with the high-concept Type O Negative. "Keyboards opened room for sampling, which is a big part of Type O Negative," Steele says. "I consider virtually every sound to be music if it's used properly, and that includes fifty-five-gallon drums being thrown down a flight of stairs, tires screeching, or babies crying."

Type O Negative formed a gloomy merger of thrash metal and

gothic rock on the basis of a half dozen unused Carnivore songs. They were unafraid to combine pounding guitars and saccharine balladeering within the same song. "We were really excited that we had Pete under contract and were able to do it," says Monte Conner of Roadrunner Records. "We saw Carnivore as very limiting and Type O as something with a much wider appeal."

Likewise, the long-laboring White Zombie indoctrinated the new decade in 1992 with its visionary *La Sexorcisto: Devil Music Vol. 1*, peppered with hundreds of sampled sound bites from horror movies and less recognizable sources. Benefiting from the prior success of the eclectic Faith No More, these musical magpies surfed culture deftly, fusing Exodus riffs with hardcore rap in a mass of handpicked sonic elements, attaching fragments of metal found while touring with heavy hitters like Slayer, Megadeth, and Anthrax. They ascended the pop charts after overtaking MTV with a bedraggled Day-Glo horror show honed for years—since singer Rob Zombie was a production assistant on the first season of *Pee-wee's Playhouse*.

White Zombie, metal ragamuffins
(Geffen Records)

As a measure of the changes, Metallica returned to Oakland's Day on the Green festival in October 1991, headlining to 50,000 sold-out seats. Supporting acts Queensryche, Faith No More, and Soundgarden were all alternative metal acts—and, significantly, bands, like Metallica, who rose through the ranks of independent metal labels in the 1980s. They represented the colorful results of metal opening up to face the outside world. Almost forgotten were the 1985 headliners—Ratt, Yngwie Malmsteen, and Y&T—who had then loomed over Metallica on that same stage. All were vaporized at the close of the 1980s like so many Members Only jackets and Delorean sport cars.

ALTERNATIVE METAL

The influence of heavy metal after the 1980s was so great that virtually every new band bowed to its sound, no matter what the intentions. While Metallica deserted thrash metal in 1991 with its commercially powerful Black Album, new groups like Soundgarden, Ministry, and Faith No More seamlessly combined metal with alternative rock, synthesizers, and dance music. Though seemingly a hodgepodge of styles, the adventurous avenues presented by alternative metal bands all pointed to Black Sabbath and Metallica. The well-scrubbed Helmet looked like New Kids on the Block, and its hybrid of pounding pop and brutally meticulous guitars was a huge influence on the upcoming decade. Yet the band didn't consider itself just a transition from Iron Maiden. "We fell into the whole metal thing by accident," says drummer John Stanier. "We always hated it when people mentioned metal in conjunction with us." Public image aside, the 1990s proved even short-hairs could play metal to the max.

Strange Attractors

❖ Butthole Surfers, *Locust Abortion Technician* (1987)
❖ Faith No More, *The Real Thing* (1989)
❖ Helmet, *Meantime* (1992)
❖ Jane's Addiction, *Nothing's Shocking* (1988)
❖ Kyuss, *Blues for the Red Sun* (1992)
❖ Metallica, *Metallica* (1991)
❖ Ministry, *The Land of Rape and Honey* (1988)
❖ Soundgarden, *Screaming Life/Fopp* (1992)
❖ Type O Negative, *Bloody Kisses* (1994)
❖ Voivod, *Angel Rat* (1991)
❖ White Zombie, *La Sexorcisto, Devil Music Vol. 1* (1992)

Prior to Metallica, the career arc of nearly every successful heavy metal band involved a noticeable wimping out—some slow and steadily, some precariously quick. Celtic Frost took a drastic slip in 1988 with *Cold Lake,* transforming from the hellishly powerful Swiss demons of 1985 into stomach-churning L.A. glam metal imitators. Regal album artwork gave way to hair spray and public displays of pubic hair, while classic literate themes dissipated into banal love songs to Marilyn Monroe. Though leader Tom Warrior now calls *Cold Lake* "a mistake," mystified fans pondered whether the puffy-haired escapade was the ultimate enigmatic high-concept twist from a band whose career perpetually reeked of surprise—or just the unfortunate result of radically misguided commercial hopes.

Although they had paid their dues, thrash metal titans like Metal Church were not automatically entitled to inherit the success of Iron Maiden and Judas Priest. Soon after deposing traditional heavy metal, thrash metal was decidedly no longer a lean contender. In some cases the changes were visible to the eye, as more than a few overfed bangers began watching their beer bellies. Slayer famously switched from full-bodied Belgian beer to watery Coors Light. According to guitarist Gary Holt, Exodus singer Steve Sousa shed forty-five pounds after beginning a NutraSystem diet. "He got the idea because Chuck Billy, Eric Peterson, and Louie Clemente from Testament all went on it," says Holt. "He showed me one of the NutraSystem hamburgers, and I was like, 'Man, I'd eat the box, too!'"

In the wake of the Black Album, wimping out was no longer the problem. Yet as Faith No More and Soundgarden were heavy without necessarily being metal, there were now scads of second-division Anthrax and Metallica imitators who played metal but lacked the depth of spirit. Overpolished commercial bands began bogging down thrash metal, underwhelming new audiences who should have been eager for more bands that sounded like the Big Four. "The major labels killed thrash metal," says indie A&R man Monte Conner.

Warner Brothers flooded stores with 20,000 free copies of the debut EP by the competent Powermad and placed them in David Lynch's film *Wild at Heart.* But imitating old-school Metallica was no longer enough to make the grade. "There was the Big Four: Anthrax,

Metallica, Megadeth, and Slayer," says Conner. "All those bands were doing well, and the majors were like, 'Hey, we gotta get in on this!' Then, overnight, two hundred generic fifth-rate bands like Gothic Slam and Powermad got signed and flooded the market. None of those bands sold anything, because none were any good. Kids got sick of it, because there were too many records coming out, and eventually those bands disappeared."

A less visible reason for the stalling of thrash metal was narcotics, as success brought the onset of heavier drug habits. Black Sabbath had survived its first decade despite excessive chemical abuse, but by and large heavy metal had been content with casual alcoholism of the kind trumpeted by Metallica's pet name—Alcoholica. Hard drugs seemed to be an affliction reserved for the Hollywood music industry and its star-tripping bands—such as the heroin-ravaged Mötley Crüe, whose manager, Doc McGhee, had been caught smuggling several tons of marijuana into America in 1988. "Mostly we were about writing positive stuff and not writing a lot of dirt," says journalist Ben Liemer, who covered all breeds of heavy metal extensively for *Circus*, "but we saw all kinds of stuff that didn't go in the articles."

Heavy metal certainly had a few skeletons in the closet. "I think you should go out there and do your drugs, and do your booze, and stay up late, and fuck your brains out, and do all the things that you want to do," says Rob Halford. "Those things are great only in terms of living, and life is a great gift. However, falling into the trap of addiction and fucking yourself up is a bad thing to do. I've been down that road. I hit the wall, like a lot of musicians do. I had obsessive personality traits that I didn't discover until I became addicted to booze and drugs. It was affecting what I love to do with music because it was screwing with my voice, so I did something about it in January 1986. Now I see other people that are my age, and I thank God that I don't look like that."

While Metallica still openly celebrated their love of vodka, former guitarist Dave Mustaine's angry alcoholism had accelerated into a never-ending appetite for speed, heroin, and freebase cocaine as Megadeth accumulated gold and platinum albums. Only bassist David Ellefson stayed with Mustaine during Megadeth's ascent. "The first two guys were asked to leave because they were using drugs and stealing equipment," Mustaine says. "The second two were asked to leave for real, real bad drug problems. One of them clicked into a phone call with my fiancée and told her he fantasized about having sex with her when he's having sex with his girlfriend. I said, 'You're outta here!'"

Later Lars Ulrich described his own lifestyle during the period to VH1 as "staying up all night partying with Guns N' Roses." Such revelations did not bode well. "There's always drugs in the music business," says King Diamond. I don't want to associate with it. I've seen its damage, and it brings a lot of stupid things with it."

Metallica's friends and labelmates Metal Church spiraled entirely out of control after relocating from sleepy Seattle to the badlands of Los Angeles. "When I left Metal Church, there were a lot of drugs going on," says vocalist David Wayne. "I've never put it on them, but there were a couple guys in Metal Church that [flopped on the floor like] fish. I saw some overdoses, and I overdosed. As much as Hollywood and rock and roll glorifies this crap called cocaine, I'm done. The addiction factor on this drug is so off the scale as to not be believed. You just keep wanting more and more, as Metallica wrote on their song 'Master of Puppets.'"

Superstars like Megadeth cleaned up and prevailed, selling 6 million albums in America during the 1990s. Likewise the squeaky-clean Anthrax recruited former Armored Saint singer John Bush—courted years earlier by Metallica—and signed a new $10 million deal with Elektra in 1992. Yet many former peers were falling like heavy flies. Even proven major-label mainstays Metal Church and Exodus were left wandering the treacherous back burners of record companies that no longer cared about their careers. "Metal Church [was] handed the CD of 1993's *Hanging in the Balance*," recalls former singer David Wayne, who left several years earlier, "and the artwork was a fat woman on a tight wire wearing what looks to be Viking-type opera diva stuff. It's quite possibly the ugliest heavy metal album I've ever seen. They weren't even given a choice."

The key to survival in the 1990s was adaptation and transformation in an overexcited musical environment. Slaving away in the metal backwaters since their *Metal Magic* album in 1983, the Texas power metal act Pantera finally became successful by smartly riding the changing times. Shortly after acquiring New Orleans singer Phil Anselmo, Pantera ditched mascara, pink scarves, leopard-print spandex pants, and hair spray and settled on a tougher, precision-metal approach. The key was replacing "tuff" with tough, as guitarist "Diamond" Darrell Abbott changed his stage name to Dimebag Darrell, bassist Rex "Rocker" Brown became just Rex, and so on.

Released in 1990, Pantera's *Cowboys from Hell* was a thrashing departure from Metallica's imperfect *. . . And Justice for All,* synthesizing metal's abrasiveness and rap's sparse song structures to create a percussive, angry sound, with a trace of the deathly growls popular on the underground. The new Pantera fused metal and rap in a more fluid manner than Anthrax did and soon

Power metal Pantera flyer

eclipsed the New York band in popularity. A black-and-white photograph of the barking singer, Anselmo, looking like a punk rock quarterback tattooed with the words STRENGTH and SHATTERED SOUL, won a Pulitzer Prize for photographer John Kaplan in 1992. Perfectly in stride with the times, Pantera next perfected its rhythm-heavy headbanging plan on *Vulgar Display of Power,* later extended through the erratically groovy and elegantly powerful *Far Beyond Driven.* After striving in the South Texas trenches for almost a decade, Pantera had become a group of market-savvy realists, rejuvenating the skills and boisterous attitude of the 1980s with a fresh, clenched-teeth approach.

True to the title of the band's later album *Reinventing the Steel,* official biographies tended to omit any mention of Pantera's activities during the 1980s. "Of course, Pantera was something more before they did *Cowboys from Hell,*" says Rob Halford from Judas Priest. "They obviously wanted to survive, and they obviously felt they had something more to say than what they were doing in the very early days. They were just a great example of taking that metal development and bringing in a new definition in terms of the sound. I remember first listening to *Cowboys from Hell* and thinking, 'Oh, my God, what's this?' It was just amazing in terms of what Dimebag was doing.

It's still always all about the singer and guitar player—and I was inspired by them."

Members of the elaborate Queensryche from Bellevue, Washington, also survived in the 1990s by using their heads. The quintet debuted in 1984 as a classy Iron Maiden knockoff, and, much like Florida's Savatage and Connecticut's Fates Warning, they vaulted from an early power metal style into a heady new progressive metal realm—never dirtying their legs in the gutters of thrash metal. In 1988, while Voivod and Celtic Frost were undergoing similar changes, Queensryche abandoned black leather and chains and conceived the science-fiction-influenced mini-opera *Operation: Mindcrime.* With its successor, *Empire,* the group garnered multiple-platinum sales awards, enjoyed an enduring hit with "Silent Lucidity," and fostered a maturing metal audience for whom literate musicianship mattered more than the image of heavy metal in the mainstream.

The runaway story in the Pacific Northwest in 1991 was not Queensryche, however, but the grunge phenomenon—first sighted in Soundgarden, whose late-1980s arrival ushered in the era of Pearl Jam, Mudhoney, and Nirvana. Presented on the regional Sub Pop Records label, these odd groups were bred in Seattle and neighboring Tacoma and Aberdeen—hard-rock strongholds where longhaired garage bands venerated forgotten 1970s groups like Grand Funk Railroad and Black Oak Arkansas, and threw in liberal doses of punk rock and heavy metal. Infused in the beer- and coffee-bar culture of the region, grunge was a distortion-rich musical hybrid that saluted the simple spirit of Blue Cheer and Stooges, along with the mountainous riffs of Black Sabbath and Led Zeppelin. Grunge bands also had a streak of

Hairy metal: Seattle's Soundgarden
(Charles Peterson)

record-store clerk in them, citing debts to jagged postpunk critical favorites like Gang of Four and the Minutemen.

Widening the emotional range of heavy music just as James Hetfield was beginning to sing from the heart, grunge bands returned to more elementary ethics in the face of increasingly technical and flashy popular rock. Unlike hyperactive metalcore acts from the region, like the Accüsed and Wehrmacht, who crossed genres by aggressively stabbing forward, the self-effacing grunge slackers allowed metal influences to slowly steep into the mix. "I didn't like Led Zeppelin or Black Sabbath until after the punk rock thing," explained Soundgarden guitarist Kim Thayil to *Sheet Metal.* "I hated heavy metal for years. I couldn't even listen to my old Kiss and Aerosmith albums because I thought it stood for everything I hated about the rock industry and about all the jocks, musicians, and jerks in high school."

Many of the grunge musicians were late bloomers, teenage punks who grew up and grew hair. They learned to love hard rock but were intent on not repeating its mistakes. With reactionary simplicity designed to overthrow former glam idols, grunge bands looked down the coast to Los Angeles with a philosophy best described as "if you can't join them, beat them." For instance, when Seattle glam metal group Mother Love Bone lost singer Andrew Wood to a heroin overdose on March 16, 1990, the members recruited singer Eddie Vedder and reformulated as Pearl Jam— wearing low-key sweatshirts and sneakers in place of leather jackets and silver boots.

Grunge groups saw themselves as upstarts attacking the excesses of heavy metal in recent years, and indeed these flannel-flying bands stepped into the void, replacing Warrant, Winger, and White Lion. Those lightweights had been hit hard by the popularity of Metallica, and now grunge helped wipe away the remains. Still, metal purists were reluctant to embrace the downscaling of image and musical technique. "Thank God I was in L.A.," says David Wayne of Metal Church. "I didn't mind grunge all that bad, but I missed guitar players who could play more than three-chord rock. I preferred my K. K. Downing and Glenn Tipton [of Judas Priest] dual-guitar riffs as opposed to Nirvana's 'Smells Like Teen Spirit,' which is just okay."

While Metal Church sat by and watched, a young and restless MTV audience segment already enamored of Soundgarden found salvation in Nirvana's breakaway success *Nevermind*—a Beatles-influenced version of heavy metal screaming full throttle. Nirvana's abrasive front man, Kurt Cobain, was a gifted and troubled songwriter raised on Celtic Frost and his local heroes Metal Church. "Kurt and [bassist] Krist Novoselic would listen to Celtic Frost and the Smithereens, and that's what they imagined themselves to sound like," said Nirvana drummer Dave Grohl to *Stance*. Though a redeeming figure to record companies and street punks alike, Cobain was too vulnerable—snapped in half by the dueling demands of the commercial machine in which he operated and the underground milieu with which he identified. After three albums the group's revolutionary promise ended when Cobain was found dead of an apparent suicide, holding a shotgun in his lap on April 8, 1994.

Metallica soared above the fray, as their phenomenal success eclipsed musical trends. No longer coy about being filmed, the band blessed MTV with videos for "The Unforgiven," "Nothing Else Matters," and "Enter Sandman"—and album and CD sales continued to multiply spectacularly. For the first time, grandparents and homemakers were part of the Metallica fan base, and the band's concert audience showed certain signs of gentrification. "When there's fifty percent chicks in the house," says Lars Ulrich, "that's the sign of making it."

Though officially rock stars beyond a doubt, Metallica continued to act as if nothing had changed. Taking its relationship with its audience to the point of micromanagement, Metallica coped with megaplatinum success by reaching out compulsively to the crowd. As a teenage superfan, Lars Ulrich had latched on to his idols in Diamond Head and Motörhead in an intensely personal way. Now as star drummer he reversed roles and offered Metallica fans similar access. Nine days before its official release, Metallica previewed the Black Album at a packed free listening party for 17,000 at Madison Square Garden. "The only annoying thing is that our album played the Garden before we did," Ulrich told *MTV News*.

Metallica was amazing at getting the message through to its metal militia. First, the *Metallica* sessions were examined through a long-form home video documenting the trials of nine months of recording. The film laid bare the working process: Lars Ulrich suggesting ideas,

James Hetfield silently working through changes, Kirk Hammett glibly adapting to any situation at hand, and Jason Newsted apparently struggling to survive. Though forthcoming about the rigors of the musical process, the self-produced video hid well the debilitating downside of the yearlong recording ordeal: the grueling sessions had cost the band $1 million and ended three marriages.

The footage depicted a grown-up, more responsible Metallica—a far cry from the obnoxious exploits of Hetfield's drunken punk band, Spastik Children. Contacted by the Make-A-Wish Foundation, the band invited teenage chemotherapy patient John Smith to the studio. Smith arrived with his family in tow, wearing a *Ride the Lightning* shirt and a bandanna over his hairless scalp. He plugged in his guitar and led Metallica through a sit-down version of "Four Horsemen," a bright moment before his short life came to a close a few months later.

Each fan with whom the band had personal contact brought Metallica a hundred new converts. To make true believers out of crowds who had been introduced to the group casually through radio and videos, Metallica embarked on an incredible three-hundred-date world tour, from which another documentary was produced. Totaling four hours, the studio and tour documentaries, collectively titled *A Year and a Half in the Life of Metallica*, were among several indulgences, committed in the name of the fans, which contrived to make the band appear larger-than-life for the first time. The music and methods defied all expert prognostication, as *Metallica* sales escalated steadily toward the eventual whopping tally of more than 20 million copies worldwide.

Such success irredeemably altered the relationship between performer and audience, but Metallica fought to preserve its informal rapport. Looking to "challenge the way that people see arena rock shows," Lars Ulrich and the band devised the "Snake Pit," a diamond-shaped stage containing two drum kits that slid into different configurations for each song. Instead of blasting at the audience from a fixed, fortified direction, the musicians would play a dynamic game of musical chairs through all the clock positions— giving every fan in the house an equal dose of face time. Adding to this unconventional in-the-round dynamic, the center of the Snake Pit was filled with 120 overwhelmed maniacs, handpicked for the crazed look in their eyes.

Meanwhile, in a separate section behind the soundboard, the band freely allowed recording devices, a nod to tape traders who exhaustively documented the band's stage career. Even without inflatable dragons, Metallica's touring machine now required a force of twelve semi trucks, six bus coaches, and a crew of sixty—not including Lars Ulrich's bodyguards. Thus sustained, James Hetfield developed a permanent grin, the countenance of a man who was spending six nights a week running to meet the welcome cheers of ten thousand outstretched arms. It was all becoming very easy.

Major rewards were increasingly common. While making the Black Album in 1990, Metallica won its second Grammy for a toss-off recording of Queen's "Stone Cold Crazy." Recorded in half an hour, the track was included on an anniversary disk of current Elektra Records artists revisiting the label's back catalog. With the help of its managers at Q Prime, Metallica was taking its first steps onto the red carpet of rock and roll royalty. At "A Concert for Life," an April 1992 AIDS benefit in honor of deceased Queen singer Freddie Mercury, Metallica performed and socialized with rock aristocracy like Roger Daltrey and David Bowie. Of greatest personal importance to James Hetfield, he joined Black Sabbath's Tony Iommi and the three surviving members of Queen onstage at London's Wembley Arena to perform "Stone Cold Crazy."

In *Guitar for the Practicing Musician*, Black Sabbath bassist and lyricist Geezer Butler soon speculated on whether Metallica's influence would eventually match that of Black Sabbath: "It's hard to say because it's so faddish now. It depends on what they do. *Metallica* is one of the best albums I ever heard. That's a classic album. That's the sort of music I really like listening to—something that is heavy but has got melody at the same time. It's still in the Sabbath sort of vein. It's not too extreme, where the singing sounds like he is puking. I like to hear an actual song, great riff, good vocal line and good lyrics. I'm too old-fashioned really, but it still works."

While in London for the Wembley benefit, Metallica sketched the details of a mammoth tour with Guns N' Roses. Though they exaggerated their differences to the press before the tour, the two were at kissing distance: Guns N' Roses the nastiest and longest-lasting of the

MTV-sponsored glambangers and Metallica the most public face of the metal underground. The first obstacle to this twenty-four-city multiplatinum metal matchup was indicative of the culture clash: whether the stage set would allow Axl Rose a fifty-foot "ego ramp" over the audience's heads, or follow Metallica's more accessible theater-in-the-round "Snake Pit" scheme.

Several 50,000-seat shows into the summer of 1992, Rose's frequent fits and cancellations were straining the goodwill of everyone from backstage to the back rows. Eighty fans were arrested in Boston and a hundred injured after an ice-throwing war erupted during the long delay before Guns' set. Then, in Montreal on August 9, James Hetfield walked into an exploding magnesium flare during the *Ride the Lightning* ballad "Fade to Black." He suffered second-degree burns on his face, hands, arms, and legs. "James Hetfield looked like the torch that they bring up the stairs to light the Olympic fire," Lars Ulrich told VH1. Added Jason Newsted with typical Metallica sensitivity, "His skin was bubbling like the Toxic Avenger."

Pyrotechnic accidents were not uncommon in heavy metal— seven years earlier Cronos of black metal godfathers Venom had been nearly roasted to a crisp during one of his band's bombastic shows. Neither was W.A.S.P.'s Blackie Lawless a stranger to flame. "You get in the wrong place at the wrong time," he says, "and you'll get your ass blown off, as James found out. One time my exploding codpiece got away from us and lifted me three feet off the ground. It burned all the hair off my legs and cracked the quarter-inch fiberglass codpiece so it would flex like an accordion. I don't know any of the pyro guys working in Hollywood that have all their fingers or don't have half their face blown off!"

Disorder reigned in Montreal as James Hetfield was rushed to a French-speaking hospital. Lars Ulrich the diplomat struggled to explain the situation to 50,000 confused and disappointed fans. As he apologized and promised a quick return to Montreal, all eyes turned to Metallica's unruly coheadliners, now responsible for rescuing the night. Just after taking the stage, however, Guns N' Roses singer Axl Rose stormed back to his dressing room. Rose complained of a damaged throat and refused to continue, though Jason Newsted recalls seeing him relaxing backstage with a cigarette and a flute of champagne. Metallica had fled Los Angeles long ago to escape such self-involved rock-star antics. The disenchanted fans made their own entertainment, trashing the concert hall and overturning cars. Eight policemen and at least ten concertgoers were injured in the fracas, and the Montreal Olympic Stadium took over $300,000 in damage.

Metallica was able to return to the road within a month of the incident. The tour survived despite skyrocketing insurance and security costs, most nights grossing more than $1 million at the box office. Incredibly, *Pollstar* ranked both the span of time Metallica spent with Guns N' Roses and Metallica's separate headlining tour among the ten highest-grossing tours of 1992. Though the pyro accident brought only a brief break in the band's remarkable ten-year ascension, the following summer Metallica took its only vacation ever. Some events were still beyond its control. For the immediate future Metallica's next move was thus prescribed: physical therapy for Hetfield's hand and much-needed rest and reassessment for the band, its pyro equipment, and its endless ambition.

Though grunge imitators wearing lumberjack shirts now outnumbered spandex pants on MTV, the Seattle scene did not bring down the metal successes of 1992, Metallica and Guns N' Roses. The superstars remained superstars. In spite of *Time* magazine's assessment of a great grunge takeover, Nirvana's *Nevermind* sold only 5 million copies in America by the end of 1993, while the Black Album sold 7 million. This ratio tilted more extremely in Metallica's favor as the 1990s progressed. Grunge could not even shake the hold of Hollywood bad boys Mötley Crüe, who squeezed another 7 million in sales out of the American public even after the release of *Nevermind*.

What grunge did accomplish in the early 1990s was making a large enough splash to permit the mainstream media an excuse to once again ignore heavy metal. With Judas Priest and Iron Maiden missing in action in the early 1990s, there was a feeling in the metal world that the triumph of Metallica superceded a golden era of heavy metal. There would never again be a decade like the 1980s, which saw the music rise from near oblivion to inescapable dominion. Though heavy metal in truth had yet to see its greatest financial success, the origin of heavy metal would always be tied to the time period of dragons, headbangers, and spiked leather belts. Still eager to evolve, the metalheads looked forward—the world beyond in the 1990s remained a vast, inviting frontier.

⊰ XIV ⊱

Death Metal Deliverance

Metallica had held the tape traders together until ... *And Justice for All,* but after years of filling fanzine pages with his ambitious predictions, Lars "Motorbreath" Ulrich after the Black Album fell temporarily silent. With all that his band had achieved, the passionate cause of inspired metal had proven its righteousness. Yet the story was far from over. Throughout the rising and falling fortunes of metal, there remained an active underground, which by 1991 was thriving and impossible to ignore. The changes of the past several years left vacant space in the heavy metal scene that could never be filled by alternative metal synthesizer bands or grunge martyrs.

Rather than simplify its approach to attract new fans in the 1990s,

Metallica's familiar nemesis, Slayer, turned away from its increasingly lukewarm peers and concentrated its devastating efforts. Between Thanksgiving 1992 and Easter 1993, the third through fifth Slayer CDs, *Reign in Blood, South of Heaven,* and *Seasons in the Abyss,* were all certified gold in the United States. This indicated that at least half a million loyal U.S. fans considered the medium-rare metal of *Metallica* black too light a step. For such scourge as Slayer to succeed was a vote of confidence for new extremes.

With widespread awareness of tape trading—now a part of the Metallica legend—thousands of new fans continued to stream like rats into the deep cellars of metal. There, in obscurity, legions at the grass roots discovered that during the prior decade, while heavy metal modernized from Judas Priest to Metallica, a strong undercurrent was developing in darkness if not silence. The cult forms of black metal and grindcore had mated to breed an astonishing cast of exotic new idols—the early 1990s brought their ultimate fruition in the form of death metal.

Crude blueprints of death metal had been sketched since the appearance of Venom in 1981, leading to a solid foundation in the more skilled satanic metal of Slayer and Possessed. In the mid-1980s "Death Metal" was a Possessed song, and a 1984 German compilation LP called *Death Metal* featured the deathly Hellhammer among a slew of European speed metal bands. Staunch characters at the root of the evil form, Slayer held mighty sway over death metal's development in the late 1980s. They laid the groundwork with ghoulish imagery; catastrophic, pyrotechnic riffs; Kerry King's flailing, atonal guitar solos; and Dave Lombardo's breathless double-bass drum rumble.

Once ignited by the furious, annihilating speed of grindcore in the late 1980s, the massive death metal conflagration pushed everything else into oblivion. The final traces of heavy metal that still resembled traditional rock and roll were utterly obliterated by the new masters—the triumvirate of Death, Morbid Angel, and Deicide. Born around the time of Black Sabbath's debut, these musicians lived nearly their entire lives in the era of heavy metal. They built their sound from the complex, high-speed explosions of Exodus and Kreator, not the rudimentary blues scales at the base of common rock.

Though its sound was a constant propulsion often likened to a hailstorm, death metal was not an antimusical assault. Nothing could top the basic speed of grindcore, but death metal expanded the fastness with something artful. The heavy metal guitar-hero culture of the 1980s trained a huge pool of players in the techniques and methods of screaming strings and pure excitement. Death metal brought these musical chops to the fore, as guitarists expressed emotional turmoil through wild shredding and gesticulating solo breaks. With constant acrobatic hammering upon two huge bass drums, drummers blazed neck-snapping breaks and polyrhythmic rolls like one-man percussion ensembles.

To appreciate the music, fans first had to accept a merciless sonic signature: guttural vocals that were little more than a menacing, subaudible growl. James Hetfield's thrash metal rasp was harsh in comparison to Rob Halford's heavy metal high notes, but creatures like Glen Benton of Deicide tore out their larynxes to summon images of decaying corpses and giant catastrophic horrors. This created a nearly insurmountable barrier to entry for the casual listener. "I'm not a big death metal fan," admits Dee Snider of Twisted Sister. "I like the music, the riffs, but as I'm more of a melody singer, it kind of leaves me in the cold."

A drastic mutation of the metal gene, death metal was an ugly duckling overlooked in its infancy and mocked in its adolescence as extreme and ridiculous. Yet as much as thrash metal was a substantial second wave of heavy metal, so death metal represented a third evolutionary stage. When it finally rose to the fore in the early 1990s, death metal elevated metal songwriting to a brutal new level of melodic depth, compositional prowess, and technical skill.

Few took this mission as far as Morbid Angel guitarist Trey Azagthoth. "Some people think death metal is all about a sound," he says. "They think if you get a heavy, distorted guitar and growling vocals, you've got death metal. Death metal is a feeling—it's not just a sound. The way the rhythm attacks and moves is what matters. I mixed up a groovy extreme—a chaos, a madness, a bunch of piranhas that would be jumping out of the speakers and chewing you as you listened. That's what I wanted to pursue with my playing. I wanted to get something that was like listening to Black Sabbath on an eight-track tape that was dragging or a warped record. Like a storm moving forward, something triumphant."

DEATH METAL

The musical pinnacle and stomach-churning depth of heavy metal, death metal bands used speed and intensity to squeeze an album's worth of ideas into a single song. All of the bombastic flash of prior forms was amplified considerably, from guitar solos, double-bass drumming, and occult-inspired imagery. While Deicide and Cannibal Corpse remained steadfastly addicted to power, others, such as Napalm Death and Morbid Angel, evolved into technical and interesting new forms of expression. Hair flying and fingers wrestling with chaotic chord combinations, band members took to wearing sweatpants onstage, an indicator of their athletic, atheistic sound. Because many death metal bands hailed from Florida, this wardrobe was mocked by European metal purists as "retirement wear." Yet the bands flailed on, in search of extremes as impenetrable as their own band logos.

The Insalubrious

- ❖ Brutal Truth, *Need to Control* (1994)
- ❖ Cannibal Corpse, *Tomb of the Mutilated* (1992)
- ❖ Carcass, *Heartwork* (1994)
- ❖ Carcass, *Necroticism: Descanting the Insalubrious* (1991)
- ❖ Death, *Scream Bloody Gore* (1987)
- ❖ Deicide, *Once Upon the Cross* (1995)
- ❖ Dismember, *Indecent & Obscene* (1993)
- ❖ Morbid Angel, *Blessed Are the Sick* (1991)
- ❖ Morbid Angel, *Formulas Fatal to the Flesh* (1998)
- ❖ Mortician, *Hacked Up for Barbecue* (1997)
- ❖ Napalm Death, *Fear, Emptiness, Despair* (1994)
- ❖ Sepultura, *Arise* (1989)
- ❖ Sepultura, *Chaos A.D.* (1993)

While heavy metal was born in England and thrash metal had its heart in San Francisco, the seeds of death metal were planted throughout the world. The phenomenon was a pure product of the tape-trading underground. Cultured on grotty little demo tapes decorated with skeletons, blood, and guts, early death dealers sent listeners hunting for maps: Possessed from San Francisco, Deathstrike from Chicago, Slaughter from Toronto, Necrophagia from Ohio, Cryptic Slaughter from California, Sepultura from Brazil, Sodom from Germany, and Repulsion from Michigan. For this widespread metal minority the post office served as site for sacred rituals until the bands were ready for concert halls.

Often credited as the original death metal band, the band called Death rose from the muggy swampland of Florida in the early 1980s. They began as Mantas in 1983, the product of fifteen-year-old "Evil" Chuck Schuldiner's guitar and Kam Lee's outrageous screeching voice, and eventually became as heavily distributed by tape traders as more established groups, including Metallica. Epitomizing adolescent horror, the intro to their inspired 1985 "Infernal Death" demo was a sludgy riff over rolling drum tubs, while Lee screamed "Die! Die! Die!" as shrilly as possible at the top of his lungs. It sounded like a torture session in a suburban basement, the graphics looked like a kindergartner's Halloween project, and it all worked terrible wonders.

With hotheaded "Evil" Chuck taking over vocals after quarreling with Lee, the 1987 Death debut LP, *Scream Bloody Gore*, emulated hardcore punk. It also evoked the dark moods of horror sound tracks from the drive-in zombie and cannibal

Terrifying original logo for the band Death

horror films of George Romero, Italian director Lucio Fulci, and Florida's own gore pioneer, Herschel Gordon Lewis. Schuldiner urged a unique cruelty from his B. C. Rich guitar—coupled with his growing technical skill, the effect was creatively lethal. Meanwhile, the band's roster, a victim of Schuldiner's erratic administration, rotated with such consistency that the band staffed its own farm-team band, Massacre, led by guitarist Rick Rozz—that released three albums of its own on Earache and Combat.

The international attention afforded Death following its debut turned the Tampa area into a death metal hotspot. Also home to Deicide and occasionally to North Carolina transplants Morbid Angel, the Sunshine State soon gave sanctuary to Hellwitch, Obituary, Brutality, Cynic, and Atheist. Maybe the boundless energy came from the water—as Ponce de León believed centuries earlier during his doomed search for the Fountain of Youth. In any case the climate was a torrid cauldron for musical agitation, an unholy promised land as far from the cool mist of grunge Seattle as geographically and philosophically possible.

The strangely synthetic southernmost U.S. state became a global magnet for metal refugees. Cannibal Corpse relocated to Tampa from Buffalo in the summer of 1994, and Malevolent Creation soon headed south from Buffalo as well. Gargantuan drummer Gene Hoglan, a former Slayer roadie, left his faltering group, Dark Angel, behind in Los Angeles and moved to Florida to serve his time in the influential Death. For most, career opportunities did not necessarily abound, but Florida was an address with death metal cachet. Furthermore, these were musicians whose connection to the metal world was stronger than their allegiance to their hometowns. They wanted to be near the original source—even if the action was still mostly in the mind.

Life in Florida did not revolve around any significant social scene, but dozens of bands had their albums produced or engineered by Scott Burns and the staff at Tampa's Morrisound Studios. Formerly a hangout for the early Metal Blade act Nasty Savage, the commercial studio transformed into a death metal gateway. Virtually every death metal act with a recording contract journeyed south for a splash of the Morrisound mystique. As death metal became a popular curiosity, the name attracted other odd characters. "Warrant recorded here, Savatage also, and a week ago Bon Jovi called to mix some stuff for a live EP," said Burns in the Dutch magazine *Watt*. "We even didn't have time for them because Morbid Angel and Death were already here."

Though Deicide was not always as dexterous or evocative as

Death or Morbid Angel, death metal found its perfect spokesman in Deicide's vocalist, Glen Benton—a maniac willing to freshly brand his forehead regularly with an upside-down cross. He boasted of raising his infant child a Satanist; and his playing was just as impassioned and wild as his image—the way he strained physically with his bass as if wrestling with a mule. At a 1995 Long Island show where an unlucky stage diver was taken away by ambulance during the opening band's set, Benton quipped heartlessly to the crowd, "I heard someone tripped over Satan's dick and broke his neck."

Deicide (left to right): Eric Hoffman, Steve Asheim, Glen Benton, Brian Hoffman *(Roadrunner Records)*

Deicide's brutal bluntness and hardcore-influenced song-writing on 1990's *Deicide* and 1992's *Legion* were steeped rich in evil mood. Guitarist brothers Eric and Brian Hoffman were barbarian virtuosos with ob-scenely muscular builds, pulling off superhuman feats of eerie musicianship while secreted behind veils of bleached-blond hair. Bug-eyed drummer Steve Asheim bore the weight of the band's tremendous power, struggling against all physical laws with insane mathematic agility. On their crowning triumph, 1995's *Once Upon the Cross*, with its anthemic title track and the rousing "They Are the Children of the Underworld," Deicide drove the impact of early Slayer fully ten years deeper into hell.

Metallica, Megadeth, and Anthrax had disavowed Satanism early in their careers, but death metal was all about the mythic interpretation of Satan. The music was a frenzied, chaotic, and amoral depiction of total lust and abandon. The fascination with evil was cultivated by younger metallers weaned on the goats and pentagrams of Venom's *Welcome to Hell*, Slayer's *Hell Awaits*, and Possessed's *Seven Churches*. "Vomit on the cross, and burn the book of lies," urged Morbid Angel on "Unholy Blasphemies." It was a liberating expression of pure abstraction—similar to when free-jazz musicians in the 1960s embraced Eastern religions that distanced them from traditional gospel-derived music.

One of the first bands to delight in a hard satanic image was Possessed, a mid-1980s group of California high-schoolers. "It was basically the draw of Satan—it was cool," says singer/bassist Jeff Becerra of the allure of the dark side. "It was definitely not drugs, because we were too young, and we weren't really into that. We knew of Venom and Black Sabbath, but it was just before Slayer. Everybody was into the occult in a way but didn't know too much about it. It just looked cool, and it was tough. And of course we were all Catholic except for Larry Lalonde."

Depicted in countless extremely provocative examples, the demonic imagery was a metaphor that ripped listeners out of complacency in order to raze the past and begin anew. "Satanized, crucified, feel the wrath of suicide," sang Glen Benton on Deicide's first album. Transformed by violence, listeners could almost feel their flesh being ripped apart by overwhelming death metal music—yet this violent imagery was never more than an abstraction. Playing a form of music as difficult as death metal required discipline, artistic sensitivity, and physical endurance that was anything but an act of negation. Metal fans did not take religion quite so literally.

Satanism as practiced by most heavy metallers had very little to do with black candles and incantations. In fact, their beliefs were astoundingly in tune with red-blooded American values—only their voices were more self-aware and honest. "I don't believe in any inherent right and wrong," says Morbid Angel's Trey Azagthoth. "I believe everyone has the right to put together their own formula that makes them feel great. All these values and beliefs we have are supposed to be put together like a computer, so we can run efficiently and be happy. The bottom line is, life is a game to be enjoyed."

As their popularity grew in the early 1990s, the original Florida bands evolved into more florid displays of the death metal form. Death's labors reached a pinnacle with 1993's *Individual Thought Patterns*, where Schuldiner's pioneering sound was extracted into a nightmare of solos, weird chord structures, and studio experiments. The songs would crouch into a low growl, then spring out in a wild, flailing attack that throbbed with bizarre genius. Neighboring bands Atheist and Cynic also channeled their unholy spirit into instrumental proficiency, branching out from basement-noise roots to play laboriously finessed, progressive death metal.

Hot on the trail of Death came Morbid Angel with a brilliant streak of albums. The first two records—1989's *Altars of Madness* and 1991's *Blessed Are the Sick*—formed a canon of Satan-infested madness and unrepentant skill, including the trinity of deathly tracks "Thy Kingdom Come," "Chapel of Ghouls," and "Blasphemy." The following two releases—1993's *Covenant* and 1995's *Domination*— were slick, professional, and masterfully disarming. The sublime religion of the unexpected that permeated Morbid Angel's music would be phenomenally refreshing in any genre. The band had a second beginning following the departure of longtime front man David Vincent, and every song on 1998's formidable *Formulas Fatal to the Flesh* flew in eight chaotic directions at once.

After Vincent left Morbid Angel, the band's worship of the unpredictable took an interesting spiritual twist. Taking over the songwriting, guitarist Trey Azagthoth replaced the band's virulent Satanism with an inventive fusion—ancient Sumerian mythology from the Middle East and 100 percent American infomercial boosterism by self-improvement gurus Tony Robbins and Deepak Chopra (much as the hardcore Bad Brains had cribbed their positive message from a 1970s self-help book). "The truth really happens when you go beyond the analytical mind," explains Azagthoth, "and you go up to the intuition, and become one with everything through subjective experience, instead of an objective one that creates difference. It's like going out and experiencing nature without talking about it to yourself. There's a lot to that."

After suffering from constant lineup turmoil in its larval stage, Napalm Death also stabilized and evolved impressively, turning wild moments of hyperactive abandon into wicked, minor-key death metal. Not only was the band influenced by little-known demo bands like Repulsion, but the 1990s version of Napalm Death was itself a product of tape trading—the musicians themselves had been traded from other bands. "I know it's kind of weird," says guitarist Jesse Pintado, who left Los Angeles for Birmingham, England, at age eighteen. "I never met [bassist] Shane Embury face-to-face before I joined the band, but we were into the same trip. We were corresponding and made some phone calls to each other. When we would talk, we knew exactly what we wanted to do."

The band's second American guitarist, Mitch Harris, was recruited from Las Vegas's Righteous Pigs by pen pal and drummer Mick Harris, no relation. "A lot of people don't understand," explains Jesse Pintado. "They've heard about the underground and corresponding through the mail, but unless they've done it, they don't understand that sometimes that can be really powerful. You can do a lot of things by just writing on a piece of paper or putting your ideas on a tape to another person. If it wasn't for that, I wouldn't be in London today. That's a really strong tool."

Napalm Death's 1990 release, *Harmony Corruption*, was recorded at Morrisound and sounded like a derivative attempt by the band to milk Florida death metal. However, the group quickly synthesized its early grindcore assault with death metal to produce something great. *Fear, Emptiness, Despair*, their seventh album, started a fresh chapter in the history of a band whose membership half-life had once lasted no longer than an album side. Previous urban hardcore noise blasts were mowed by sophisticated guitar layering and innovative drum patterns. Their dissonance became a conscious component of the composition, not merely a side benefit of chaos, and the marriage of intense anger and calculation yielded a masterpiece of passionate, politically minded, negative realism.

The first several albums of Carcass, formed by runaway Napalm Death guitarist Bill Steer, were too brutal and amorphous to be properly called death metal. Yet the band's major-label debut, *Heartwork*, was a brilliant standard-setting accomplishment. It was the Metallica Black Album of death metal, retaining the internal pulse and dynamics of brutal death metal while reducing the number of notes. The album was a meticulously constructed masterpiece that revisited traditional metal harmonies, uniting Iron Maiden and Napalm Death in evolution. All of the bludgeoning melodic progressions that made Carcass a cult favorite were intact, but they seemed to swoon rather than suffocate.

Where Carcass had buried its technical perfection beneath baffling layers of grotesque wet noise on previous albums, *Heartwork* shone as cleanly as the skeletal surgical-steel H. R. Giger sculpture on its cover. Prior album covers had been dripping with photographs of raw meat—now the gore was left to implication. Jeff Walker's deathly vocals were audible without betraying their throat-shredding intent. As could be expected, the band generated some crossover appeal among other adventurers: The hit UK single for "Isobel" by Icelandic waif Björk included a version of the song remixed by Carcass.

After operating in the underground for many years, death metal bands were selling hundreds of thousands of albums to dedicated fans in the 1990s and represented a tremendous opportunity for independent metal labels. Metal Blade scooped up Cannibal Corpse to complement a roster of balanced metal styles that ranged from the traditional Fates Warning to the gory performance group Gwar. The metal indie Roadrunner Records went whole hog, joining forerunners Death and Deicide with the popular Sepultura, Brujeria, and Fear Factory, plus the heavy-hitting Immolation, Suffocation, Gorguts, Obituary, and Sorrow. "Bands like that were cheap to sign, and they basically sold themselves," explains the label's A&R head, Monte Conner.

Meanwhile, England's Earache Records attracted Morbid Angel, Nocturnus, Carcass, and a prolific panoply of others to a label roster anchored by flagship act Napalm Death. Though not as well organized as Roadrunner, Earache had marketing power great enough to break new bands based on brand recognition, ushering in the era of designer labels just as Sub Pop Records was striking it rich with grunge. Earache also fed the collector impulse of its customers with picture discs, singles, and special releases in a way that was savvy and a little nostalgic for the rarity of NWOBHM and hardcore punk records.

As the music grew more sophisticated and difficult, so did its representations. Occult symbols proliferated as Deicide and Morbid Angel delved into arcane, witchy texts to find ever more convoluted symbolic expressions of the death metal mind-set. With hundreds of bands looking to stand apart, band logos became cryptic, unreadable semaphores. Lyricists went far beyond the thesaurus abuse of typical songwriters, appropriating the most fearsome and unacceptable language from medical dictionaries and old religious documents—a typical early Carcass opus was titled "Embryonic Necropsy and Devourment."

Such gurgling blasphemies and imperceptible iconography were intended to be 100 percent immune from any kind of mass acceptance—even *Kerrang!* initially dropped the ball, awarding Death and Deicide one-star reviews for their recording debuts. Yet despite the egregious obscenity acting as an insurance policy against corruption, the music business eventually beat a path to the doors of death metal. A dozen of the world's most intense bands entered short-lived recording deals with major labels, as record executives wondered aloud whether the caustic rumblings of the metal scene could cough up another "surprise" success à la Metallica.

Morbid Angel was the first to go public, signing with Giant Records in 1992 and hiring Metallica producer Flemming Rasmussen to record the uncompromised *Covenant*. Soon afterward Cannibal Corpse went to Warner Bros., and South American act Sepultura was bargained away from Roadrunner to Epic Records. As part of a far-reaching alliance crafted by Earache, the bands Carcass, Cathedral, Napalm Death, Godflesh, and Entombed all became part of the mega-conglomerate Sony/Columbia roster. "We were never naïve enough to think we were going to become the next Metallica," insisted Jeff Walker of Carcass to AntiMTV.com—but if Metallica could thrash its way multiplatinum, these bands might have at least a chance of grinding to gold.

The first death metal group to trespass into the *Billboard* chart was Cannibal Corpse, which processed rawer influences into a manufactured, powerful version of the sound. As singer Chris Barnes took the "Cookie Monster" death metal vocal style over the top, songs like "Entrails Ripped from a Virgin's Cunt" played shock value to the hilt. "For me, Cannibal Corpse went too far," says Dee Snider, who had defended heavy metal against the PMRC in 1985. "I read lyrics that literally said, 'I fucked a nun in the ass,' and I said, 'What the fuck is that?' It's not a fantasy, it's just heinous. They've sold hundreds of thousands of albums, which is a little disturbing, but then again, does anyone really know the lyrics?" Nonetheless, comic Jim Carrey found the over-the-top bravado hilarious and hired Cannibal Corpse to appear in *Ace Ventura, Pet Detective*.

From the dirt of the grass roots the popularity of death metal piled up steadily. When Cannibal Corpse blighted *Billboard*, those hundreds of thousands of album sales represented not general music-buying audiences but a formidable number of exclusively pledged metal fans. These were cultivated consumers who would more likely seek out demo tapes and underground LPs than buy other popular music—and they were richly rewarded for the search. By the end of the 1990s, Earache Records claimed that both Napalm Death and Morbid Angel had sold more than a million albums apiece—tallied not in smash-hit gold records but in handfuls of steady releases seen by fans as nothing less than mandatory.

In need of a nerve center, metal fans in the early 1990s could barely have hoped for a better chronicle of the tumultuous scene than *Metal Maniacs*, a quasi-corporate music magazine run with the heart of a fanzine. Published by Sterling/MacFadden, whose other titles included the newsstand fodder *Yo!* and *Country Hits, Maniacs* was launched during the late 1980s as an infrequent offshoot of the glam-centric pinup magazine *Metal Edge*. An early issue captured metal icons Ozzy Osbourne, Gene Simmons, and Vince Neil in lewd poses. When a new editor, Katherine Ludwig, entered the picture, she immediately changed direction. "The former editor's idea of what should go in the magazine was a pinup of Blackie Lawless in a diaper," she says. "I was into having a magazine that didn't talk down to people."

Ludwig tailored Sterling/MacFadden's fan model to fit the hungry metal underground, combining the mass-market approach of *Circus* with the information overload of *Metal Forces*. Pen-pal listings in the magazine were converted to "Shorts," a collection of hundreds of ads for tape traders and amateur bands. The color pinups mandated by the publisher were subverted to feature untraditional icons like the drum-machine pioneers Godflesh or the decimating girl bassist Jo Bench of Bolt Thrower. In addition there was a lively letters section, which became a forum for debating everything from scene politics to abortion rights. "I also liked to get in something about vegetarianism, hemp, feminism, and freedom of speech when I could," says Ludwig.

As a first-time editor, Ludwig resisted the degree to which record-company publicists could set agendas at music magazines. Against the wishes of Carcass's handlers, a typically controversial story on the band took up the issue of its members' belief in the ethical treatment of animals. To Ludwig, the public-relations people appeared afraid that the plant-eater tag would ruin the reputation of a band whose gory 1988 *Reek of Putrefaction* meat-collage album cover had been banned in England. "I don't think a lot of people really got what Carcass was saying," says Ludwig. "They took them at face value and didn't get the irony, the obviousness, of the meat."

Ludwig found that metal fans were dying for a public dialogue that gave dimension to their love of music. "I got the feeling that a lot of kids were starved for someone older to treat them like human beings that might possibly have something to say," she recalls. "A lot of the readers were kids who felt they had nothing but metal, the same way I had felt about hard rock and then punk rock when I was growing up in the 1970s. I felt like I had an obligation to them not to glorify sexism or cruelty; basically to be conscious of the fact that someone was listening. I got marriage proposals. I got phone calls at home. Later on we started getting hate mail. Someone called it *Metal Brainiacs*, which I didn't really take as an insult."

Not only fans responded. Though the freelance budget was a puny three hundred dollars per issue when the magazine began, there was no shortage of writers happy to support something intelligent. Three prominent metal singers—Kevin Sharp of Brutal Truth, Mark "Barney" Greenway of Napalm Death, and Michael D. Williams of Eyehategod—became regular and surprisingly insightful contributors. Staff writers included Borivoj Krgin, a metal encyclopedia who helped discover and promote the career of Sepultura—the Brazilian band that later turned to Katherine Ludwig for help writing lyrics.

Metal fans showed their loyalty by pumping circulation during Ludwig's five-year tenure to a peak of 90,000 in 1995, matching higher-profile alternative music magazines like *Raygun*. Even better, as *Metal Maniacs* survived on subscriptions and sales in 7-Elevens the editorial department remained more beholden to the fans than to the advertisers. It proved that seemingly unwieldly underground metal could be lucrative for anyone who would champion it wisely and creatively. The broad scope of the magazine continued after the departure of Ludwig, but its two very unusual exclamatory subheads slid off the covers into memory: NOT FOR EVERYBODY! and IT STANDS ALONE!

As death metal giants took their place alongside traditional heavy metal heroes in European magazines and at summer festivals, interesting new heavy-death fusion by the likes of Germany's Bethlehem and Tiamat and Finland's Amorphis began tying together the decades. After death metal had nearly purged rock and roll from its bloodstream, the Swedish syncopation fiends in Entombed even brought back some boogie, turning guttural melodies and blast beats toward sinister hip motion. The imitative but satisfying Dismember likewise let detuned guitars, hoarse vocals, and agile guitar slip around in a wet stew of well-engineered sonic gore. Entombed, Dismember, At the Gates, Grave, Dissection, and In Flames—these energetic administrators of the regional Götheborg, Sweden, sound emphasized power alongside grotesqueries and lured many willing mainstream rock fans down to depths of death metal.

Meanwhile, groups like Montreal's Kataklysm, Wyoming's Mona-stat 7, and New Jersey's Human Remains invigorated fans with mind-clearing scientific chaos, standing out as jaw-hangingly unique even in an atypical atmosphere. In 1989 saxophonist John Zorn, a fixture of the New York avant-garde music scene, had launched Naked City, a jazz-influenced death metal genre study featuring himself, guitarist Bill Frisell, bassist Fred Frith, keyboardist Wayne Horvitz, and drummer Joey Baron. That group took basic extreme metal tenets—blast beats, gurgled vocals, and chaotic guitar—and intentionally rearranged them in a tightly structured formal context. The results measured up well—though they were somewhat academic in comparison to the inspired amateurism of death metal in its purest forms.

To claim superiority at the pinnacle of heavy metal's long evolution, death metal could not sit still for one hyperactive, overstimulated second without stretching toward new revelations. While Napalm Death presented a string of unusual side projects, the like-minded Painkiller, Brutal Truth, and Mr. Bungle expanded the scope of sonic assault in a headstrong, almost surreal way. In 1991 John Zorn joined bassist Bill Laswell and Napalm Death drummer Mick Harris to form Painkiller. Though it began as a contest in abrasive non sequiturs similar to those of Naked City, the project quickly evolved beyond sonic extremes into a black-hearted form of ambient electronic dub. At the invitation of Laswell, Mick Harris next guested on a 1993 album, *Sacrifist*, by Praxis, oddly joining Parliament-Funkadelic icons like Bootsy Collins with a battery of bloodcurdling screams. "I'm always down for a bit of that," says Harris. As such departures found wings, they untied death metal from the pentagram.

Continuing to leap ahead musically with a flickering attention span, death metal branched out in the mid-1990s into computers, noise, opera, and the avant-garde. Brutal Truth's creative crossover fantasies coupled singer Kevin Sharp's overview of the genre as metal columnist for the *CMJ* music journal and bassist Dan Lilker's frontline experience as a founder of Anthrax, S.O.D., and Nuclear Assault. Super, piercing speed freaked out atop slow, distorted lurching while cover versions of songs by Celtic Frost and the eccentric jazz composer Sun Ra put the band in outer space. One crushingly original example, the song "Godplayer" from *Need to Control*, pounded over the gurgling, deep-end belch of a didgeridoo, a four-foot-long tube of Aborig-

Departure from death metal: Brutal Truth
(Relapse Records)

AVANT-GARDE METAL

As death metal took conventional music to the outer strato-sphere with its whirling speed and intensity, a number of mu-sicians abandoned the tightly wound structure of the music and experimented with abstractions of its founding elements. Among the success stories of death metal fusion were the clas-sical exploits of Master's Hammer, the jazz screech of 16–17 and Painkiller, and the weirdness of Pan-Thy-Monium and Old—bands in which the influence of Voivod became essen-tial. In many cases these were some of the first metal bands to be seen wearing glasses. In other cases, as with Masters Ham-mer, the mixed-up metal influences were part of an exit strat-egy, the sign of metalheads leaving crumbs behind as they dis-appeared into strange new dark forests of experimentation.

Head Cases

- ❖ Arcturus, *La Masquerade Infernale* (1997)
- ❖ Breadwinner, *The Burner* (1994)
- ❖ Flying Luttenbachers, *Revenge* (1996)
- ❖ Master's Hammer, *Slagry* (1996)
- ❖ Naked City, *Naked City* (1989)
- ❖ Old, *Lo Flux Tube* (1991)
- ❖ Painkiller, *Execution Ground* (1995)
- ❖ Pan-Thy-Monium, *Khaos and Konfusion* (1996)
- ❖ 16-17, *Gyatso* (1994)
- ❖ Treponem Pal, *Treponem Pal* (1989)

inal Australian heritage, whose drone gave any grinding bass on earth a run for the money. Says Yamatsuka Eye of the experimental Japanese band Boredoms, "Brutal Truth play so good in Osaka, I cry."

Concurrently, Faith No More singer Mike Patton took advantage of his celebrity clout to resurrect and promote Mr. Bungle, the Frank Zappa–influenced crossover band he formed during the halcyon days of Cryptic Slaughter and Hirax. After an infantile 1991 debut CD, subsequent outings showed a team of thrashers who had outgrown their genre, tackling disco, electronics, and lounge music in a gory, scatological package. "So many people are so turned off with what they're doing, but they're so tasteful and so ingenious," praises Shawn Crahan of Slipknot, an eclectic band formed in the early 1990s. "Watching them, you also realize, 'Hey, this is the guy who sings in Faith No More and made some of my favorite songs ever.' It's quirky and it's way out there, but so few people can do it from their heart."

On a similar postmodern metal journey was Switzerland's 16–17, a crisp grindcore combo sponsored by Apple Computer, with tearing saxophones in place of guitars. Another highbrow strain of mayhem came from the Prague group Master's Hammer, which ventured from operatic black metal toward modernist electronic music. On *Slagry* they covered Carl Czerny, Otto Katz, and Giuseppe Verdi, mixing bits of metal, folk, and musique concrète into an abstraction of death metal. The bewildering result had nothing to do with evil but demonstrated that metal breeds more than its share of visionaries—living up to the funny slogan of the band's French record label, Osmose Productions: "Extreme Artists Make Extreme Music!"

A hearty number of metal fans in the mid-1990s also seized upon Japanese noise. As the moniker indicated, these recordings were produced using piles of distortion pedals and modulators to create layers of feedback and white noise, presenting a purity and freedom of form impossible in commercial music. While producing the Nirvana album *In Utero*, guitarist Steve Albini traveled to Japan to play with the metallic noise act Zeni Geva. "There's just so many layers to how fucked up Japanese bands are" Albini says. "All rock music in Japan seems to start with a Western influence; then, due to their isolation and enthusiasm, and crappy equipment and environment, they end up making these really idiosyncratic adaptations of this Western music. A heavy metal band that is really into Pantera might also be really flamboyant and queer looking, and have sort of a Liza Minnelli front man."

Metal fans had experienced a long, multitiered acceleration and acclimation to increasing returns of heaviness. Now, using death metal as a base, they were looking for the same intensity of expression in all forms of music. Two tape-trading friends who founded the label Relapse Records, Bill Yurkiewicz and his partner Matt Jacobson, signed Japanese noise bands like Merzbow and Masonna to complement the grindcore and death metal acts in their roster. "We started off as total metalheads," says Jacobson, "and a lot of people that we know were the same. It was just a natural progression to become fans of the industrial and noise stuff."

While acoustic and indigenous music found favor, noise music was an irresistible challenge to the listener—a total blackout. "We see it already, the people that were into early Napalm Death and Carcass are listening to [Japanese noise performer] Masonna," says Yurkiewicz. "Death metal can only go so far being brutal, and the Japanese noise bands just reduce them to nothing within the first five seconds. People always want to keep going one step further."

While death metal proliferated and superstimulated the true believers, the scene was large enough so bands could survive nicely catering to the core audience. For established aboveground music companies, however, the subterranean caverns proved too treacherous to navigate. There was almost no hope of radio or video play to begin with, and widespread resistance among bands to changing for the sake of commerce only made the situation worse. Death metal bands were pursuing their selfish individual thrills, and past a certain point all the record company could do was pay the bills and hope for the best.

As might have been expected, given the extremity of the milieu, the major-label Earache/Columbia Records pact fell through within a year, largely as a result of incompatible business cultures. Soon Napalm Death, Entombed, Carcass, and Cathedral were once again independent bands in the Earache stable. After its separate deal with the major label Giant disintegrated, Morbid Angel also returned to Earache—after selling just short of a million albums during three years in corporate cahoots. Though not what the partners had once hoped, the unification of corporations and cultural destroyers remained historic.

Dumped from the majors, the big death metal acts found themselves still contractually beholden to their original independent labels. Even in the notorious sphere of record-industry contracts, the agreements signed by metal bands appeared especially harsh. After experiencing artistic success and earning a gold album on Epic Records, Sepultura reverted to Roadrunner, honoring a multialbum contract signed when they were still teenagers living in South America. "I think most metal indies try to sign bands long-term," explains Roadrunner executive Monte Conner, "because when you're talking heavy metal, there's a lot of development. It takes five or six years sometimes. If you're going to sign a band and invest all this money up front, you need to ensure that you'll still have the band on your label when they finally become profitable."

In metal there was also incredible money to be made beyond CD sales. Great business flowed from Roadrunner to manufacturers of blood-colored ink, as the label's merchandising operation offered fans dozens of gory T-shirt variations for each band. "Let's face it, merchandising is an incredible thing," says Conner. "You can make more money selling T-shirts than you can selling records. We recognized that and decided to get into that business from the start." Not at all unusual among metal labels, a typical Roadrunner contract was an omnibus deal that assigned merchandise rights to Blue Grape and song publishing to The All Blacks, both sister companies of Roadrunner.

If not exactly living up to Metallica's sales precedent, death metal remained profitable into the mid-1990s. Still, after operating on an underground level for almost ten years, many metal indies wanted out of the niche. Metal Blade's eyes were widened by the success of its signing of the bar-rocking Goo Goo Dolls, and Megaforce languished as a label while its owners focused on managing the tumultuous career of Ministry. Monte Conner claims that Roadrunner was easily able to sell 100,000 copies of any death metal record, but breaking beyond that ceiling was frustrating. "With Obituary, whether we spent twenty thousand dollars promoting something or two hundred thousand dollars, we'd sell the same amount of records." They were ready to give metal back to the tape traders.

The mail-order company Relapse Records added up the numbers

in a different way, assembling thousands of unknown bands into a bewildering force without counting on gold albums. Founded by two tape traders in Colorado in 1990, Relapse was both a record company and a distribution source. The company assailed shelves with an international array of artists, acting like a superpower tape trader that offered specialized music for sale instead of trade. It was a pure product of the underground and thus completely in tune with its audience. Besides direct sales to fans via mail order and the Internet, the organization sold directly to about a hundred mom-and-pop stores. It was a lifeline. "Ohio, California, Texas, and New York are really big for death metal," says Relapse cofounder Bill Yurkiewicz. "But our catalogs have made it over to every obscure country in the world. It's mindblowing."

With the entire world as a marketplace, Relapse was a success of limitless supply years before the launch of Amazon.com. Its staggering mail-order catalog presented thousand of items from every phase of metal's long, illustrious history—and then some. Besides metal artifacts, the catalog shifted headbanger tastes toward the esoteric, incorporating Indonesian field recordings, voice poet Ken Nordine, and protoambient psychedelic bands Amon Duul and Popul Vuh—even Ella Fitzgerald, for those who preferred torch songs to power ballads. As the largest of a giant network of similar operations, Relapse proved there was a self-sustaining strength and richness in underground metal in the mid-1990s that barely needed the outside world or even the mainstream music industry to prosper. The metal milieu was now an entrenched network of regional scenes that refuted all recognized musical limits and often discarded social constraints to a shocking degree.

❧ XV ❧

Worlð Metal:
The Globalization of Heavy

➤ **August 1984:** Iron Maiden's *Powerslave*
tour visits Eastern Europe

➤ **1986:** Sepultura releases *Morbid Visions*
in Brazil

➤ **April 10, 1993:** Rioting at Metallica shows
in Indonesia prompts ban on foreign bands

➤ **October 19, 2000:** Sepultura *Chaos* A.D.
goes gold in the United States

➤ **April 2001:** Brujeria's *Brujerizmo* nominated
for Best Rock Album at *Billboard* Latin
Music Awards

Beyond Grammy winners and other morbid millionaires, there remained thousands of bands that seemingly existed solely for the sheer joys of extremist expression. Throughout the global metal diaspora, heavy metal outposts remained in constant contact via always lively international channels. Metalheads of all kinds were banging on guitars, typing fanzine articles, and scribbling each other notes from every nook and cranny of the earth. Between map points flowed a never-ending stream of touring bands. If rap music in the 1990s was, as Chuck D once said, the CNN of black America, metal was an unflinching broadcast of international affairs.

Whether living in Ohio or Oslo, headbangers had a more accurate awareness of life in Third World countries than did the majority of Westerners. "I know not to believe what you see on TV, that's for fucking sure," snorts Napalm Death's singer, Barney Greenway. "The different levels of class around the world are quite noticeable, the way different societies treat their citizens. I find Americans so fucking strange. I find them very twee. Then, going to Russia, people walk with their heads down. It's like they're just walking in circles because they've never known anything different."

Heavy metal had established itself early as an international voice. Iron Maiden's film, *Iron Maiden Behind the Iron Curtain*, documented the band's 1984 tour through Poland. There, heavy metal of any kind had previously been contraband, thus necessarily underground and tightly cherished. As the English group

Join the party: official heavy metal union pin from communist Poland.

and its touring armada entered Warsaw, Polish metalheads swarmed over public buildings, deluging the band with homemade gifts—offering a joyous reception to the country's first British invasion.

Even among American bands there was a huge metal immigrant population, starting with the Van Halen brothers from Holland and Lars Ulrich from Denmark. Rudi Sarzo of Quiet Riot and Ozzy Osbourne's band came from Cuba. Tom Araya and Dave Lombardo of Slayer were both born in South America. Tommy Lee of Mötley Crüe was Greek—the son of a nationally known beauty queen. Along with countless others, these foreign-born musicians came to America as children. The grandiose expressions of heavy metal probably helped reconcile their experiences in life among an adopted culture—it was something big enough to bridge the gap. In any case, heavy metal brought opportunity.

Though Metallica's music was no longer at the cutting edge of development in the mid-1990s, the band's incredible touring regime reached out to every country with a soccer stadium. As the good ship Metallica sailed around the world to promote the Black Album, the band played more than three hundred shows in thirty-seven countries, most performances lasting longer than three hours. In North America excitement over heavy metal was measured by showers of money. In less affluent parts of the world, where troubled youth sought salvation in vociferous discontent, there could be havoc. At a free outdoor show at Moscow's Tushino Airfield in September 1991, a small city of half a million, Metallica fans were beaten down by moonlighting Russian army soldiers. These were unseasoned security guards who panicked at the first sight of thrashing and wild slam dancing, and their methods of crowd control led to eleven deaths.

Then, on April 10, 1993, over a hundred people were arrested after a Metallica show in Jakarta, Indonesia. According to UPI reports, rioting broke out between the ticket-holding haves and the less fortunate have-nots, causing a regional melee that left thirteen people hospitalized, thirty-eight others injured, eight cars and a number of palm trees burned, and several houses damaged. "Indonesia was the first date of a three-week tour," says Lars Ulrich. "We played Singapore and the Philippines for the next couple weeks. Everywhere we went, we were the big bad Western satanic metal band from hell, causing riots and disturbing the peace. The media followed us around, writing front-page headlines like HERE COME THE RIOT-INDUCERS METALLICA! There we were, just four friendly guys."

In America and Europe rock and roll had become largely safe, professional, and controlled. In Jakarta government officials denounced Metallica and vowed to crack down on permits for all future rock concerts. Heavy metal served as a spontaneous expression of instant liberty, dangerous in areas with very different cultural climates from those in London or Los Angeles. "I've seen the aggression of music bring people to the point where they understand the struggle against the powers that be," says spokesrapper Chuck D of Public Enemy. "Worldwide I think people are more aware of how the music is being put down than I guess the people in America give them credit for."

The global response to underground heavy metal was enthusiastic, coming from audiences who related to bands as blessed peers. Anywhere young people lived without illumination, Napalm Death's corrosive metal ate into musical consciousness. Like Iron Maiden and Metallica before it, the band toured until British-bred singer Barney Greenway reckoned he felt more at home in Tel Aviv than in Tennessee. In 1992 the band hosted 9,000 people in Czechoslovakia and a combined total of 15,000 over two days in Moscow. "We're playing places that we never thought in a million years we would," says guitarist Mitch Harris.

These were musicians at long last—Westerners, no less—who understood systemic conflict and lifelong frustration. Increasingly the harsh messages and typically gory illustrations of death metal were seen on the black T-shirts of disenchanted teens in cultural war zones like Poland, Puerto Rico, and Thailand—as well as the back streets of New York, Miami, and San Antonio. The language was often as indecipherable as graffiti, but the meaning to outsiders was clear: "Stay away—I hate your lying, hypocritical world."

Outside of America metal bands were often motivated by values other than riches or fame. In Russia, Napalm Death was supported by Korrozia Metalla, an outrageous Motörhead-inspired performance-art revue whose act included seminude women, wooden barricades, and automobiles for clobbering with hammers and setting ablaze. Highlights among the band's repertoire included "I'm President," "Russian Vodka," and "Trash Around Kremlin." Vocalist Sergei "Spider" Troitsky's strange shockpolitik was clearly an attack on the country's post-Soviet cultural vacuum and was unheard music to Western ears.

Though black-market sales were shady and impossible to track, heavy metal appeared to totally dominate youth culture in the Eastern Bloc during and after the fall of the Soviet Union. "Dio played Romania, Bulgaria, Hungary, Estonia, and I loved all those places," says Ronnie James Dio. "Those kids know more about metal than anybody I've ever heard. These kids had to hold the stuff really dear, because the laws a lot of times said that if you get caught with a record, it's prison, pal. That's brave, and it's somebody that really cares a lot about music. I don't think I would have done that."

DIY in the Third World

With the dissolution of the Soviet Union in 1991—coinciding with the early peak of metal's mainstream popularity—the former communist countries joined the rest of Europe in exporting metal to the global vortex. Earache Records signed the Polish death metal band Vader in 1992, while the cult black metal band Behemoth charred their heels with a series of demos. In the 1990s strange, homegrown metal flourished in every pocket of every continent where civilization and its discontents were possible.

The middle of the decade brought the spread of intense metal across the Far East, to Singapore, Malaysia, Indonesia, and Taiwan. Japan had participated in heavy metal's evolution with relish since the start, offering the huge fan support evidenced on 1970s live albums by Judas Priest and Scorpions, and periodically exporting key bands like heavy metal act Loudness and grindcore group S.O.B. Now the extreme act Impiety joined a black metal revival in the Pacific Rim, sparring in Hellhammer-style atrocities with Australia's Sadistik Execution and Destroyer 666 despite threats from Islamic mufti holy leaders in nearby Malaysia.

The metal underground provided a conduit from countries where little rock music had previously escaped. Greece, home to Rotting Christ and Varathron, saw the rise of dozens of doom-inflected black metal bands and thriving record labels. Even in Turkey bands like Ziggurat and also Pentagram—later called Mezarkabul—combined heavy metal tradition with the unique inflections of Mesopotamia.

Along with European classical music, the Middle East had been a popular source of ideas since the 1980s, when Mercyful Fate recorded "Curse of the Pharaohs" and Iron Maiden titled an Egyptian-themed album *Powerslave*. In the 1990s the Mediterranean produced its own metal, imbued with the rich accents of the region. In Tel Aviv, Israel, the five lads in Orphaned Land wove romantic dark metal forms elaborated by Middle Eastern modalities, instrumentation, and devotional singing styles. An odd group called People combined grindcore with Israel's other famous musical export, disco, to create a sound that mixed Morbid Angel with Miami Sound Machine. Meanwhile, the eccentric Israeli band Rabies Caste, signed to Earache in the late 1990s, consisted of refugees from Russia who were refused asylum in America as children, thus rerouted to a life in exile in Israel, like the fabled strangers in a strange land.

From the other side of Jerusalem came Arallu, an Arabic black metal band that took pride in the similarities between the origins of the *Necronomicon*—the mystical book of the dead and a favorite heavy metal literary source—and the beliefs of a group of ancient pre-Islamic magicians called the Muqarribun. As told on *The War on the Wailing Wall*—accompanied by photographs of the band feigning a defilement of the holy ancient West Wall of Jerusalem—the band's satanic attack on Christianity and Judaism had a much more tangible dimension than the fantastical devil semiology of Florida death metal bands.

Neither was Africa's metal scene limited to Westernized countries. Lagos, Nigeria, hosted a small metal cluster spread by the children of foreign diplomats. Though gory imagery remained a constant, the level of sedition in each country's metal scene was highly relative. "Our metal scene is made up almost entirely of whites," says guitarist Shukri Adams of the South African grindcore band Cauterized. "Nonwhite people do come to gigs, and there isn't any obvious racial friction, but people keep to their own groups. I am the only nonwhite metal band member I know of in this country. I've had two white vocalists in the band, but while we're friends, they don't really share my enthusiasm for lyrics that lambaste racist South Africans."

A sophisticated network of metal cells tied all of these disparate entities into one global web. Each country had specialty labels and distributors, like Relapse Records in America, Cogumelo in Brazil, and Siam Pacific in Thailand. It became possible for a band from India to share promotion with a band in Islamabad, Pakistan, then have its music released by a Brazilian label for sale in America and Europe. Internet contact hastened the process of networking and publicity. The bootstraps approach of *Metal Massacre* was happening a thousand times over as metal become borderless folk culture, the first voice of dissent and disaffection.

While American and European death metal acts went adventuring in the world, Brazil's brilliant Sepultura came from a cultural backwoods to become the international metal success story of the 1990s. On 1989's *Arise*, its fourth record, the teenage members of Sepultura combined the snarling aggression of Slayer with the powerful multi-layered composition of *Master of Puppets*–era Metallica. Even while developing an activist message on later albums, the band remained unpretentious and approachable. Following a brief feud between the two parties, Sepultura was the one death metal act that Slayer deemed worthy of having influenced. "In the beginning they were Slayer babies," says Kerry King. "They just had the lower voice. There was some serious Slayer influence. Then, around *Chaos A.D.*, they got their own direction, and they were good at it."

Sepultura threw deathly thrash back at the Europeans while keeping its South American identity. Even the satanic character of early albums like *Morbid Visions*, recorded when the members were fourteen years old, responded to the realities of their Third World environment. "In Belo Horizonte, where we lived," explains singer/guitarist Massimiliano Cavalera, aka Max, "almost everybody that's born there goes to church and starts praying and is a Catholic already. Like I used to be, until I really started to understand things and found out it's just a bunch of shit. Everything is just unreal. They were so rich in the church, and they were doing nothing to help people, really. There's more churches than houses there."

Sepultura 1987 (left to right): Paolo Jr. (wearing calculator watch), Max Cavalera, Igor Cavalera, Andreas Kisser
(Roadrunner Records)

As close to death metal as any other gold-selling record before it, *Chaos A.D.* stripped down Sepultura's sound into a coarse metallic loop. The CD sold half a million copies, and alongside Pantera the band forged a streetwise, death-derived groove metal that inspired an upcoming generation of mavens in the 1990s. "One thing I love about Max Cavalera of Sepultura," says Shawn Crahan of Slipknot, "he plays with three or four strings on his guitar, because he has no need for two of them. I love that philosophy."

Not merely a metal success story, Sepultura was the most popular rock band ever to embark from Brazil, a country with a vast musical landscape. As it toured the Northern Hemisphere, the group brought its hometown roadies and soccer balls, retaining a distinctly familial Brazilian atmosphere. On the acoustic protest hymn "Itsari" the band recruited native Amazon drummers from the troubled Xavantes rainforest tribe. The marriage of Max Cavalera to the band's manager, Gloria Bujnowski, was a paparazzo event in Brazil compared by one guest to the royal wedding of Prince Charles and Lady Diana. Yet Sepultura's vision remained focused on the impoverished Brazil portrayed in "Kaiowas," a raging memorial to an Amazonian tribe that committed mass suicide rather than Westernize.

Fans repaid Sepultura with devotion, especially in South America, Mexico, Spain, and Portugal—all regions with rampant metal scenes. Though Brazilians speak Portuguese as a remnant of their colonial heritage, Sepultura considered all Hispanic fans "the same Latin American kind of blood, the same kind of people," according to guitarist Andreas Kisser. "It's the same kind of feeling when you play in Mexico

The members of Sepultura visit their home fan club
(Katherine Ludwig)

and Brazil. The people are really hungry to see shows. They kind of identify with us, because we are from Brazil, in South America."

Even as New York City exported rap music to the world in the 1990s, a group of Spanish-speaking women from Spanish Harlem and the South Bronx spawned the fanzine *Endemoniada*. The creative endeavor lovingly cradled metal-romantic amateur art and poetry along with the usual interviews and reviews. Editors Lucifera and Xastur, a pair of self-professed witches, oversaw highly personal explorations of the occult, gender issues, and somber unknown sounds. "You should see the look I get when I say I'm into metal," says Lucifera. "Espe-

From Spanish Harlem and the Bronx,
the editors of *Endemoniada*
(*Endemniada 'zine*)

cially in my area, since I'm Hispanic. People are so closed-minded. They swear I'm trying to be white! Go figure."

Yet for many young people in Colombia, Argentina, Mexico, and Brazil, metal was the music that mattered. In the wake of Sepultura's success, the cities of Bogotá and Medellín, Colombia, spawned more than a hundred underground death metal and black metal bands. Signed to a French label, the Colombian band Masacre (not to be confused with Florida's Massacre) was one of the most successful. Beginning in 1988, with its demo *"Colombia . . . Imperio del Terror"*—"Colombia . . . Empire of Terror"—the band dealt in its lyrics with the violence that was the scourge of that war-torn country. Masacre toured South America extensively, playing Colombia, Ecuador, Venezuela, and Peru, sometimes performing in strange venues but always reaching an informed local death metal scene, each with its own magazines, radio programs, and record labels.

Metal reached through cultural and national borders. The mountainous crucible of Mexico City was home to thudding thrashers Transmetal, Drakkar, and Death Warrant, influenced by early Los Angeles speed metal bands like Slayer, Agent Steel, and Hirax. Following a 1998 tour by Death, where Chuck Schuldiner was photographed amid Mayan temples, the Mexican headbangers began leaning toward death metal and exploiting the legendary heart-ripping blood-sacrifice rituals of their Aztec ancestors. Even the former Mexican provinces of Texas, New Mexico, and Arizona were filled with headbangers and *metaleros* from the thriving Mexican metal universe. In Gallup, New Mexico, the largest U.S. city on a Native American reservation, Mitch Harris of Napalm Death recalls finding discarded fistfuls of long, black Navajo hair on the floor after a frenzied show.

A world apart from the rich glam metal playground in West Hollywood, the backyards and wedding halls of East L.A. spawned their own Hispanic metal scene. There, raging death metal bands like Sadistic Intent and Profécia spewed vile prophecies in Spanish to small audiences, including toddlers, grandparents, and skeptical groups of men huddled around beer kegs. Before being whisked to new bands far away, both drummer Oscar Garcia of Morbid Angel and guitarist Jesse Pintado of Napalm Death played in Terrorizer, which Pintado characterizes as "a bunch of Mexican kids thrashing away in their backyard." During the late 1980s the band never played for more than twenty relatives and neighborhood kids—yet Terrorizer's demo and rehearsal recordings remained a staple of underground tape traders, leading to a 1989 Earache release, *Endless Downfall*, which captured a lethal, slippery, thrash-based style.

Furthering the spirit of Terrorizer was the mysterious Spanish-language project called Brujeria. Formed by Fear Factory guitarist Dino Cazares, himself a veteran of the East L.A. backyard bashes, Brujeria extrapolated a terrifying worldview from the bizarre 1989 discovery of a cult of Matamoros, Mexico, drug lords who killed competitors via ritual sacrifice. Glorifying the dark arts of blood worship and heroin trafficking while dressed in a ski mask, the singer bellowed livid lines "*El norte quiere nuestro cosecha de oro / Trafficiando drogas, coca y mota / La benedición satánica,*" or "The north wants our gold / Trafficking drugs, cocaine and pot / Under satanic blessing."

Even in death metal the Brujeria album *Matando Güeros*—"Killing White Filth"—was a landmark in aural atrocity, employing the everyday violence of Latin America as a backdrop for a blistering onslaught of greed-induced horror. Color photographs on the CD sleeve depicted a decapitated body and bales of narcotics, images filched from the bloody tabloid *Alarma!*, a weekly dose of gore funded by the Mexican government. The part-time group managed a second album, *Raza Odiada*—"Hated Race"—featuring equal doses of slow, pounding numbers and pressurized speed bolts. On the opening song an assassin cuts down California governor Pete "Pito" Wilson, portrayed by punk singer Jello Biafra, in the midst of an antiimmigration speech. In search of heroes of revolt, the band toasted brazen idols like the rebels of the Chiapas uprising, Colombian drug boss Pablo Escobar, and that scourge of Catholicism, Lucifer.

An underground scene was no place for secrets, and it soon became known that Brujeria's spurts of activity came only when its members could sneak away from their day jobs in Fear Factory, Faith No More, and Napalm Death. Brujeria might have been an in-joke among the prominent bands that lent it members, but the topics and approach were confrontational, disturbing, and real. Even in jest Brujeria represented truthfully the degree to which Latin America was a death metal stronghold. When the mainstream finally caught up with metal's Latin flavor, Brujeria was nominated for the Best Rock Album at the 2001 *Billboard* Latin Music Awards.

So in the 1990s the tendrils of extreme metal unfurled via fanzines, regional distributors, and computers to implant themselves firmly in every hidden crevice of the globe. Metal was instinctively against many things, but wrapped up in all the blood and guts the belief that mundane individuals might aspire to immortality. Fans everywhere continued to play their crucial role, creating a culture whose values often strayed from the popular marketplace and normal behavior. If mainstream social structures could communicate such ideas half as fairly and effectively, groups of teenagers in gory T-shirts would not gather to listen to Slayer on every street corner from Chicago to Calcutta.

The Teen Terrorists
of Norwegian Black Metal

➤ **1985:** Mayhem releases "Pure Fucking Armageddon" demo

➤ **April 1991:** Mayhem vocalist, Dead, commits suicide

➤ **June 6, 1992:** Fantoft stave church burned by arsonists in Norway

➤ **August 1993:** Emperor records *In the Nightside Eclipse*

➤ **August 10, 1993:** Mayhem guitarist Euronymous killed at his apartment

➤ **Fall 2000:** Cradle of Filth signs with Sony

Rarely registering with the mainstream except when lumped together as a mass phenomenon dressed in black, the differences between metal subgenres were huge nonetheless. Even as death metal decimated artistic and commercial frontiers the world over, a cadre of talented, violent, and ultraserious black metal bands pulled the locus of metal power away from swampy Florida to the dark, cold countries of Scandinavia. There, all of the speed and experimentalism of the metal fringe regrouped with primal passion in what practitioners called pure Norwegian black metal.

Black metal in the 1990s was much faster and more orchestral than death metal, with fewer curving riffs to complicate its unrelenting assault. In the 1990s, this wave of bands imported the crude beginnings of 1980s black metal forefathers—Venom, Hellhammer, and Bathory—to capture their own evocative wash of night skies, natural wonder, and Nordic myths. A pronounced influence in this regard was the Swedish group Bathory, whose early-1980s albums were the ultimate sonic blend of speed and atmosphere. Even while looking to the American bands, Bathory founder Quorthon Seth found developing in cultural isolation in Scandinavia to be a creative asset. "Had we been from New York, we would have gotten gigs and contracts and gotten caught up in trends," he says. "We didn't have those kind of pressures—so we were able to add acoustic guitars and backing harmony vocals and the sound of a seagull flying by. Slayer would never get away with doing that, but we could."

In Norway the second generation of black metal began with Mayhem—called "The One True Mayhem" to differentiate itself from bands in Oregon and New York using the same name. Founded in 1984 by sixteen-year-old Oystein Aarseth, aka Euronymous, Mayhem initially mimicked the simple satanic noise of Venom, whose 1982 opus, *Black Metal*, gave the style its name, and the Swiss band Hellhammer. Through tape trading Euronymous came to admire also the speed of Napalm Death and the ferocity of South American bands like Sarcofago and Holocausto, who created incredibly savage music in lean circumstances. All these were bands from the metal fringes, who utilized extreme speed and drama to make themselves known to the underground. "Without Euronymous black metal would not be the same," says Mortiis, original bassist for the Norwegian band Emperor.

The One True Mayhem
(Mayhem)

"Back then you didn't have fifty thousand black metal albums out; you had, like, fifteen. It was different. Euronymous had this total Satan attitude. I didn't have that—he had that. He was such a devil worshipper you wouldn't believe it.

Mayhem was an emotional and ritualistic band consumed by a

wild spirit—the band characteristically adorned its stage set with skinned pig heads. Initially there was a great deal of goofing around involved, but attitudes grew increasingly serious. Euronymous was essentially a realist who possessed worldly zeal and ego, but after several demo tapes the band found its poetic and morbid dimension in Swedish vocalist Per Yngve Ohlin, aka Dead, an erratic dreamer who buried his stage clothes underground to imbue them with proper grave-like essence. Onstage Dead inhaled from a plastic bag containing a dead bird. With changing lineups growing ever more dedicated, Mayhem traveled to eastern Germany in 1990 and recorded what became the gruesome *Live in Leipzig* CD—a classic outing showcasing Dead's ghastly delivery on "Freezing Moon."

In addition to playing guitar in Norway's leading band, Euronymous also cultivated the local metal economy by operating Helvete, a black metal corner shop in Oslo, and running the Deathlike Silence record label. A flock of younger musicians thrived under the wings of his diverse interests. In the early days before joining one of Norway's greatest bands, Emperor drummer Bård Eithun, aka Faust, worked at Euronymous's store. Emperor guitarist Tomas Haugen, aka Samoth, lived in Euronymous's shop for a period of time.

Scandinavian teenagers took pride in their local extreme metal variant. In the early 1990s, fans gravitated toward the Swedish bands Unleashed and Dissection and the strong scene in Norway—spearheaded by Mayhem and including Darkthrone and Immortal. They were fatigued by the machismo and deflating dynamism of Florida death metal, which they came to see as overly commercialized and flagging in spirit. "Some imagine for some weird reason that death metal is something normal and available for everyone," Dead told the influential

Early Emperor
(Century Media)

Slayer 'zine. "If you go into an ordinary school, you will surely see half of the children wearing Morbid Angel, Autopsy, and Entombed shirts, and once again I will vomit! Death black metal is something all ordinary mortals should fear, not make into a trend!"

Formed in 1991 from the ashes of its death metal band Thou Shalt Suffer, Emperor truly realized the artistic ambition of black metal, rejoining many distinct offshoots into an intensely mood-driven style. With their proximity to Germany, it was natural for the Norwegians to adopt the melodic methods of classic German speed metal bands like Destruction and Kreator—though black metal doubled every note to increase the rushing feel. Emperor and others also added keyboards and experimented with another natural ally, goth rock, particularly Kate Bush and the gloomy Sisters of Mercy. As a direct result black metal filled its ranks with young women who had found themselves edged to the periphery of the more muscular, mosh-pit-oriented death metal scene.

Creating a bizarre and altered atmosphere, these bands also returned theatrical flair to heavy metal with a vengeance. Like their predecessors in Venom and Hellhammer, the Norwegian black metallers adopted nicknames to replace given "Christian" names. Many wore capes and black-and-white face paint in the style of King Diamond from Mercyful Fate—a great change from the anti-image times of thrash and death metal, when bands like Exodus and Cannibal Corpse performed wearing sweatpants. To further prepare for their journey into the unknown, Mayhem, Emperor, Immortal, and Darkthrone posed for group portraits waving torches, mean-looking daggers, axes, and spiked clubs. "It's the same thing as when punk and hardcore came out," says Brutal Truth singer Kevin Sharp, a former metal columnist for *CMJ*. "They used to wear the spiked armbands or whatever for total shock value, just to say, 'I'm a total shithead asshole.'"

Among other quirks there was a branch of radical environmentalism to the scene, as black metal artists populated CD jackets with natural landscapes and professed their affinity for nature—which Norway offered in powerful abundance. Trumpeting solitude as a virtue, teenage musicians began to resemble the famously isolated literary protagonists of Norwegian novels by the likes of Knut Hamsun. "Usually, we do walk to the mighty Isle of Man during the later hours," Ovl Svithjod of In the Woods told the 'zine *Petrified*. "We light a fire, put on some spiritual music or sound tracks, and talk and reflect on later happenings in life. It is indeed like balm for our souls."

Unlike fun-loving thrash metal bands Exodus and Anthrax, who never stopped recruiting converts to the metal cause, black metallers ultimately viewed themselves as elites of rarefied sensibility. Their style was less a cause to be spread gleefully than a privilege to be cultivated by the chosen few. The populist concerns of death metal were scorned, and the landscape became internal, less extroverted. They took their cause very seriously. "We were young at that time," writes Bård Faust of Emperor. "We were dedicated to the core to a vital and subcultural underground world of harsh and devilish-inspired metal."

Soon the destructive gleam of Norwegian black metal took on a malicious focus. Deicide returned from a tour of northern Europe in 1992 reporting that a bomb had been detonated at its concert in Stockholm. Allegedly the explosive was planted by animal-rights activists inflamed by the group's advocacy of animal sacrifice—or whatever anti-American urges would compel street activists to blow up a rock club. Deicide's drummer, Steve Asheim, however, speculated that the blast was actually an attack against the opening act, Gorefest, by ultrasatanic Norwegian black metallers. The bomb was an augury of events that would turn the metal world into a scary place, where being the fastest band or collecting the most obscure demo tapes was no longer the measure of credentials.

As it happened, the rise of black metal coincided with the thousand-year anniversary of Christianity in Norway, when two pagan kings, Olaf I Tryggvason in 995 and Olaf II Haraldsson in 1015, violently imposed religion on the western coast of Norway and hastened the end of the Viking era. In studying the atrocities perpetrated by the cross against their forebears, the pentagram-laden black metal bands of Norway found an ambitious aim that elevated satanic pranks to the level of religious jihad: to cast out Christianity as violently as it had invaded, returning Norway to a natural condition of spiritual harmony.

With such dramatic historical fragments in mind, the black metal

SCANDINAVIAN BLACK METAL

The distillation of death metal into a simpler, more concentrated style, black metal abandoned lurching chaos for a million-miles-an-hour assault on the senses. Later the music became entwined in the feuds and terrorist dramas of Norway and eventually bloomed into a creative flowering of orchestral angst, complete with choral arrangements and techno fugues. Black metal musicians made some of the most moving heavy metal ever created—the criminals among them also raised the most disturbing questions about the music's potential social uses. Dissection and Marduk actually hailed from nearby Sweden, also home to the genre's godfather, Bathory.

The Blackest of Hates

- ❖ Burzum, *Filosofem* (1996)
- ❖ Darkthrone, *Transilvanian Hunger* (1994)
- ❖ Dimmu Borgir, *Enthrone Darkness Triumphant* (1997)
- ❖ Dissection, *The Somberlain* (1993)
- ❖ Emperor/Enslaved, *Emperor/Hordane's Land* (1993)
- ❖ Emperor, *Into the Nightside Eclipse* (1995)
- ❖ Enslaved, *Frost* (1994)
- ❖ Immortal, *Battles in the North* (1995)
- ❖ Marduk, *Panzer Division Marduk* (1999)
- ❖ Mayhem, *De Mysteriis Dom Sathanas* (1993)
- ❖ Mortiis, *Ånden Som Gjorde Opprör* (1994)

children—mostly in their late teens and early twenties— attacked the religious landmarks of their stern Christian tradition, raiding churches in the dark of night using matches and gasoline. The first to

A 1900 stereoscope card depicting Fantoftkirke

burn was the majestic twelfth-century wooden-stave church called Fantoftkirke, torched in the predawn hours of June 6, 1992. That arson was fast followed by the burning of Ullandhaug Bedehaus Church, Revheim Church, Holmenkollen Chapel, Skjold Church, Ormøya Chapel, Hauketo og Prinsdal Church, and Asane Church. "All this is said to be of historical value," said Vegard Tveitan, aka Ihsahn, of Emperor in a 1996 interview, "though still being of Christian value, it was to be reduced to a pile of ashes."

Nonetheless, the black metal vandals were unusually articulate criminals—hand in hand with this period of literal mayhem came a series of incredible creative breakthroughs. Mayhem's vocalist, Dead, committed suicide with razors and a shotgun in April 1991, but Euronymous kept the band going. He shortly set about recording Mayhem's long-awaited debut LP, *De Mysteriis Dom Sathanas*. (Before calling police, Euronymous somewhat coldly claimed to have picked pieces of Dead's skull to make jewelry, and cooked and eaten a stew containing some small portions of brain.)

Following the tradition, begun by chronically understaffed bands Bathory and Hellhammer, of employing "session players," Euronymous summoned operatic vocalist Attila Csihar from the Hungarian group Tormentor in the spring of 1993. "I remember them waiting for me at the train station," Csihar told the 'zine *Descent*. "Euronymous was wearing a black cloak. He was a dark man, and he was very short and stout. [Bassist] Varg Vikernes was waiting for me with an iron mail cloak like a Norse viking. The other guys, [guitarist] Snorre Ruch, aka Blackthorn, and [drummer Jan Axel von Blomberg, aka] Hellhammer, were more normal. Vikernes was driving the car and listening to very fast and hard techno."

As *De Mysteriis* neared completion, the sessions pushed the artistic process to the point of epiphany. "I remember dedicating an entire day to recording 'De Mysteriis Dom Sathanas,' a most difficult song," says Csihar. "Euronymous explained to me how he wanted me to sing 'A demon flies.' They were great musicians. Euronymous and Blackthorn were playing their guitars very well, and Vikernes was a very young but good bass player, very professional as well. Hellhammer was incredible on drums. They were very nice people to me and my wife." An orchestrated and unpredictable maze of interlocking mercurial riffs, the results were cryptic and dire, yet impressive. Euronymous felt that the savagery of the recordings measured up to expectations—yet the release was delayed for the mundane reason that his self-financed record label lacked the funds to proceed.

During the peak of the church fires in 1993, Emperor recorded its triumphant *In the Nightside Eclipse* at the Memorial Hall of Norwegian composer Edvard Grieg. The album opened with a dramatic rush of rolling drums and symphonic guitars underscored by choral and organ lines, as vocalist/guitarist Ihsahn cackled a moving invocation. "As the darkness creeps over the Northern mountains of Norway, and the silence reach the woods, I awake and I arise . . ." Decorated with stark photos of the wilds of Norway, *Nightside* was dirty, destructive music, yet oddly beautiful. Though still teenagers, the band members understood juxtaposition completely, sealing the album's sinister and sensitive sides together in a lyrical net of moon worship, forest fantasy, and dark-star loneliness.

Meanwhile, the crimes escalated in senselessness, and rumors spread of an "inner circle" of a "black metal mafia." Norwegian police remained baffled by the severity and seemingly random patterns of the attacks. As with a terrorist movement functioning through independent cells, there was little evidence of a real conspiracy between metal bands, yet arson and unsolved stabbings continued. "Most of the actions were more or less 'let's do it tonight' kinds of things," recalled Emperor's Samoth in the book *Lords of Chaos*, "but that didn't make them any less serious. It was not like 'Knights around the Round Table.' There was not a formal meeting before any act would take place, where people were told what to do and things like that. For a little while there was unity and some strong ideas, but it soon became too unserious. Way too many people knew what was going on."

Stoking the fires of controversy, the Burzum album *Aske*—"Ashes"—recorded in August 1992, used a photo of the smoldering ruins of the Fantoft stave church on its cover. A limited edition was later packaged with a cigarette lighter. Though underworked and not altogether impressive, the music remained surprisingly melodic and featured a rare outside contribution by Emperor's Samoth on bass. Unlike the sophisticated Emperor, Burzum was an intensely personal one-man band, at that point sounding like the low-fidelity product of raw angst and adolescence sinking under extraordinary pressures.

The unchecked violence in the scene hit home on the early morning of August 10, 1993, when Mayhem founder Euronymous was stabbed to death in his Oslo apartment. Seven days later police arrested a younger rival, named Varg Vikernes, aka Count Grishnackh—the bassist in Mayhem at the time, whose savage Burzum was also signed to Euronymous's record label. The motive was unclear, and various rumors explained the killing as a dispute over money or rivalry over a girlfriend. There was certainly a taste of Oedipal victory in the slaying of his former mentor—Vikernes had begun openly proclaiming his view that Euronymous was a "fat, lazy communist" whose lifestyle failed to uphold his ultraevil persona.

Turning their attention to the black metal scene, authorities discovered another motivation—a twisted sense of one-upmanship on Vikernes's part. As they began questioning the black metal community, they learned it was apparently widely known that Emperor's drummer, Faust, had already committed the ultimate sin of murder, in August 1992 stabbing to death a middle-aged homosexual man who had trailed him from a pub into the Olympic Park in Lillehammer. ("I remember I thought, 'This is it, now it is done,'" Faust told an interviewer.) For this crime and his role in subsequently uncovered arsons, Faust was arrested one year and one week later. After confessing, he won a fourteen-year prison term.

As the fog of secrecy evaporated between 1992 and 1994, a dozen young people from the black metal scene were convicted and jailed for acts of violence and the arson of twenty-four churches in total. Except for its primary songwriter, Ihsahn, Emperor was especially inspired to commit wild acts: Guitarist Samoth and bassist Tchort were also imprisoned for shorter terms for arson and assault. Tabloids shocked readers with the revelation that Samoth and Ihsahn had previously been guests of the government in 1991, when their former band won a small arts grant to pay for rehearsal space.

Convicted of the murder of Euronymous plus three church arsons, Vikernes was sentenced to Norway's maximum, twenty-one years in prison. European television reported that he testified, unrepentant, in court, "I want to create a large following, burn all churches, and throw all Christians out. My church-burning army is to consist of young people." In the tradition of the great scandal sheets of London, the long-running heavy metal magazine *Kerrang!* broke the story to the rest of the world with lurid, satanic-themed headlines and photos of Vikernes posing shirtless with weapons.

Mock Burzum "church tour" promo flyer

Playing the character of "Count Grishnackh" to the hilt, Vikernes relished his new role as a media figure, baiting the mainstream papers and toying with underground fanzines from his prison cell. A longtime Satanist, though only twenty years old, Vikernes dramatically switched to preaching Odinism after an earlier arrest for arson. He attempted to reach his deeds in the Norse warrior ethic of a bygone era. "The thing with him," says former ally Mortiis, "is whenever he changes his mind, he takes all the old stuff and changes the concepts to harmonize with what he's doing now. A lot of other people would see through that. First he was a devil worshipper and then a Nazi who wants to do Norwegian lyrics, for example. Every time he does that, he twists the old style to make it look like that's what he's been doing all along. It kind of takes a mastermind to do that, but he's an intelligent guy."

The killer also had a latent talent for music. In 1993, after many of the arsons but four months before the murder of Euronymous, Vikernes created the Burzum album *Filosofem*, a masterpiece intended "to stimulate the fantasy of mortals." Not released until 1996, this tempered suite of metal-derived, folk-inspired electronic sadness used distant, raking guitars and ominous, heavily distorted and tortured vocals to evoke powerful themes of innocence, violence, and self-reflection. Dominated by simple, repetitive synthesizer riffs, the forlorn "Rundgang um die Transzendentale Säule der Singularität" was a nearly eternal four-note ambient psalm marked deeply by both beauty and horror. A glossy booklet illustrated feelings of withdrawal with etchings of sea spirits, horn-blowing widows, and frightened woodcutters—the fairy-tale protagonists of Burzum's music.

Had he been assassinated on the streets or executed by the state, Vikernes's legacy would doubtlessly have thrived as his myth grew. Instead the free press and scrutiny of prison dictated the best treatment for neutralizing his glory as a terrorist, as the troubled musician's own confused rhetoric was repeatedly exposed to be folly. Continuing to mouth off to fanzines and other media outlets from jail, the murderous Vikernes latched on to the European far-right National Socialist movement, shaving his head and donning suspenders. In 1997 a Norwegian publisher, financed by Vikernes's mother, Lene Bore, issued a paperback edition of *Vargsmål*, the young convict's version of *Mein Kampf.*

After a long period of personal change, Vikernes finally disowned black metal completely while in jail, preferring to listen to classical music and marches. He continued composing and recording bleak, fantasy-oriented electronic music as Burzum on a prison-approved synthesizer, to waning interest. "My roots have never been in metal music in the first place," he protested to the fanzine *The Seventh Scroll* in 1998, "and definitely not in black metal." Eventually Vikernes became a figure of ridicule and even contempt—but not before inspiring many waves of dangerous idol worship and achieving his goal of becoming Norway's black metal bogeyman.

The murder of Euronymous and subsequent imprisonment of so many key musicians sent discord rippling through Norway but did not stifle the notoriety of black metal. In fact, the subsequent hysteria helped Norwegian-style metal grow to much stronger. Propelled by a scandal-crazed media, it benefited from the most frenzied terrorist chic since the student upheavals of the early 1970s, when the Weathermen stormed America and the fashionable Baader-Meinhof group rocked Germany by bombing department stores. "The media really made it much it bigger than it was," says Ihsahn of Emperor. "The media also made reputations. In the beginning there were maybe twenty people in the scene [in Norway], and suddenly there were four or five hundred."

In some misguided way black metal had become the revolutionary force that rock and roll always wished to be. These events added up to more than just the Sex Pistols singing "Anarchy in the UK"—they validated what fans had always believed: that heavy metal was more than merely music. While the world was repelled and fascinated by anti-Christian actions, such radical acts impressed some peers greatly. "Those church burnings and all that stuff?" says Mortiis. "I was not in town when a lot of that happened, which I'm pretty glad that I wasn't, so I'm not in jail still or something like that. I respect that, to be honest with you. As a symbolic act? I respect it totally."

The original black metallers, over whose occult-laced record albums the younger generation pored and obsessed, wanted nothing to do with the extracurricular activities of their scions. "For them to claim my lyrics were an inspiration for those actions?" retorts Bathory's leader, Quorthon, "I went back and checked my lyrics, and there wasn't anything in there about slitting someone up because of his sexual preferences. I was talking about raping angels and masturbating on the golden throne up there, but I find it very hard to imagine someone raping an angel. I mean, these are abstract fantasy lyrics. For anybody not being able to take that as a horror story—an expansion of *Tales from the Crypt* or Black Sabbath—they're screwed up."

Metal had represented power and force since its beginning. The explicit rhetoric of violence could be traced back to the lyrics of Slayer and Exodus, musically adept thrashers who upped the excitement of Iron Maiden's horror tales, "Murders in the Rue Morgue" and "Phantom of the Opera." Though Slayer had taken heat in the 1980s for glorifying Nazi sadist Josef Mengele in the song "Angel of Death," it was all part of an act. In fact, Slayer's South American–born vocalist, Tom Araya, called the Norwegians "creepy white folks freezing their brains, thinking real slow." Although James Hetfield of Metallica claimed to have amassed a collector's arsenal of 150 guns, his primary weapons were skateboards and pyrotechnics, and he sent only himself to the hospital.

The primitive Swiss band Hellhammer was extremely influential to Norwegian black metal—Mayhem's drummer, Jan Axel Blomberg, nicknamed himself Hellhammer, and even "Euronymous" was a Hellhammer song title. Yet after the events in Norway the band's leader, Tom Warrior, declared black metal the music of primitives who would see Europe return to an age of eating with their hands. As for the crimes of Christianity mentioned in Morbid Angel's *Altars of Madness*, which Emperor guitarist Samoth praises as "something new" and "a classic," it was only meant to be a symbolic battle. "I'm not a Satanist. I'm just my own person," says guitarist Trey Azagthoth. "I don't believe in attacking Christians and burning churches. It was never about attacking Christians physically, it was about attacking their chains and illusions, their beliefs."

In the semiotic soup from which values are drawn, however, one metaller's symbol can become another's concrete reality. American heavy metal bands simply could not relate to conflict and violence in the same way as could Europeans, for whom war had been a persistent historical reality. Even the bullet-belt-laden German thrash bands Kreator and Destruction were avowed pacifists, a product of their country's post-war preoccupation with peace. Yet mustard gas and Nazi rubble directly inspired the war metal offshoot of Scandinavian black metal, explored by the groups Zyklon-B, Niden div. 187, and, yes, War. Surrounded by images and memories of war, yet never having experienced war firsthand, the Norwegians seemed intent on creating their own.

As black metal brought its homeland under assault, the long-standing ulcers of Norway's society burst open and bled. "Norway is a very screwed-up country," says Scandinavian black metal godfather Quorthon. "The church has a lot of say. They're not allowed to show this and that on the TV. The women come to Sweden to have an abortion. It's one of the most beautiful countries in the world, but it's fucked up, mainly because it lost its identity squeezed in between England, Denmark, Germany, and Sweden. Also, I think for anybody to sit down in your basement listening to your music twenty-four hours a day without having anybody knock on the door and say, 'Hey, are you okay?' is screwed up to begin with."

To their credit those Norwegian bands not crippled by court cases produced very expressive music—combining black metal fury with techno elements, folk, and other progressive approaches. Ducking the evil stereotypes altogether, Enslaved used the genre instead as a springboard for something expansive, confounding, and clever. On a series of albums titled after the Norwegian names for natural elements, the band wove unpredictable waves of guitars into a fractured, futuristic fabric filled with synthesizers, Viking battle horns, and strains of Norse folk hymns. Not coincidentally, the landmark Celtic Frost album *Into the Pandemonium* was frequently cited as influential by bands such as Arcturus, which was seeking complexity and nuance. The drum machines and operatic vocals that sounded so bizarre when introduced by Celtic Frost in the late 1980s had become standard issue for progressive black metal.

As Burzum's *Filosofem* had proved, black metal didn't always have to be bombastic or abrasive to prove its point. Besides pressing musicians to physical limits through sheer speed, black metal also explored inner depths. For example, black metal's connection to electronic music was not a recent affectation. As far back as 1987 Euronymous of Mayhem had named unusual synth acts like Klaus Schulze and the Residents as influences. The first Mayhem EP, *Deathcrush*, even opened with drumming by Conrad Schnitzler of the early-1970s psychedelic group Tangerine Dream. "Con is a fifty-year-old, bold, and a very strange man," Euronymous told *Morbid Mag*. "He once was a member in Tangerine Dream, which is well known to everyone a bit seriously into the rock business. I've always loved Tangerine Dream's music, and I am very much into the music of Con. One day I met him at his place in Berlin. He was very friendly and cool, and I asked him if he'd like to do an intro for Mayhem and he did!"

Probably the most ambitious convert to the electronic side of black metal was former Emperor bassist Mortiis, who fled to Sweden in 1993 at age eighteen. Dressed in spirit-king persona, complete with prosthetic nose and ears, he embodied the soul of metal with little of the sonic heritage. "I was trying to describe it, because there's not really a category," says Mortiis of dealing with customs officials during his first trip to America. "The guard asked, 'I don't understand, it is heavy metal? And I said, 'No, it's not! I'm bringing in keyboards, man.' They were looking at all this black stuff, and I didn't think they were going to let me in. They only wanted to know what kind of music I was doing."

Mortiis in his kingdom
(Cold Meat Industries)

The best known in a variety of other Norwegian "black ambient" projects, which included Aghast, Isengard, and Wongraven, Mortiis made a main destination of the odd electronic excursions that had appeared sporadically on metal albums since *Sabbath Bloody Sabbath*. Early Mortiis volumes like *Ånden Som Gjorde Opprör* crept slowly through twenty-minute drones, holding court with rich atmosphere. As his cult grew, Mr. Mortiis became the flagship artist of Earache Records—taking over from Napalm Death after its contract expired. Never mind that this was an electronic-ambient musician with a back catalog of meditative minimalism. The key was his image and ebullient written concepts. *The Stargate*, released in 1999, was barely as heavy as the Kate Bush LP from which it copied its artwork, yet its chants and medieval heraldry danced into the metal imagination.

With many such excursions afloat in the Scandinavian scene during the 1990s, somebody had to stick with the basics. Using a bare minimum of atmospheric interludes, Immortal concentrated on pure power. These self-proclaimed "Sons of Northern Darkness" were a blur of wickedness, baroque bombast, and foul temper, with a host of albums under their bullet belts. Their 1995 album, the blazing *Battles in the North*, was a hyperspeed assault that guaranteed evil Nordic dominance of the underground in the post-Mayhem era. Furious guitarists Abbath and Demonaz funneled energies into a barrage of Bathory-like blasters, including "Cursed Realms of the Winterdemons" and "Moonrise Fields of Sorrow." The sound had the hypnotic thrill of crushing ice in a whining blender and was possibly the fastest sustained expression of speed ever released. It was surely the most demanding—the end of Immortal's great period came when guitarist Abbath succumbed to tendinitis in both arms as a result of overpracticing. "He couldn't even wash his hair," Demonaz lamented to the English magazine *Terrorizer*.

The mid-1990s brought widespread emulation of Norwegian black metal in distant lands. Norway briefly became a mythical realm to heavy metal in the way Africa was to rap music, with Vikings and Odinist artifacts instead of Zulu warriors and Kente cloth. As Emperor and Burzum had posed for photos in the Norwegian forest wielding axes and clubs, so in Japan would Sigh and Sabbat stand among bamboo stalks waving samurai swords. From Korea to Finland corpsepainted faces and upside-down crosses became symbols of solidarity, even in countries without Christianity. "Bands from fucking Greece and Italy going pagan Viking metal—how stupid can people be?" says Mortiis. "People are always picking up things in the wrong way. A guy from Greece holding on to Thor's hammer, what's the point of that? He should have a Zeus symbol or a Cronus symbol. At least respect that, his own mythological gods!"

Further confusing the distinction between fantasy and reality, headbangers in Germany, Sweden, Japan, and Poland boasted of church arson and graveyard desecration. As legends of the murderous black metal musicians spread through various channels, 1997 brought a rash of church fires and bombings in the conflict-laden republic of Russia. "History repeats itself, even in the world of music," wrote drummer Bård Eithun from prison. "Everything moves around like a constant cycle, some sort of dialectic interrelationship between the bands, the fans, and the cultural environment as a whole."

Driven to embarrassment by this black metal bandwagon, a dedicated faction attempted to stick to the crudest sounds possible, championing spirit over obviousness. These included Norway's Darkthrone and Carpathian Forest and New York's Havohej and Hemlock, all using corrosive sound as a yardstick of brutality. Havohej's *Black Perversion* EP was probably the worst-sounding metal album ever made, seemingly recorded in the back of a van with a microcassette recorder, using low-grade samples of a dangerously neglected basement trash incinerator. Havohej leader Paul Ledney's cruel vision was carried over from Profanatica, a band infamous for releasing an interview video of themselves drinking urine and masturbating onto a Bible.

Crudeness was an exciting aesthetic choice, and not necessarily self-defeating. Strapped for cash, black metal bands often historically recorded using rather cheap recording techniques anyway. Seemingly a rejection of heavy metal grandeur, this was acceptable for several reasons. For starters, even bands like Morbid Angel and Metallica first became known to fans via copied cassettes, and part of that experience was the loss of audio quality inherent in the process of infinite dubbing. Second, groups in Greece, Brazil, and Mexico simply did not have access to hitmaking studios. The silver lining in the coffin, so to speak, was that the cloudy, muffled sound fit the often claustrophobic and intensely personal nature of black metal.

Experienced bands like Norway's Darkthrone and Sweden's chaotic Abruptum saw the humor and relished the ironic badness of being black metal slumlords. A key band in Norway since 1991's popular *A Blaze in the Northern Sky*, Darkthrone thrived on a wicked minimalist plan scribbled on sheets of rust-caked guitar. An inspiration to Burzum, Varg Vikernes returned the favor by writing folkloric lyrics for Darkthrone's desperately ripped *Transilvanian Hunger*. After years of grim faces, however, drummer Gylve Nagell, aka Fenriz, began to pride himself on comic crappiness. "We're not entertainers, we're a black metal band," he told *Terrorizer*. "There are limits to how much technical Neil Peart [of Rush] drumming there's supposed to be on an album like Bathory's *The Return*, y'know? I'm really happy about my drum sound. It's really *bad*."

It took five more years for the United States to gradually grasp black metal—as stories spread through fanzines and mass media alike, it was difficult to separate the facts from the urban legends. For Americans there remained very little firsthand exposure to Norwegian black metal bands, though they had sold hundreds of thousands of CDs. There was also unreliable distribution of music released through extremely tiny labels. Unscrupulous grave robbers capitalized greatly on Mayhem, releasing dozens of unlicensed pirate CDs of any existing scraps of tape. One famous set of live recordings featured a photo of Mayhem's singer, Dead, lying at his suicide scene.

With all their high jinks and grand expectations, black metal bands rarely played live. Save for Immortal, Sweden's Marduk, and a brief 1993 UK tour that paired Emperor with the British group Cradle of Filth, the top black metal bands had triumphed only in the studio environment. "I'm never going to sing live," said Mortiis in 1998. "Playing keyboards with the makeup, that's supposed to be timeless. I don't want too much modern technology in my stage set. It's just going to fuck things up." Instead staging a theatrical event, at early shows Mortiis pantomimed to prerecorded music and a black-and-white film of himself wandering around castle ruins.

Even as black metal riveted the record stores, Florida death metal reigned supreme in the live arena—Deicide and Morbid Angel were formidable and professional stage acts whose perpetual touring schedules earned a constant influx of new devotees. When the black metal wave hit full force in the late 1990s, a large throng of death metallers dug in their spurs against the indulgent keyboards, costumes, and romantic trappings. One memorable sign of fealty at Milwaukee Metalfest in 1998 came from a tattered metal soldier wearing a homemade BLACK METAL SUCKS T-shirt with a SUPPORT DEATH METAL baseball cap worn backward over his long, frizzy hair.

Soon paroled and reconstituted, the members of Emperor, still only in their mid-twenties, were eager to burn their tabloid infamy in a flame of ferocious black metal. When Emperor guitarist Samoth was released from prison, he and Ihsahn recruited two new members for a regenerated version of their band, which finally came to America and toured with Morbid Angel. Even Mayhem returned after the passing of its leader, Euronymous, as drummer Hellhammer recruited singer Sven Erik Kristiansen, aka Maniac, and bassist Jorn Stubberud, aka Necrobutcher—both long-vanished members of the late-1980s Mayhem.

The new Mayhem announced its first American concerts in 1998, and a throng awaited the debut like children staying up late for Santa Claus. As trademark skinned cow heads were placed on stakes across the stage, the spectacle did not disappoint. Speaking fluently in the arcane cant of Mayhem's eerie music, Maniac shrieked incantations of disaster while gray hair dye and corpse paint dripped off his face in the heat. Bassist Necrobutcher and new guitarist Rune Erickson, aka Blasphemer, spilled a blurry pool of black metal noise in reverent rendition of Euronymous's familiar blazing style, while Hellhammer pushed the procession forward with his unique, superhuman, quadruple-time drumming. To think of conventional music during this blazing chaos was impossible.

America receives black metal gifts

Soon Mayhem even returned to the studio, creating esoteric, indulgent records like *Grand Declaration of War*, which took Euronymous's primitive inspiration to a damaging intellectual realm—whether durable or not, it was impressively conceived to keep Mayhem at the forefront of the music the band helped create.

As it repeatedly influenced metal across the world and found a footing in the live concert setting, by 1999 the Norwegian black metal scene began to succumb to convention. While Emperor's awesome *In the Nightside Eclipse* stung with infernal adolescent zeal, the polished later albums, *Equilibrium IX* and *Prometheus*, were majestic whirlwinds of angry regal riffs and demonic drama, recorded in state-of-the-art 48-track digital studios. The destructive impulse had been placated by rock stardom, or simply through natural maturity.

Always more a musician than a terrorist, Emperor leader Ihsahn at age twenty-three in 1999 struggled valiantly for professionalization and found the crimes of his peers a distraction. "I see things in a different perspective," he says. "It's quite common when you're fifteen or sixteen to rebel and want to do bad things." In particular, Ihsahn expressed frustration over being continually asked about crimes—even seven years after the fact by the New York paper the *Village Voice*. "Look at Marilyn Manson," Ihsahn says. "He's a millionaire and a big star, so it's okay. He has much more taboos than we have, but he's okay because he makes a lot of money in the commercial market."

Nonetheless their reputations preceded them—the price of fame drawn from a uniquely Faustian bargain. Having served most of his murder sentence by the end of the decade, former Emperor drummer, Faust, under Norwegian law was allowed weekend furloughs to attend the odd Kiss concert—despite professing his continued admiration for Bret Easton Ellis's *American Psycho* in interviews. Yet there was little fear of reprisal. Emperor guitarist Samoth, after spending two years in Norwegian prison for his role in the destruction of the Skjold church, said he would not join a younger movement of church burners. His anger, boredom, or need for attention had mellowed. "Been there, done that," he replied, as if refusing a day trip to the Eiffel Tower.

As purists struggled with their legacy of destruction, it was up to supporting characters to sell significant numbers of records. The happy-go-lucky English black metal band Cradle of Filth, a whirlwind of players led by the impish Dani Davey, sold half a million albums in Europe by emphasizing sexual and demonic characters and stage props. The group washed down its blasphemy with a typically British sense of camp—while showing a prodigious talent for dark eroticism in heavy metal T-shirt design. Behind them came Dimmu Borgir, a Norwegian group formed while its members were still in high school in 1993, during the heat of the country's crime wave. Showing national loyalty by singing in the Norwegian language until after 1996's *Stormblast*, Dimmu Borgir streamlined and simplified black metal—and the 1997 *Enthrone Darkness Triumphant* CD in turn sold more than a quarter million copies.

In Norway at the end of the 1990s, the extreme had eased into social acceptance. The pagan war against Christianity had been pre-empted by career concerns as the bands were perversely lauded for bringing the country a musical identity. Years after the torching of Fantoftkirke—in fact, not long after the church had been entirely reconstructed—black metal bands including Emperor could be seen battling over awards at the Norwegian Grammys. Another sign of the times: Militant black metallers were parodied in a mainstream Norwegian detergent ad that featured a mock black metal band wearing full stage garb. While they were washing up, one of the actors wiped his face with the cleansing soap. When his corpse paint rubbed off clean, his bandmates mocked him, saying, "It's only ash!" The product's slogan, translated: "It all comes out in the wash."

XVII

Satan Goes to Court: The People v. Heavy Metal

➤ **1988:** Ozzy Osbourne "Suicide Solution" case tried in Los Angeles, California

➤ **1991:** Judas Priest dual-suicide backward masking case tried in Reno, Nevada

➤ **Spring 1994:** "West Memphis 3" defendants convicted in West Memphis, Arkansas

➤ **1996:** HBO's *Paradise Lost* documentary released, questioning West Memphis 3 trial

---

While dashing wildly toward unknown destinations, heavy metal earned its scars. Metallers in America often found themselves in skirmishes that erupted into destructive dramas—producing more heavy metal martyrs than metal terrorists. As the mystically powerful music and its myriad offshoots forced their way to the front of cultural change, they often crossed swords with factions of society that were dragging their feet, trying to reverse history and deny rather than embrace the new realities of the modern world.

In the simple terms of rhetorical shorthand, heavy metal remained the devil's music—a convenient and reliable scapegoat for social and spiritual ills. "It's so easy for Middle America to look to people who are slightly different and ostracize them," says Bruce Sinofsky, director of the film *Paradise Lost: The Child Murders at Robin Hood Hills*. "Then, when a crime takes place that can't be solved because there's no evidence, they can say it's an occult-related crime, and somehow it's traced to the heavy metal music scene. The logic is pretzel logic. You can never figure out where it came from until you actually live in that environment. It's scary."

By its nature heavy metal had always threatened the status quo, offering an escape from the strip malls and fast food of Middle America. Since Black Sabbath, heavy metal lyrics investigated the corners of the subconscious, and bands from Judas Priest to Metallica took their gloom and doom straight from the pages of heretical writers like Goethe and Nietzsche. Naturally young people examining the big questions of God and the devil took to heavy metal—these musicians were the only adults who respected their curiosity. "I always consider my audience to be a lot brighter than most people think," says Ronnie James Dio. "I gave them songs that I thought had a lot more fiber than most songs they'd heard, and I think they were smart enough to realize that."

Even as heavy metal figures visited Congress in the 1990s to ask for election-law reform, they were still beleaguered by the prior effects of the PMRC censorship hearings on Capitol Hill in the 1980s. Metal witch-hunts still spotted the American cultural landscape, fueled by fundamentalist Christians for whom devils and witches were as real as floods and famine. Led by many of the same religious groups who had organized record-burning bonfires in the 1970s—when church leaders gathered all heavy metal albums from their young flocks for ritualistic nighttime conflagrations—the antimetal crusade flared during the 1990s into a wave of scary accusations and indictments.

Not that heavy metal was against the church. Even musicians who attacked organized religion, like Dave Mustaine of Megadeth, returned to Sunday services after coming to terms with personal beliefs. "You have to take into consideration that I died once," Mustaine says. "I overdosed in 1992. My heart stopped, and I was dead as a doornail. You tend to be willing to look to a power greater than yourself after trying to live on your own terms fails. I've come to have my own understanding of God now. I'm not going to grow hairy palms for jerking off, and I'm not going to grow tits for smoking pot. I go to church, and my little kid goes to Sunday school, but it's at a nondenominational place where I hang out and tell jokes with the pastor."

The idea that heavy metal corrupted innocent minds was a myth. Hundreds of Christian metal groups surely demonstrated that there was nothing inherent in the music to lead civilization toward destruction. Even the music of the church-burning black metal band Emperor was once played for Dom Laurentino Saenz de Buruaga, the spiritual and musical leader of a choir of Spanish Benedictine monks whose records sold platinum numbers in the mid-1990s. Far from recoiling in horror, this holy figure assessed it bluntly: "It is the usual sort of noise in every sort of discotheque or dancing in the world. It's a rhythm only."

Yet early in the 1980s that rhythm became confused with the crimes of two famous sociopaths. Serial killer Richard Ramirez was dubbed the "Night Stalker," owing to a reporter's error based on the creepy crawler's penchant for the eerie 1979 AC/DC song "Night Prowler." Though heavy metal gave him a theme song, Ramirez's character was shaped by much worse. Troubled with health problems since childhood, he was trained to kill silently by a psychopathic uncle—a decorated Green Beret who bragged of rape and other atrocities committed during duty in Vietnam. Later, Long Island LSD dealer Ricky Casso killed a client in the woods and was arrested wearing an AC/DC shirt that matched the heavy metal graffiti found across the playgrounds and alleys of his town. Though police refused to label the case satanic—the victim owed Casso a sum of money, and drugs seemed the obvious source of the conflict—provocateurs following the PMRC were more than willing to ring the heavy metal alarms.

During that same time period, there were more than 20 million AC/DC albums sold, and two criminals hardly amounted to a statistical majority. Attacking heavy metal for its lyrics was a case of blaming the messenger. It was a mistake to equate the nonconformity of many with the actual deviance of a few, but likewise the Beatles were dragged twenty years earlier into the circus of the Charles Manson trials. Showing a disturbing ignorance of the facts, accusers claimed that rock music had been Manson's inspiration. As heavy metal became a powerful cause for the faithful, those who coveted social control realized that lack of understanding of heavy metal could be useful if played for political and financial gain.

When they first appeared, people immersed in the world of heavy metal occasionally found themselves stigmatized unfairly, targets of something resembling a homegrown heavy metal pogrom. By intensifying degree there were three basic levels of headbanger harassment: individual discrimination, lawsuits or criminal charges on a local level, and wide-ranging legislative moves that aimed to stifle heavy metal nationwide.

The most common kind of headbanger harassment was being "guilty of wearing black T-shirts," an informal badgering of people marked as aberrant by virtue of their clothes and long hair. These conflicts ranged from tacitly approved social prejudice, like being watched too carefully by store owners, to outright harassment, such as being repeatedly targeted as a community troublemaker for wearing a black wardrobe. Solutions were often benign, leading to harmless battles over school dress codes that banned blasphemous clothing in the classroom. Such cases were to be expected—the friction of freedom of speech came with the self-chosen territory of dressing in black. To be sure, many metalheads relished the confrontations, as witnessed by the rise in facial piercings and dyed-black hair in the 1990s.

Unfortunately, there were also semiprofessional oppressors who sought to ban heavy metal not only from social-studies class but from society itself. As W.A.S.P. and Venom had capitalized on the sensationalism of their over-the-top stage shows, a caste of professional witch-hunters had learned how to stoke that shock value to a different and more profitable audience. Heavy metal "experts" such as Dr. Dale Griffis, a former Ohio policeman and self-proclaimed cult expert, appeared for a fee at court cases around the country. He insisted repeatedly that murderous underground satanic cults were operating in America and recruiting young people from the heavy metal scene. "We have kids being killed," Griffis told *20/20* newsmagazine. "We have people missing. We have all types of perversion going on, and it's affecting America."

If the dark visions of heavy metal music often lacked nuance, the same was certainly true of its attackers. As John Cardinal O'Connor hurled insults at Ozzy Osbourne from his pulpit, it seemed that the press-hungry priest was praying for the worst response. "What is a

Satanist anyway?" asks King Diamond, whose dress and image would seem to fit the description. "If you say it's a person who will kill babies and drink their blood, I say those people are deeply insane. Why do you tell people that is what Satanists are like? You only give them instructions on how to behave."

Most metalheads found the misapplied analysis of such adults comical and reprinted excerpts in fanzines. Yet inflammatory bias had a way of snowballing, as law enforcement responded to mosh-pit manners with a primitive form of prejudicial profiling. An educational tract used by police departments, *Youth Subcultures,* identified "Heavy Metalists" as follows: "This category covers a wide age range, perhaps from 8 to 24. Currently it is the largest group in most schools. . . . They are heavy drug users. . . . Many are not motivated to do much of anything constructive. They get their drug money from thefts, and from dealing in drugs themselves."

"HEAVY METALISTS"

In the crosshairs—from *Youth Subcultures*

Through the feeding cycle of misinformation, heavy metal became targeted as a problem, and broadly inaccurate propaganda soon became probable cause to detain and search any high-schooler in a Ratt T-shirt. Companies like the Back in Control Training Center explicitly advertised their expertise in cult deprogramming techniques to "depunk" or "demetal" troubled teens and bring them in line with fundamentalist Christian beliefs. "Once kids become part of the heavy metal or punk culture," said Back in Control's founder in the book *The Satan Hunter,* "there is an attitude they frequently pass on to the parents: 'I'm going to do what I want, the hell with you, leave me alone,' and with the metallers, in particular, better than 90 percent are involved with drugs." Just as

Satan chasing proved effective in mobilizing fundamentalist Christians, the prejudiced presumption of drug use was alarming to adults everywhere—leading to cures that were often worse than the symptoms.

The most antiyouth growth industry of the 1980s, the private adolescent detention centers, used the heavy metal scare to pad their profits. Thanks to the testimony of antimetal experts in juvenile trials, frustrated parents and municipalities were persuaded to enroll problem children for costly doses of tough love and group encounter therapy to shake off the influence of the occult—the amorphous source of all problems. Like a scene from Samuel Fuller's *Shock Corridor*, in which a journalist investigating a corrupt mental asylum is trapped as an inmate, these expensive and often privately owned campuses were soon populated with benevolent metalheads guilty of little more than listening to Slayer or growing long hair.

Well-meaning as the parental intentions were, the scenario repeatedly led to abuses of power against their captive populations. Many of the centers were shut down for rights violations in the 1990s, following investigations by the Department of Justice.

In fact, concerned parents could have done much worse than discover that their children had fallen under the influence of heavy metal. As Dave Mustaine promised *Kick Ass Monthly* about Megadeth, "The crowd that we play to, whether they're 12 or 20, they're the leaders of tomorrow for us. If we poison their minds or intoxicate their thinking in any way, or leave their curiosity untapped without making them think or expand their education by looking up words that are more than the basic words they learned in sixth grade—the average education of an American—then we'll have failed."

Whether successful or not, each attack on heavy metal fed the next in an incestuous soup of insinuation. Accusations of Satanism and drug use led to a second and more consequential breed of problems, when personal-injury lawyers and prosecuting attorneys played on these prejudices to bring heavy metal to court. After the PMRC opened the door to labeling records with warning stickers, opponents began to argue that heavy metal was a dangerous product and that musicians who created it could be liable for damages or criminal charges when the behavior of fans went astray. These were perilous cases—loaded with courtroom hysteria that proved hard to dissipate.

Heavy metal first had its day in court in 1988, when a personal-injury attorney named Kenneth McKenna alleged that a California boy had committed suicide as a result of exposure to Ozzy Osbourne songs, namely "Suicide Solution." The album *Speak of the Devil*—a collection of live Black Sabbath material *not* including "Suicide Solution"—was found spinning on the record player in a room with the young man's corpse. Previously McKenna had lost a case against Paul Revere & the Raiders, brought on behalf of a woman struck in the head when Revere tossed his trademark three-cornered hat into the audience at a concert. In setting his sights on the madman of rock, McKenna apparently thought he had found an easier target.

The crux of McKenna's suit was bizarre evidence obtained through extensive computer analysis that "Suicide Solution" contained hidden messages. What sounded to normal listeners like Ozzy singing "suicide" into an effects box during the guitar solo became "get the gun and shoot it"—incitement to a final solution. Presenting the actual lyrics, plainly printed on the record sleeve, Ozzy's defense attorney successfully explained that the song was concerned with a liquid solution, namely alcohol. In fact, the words lamented the excessive drinking that had nearly killed Ozzy and took away his friend Bon Scott: "Wine is fine but whiskey's quicker / Suicide is slow with liquor."

Furthermore the judge found that creative expression could never be equated with harmful criminal speech, such as yelling fire in a crowded theater. He concluded, "Reasonable persons understand musical lyric and poetic conventions as the figurative expressions which they are." But with tens of millions of heavy metal albums going over the counter, there were plenty of unreasonable people listening to the music. Many of them were right-wing zealots with axes to grind. They did not wait to hear that McKenna's backward masking was nonsense—the appearance of the case in the newspapers was enough to legitimize their belief in subliminal programming.

Buoyed by the publicity from the failed "Suicide Solution" case, McKenna returned in 1991 with a lawsuit against Judas Priest in Reno, Nevada—a less favorable venue for freedom of speech than California.

The Reno suit was a wrongful-death action, holding the band responsible for a dual attempted suicide. Apparently after drinking and listening to the album *Stained Class*, two teens went out to a playground with a shotgun and desperate plans. In the bloody hours that followed, one died of self-inflicted wounds. The other survived for a short time, with half of his face damaged, before expiring.

Summoned to a Nevada courthouse, the members of Judas Priest were greeted by cheering fans holding album covers and cardboard guitars, many of them friends of the deceased. In court, according to analysis in the book *They Fought the Law: Rock Music Goes to Court*, McKenna's complaint altogether ignored the actual song lyrics, which were protected by the Constitution. He hammered away instead at his belief that the band had inserted subliminal and backward messages to drive the disturbed teens to suicide. "It's like we're ghostbusters or something," commented a lawyer from McKenna's team.

As chronicled in the documentary film *Dream Deceivers*, the members of Judas Priest were confused by the inquisition as they defended themselves against charges of mind control, dangerous negligence, and cult conspiracy. They found themselves victims of the occult loophole in post-PMRC music attacks—the irrational idea that heavy metal had supernatural power over its listeners. Yet despite claims of a secretive cult conspiracy, there was simply no factual basis for the charge, and the band prevailed. "You just don't back away from those things," says Judas Priest singer Rob Halford of the experience. "Firstly, you can't back away when you're given a subpoena, but it's more than that. It's basically standing up [when] being accused of doing something that we did not do. In the Reno trial we defended ourselves, and we defended the music, and we defended our fans."

Heavy metal did not shy away from the disaffected. As would often prove true, when heavy metal appeared at a crime scene, its role appeared to be a last-ditch safety net against a harsh existence. *Dream Deceivers* revealed that prior to finding Judas Priest, the two Reno boys had both suffered miserable lifelong physical abuse at the hands of their alcohol-ravaged families. The bands' interests were certainly in keeping the fans alive. "I never sat down to write lyrics with the intent that anyone should kill themselves," said Ozzy Osbourne of the

"Suicide Solution" case in *They Fought the Law.* "I feel very sorry for these kids. But why can't you sing about suicide? It's a thing that really happens."

These grandstanding attempts to vilify heavy metal by alleging subliminal messages and other hocus-pocus had increasingly real effects. They served to build an unwanted mystique that completely obscured the benefits of the music. In 1996 an appalling case of persecution in West Memphis, Arkansas, came to widespread attention following the release of *Paradise Lost,* an HBO documentary directed by Bruce Sinofsky and Joe Berlinger. "We work in New York," says Sinofsky, "and though many people think New York is crazy, it's a very civilized society. When we got down to West Memphis, we'd be sitting in our hotel room watching the evangelists talking about the evils of heavy metal, and it would come up when we'd be talking to people at Burger King and Wal-Mart about the case. We couldn't believe they were thinking that Metallica and Megadeth and Slayer could ever possibly have something to do with this crime."

The crime in *Paradise Lost* was the horrendous group murder of three little boys, discovered stripped and mutilated one afternoon in May 1993 after a frantic overnight search. Police had few leads, and most of those were cast aside as investigators focused increasingly on three teenagers in black T-shirts: Jessie Misskelley, Jason Baldwin, and Damien Echols. Although no physical evidence or witnesses connected any of them to the crime, during the subsequent trial the district attorney presented lists of occult-related books Echols had checked out from the local public library. Though aggressively challenged by the defense attorney—the accreditation of his alma mater was later taken away by the state of California—the testimony of familiar satanic "expert" Dr. Dale Griffis clouded the judicial process with dire proclamations and misinformation.

Ozzy Osbourne and Judas Priest could afford to battle career-minded district attorneys and Christian crusaders, but not so the three young defendants in Arkansas. In the spring of 1994 all three were convicted. Echols received the death penalty. The West Memphis jury may have sacrificed its outcasts in order to seal away the pain of its ghastly hometown murders. "Damien Echols was intelligent," says Bruce Sinofsky. "He was thoughtful. He experimented with a lot of religions, which is common if you're fifteen, sixteen, seventeen years old. I think his being different scared people, because he wasn't the clean-cut football player following what was happening with the University of Arkansas team. Down there wearing a Metallica or Megadeth shirt is a crime. It was scary to them. He might as well have been Godzilla marching through a Japanese town."

In fact, *Paradise Lost* showed that rural America was where Metallica most dignified the lives of "unforgiven" kids as they sought relief in a stifling environment. The directors edited *Paradise Lost* to a score of Metallica songs before appealing to the group for permission. "We figured we'd have to end up with some cheesy knockoff metal group," says Berlinger. But Metallica took a personal interest and granted free use of a range of songs, the first time they had allowed their music in any movie. "Lars explained to us that there was a truth in *Paradise Lost*," says Sinofsky. "They have that kind of relationship with their fans. They wrote to Damien in jail."

Metallica again donated music for a sequel, *Paradise Lost 2: Revelations*, released in March 2000. "There's a wonderful moment where two mothers are talking about their children in jail," says Berlinger. "One says, 'I sort of dedicated my life to Jason, and the song "Nothing Else Matters" is what my life is all about now. Nothing else matters but getting Jason out of jail.' We showed Lars a rough cut, and he said he was moved to tears."

Paradise Lost 2 brought further attention to the mishandling of evidence in the trials of the so-called West Memphis 3, and, unlike the evenhanded approach of the first film, it suggested a possible culprit—the erratic stepfather of one of the little boys (the stepfather vehemently denied any involvement). After viewing the movies, the boy's biological father contacted the West Memphis 3 website. "I am not satisfied with the investigation of my son's murder," he writes. "I am not satisfied with the verdicts of the trials, and I want everyone to know that I believe the wrong people are in prison for this crime."

In its review the *New York Times* compared the film to the Denzel Washington social-justice picture *The Hurricane*, which dealt with the ten-year imprisonment and subsequent acquittal of an African-American boxer wrongly accused of murder in New Jersey in the

1970s. Despite its critical success, *Paradise Lost 2* did not achieve the ultimate accolade scored by the 1988 death-row documentary *The Thin Blue Line*, which successfully secured a reversal of conviction for an innocent man. "I'm very disappointed that those kids are still rotting in jail," says Berlinger. "To me the film failed because it never moved this story from the arts section of the newspaper to the front page."

Disgusting and confusing as the charges in this case were, and worthy of intense scrutiny, the fog of occult allegations should not have trumped the basic legal right of innocence until proven guilty. Despite mounting questions—and no physical evidence of guilt—the West Memphis 3 remained victims of satanic panic, the poster children for heavy metal discrimination. "I think maybe for the general public, it's not quite as scary to believe that bloodthirsty Satanists are murdering children," said Damien Echols in *Paradise Lost 2*, "as it is to believe that parents are actually murdering their own children."

⟲ ✦✦✦✦✦✦✦✦✦✦✦ ⟳

Apart from Arkansas most of America had grown less afraid of devil-worshipping metalheads by the mid-1990s, as attention shifted to the street violence of gangsta rappers. While heavy metal embraced sorcerers and barbarians, hardcore rappers now emulated the fictions and moral codes of inner-city pimps and drug pushers. When rap musicians put on gang colors and garnered arrest records, the strongest criticism initially came from within the black community. "I just thought NWA [was] doing aggressive music based on what Public Enemy was doing first," says Chuck D of Public Enemy. "They just talked about themselves and killing black folks more. Shrinking yourself to negativity and talking about killing niggers is just the same old racist game anyway. I guess to white folks it might be on the edge. To black folks it's counterproductive."

The first national assault on heavy music since the PMRC was incited by a merger of gangsta rap and thrash metal. Though the press focused on its rap image, Body Count was a live thrash metal group fronted by vocalist Tracey Marrow, aka Ice-T. As a solo artist he cultivated a pimp image on several hard-edged albums in the 1980s—after writing lighter rhymes for the break-dance movie *Breakin' 2* and a

Mr. T motivational video for kids. In Body Count, flanked by shirtless black men hammering metallic ghetto nightmares on guitars, Ice-T became the first metal singer to dedicate his gut-chugging music to "people of color throughout the entire world."

In 1992 a national uproar followed the release of the Body Count song "Cop Killer," a graphic revenge fantasy against police brutality that advocated fighting back against the men in blue. Police groups protested in the parking lots of Six Flags amusement parks, a corporate relative of Body Count's record label. President George Bush and Vice President Dan Quayle both decried Body Count's music from the campaign trail as an incitement to violence and a threat to the safety of law-enforcement workers.

Defending his right to express angry political thoughts, Ice-T fought for freedom of speech while teetering on the brink of danger. That July police officers and NRA spokesactor Charlton Heston disrupted the annual Time Warner shareholder meeting in Beverly Hills. A coalition of sixty members of Congress wrote a letter to Warner Bros. to persuade them to drop "Cop Killer" from the album, and more than a thousand record stores returned their copies to the distributor. Under heavy pressure from corporate brass, Ice-T ultimately removed the song voluntarily and excused himself from his contract with Warner Bros. "I learned that lesson in there," Ice-T told *Rock Out Censorship*, "that you're never really safe as long as you're connected to any big corporation's money."

Corporate help for challenging music dwindled as the Body Count debacle ushered in a new age of conservatism in the music business. Metal bands were among the first to go as big business faced boycott threats by religious protesters, many of whom were veterans of past censorship shakedowns. Metal Blade Records, partnered with Warner Bros. since 1989, felt the ripples as it was forced to justify the lyrics of death metal bands like Cannibal Corpse. After the Body Count fallout, the label's next slated release was from Gwar, former art students from Virginia whose gleefully offensive stage act involved castration, decapitation, cannibalism, and other acts perpetrated in jest with the help of foam rubber, latex, and untold gallons of fake blood and other stage ooze. "All of a sudden there was a guy at Time Warner, and you had to give him all the lyrics to all the records coming out," says Metal Blade's founder, Brian Slagel. "We'd give him a set of lyrics, and he'd come back and say which songs had to come off. That didn't work for us."

Metal Blade wanted major distribution for its records, but it did not need mandated morality from a corporate baby-sitter. "We went to [label executives] Mo Ostin and Lenny Waronker," says Slagel, "and we told them if it was going to be a continuing problem, we didn't think it was going to work for us. I'm not going to tell bands to take songs off the records. We worked out a deal. The Goo Goo Dolls stayed at Warner Bros. and have obviously gone on to some success— and we went back to independent distribution, which has been a blessing." Indeed, without major-label backing, Cannibal Corpse soon became the first death metal band to debut in *Billboard*'s album chart.

The government's intervention and efforts to influence the music business in the Ice-T case was an example of the third, and most heinous, facet of organized attacks on heavy metal: direct government attempts to censor or restrict the sale of metal albums. The spirit of these complaints against heavy metal had been discredited by prior court cases, but sometimes the political currency of having shocking music simply appear in court was more important than the outcome. From circular logic again came a familiar self-propagating conclusion: If there were parental-advisory warning stickers—themselves the product of government meddling—there must also be inherent danger and a need for further regulation.

With its explicitly obscene album covers and lyrical blasphemies, it was inevitable that Jim Carrey's favorite band, Cannibal Corpse, would become a target for political posturing. At the end of 1997 Senator Joseph Lieberman of Connecticut chided the band during a renewed congressional attack on the entertainment industry, also citing other diverse signs of cultural decay, such as Fox Television's *When Animals Attack*, the computer game Postal, and Calvin Klein's "heroin chic" ad campaigns. In a statement titled *The Social Impact of Music Violence*, he testified, "Consider the vile work of the death metal band Cannibal Corpse, distributed through a Sony subsidiary, which recorded one song describing the rape of a woman with a knife and another describing the act of masturbating with a dead woman's head. This is extremely awful, disgusting stuff that kids are listening to."

Cannibal Corpse could not have asked for a more precious authentication of its shock value. The more the inhuman image of such bands was taken at face value by politicians, the more curious new fans sought out the band's sensationalized CDs. Both Lieberman and the group saw their careers advance—the senator's profile was raised, and he was tapped as Al Gore's vice-presidential running mate in 2000. Meanwhile, hapless headbangers were caught in the crossfire back in their hometowns, where rhetoric could turn into police warrants and court dates.

Government intervention continued to intimidate people and inhibit sales at small metal specialty stores in Florida, where district attorneys facing reelection threatened to arrest clerks who sold stickered records to minors. At least six states during the 1990s sought to enact legislation that would criminalize sales to minors of CDs bearing the supposedly voluntary stickers. On the verge of giving up their courtroom assaults, heavy metal's opponents were suddenly recharged to attack with the help of lawmakers.

In September 2001 those going after heavy metal for philosophical reasons or financial gain in the United States were buttressed by a Department of Justice report that charged negligence not on the part of artists themselves but on the part of the distribution companies that sold objectionable material to minors. This federal report reopened the doors to a dormant 1995 wrongful-death case against Slayer and its record label. A new legal strategy was formulated that attempted, instead of targeting the creation of the music, to frame the widespread marketing of Slayer CDs as the illegal sale of a dangerous substance. Thus the misguided attempts at moral cleansing continued.

Government crackdowns on heavy metal were to be expected in police states like North Korea and the Taliban-controlled Afghanistan. In Malaysia the government even barred heavy metal outright from radio and television in 2001 and sought to block performances by Megadeth and Scorpions on the basis of "black metal cults" they claimed were sacrificing small animals and burning the Koran in secret forest rituals. Primitive and antidemocratic as such crackdowns seemed, the same approaches were used in attempts to control heavy metal in America—only the gloves were softer.

XVIII

The Antimetal Era:
Haircuts & New Roots

1995: *Headbangers Ball* canceled by MTV

April 10, 1996: Metallica appears with haircuts at Alice in Chains' *MTV Unplugged* taping

June 27, 1996: Metallica, Ramones, and Soundgarden launch Lollapalooza '96

Death metal raged, black metal burned, and good old-fashioned heavy metal continued to sell tens of millions of CDs during the 1990s—yet the public spotlight moved elsewhere. In the dull eyes of the mainstream, metal was dead. Popular culture in the Prozac-gobbling era of Bill Clinton could scarcely have been less committed to anything. Attitudes in this prosperous and gentle time tended toward moderation and self-restraint—two of metal's admitted weaknesses. Though metal still reigned in Europe, Americans were lulled into thinking they no longer had need of dissent. "People are getting a little too much into political correctness now," Slayer's Jeff Hanneman told *Tales from the Pit*. "That may be why people like to say metal is dead, because metal is about freedom and saying what's on your mind—not curbing your thoughts."

The cancellation of the long-running *Headbangers Ball* video show in 1995 was a crushing blow. As MTV purged Poison and other heavy metal ills, the entire glam metal party began to feel like an unwelcome 1980s hangover. In its place romped Green Day and the Offspring, leaders of the squeaky-clean wing of the still-active hardcore punk scene. Stepping up to represent several generations of dyed hair, Green Day's child-safe *Dookie* sold a whopping 8 million copies by 1995 and dominated magazine and newspaper music coverage for more than two years. Punk's importance to rock and roll was finally being acknowledged, though the music was now being delivered by sterile new messengers. "I hope they took that money and invested it," says Richie Stotts of the Plasmatics, "because they had some good hits. I had no problem with it. Green Day wrote pop songs. Were they trying to be anything more than what they were? It was like the Knack—it was fun!"

With aggression and frustration conveniently excised, this was over-the-counter counterculture—not the confrontational, scary music that excited metalheads. Punk had become a Southern California lifestyle product, settled in a subdivision of the entertainment industry. "For me, punk always represented sociopolitical lyrics and some kind of an edge," says Alycia Morgan, an editor of *Metal Maniacs.* "Some kind of angst made it different. Those Berkeley bands that sing about masturbating on the couch and [about] girls are safe. They're not threatening to the status quo at all. Nirvana to me was more threatening—they had real angst and real seriousness to their lyrics that these bands don't have."

Yet heavy metal had lost its mandate, and its values were being cast aside in many ways. Very different from graduates of the heavy metal school, the happy punks and their older siblings the alternative rock bands were cautious not to appear too friendly to the system. While Quiet Riot had capitalized on the overnight success of *Metal Health* in 1984 by instantly jumping aboard a Black Sabbath tour, platinum punks the Offspring turned down arena gigs with Metallica and Stone Temple Pilots in 1994. "It just really didn't seem like the right thing to do," says Offspring's singer, Bryan Holland. "I still like the club thing, even if it's a big club. I like Stone

Temple Pilots—it's not like we're saying we're too punk for that."

Never entirely comfortable with heavy metal, the music press soon lost interest in headbangers. Instead they courted alternative rock bands who believed they had outsmarted the record industry by affecting a critical attitude toward career advancement. Rather than deliver musical landmarks like *Master of Puppets* and *Reign in Blood*, bands like Sebadoh passed off musical monotony as ironic disaffection. "Someone came up with the idea that it's uncool to try and entertain the audience, so those shows are so boring," says Rob Zombie. "Liz Phair and all that stuff—who cares?" The alternative rock band Pavement satirized the changed music world in "Cut Your Hair," an ode to the increasingly desperate world of musicians' classifieds— once the lifeblood of the Hollywood metal scene.

While the media ignored metal's continued vitality, the numbers told a different story. The dirty little secret: When it came to record sales, the pop machine could not destroy something it had not created in the first place. While *Spin* feasted on the fall from grace of Skid Row and Poison, it was never more obvious that heavy metal did not judge its success by the burn rate of monthly magazines. For instance, the starting point for all MTV metal, Quiet Riot's *Metal Health*, sold 2 million copies during the 1990s. Mötley's Crüe's sleazy *Dr. Feelgood*— as raunchy a celebration of crotchless underwear as ever emanated from Hollywood—after 1991 continued to rack up triple-, quadruple-, quintuple-, and ultimately sextuple-platinum sales, measuring 4 million records sold after the alleged housecleaning of glam. In comparison, though seemingly ubiquitous during the 1990s, the *Doggystyle* CD by L.A. rapper Snoop Dogg sold only 4 million copies total.

Even with its pretty flowers clipped, the dirty roots of metal remained to reach out to new audiences. Black Sabbath's *Paranoid* crossed the 4 million mark in January 1995. Slayer rode a commercial high in 1994 as *Divine Intervention* went gold in six weeks, the evil band's fourth gold record since 1992. Afterward Pantera, now an undeniable force, returned ever heavier with its own *Billboard* Top 10 album. The very traditional *Youthanasia* CD by Megadeth went platinum in early 1995, complete with piles of guitar solos and billowing volumes of hair. Even *Ozzmosis*, released by the indefatigable Ozzy Osbourne in 1995, sold 3 million copies within one year.

Nonetheless, Tower Records put its spiked wristbands on clearance sale, oblivious to how extreme acts, like Morbid Angel, Emperor, and Deicide, were still strapping on their leather and selling millions of CDs. As always, the black T-shirts on the street told the true story of metal's durability, "Looking at MTV, I get pretty disgusted," says Relapse Records' Matt Jacobson. "What can you do? You're always going to have a lot of people who are just going to listen to whatever is accepted by mass culture. There's no way you can change that, so all I can say is I feel bad for them. When the mainstream media killed cock rock, people thought metal was dead. It wasn't. We've always been in touch with it and involved with it, and consequently we'll always grow."

Once again, fans became rats scurrying underfoot. While metal suffered in the public eye, Metallica helped matters very little. For years they put the heavy metal world first. Now jumping uncharacteristically into the limelight at every television awards show and video opportunity, the band traveled with alternative acts Hole and Veruca Salt in September 1995 to perform at a publicity festival for Molson Ice beer in the Arctic hamlet of Tuktoyaktuk. The band that had refused for more than seven years even to make a video was now accepting promotional engagements.

The Black Album cleverly calmed the overkill of Metallica while remaining heavy metal at its essence. With its successor, released five years later in June 1996, the band broke its trademark crunching sound down completely, crashing through the stained-glass ceiling and leaving heavy metal behind. Beckoning pejorative puns with its title, *Load* featured a respectably meaty production, yet classical European metal songcraft was abandoned in favor of simple blues-based riffs. This conversion earned widespread radio play that had always eluded heavy metal, but it was a lazy victory. "I felt a little betrayed," recalls Ronnie James Dio—whose band, Dio, was derailed in the late 1980s in part by the juggernaut of a hungrier Metallica. "I thought they started sounding like they wanted to be Deep Purple, and that wasn't the Metallica that I remembered and really cared for."

In the thirteen years since *Kill 'Em All*, Metallica's early headbanger accoutrements—jean jackets, Saxon pins, and the pubescent mustache on Lars Ulrich's face—had given way to a uniform of match-

Shorn: James Hetfield at Lollapalooza
(Stew Milne)

ing black jeans and shirts. Now, in one fell swoop, Metallica's members cropped their long locks—the traditional signifier of a metaller's commitment to the cause. With sideburns shaved high into freakish Mohawks, Jason Newsted and James Hetfield had been halfway shorn since 1992. In Newsted's case the final, complete cut was typically practical. "I was busted for possession of psychedelic mushrooms," he told *Melody Maker*, "and I spent Saturday night in the West Hollywood sheriff's jail. I paid a thousand dollars bail, cut my hair, went to court, case was dismissed."

After years of impassive anti-image, *Load* presented dozens of photos of Metallica dressed up in a bizarre fashion show of costumes. The group presented itself alternately as errand runners for the Cuban mob, Canadian hairdressers, tourists in Times Square, or simply Metallica wearing eyeliner. Metallica was finally dressing to suit its bank account. "I haven't worn underpants for the last fifteen years," Lars Ulrich told *Melody Maker*, "but about nine months ago I decided I was never going to wear jeans again. Because I'm not circumcised, unlike most Americans, there'd be a considerable amount of urine splashed over my expensive non-jean pants caused by my excessive consumption of alcohol. So my wife suggested I wear underwear so I wouldn't piss in my nice expensive designer-label pants all the time."

This affluent metalhead mind-set caught longtime fans in a struggle between lingering affection and apathy. "I understand all the new hairstyles and trends, but Metallica's one band that didn't need to do any of that shit," says longtime friend and fan Katon W. DePena ruefully. "But I guess they figure if they're going to sell out, they might as well do it rad." Even upgrading the price range of its artwork, Metallica relegated on-call illustrator Pushead to merchandise design, and for *Load*'s CD cover reproduced the expensive photograph *Blood and Semen III* by Andres Serrano, a collectible New York artist notorious for suspending a crucifix in a jar of his urine.

Though its music was lighter, on the plus side the lyrics on *Load* were more personally revealing than anything previous, as James Hetfield worked through his anger at his parents carefully instead of simply lashing out with fury. The metal gods were mellowing into mortal human beings. "Going back listening to the Black record, it sounds so tight and so constricted," James Hetfield told *Addicted to Noise*. "We thought, 'Boy, that's the loosest, livest-sounding thing we've done.' Compared to this one, it's like anal."

Put simply—after dealing with exhausting lyrical subjects, the death of Cliff Burton, years of touring, and bearing the weight of metal credibility while opening commercial opportunities for heavy music, the band finally allowed itself to relax publicly. Fifteen years was long enough for James Hetfield and Lars Ulrich to scowl—in many eyes the members of Metallica deserved to enjoy their hard-earned rock-star retirement. "Metallica can do whatever they want," says Shawn Crahan of the band Slipknot. "They won. They earned the right to do what they want today."

Among the strange changes of the mid-1990s, Metallica's cutting its hair and opting for a normal life nearly paled in comparison to the odd saga of Judas Priest. Singer Rob Halford departed Judas Priest in the early 1990s and formed the leaner, Pantera-themed project called Fight. While debating Halford's replacement, Judas Priest discovered Tim Owens, aka Ripper, nicknamed after one of their own signature songs. Incredibly, the twenty-eight-year-old Ohio resident had "played" Rob Halford in a Judas Priest cover band called British Steel and had exactly patterned his natural range after Halford's. "It's a one-of-a-kind story," explains Ripper. "I was in a Judas Priest tribute band. Some girl from Rochester, New York, shot video footage of my next-to-last performance with them in Erie, Pennsylvania, and forwarded it to Priest. I don't think anyone that's ever been in a tribute band ever made it to the band that was being tributed."

Giving the strange situation a further turn for the peculiar, on the same day that Judas Priest announced plans to introduce its new singer to fans through a world tour, Rob Halford upstaged his old crew by holding a press conference to blow the cover from his thinly veiled homosexuality. Halford had dressed like an S&M leather daddy since the mid-1970s, and his coming out was small surprise to anyone who had seen the man wield a riding crop. Still, after twenty years of "Don't ask, don't tell," it was astonishing to hear a definitive answer to one of the great unanswered questions of metal.

Early Judas Priest concept videos had alluded to Halford's gayness by placing the singer in a variety of homoerotic roles—in "Hot Rockin'" he was pushed aside by his sweaty bandmates as they entered a room of scantily clad women without him. The titles of Judas Priest's *Screaming for Vengeance* and *Ram It Down* took on new meaning, as did the urgent delivery of many classic songs. In particular the band's 1980 hit, "Breaking the Law," was written while what was then called "buggery" was still illegal throughout most of the United Kingdom and the subject of political debate. Certainly the words of the 1976 anthem "Genocide" assumed prophetic new meaning following the AIDS epidemic: "Sin after sin, I have endured. Yet the wounds I bear are the wounds of love."

As the legacy of Judas Priest was cast in a new light, the biggest surprise was how the tougher-than-leather metal community took the news in stride. Halford told the *Boston Phoenix* in April 1998 that he did not consider heavy metal a homophobic genre of music. "I think it would be unfair to pin it down exclusively to the world of heavy metal," he said. "I think that metal is still perceived by most people as being a very macho, straight, male, drinking-and-chicks kind of environment, so people make assumptions about it."

Halford's iconic status remained firm—to deny him would mean repressing a huge portion of heavy metal's sound and imagery. "Maybe because of who I am and what I've shared with people," Halford said, "a majority of people have been able to handle it in the metal community." Needless to say, the announcement did not start a wave of heavy metal unclosetings. If other flamboyant front men were also eking out a secretive life, they held their tongues. The complex drama of this story led to a lengthy *GQ* article examining Ripper's unusual role in Judas Priest, which in turn inspired a screenplay titled *Metal God*—released later as *Rock Star*.

With Lars Ulrich and Kirk Hammett themselves wearing makeup and playfully tongue kissing for cameras, Metallica took another step into the times by invading the successful Lollapalooza touring festival in 1996, sharing the bill with the Ramones, Soundgarden, Rancid, Screaming Trees, and a group of Shaolin fighting monks. In a world where punk temporarily reigned, Ulrich rallied to distinguish between his new allies and the Sex Pistols, who were undertaking a lucrative reunion tour at the same time. "I always thought the Sex Pistols were a little fluffy," he says. "After all the small talk, there just really wasn't all that much back there. I'd take the Ramones in a heartbeat."

As *Load* had demonstrated a less strenuous approach to songwriting, Lollapalooza relieved Metallica of its heavy-touring dogma. "I look at this as the most fun you can have when you're in a band," Ulrich says, "playing outside in the summer in America for ninety minutes. It doesn't get much more A-plus than this. Burnout is what happens when you have to do twenty-two gigs in Germany in November. Summer outdoors in America is pure, unadulterated fun."

Alternative Kirk Hammett
(King Django)

Metallica was cruising through a working vacation, and even before the Lollapalooza tour began Ulrich promised more of the same: "The stuff on *Load* is only half of what we've been recording in the studio. We more or less cut two records, so a second one should show up in about eighteen months. They just need some vocals and guitar bits here and there."

More adventurous than its warmed-over predecessor, *Reload*, released in November 1997, was a slightly more committed attempt at branching out, even recruiting smoky-voiced Marianne Faithfull for a duet on "The Memory Remains." "We've got such carte blanche at this point," James Hetfield told VH1. Among the erratic suite of songs on *Reload* was "The Unforgiven II," revisiting the outlaw theme from the Black Album. Inspired by Clint Eastwood's antiwestern, the songs became personal anthems for Hetfield—now a grown man and not the pimple-faced ingrate whom *Kerrang!* had observed in 1985 drunkenly urinating on a television set that housed the face of cowboy actor John Wayne. Times—and political views—had changed.

With so much monkeying around, a long-brewing backlash and breaking away from Metallica was inevitable. Their former Megaforce labelmates Manowar had built a tremendous worldwide following by pounding solid iron for twenty years and did not view the conversion to martini metal charitably. Like Fates Warning, Overkill, Savatage, and other surviving power metal bands, Manowar never sacrificed traditional chops for the greater noise and speed of death metal. These were true-blue practitioners of the old school, for whom even thrash metal was something of a passing fad.

Manowar sweated out trends and a difficult record deal with Atlantic Records by touring abroad extensively and perfecting its oeuvre, pressing the rebel imagery of bikers and barbarians into a taut metal wafer for orthodox heavy metal communion. Even within the austere world of traditional metal, Manowar was a sealed entity—a group of self-made statues singing songs about blood, fire, steel, and patriarchy in absolute terms. For this band every adversity faced was a battle and every triumph a supreme victory against all odds. As decreed in the searing liner notes to *Hell on Stage*, an exhausting live double CD: "There is no 'If' in our world." With the turning of Metallica they found a focus for their anger.

Manowar moved in and regrouped the crowd left to founder by the nonmetal Metallica. Touring for *Louder Than Hell* during a short-lived deal with Geffen Records, Manowar enacted a nightly stage ritual, one of a slew of stunts seemingly inspired by a Christian tent revival. Scouting the crowd for a youngster in a Metallica shirt, bassist Joey DeMaio would haul him onstage to mock those who "turned their backs on true metal." When the fan was shamed thoroughly and near the verge of tears, the stern metal fighters would exchange his Metallica rags for a brand-new Manowar shirt, pass around a symbolic can of communal beer, then kick him back into the crowd—reborn a Manowar man.

Yet while heavy metal searched for a new center, fans were not necessarily interested in reliving the sword-wielding glories of Manowar's classic canon. The band's poser-crushing battle cries maintained tremendous popularity, yet they were confined in anachronisms. Instead heavy metal reached for new discoveries on the periphery, as the disappearance or apparent defection of its influential leaders pulled off the lid from the wide-ranging scene now scrambling in several seemingly incompatible directions. Even as black metal incited and inspired the underground the world over, other young bands from outside the hardcore metal loop took inspiration from the environment immediately around them.

With heavy metal marginalized during the mid-1990s, the influence of hardcore rap music on hard music was enormous. Even a stalwart independent label like Roadrunner, which hosted more than a dozen death metal acts just five years earlier, began throwing in its lot with rap metal bands who were seen as having commercial potential. In Biohazard, Dog Eat Dog, Machine Head, and Life of Agony, the label believed it had discovered bands who represented the anger and spite of hardcore punk, not just the hair coloring. By 1996, however, the fusion of hardcore and metal in these groups had become less remarkable than their rap-inflected vocals and attitude.

In this thuggish, combative form of metal, Pantera loomed large. As Pantera netted six gold albums between 1993 and 1996, newcomers Biohazard and Machine Head crept up the charts with a similar convulsive style—incorporating the pounding groove of rap music

A show of hands: Pantera live in the 1990s

while sticking to a basic guitar-based thrash metal drive. These urban squads rolled from the streets of Brooklyn and Oakland, and their aggressive fusion took naturally to the indomitable influence of hardcore rap. At the same time pot-smoking, gun-praising rap group Cypress Hill met them halfway—treading tough turf with haunting, paranoid rhymes and versatile music by producer Mixmaster Muggs, a steady user of Black Sabbath samples. In turn, all of these acts influenced a brand-new smattering of little-known regional bands like Korn, Slipknot, and Limp Bizkit, all of whose self-released debut albums in the mid-1990s showed that the heavy metal spirit survived in ways that were increasingly hard to identify.

As its hair slowly grew back, Metallica rediscovered its metal roots. An elaborate stage show concocted for its 1997 North American tour reenacted the archly constructed reality in which the band now lived. Recalling James Hetfield's dramatic accident in Montreal, a rigged piece of lighting exploded halfway through each nightly set, sending a flaming spotlight technician swinging through the air by a safety cable. With the deconstruction sequence and storyline initiated, lighting towers fell into a preset semicollapsed position, and roadies rushed to extinguish the flames. The lighting technician was toted away by stretcher to an ambulance waiting by the stage, while the sound system played a loop of crackling static noise.

Their equipment thus devastated, the band members pretended to improvise a makeshift solution to the catastrophe. Reconvening on a remote corner of the stage, where small, two-speaker combo guitar amps sat beneath a few bare lightbulbs, they bashed out a homey medley of "Four Horsemen" and other oldies from *Kill 'Em All*. Slowly the soundman fortified the mix to proper arena volume. It was a tremendous event that played on disaster fantasies and told the story of the band's now-legendary origins. More logistically complex than any of Iron Maiden's mammoth stage sets of the 1980s, the production was pure Metallica genius, pretending to mock rock and roll convention even as it played into it wholeheartedly. Indeed, the special-effects company won a Designer of the Year award from the leading stagecraft industry magazine.

As Metallica kept itself entertained, they tapped the credit line of their creative carte blanche—and avoided writing new songs—with a return to heavy metal form. As *Load* and *Reload* were attempts to get back to basics by playing simple rock, *Garage Inc.* returned the band to its true origins: classic NWOBHM metal and hardcore punk. Since the *Creeping Death* EP in 1984 and the *Garage Days Re-Revisited* EP in 1987, the band had always had great luck with cover songs stroked with heaping quantities of trademark Hetfieldisms and Metallithrash. Now the double CD *Garage Inc.* made new payments on old artistic loans by exposing Metallica's interests and influences to a new generation of listeners.

Combining one disk of sixteen previously available cuts with a second disk of new recordings, the *Garage Inc.* double CD gave Metallica a chance to further exhaust the catalog of Diamond Head and the Misfits, while throwing in a couple of overlooked classics by Black Sabbath and the British hardcore band Discharge. Wild cards were Bob Seger's "Turn the Page," Nick Cave's "Loverman," and an acoustic version of Lynyrd Skynyrd's "Tuesday's Gone"—with Kirk Hammett's old friend from algebra class, Les Claypool, on banjo.

One simple cover from a band as full of riffs as Mercyful Fate did not suffice. Metallica worked five songs from the hallmark *Melissa* and a preceding EP into an eleven-minute medley. "They captured the essence and still sounded like Metallica," says Fate singer King Diamond. "I was surprised when they did that. They thought our publisher would have told us, but it was Lars calling me out of the blue. He started playing the tape for me over the phone the first time, and my hair started standing on end. It was so authentic."

Former Misfits leader Glenn Danzig willingly handed over permission to rerecord his songs after denying the same rights to the Misfits, now re-formed with a new singer and signed to Geffen. "Kirk Hammett called me before they did the covers album," Danzig says, "and told me they wanted to play 'Die Die My Darling,' 'Last Caress,' and 'Green Hell.' It was cool with me." Cooler yet was his percentage of royalties on the three songs from an unexpected 4 million CD sales of *Garage Inc.*

Since they did not play any of their own songs during a short tour to promote *Garage Inc.*, Metallica fittingly hired a Metallica cover band called Battery as opening act. At Grammy time in 1999, Metallica took home the Hard Rock Performance award for *Garage, Inc.*'s "Whiskey in a Jar," beating out a slew of new names, including Korn, Kid Rock, and Limp Bizkit. Metallica now represented the establishment vote—a familiar face when it came time to pick industry honors. Metallica's millions had made rich men of many in the music business, and thousands of lawyers, photographers, security guards, and record-store clerks were served by the economy the band generated. This fifth Grammy was an especially sweet award, honoring a traditional Irish folk song that had been a hit in 1973 as played in Thin Lizzy by the late Phil Lynott, one of Cliff Burton's favorite bassists and an underrecognized influence on countless metal greats.

Not content to retire and collect publishing checks from Metallica performances, the revived NWOBHM label Neat Records responded to *Garage Inc.* with *Metallic-Era Vol. I* and *Metallic-Era Vol. II.* These were collections of original versions of the Motörhead, Diamond Head, Holocaust, and other early British heavy metal tracks covered by Metallica. On the second volume Holocaust turned the tables with its own interpretation of "Master of Puppets." Metallica had previously been treated to several reinterpretations of its music: first by the industrial band Die Krupps, then by *Apocalyptica Plays Metallica by Four Cellos*, a classical music project by a Finnish string quartet. The *ECW Extreme Music* wrestling soundtrack CD in 1998 offered the ultimate headbanging honor: a faithfully meaty cover of "Enter Sandman" by Motörhead.

Meanwhile, floating in the Persian Gulf on the aircraft carrier USS *Constellation*, naval and marine officers passed the time playing Metallica cover songs in a "classic alternative rock band" called One Ball Low. The film *Paradise Lost* proved that Metallica was popular with captive audiences, and the 5,000-person crew of the *Constellation* was no exception. Still, there was more than a little irony in soldiers copying songs by the band that wrote impassioned antiwar hymns like "Disposable Heroes" and "One."

"Enter Sandman" was treated differently by the great-grandfather of Christian rock, Pat Boone. On his *In a Metal Mood: No More Mr. Nice Guy* CD, Boone found the schmaltz in twelve metal chestnuts, in-

ꟿETAL TꞦIBUTES

Dating back to the first records by Black Sabbath and Judas Priest, heavy metal used cover songs as a measure of its distance from what came before. The soaring voice of Rob Halford on Priest's version of "Green Manalishi (with the Two-Pronged Crown)" sounded like it came from a different century than did the Fleetwood Mac original. With thrash metal, cover versions became a full-fledged mania, as Slayer covered Iron Butterfly's "In-A-Gadda-Da-Vida" for the *Less Than Zero* sound track, Megadeth covered Nancy Sinatra, Exodus covered War, and Xentrix lamentably covered the theme from *Ghostbusters*. Metallica was among the most prodigious raiders and careful selectors of back catalog, illuminating obscure influences through limited-edition releases. In the late 1990s the practice extended to full-length albums of covers by major metal artists, as well as lesser tribute albums of metal greats by unknown bands. One tribute album was not enough for the most legendary, as Black Sabbath, Mercyful Fate, Metallica, Judas Priest, Slayer, Venom, and Iron Maiden tribute albums ran into multiple volumes.

The Masters' Call

- ❖ *A Tribute to Abba* (2000) With Therion, Morgana LeFay, and other tongue-in-cheek tributes

- ❖ *In Memory of Celtic Frost* (1996) With Emperor, 13, Mayhem, Opeth

- ❖ *Nativity in Black: A Tribute to Black Sabbath* (1994) Type O Negative proves it is possible to slow down "Black Sabbath"

Metal Tributes (cont'd)

Answering to the Masters

- ❖ Pat Boone, *No More Mr. Nice Guy: In a Metal Mood* (1997) Easy-listening Metallica, Dio, and Judas Priest

- ❖ Cutthroat, *Rape Rape Rape* (1998) Japanese attacks on Hirax, Mace, Exodus, and Warfare

- ❖ Guns N' Roses, *The Spaghetti Incident?* (1993) Primal-therapy LP covering Damned, Charles Manson, the Stooges, and Hanoi Rocks

- ❖ Metallica, *Garage Days Re-Revisited, the $5.98 EP* (1987) Original covers of Holocaust, the Misfits, Killing Joke, and Budgie

- ❖ Metallica, *Garage Inc.* (1998) Adds Nick Cave, Motörhead, Bob Seger, and Mercyful Fate

- ❖ Overkill, *Coverkill* (1999) Thrash kings cop Motörhead, Kiss, Judas Priest, and the Sex Pistols

- ❖ Rage Against the Machine, *Renegades* (2000) Taking Afrika Bambaata to the metal

- ❖ Slayer, *Undisputed Attitude* (1996) Metal kings send alms to Minor Threat, Dr. Know, DI, and the Stooges

- ❖ Six Feet Under, *Graveyard Classics* (2002) Cookie Monster does Venom, AC/DC, Exodus, and Accept

cluding Judas Priest's "You've Got Another Thing Coming" and Dio's "Holy Diver." "That was funny to hear 'Holy Diver' done that way," says Ronnie James Dio. "I don't think a lot of people got the joke, but he certainly did." With the camp factor cranked up to eleven, Boone crooned his way through the titanic themes, accompanied by backup singers, a horn section, and an outrageously wimpy lead guitar.

Vigilant and unamused, the religious right temporarily turned against the figurehead of wholesomeness, as Boone's *Gospel America* program was suspended from the Trinity Broadcasting Network. Yet despite the Christian industry's longtime bullying of politicians and corporations with threats of boycotts, their supposed blocking power looked anemic as *In a Metal Mood* became the first Pat Boone record to crack the *Billboard* 200 in more than thirty years.

After taking a beating in the mainstream during the 1990s, supporters of heavy metal were not surprised that the music still had market power. Dedicated back-catalog labels like CMC International and Spitfire Records snatched the opportunity to acquire from major labels at bargain prices the previously recorded back catalogs of Iron Maiden, Twisted Sister, and other faded giants "With the perceived heyday of metal long since gone by, the majors have turned their focus to other forms of music," announced the Spitfire Records mission statement. "With the majors almost entirely out of the picture and the simple fact the record business is cyclical in nature, a growing trend back to the harder-edge music is emerging. Actually, metal and hard rock music have never gone away."

Free from the marketing plans of large record companies, metal in the mid-1990s remained vital and self-directed. The spirit persevered in a fresh generation intent on recombining heavy metal traditions reverently. Young bands like Hammerfall, Blind Guardian, and Iced Earth reverse-engineered the 1980s metal style into a vintage reproduction called legacy metal, combining the fantastic grandeur of straight-ahead bands like Fates Warning and Manowar with the fluency of German speed metal. To them, the early heavy metal pioneers had achieved immortal status—the faces of Ozzy, Halford, and Dio could be carved on an imaginery Mount Rushmore.

Other retro treatments demonstrated heavy metal's often-underestimated ability to laugh at itself. As much as armor and long-winded pageantry, metal's sense of irony was always part of its attraction. Cranium's music in particular was a hyperactive master's thesis on the joys of wearing leather and spikes. Worshipping mid-1980s speed metal records by Violence and Living Death, the band purified and pilloried the form. *Speed Metal Slaughter* featured as many outrageous riffs and silly solos as the entire Combat Records back catalog. On the antidisco "Slaughter on the Dance Floor" and the anthemic "Satanic Rescue Team," vocalist Chainsaw Demon purposely exaggerated his European accent in tribute to the great voices of German speed metal.

Ohio's Boulder took nearly the same approach, cramming Melvins and Motörhead riffs into a package adorned by Flying V guitars, tributes to Michael Schenker, and artwork sampled from old Riot albums. Boulder and Cranium both demonstrated a metal paradox: They gave their all without taking themselves too seriously. Not surprisingly, these bands emerged during a transitional time when Iron Maiden was oddly touring America in support of Ed Hunter, a video game starring its mascot.

Forced to recognize their own value in the wake of a media blackout, metallers developed a real nostalgia for battles won. Fans and musicians who for so long had been focused on the next big thing, looked back and discovered that an admirable number of metal records stood the test of time. "As Megadeth became successful," says Dave Mustaine, "a lot of the bands that we passed up, I oddly enough thought, 'Why should I listen to them anymore, we're bigger than them.' But if you open up my suitcase today, there's a bag in there with *Ride the Lightning*, the Metallica Black record, Megadeth *Rust in Piece*, Diamond Head *Behold the Beginning* and *Lightning to the Nations*, and Mercyful Fate *Melissa* and *Don't Break the Oath*."

With that wistful feeling in the air, it was not long before *Metal Dreams*—a fanzine entirely dedicated to restoring 1980s-style metal—shot to prominence. Editor Chris Dugan supported languishing metal acts generously, passionately charging through interviews with Anvil, Accept, Dokken, and Savatage. Death metal was not especially relished, but alternative rock was viewed as a scourge akin to leprosy. Not entirely seduced, the older generation kept its success in perspective. "Musically, the eighties generation is gone," says Ronnie James Dio, whose most recent platinum album came in 1989. "Never in a million years will it be as big as it was. That was the music that built MTV, never will that be again. People who say, 'Yeah, it's coming back, it's coming full circle'—those are the people who don't understand the world as it is. I've looked in the mirror recently, and it doesn't bother me."

Without merely reveling in the greatness of the past, however, there was a feeling of continual renewal and renovation of heavy metal's incredible propulsive energy. "The way I see the genres and subgenres evolving, I think there's just going to be more of everything," says Matt Jacobson of Relapse Records. "More classic metal, more power metal, more death metal—there's just more diversity across the board. I think it's happening with all music. There are more influences than ever before. I think there's room for a handful of bands from each subgenre to be pretty big and for each subgenre to thrive, ultimately depending on the strength of the bands."

Powered by the late-twentieth-century boom economy, the amount of available heavy metal choices soon grew almost surreal. Reunions by long-lost metal heavyweights Exodus, S.O.D., Venom, and Saxon competed for flocking crowds with insurgent tours by still-thriving death metal and black metal acts. The diversity was overwhelming. At the annual Milwaukee Metalfest—a long-running meeting of headbangers from Japan, Europe, Australia, and anywhere in North America with interstate highways and a caffeine supply—fans roamed freely between rooms and multiple stages—gorging across decades on power metal greats Anvil, intricate and

Logo à go-go: Metal overload in L.A., November 2000

jazzy rap metal upstarts Candiria, and Norwegian black metallers Enslaved as if flipping television channels.

Despite the uncertainty of the mid-1990s, there remained an ever-emerging new young audience for heavy metal that would only be confirmed in the coming years. This fresh audience kept Metallica at the front line of music sales during the second half of the 1990s. SoundScan, the record industry's sales meter, reported Metallica Black the third bestselling album since it began counting. Even though the band had barely lifted a creative finger, the *Load* and *Reload* CDs together sold an impressive 7 million copies by the end of the decade. Eclipsing the popularity of the entire grunge and lite punk genres, Metallica sold more than 22 million CDs in America just between 1995 and 2000, while touring and remaining internationally popular. Meanwhile, the concert trade magazine *Pollstar* calculated Metallica's total career headline gross for North American shows at $218 million.

By the late 1990s Metallica was arguably the most popular modern rock act in the world, competing only with U2, R.E.M., and Madonna. Yet its live performances were still riddled with songs by obscure heavy metal giants like Diamond Head and Mercyful Fate. In late 1998 Metallica performed at the Playboy mansion, the showbusiness equivalent of being invited by the president to play at the White House. According to the RIAA, the organization that accounts for gold and platinum record awards, as of 2000 Metallica had sold as many records in America in fifteen years as the Rolling Stones could muster in all their legendary four decades. Though the world was late to realize it, heavy metal had become the new rock and roll.

❧ XIX ❦

Virtual Ozzy &
Metal's Digital Rebound

- ➤ **October 25, 1996:** First Ozzfest held in Phoenix, Arizona
- ➤ **July 29, 1997:** *Spawn* sound track includes Slayer remix by Atari Teenage Riot
- ➤ **May 2, 2000:** Slipknot goes platinum in the United States, royalties split nine ways
- ➤ **July 11, 2000:** Lars Ulrich testifies against Napster.com before U.S. Congress

While Metallica's twenty-two-show Lollapalooza summer 1996 tour grossed a respectable $16 million, the former Bay Area bashers had no intention of reinventing the festival as a roaring heavy metal summit. That job was taken by Ozzy Osbourne—himself snubbed by Lollapalooza promoters the previous year. Although Ozzy saw 10 million CD sales in the 1990s, compared to 6 million albums in the 1980s—the alleged heyday of heavy metal—the beloved singer's career was due for a face-lift. His public antics during the 1990s included stumbling comatose across a WWF wrestling ring, demonstrating exercise equipment to befuddled magazine editors, and recording a romantic duet with the Muppet Miss Piggy.

In the second half of the decade, the long-lived madman put his enduring charisma to better use. Ozzy's band played more than a hundred dates in 1996, anchored by a spectacular pair of minifestivals in Phoenix, Arizona, and San Bernardino, California. Dubbed "Ozzfests," the two shows brought Ozzy Osbourne together with top metal acts such as Slayer, Sepultura, and Biohazard, plus the unconventional wild cards Neurosis, Powerman 5000, and Coal Chamber. These all-day happenings drew tens of thousands of metal rats out of the woodwork and resurrected the prominence of the slightly doddering Ozzy. After suffering metal neglect in recent years, a popular culture scene was starved for exactly such an iron-plated celebration of excess and power chords.

Suddenly, there was talk of a resurgence of metal, the millions-selling genre that had never gone away. Expanded into an apocalyptic coast-to-coast caravan in subsequent years, Ozzfest, with its sun-drenched twelve-hour stretches of adrenaline and aggression, revitalized the concert industry. While box-office receipts suffered during the reign of pop punk, alternative rock, and rap music—leading to wide concern over the imminent collapse of the concert medium—Ozzfest affirmed that huge audiences existed for live music, particularly hardcore heavy metal. "We don't try to outsmart ourselves," Ozzy's longtime wife and manager, Sharon Osbourne, told *Billboard*. "We don't try to bring in forty singing monks or Tony Bennett. We just do what we do. A lot of times when people get successful, they try and get too smart and put stuff on that impresses themselves and the people of their age group—yet it doesn't work with the kids on the street."

As when he helped along Mötley Crüe and Metallica a decade earlier, Ozzy Osbourne again put his symbolic approval behind adventurous young bands with momentum just beginning to manifest. In this case he took the cream of the crop of an entire field of bands. They all had been hovering around the periphery of the music scene looking for a niche while releasing music on tiny regional labels—or in many cases on their own. They were exceptionally angry, and two years earlier their career prospects were virtually nil.

Dubbed "nu metal," the Ozzfest bands whipped together a new and improved formula that raged with the thunder of heavy metal while swaying to the funky pulse of rap music. Then they struck a compromise between that mixture and the gruesome sonic assault of death metal. Harking back to the alternative metal wave of 1991, the nu metal bands were grinders of a slam-dancing musical sausage—picking and choosing influences like the aggressive cable-ready channel surfers they were.

The mix of raw guitars, emotional singing, and sonic trickery introduced a popular explosion that had been waiting since the early 1990s, as nu metal bands put a stylish face on the endless, undying desire to lash out. To a band like Korn—initially labeled rap metal—the original metal icons Iron Maiden and Judas Priest were already past the vanishing point. Their memories of live music began during the time when rap and metal began to clash in the early 1990s—the era of the historic live collaboration between Anthrax and Public Enemy. "Our musical history starts with the Red Hot Chili Peppers and early Faith No More," said Korn bassist Reggie Arvizu, aka Fieldy, to the *Akron Beacon Journal*. "As a band, that's where we begin."

In the decade since the Bay Area thrash band Mordred first added a DJ to their lineup, the funk metal mix had grown much more formidable. Founded in the hinterlands of Bakersfield, California, before relocating to Los Angeles, Korn intensified the precision assault of Pantera and added funky electronic sounds. An energetic live act, the band rode a repetitive rhythmic churn of low-tuned guitar riffs while pantomiming and exaggerating the poses of rappers. Bringing greater contrast to the erratic technique of Mike Patton from Faith No More, kilt-wearing singer Jonathan Davis alternated between a pained growl and a sarcastic, tuneless whine, pioneering a new vocal style.

Nu metal shared some tonal qualities with death metal, but was much more accessible. By 1997 Korn had earned platinum sales of its self-titled debut and the follow-up, *Life Is Peachy*. Putting anger to a beat, the band grabbed the attention of the affluent suburban teen audience that had previously identified with the antisocial outlook of rap music. As longtime rap scene also-ran Kid Rock began rhyming over Metallica riffs, he also tapped the incredible market power in the rediscovery of guitars. "Limp Bizkit's Fred Durst and Kid Rock are rappers," says Chuck D from the influential rap group Public Enemy. "They probably rebelled against rock in their teenage years, because it was too white-boy or something. Now it's available to them, and you have to tip your hat to these guys for doing it."

Image-savvy and raised on MTV since early childhood, members

Rap rocker Kid Rock, pre-Metallica samples (*Jive*)

of the nu school embraced and exaggerated the stereotypes of heavy metal instead of defying them. Like the nightmarish child of glam metal, they relied heavily on image—replacing the hair spray with facial piercings, custom contact lenses, and made-to-order dreadlocks, and tossing into the mix an unsettling slew of masks, midgets, and other randomly appropriate props. As Mötley Crüe and Poison escorted models and strippers on Sunset Blvd. in the 1980s, so in the 1990s Korn and Limp Bizkit showed status by mingling with porn stars on Melrose Ave.

Awakened to the fad in full swing, MTV recast itself in nu metal's image at the end of the 1990s, yet cable television was no longer the insurgent medium. The Internet created a nationwide network of all metal fans, not just those willing to wade through the back pages of magazines for tape-trader ads. Korn and its peers were fully aware of the computer age, and they invested heavily in Internet promotion, using new media and e-mail to personalize their relationship to fans in the hands-on style of Metallica and other underground bands. On their websites fans wrote the bios, voted on playlists for live shows, and picked up music for free.

Ozzfest became the physical host for this scene—a rolling virtual nu metal city on wheels. In 1998 Ozzfest launched the career of the transitional band whose success sounded a death knell for the 1990s, Limp Bizkit. Previously the band's ever-present DJ, Lethal, had survived as a hip-hop hitmaker with House of Pain. Now Limp Bizkit twisted the rap-rock dial confidently in the direction of metal, absorbing the bravado and rhythm of hardcore rap into a saturated framework of guitars and fist-pumping anthems. Their catchphrase-laden songs, like "Show Me What You Got" and "Take a Look Around," seemed based on slogans cribbed from bumper stickers and county-fair novelties. In the sweaty churn of the slam pit, however, the band worked wonders—its physical effect could not be denied.

After Limp Bizkit and Godsmack in 1998, the Ozzfest in 1999 introduced the eclectic System of a Down, whose down-tuned guitars and scattershot drum arrangements wove threads of Carcass into an eclectic Zappa-esque mix. Wearing face paint and a huge Afro, System's Lebanese-born front man, Serj Tankian, sold agitated political lyrics with grindcore growls, feral barking, and nervous squeals. In 2000, the most impressive Ozzfest newcomer was Kittie, from London, Ontario, an all-female band formed after two members met in gymnastics class. As their band's debut, *Spit*, sold more than half a million copies, its gimmicky pink hair and barrettes gave way to leather belts and a more mature sound on the follow-up *Oracle*. "Of course we have a lot of aggression," said vocalist Morgan Lander to *Rolling Stone*. "It's an aggressive style of music, and it's easier to get your point across."

The nu metal bands understood adolescent rage, but they were too young to remember the time when heavy metal was truly outsider music. Not surprisingly, many traditional metallers remained slow to embrace a form whose biggest musical contribution was oversimplification. The success of nu metal stars like Papa Roach—whose song "Last Resort" was based entirely on a looped Iron Maiden guitar lick—irritated the old guard immensely. "In the past eight or nine years music has gotten really atonal," says Megadeth's Dave Mustaine. "The bands all sound identical, whether it's the alternative bands or even the nu metal bands. I think a lot of it has to do with the music industry—they're not looking for originality."

Mercedes Lander and Fallon Bowman of Kittie
(Jeanne Mitchell)

Yet veterans were perhaps guilty of forgetting how simple and charming basic heavy metal had been a generation earlier. There was originality and freshness in the nu metal sound, and its influence inevitably seeped into the underground, drawing old metal into healthy new hybrids. Slayer and Napalm Death remained popular in the late 1990s by stripping the number of musical ideas in their songs to an attention-deficit minimum. Likewise, after Sepultura chose not to renew a management contract in April 1997 with singer Max Cavalera's wife, Cavalera left his brother and bandmates and formed Soulfly—an

Ozzfest favorite whose grinding guitar metal was layered within a state-of-the-art cut-and-paste of sound.

As the wheels turned forward, nu metal reinvigorated heavy metal for an enthusiastic young generation. "Those bands are commercial music," explains Matt Jacobson from the underground label Relapse Records, "but they're great for what we're doing in general. It prepares people for heavier music. I think bands like those are opening people up to underground music. I certainly didn't go from pop radio to Napalm Death. It was like Black Sabbath and ZZ Top into Mötley Crüe and Iron Maiden, then Slayer, and then Napalm Death. Everyone needs a transition."

<hr />

By the end of the decade the distinction between nu metal and traditional metal began to vanish as package tours and festival bills brought genres and fans together. The ultimate bridge between the camps was Slipknot—the band whose rabid countenance most closely embodied the spirit of Ozzfest. "I don't think jumping up and down and wearing baggy pants have anything to do with metal, but that's just personal taste," says Dan Lilker, whose hard-crunching S.O.D. was a major influence on nu metal. "But I know I can definitely tell the difference between Limp Bizkit and a band like Slipknot."

Appearing from the post-Scandinavian badlands of Des Moines, Iowa, the nine-member Slipknot delivered bullet points on the complex treatises of death metal, showing technical finesse while remaining dedicated to chaos. Including former members of the death metal groups Body Pit and Anal Blast, Slipknot was the result of years of rabid late-night brainstorming while its members worked dead-end jobs in their hometown. The minimum-wage post behind the cash register proved a powerful incubator. Claiming the influence of every style of music save modern country, the band twisted percussive arrangements with scorching groove, weird guitar, DJ squiggles, and a graveyard sense of humor. With cuts like "Left Behind" and "People = Shit," they digested underground metal for mass consumption and dragged down every other form of music into the muck. "We're going to take all the genres of music that we love," says percussionist Shawn Crahan, aka 6, "death metal being one of the highest, and incorporate it in everything we've done."

ПU METAL

Somewhere around the time that Biohazard hit the scene, funk metal stopped being a joke. Combining the spectral influence of Faith No More with snippets of the hardest death metal, the nu metal bands proved that pancultural metal could pay off. Given a perfect platform in Ozzfest, a yearly summertime touring moshfest, the Deftones, Limp Bizkit, and Kittie turned in multiple-million sales by the end of the 1990s. Though the skater clothes and rap-inflected lingo were a world apart from the medieval garb of a previous generation, the effect on audiences was just as fervent. Slipknot especially retained the whirling chaos of its death metal roots—adding clean vocals increased the potential audience nearly tenfold.

Play That Funky Music Redux

- ❖ Biohazard, *State of the World Address* (1994)
- ❖ Deftones, *White Pony* (2000)
- ❖ Fear Factory, *Demanufacture* (1994)
- ❖ Kittie, *Oracle* (2001)
- ❖ Korn, *Life Is Peachy* (1996)
- ❖ Limp Bizkit, *Significant Other* (1999)
- ❖ Papa Roach, *Infest* (2000)
- ❖ Slipknot, *Iowa* (2001)
- ❖ Slipknot, *Slipknot* (1999)
- ❖ Soulfly, *Soulfly* (1998)
- ❖ System of a Down, *System of a Down* (1998)
- ❖ Tool, *Aenima* (1996)
- ❖ Rob Zombie, *Hellbilly Deluxe* (1998)

Slipknot members wore rubber costumes reminiscent of horror-film monsters and used bar-coded numbers instead of names. Alongside the shock value was a scrap of meaning: The repulsive masks were intended (as with the eyeball-clad avant-garde group the Residents) to breed anonymity and subvert the cult of the rock star. Of course, as with Kiss, the masks only created a huge mystique around the band. Following trickling sales of the self-released 1996 LP *Mate, Feed, Kill, Repeat,* the band joined Ozzfest, and the breakthrough 1999 *Slipknot* CD clicked with a pissed-off public and went platinum—the first million-selling honor for the longtime metal indie label Roadrunner. "Every day that we do this, I become more of what I've tried so hard to be my whole life," says Crahan. "I'm getting the opportunity to live my dream, and I'm getting to be what I really am. I don't exactly know what that is. But I know I love it. I come home and draw pictures with my kid, and then I go out onstage and set my DJ on fire."

With popularity came the expected public attacks. After student Robert Steinhaeuser shot thirteen teachers, friends, and a policeman in Germany in 2002, media critics fingered Slipknot's lyrics as a cause—particularly a song allegedly titled "School Wars." Slipknot indignantly defended itself and asked for a fact check. "It is ludicrous to place the blame on our band or any other form of music," read their official statement. "Slipknot does not have a song called 'School Wars,' we have never written a song called 'School Wars,' and we certainly would never encourage people to kill others. We are a blanket of hope for our kids, not a scapegoat for attacks like this, and while we send our most sincere condolences to those affected by this, we will not take responsibility."

Too harsh for MTV and radio, in the metal tradition Slipknot turned its Ozzfest success into a well-publicized, hard-touring cottage industry. The costumed antiheroes created a circuslike spectacle of aggression, turning their stage into an amplified mosh pit that completely immolated the safety barrier between band and audience. "If you're not convinced that a band can go out and win kids on the road, then you shouldn't sign them," says Roadrunner Records' A&R director, Monte Conner, who also brought Soulfly and the Korn-like Coal Chamber to the former label of King Diamond and Death. "Traditionally the way Roadrunner sells records is by bands on the road, not through radio. There is very little MTV for a band like Slipknot. They've gotta just sell it."

In true heavy metal fashion the focus was on the fans—disgruntled young people growing up during an Internet-driven financial boom, fully expecting to be left holding the bag when the bubble burst. "The crowds sing the fucking words," says Crahan, "and you can tell that the words mean everything in life to them. We've got the jocks sitting right next to the scumbags and the total metal dudes sitting next to the hip-hop guys. No matter how sore I am, when I see those faces in need of a break, I make sure I indulge as hard as I can."

As the collision of metal and nonmetal styles intensified and headed toward destinations unknown, the changing terrain of metal became a curiosity even to veterans of the underworld. Legions of new fans began appearing at Ozzfest looking like vampiric ravers from Japanese cartoons, combining the baggy pants of urban homeboys with the gothic white face paint of black metal. "I don't know what that is supposed to be," says Type O Negative's Peter Steele, "but it's pretty interesting."

Beyond nu metal, pop music at the end of the 1990s was about coalition building—whether between genders and races or by mixing underground influences with mainstream genres. As the prevalence of computers gave hungry young musicians unprecedented perspective on the world around them, boundary bouncing became evident in the techno-metal of Prodigy, the rap-rock of Beck, and the punk-folk of Ani DiFranco. In 1997 headbanger authority *Metal Maniacs* reported that Moby, the first techno DJ to reject anonymity and develop a star persona, was shocking summer music festivals in Europe with a live metal-oriented band that reckoned from Slayer in terms of deathly attack.

It seemed that a union of the club dance floor and the mosh pit was inevitable—the ultimate crossover between heavy metal and disco. As samplers and drum machines found their way into guitar stores and became the new standard media of musicmaking in the late 1990s, so did Korn, Limp Bizkit, and System of a Down arrive at metal with MIDI-based sequencing already on the mind. It was a completely renovated approach to headbanging. As a by-product of nu metal's reliance on rap music, the defining musical traits—repetition, highly processed production style, and pastiche songwriting—were also the essence of digital music production, brought into bedroom-based home studios in the 1990s via computer programs such as Cubase, Logic Audio, and Pro Tools.

Instead of carving decibels with giant mountains of equipment as did Judas Priest, nu metal bands used digital guitar effects that emulated the enormity of vintage amplifiers through algorithms. "We kept up with what was available in terms of technology," says former Judas Priest singer Rob Halford. "Now it's all done with Pro Tools, it's all done with computers. It doesn't really matter how you get to the point that you're aiming for. You just use the gear that you want. You no longer need to go into a full-blown studio—you can make a record in your bedroom. A lot of what musicians need is atmosphere, and emotional support to get the right things happening. Studios are terrifying places for bands—when they go in, they just kind of lock up and are fearful of it. Now they have access to all this sophisticated but easy-to-use software and recording gear. You don't need to spend gazillions of dollars to do what you require."

Life after Napalm Death:
Nick Bullen and Mick Harris of Scorn
(Earache Records)

There was certainly precedent for machine-assisted metal. The Birmingham, England, band Godflesh, formed in 1989 by Justin Broadrick after his exit from Napalm Death, proved that the definition of heaviness could waver into stark industrial turf far outside the colorful grasp of Van Halen and Mötley Crüe. Dressed like communist Chinese factory workers, the pioneering two-man band bludgeoned intrepid listeners with the sound of a monolithic machine press. After their digital sampler was dropped during the first American gig, Broadrick frantically rebuilt the basis of his band's repertoire from memory in forty-eight hours. Afterward he traveled with backup disks of his precious data—weathering both technical and cultural storms to create a new direction for metal.

For many years, most headbangers resisted technical changes, allowing commercial electronic acts to steal their thunder. In the early 1990s the wholesale cultural sampling of heavy metal was commonplace, as when Düsseldorf's Die Krupps released a CD of Metallica standards. Best described as "Metallica on *Sprockets*," *A Tribute to Metallica* contained robotic versions of "For Whom the Bell Tolls," "Nothing Else Matters," and seven more techno-tallica takes on music that was already drum-machine tight in original headbanging form.

Toying with sacred cows, there were converts to the digital sound. With computer technology, the precision of top bands could be counted on a microchip-controlled time clock and no longer needed to be cultivated through live practicing and playing—a huge departure from metal tradition. Mick Harris, the longtime leader of Napalm Death, baffled peers as he abandoned his drum throne in favor of a sampler and a mixing deck to form Scorn. "I just think they're scared that people won't accept them if they take in new ideas," he says. Offering a sound track for bassist Nick Bullen's films, Scorn brought metallic intensity to the electronic arts. "When we were young and looking for music," says Bullen, "Joy Division, Birthday Party, and Throbbing Gristle were the bands that were around for people like us. And then we'd go out with girls who'd be into funk and rap, and they'd get us into that as well."

The adventurous Brutal Truth and Napalm Death also threw electronic elements into their roaring morass of sound, mainly with side projects like Meathook Seed, Blood from the Soul, and Malformed Earthborn. Influenced by the angst-laden scrapings of Skinny Puppy and Nine Inch Nails, these groups used drum machines, sampled sequences, and distorted guitar and vocals to create a psychedelic techno-metal hybrid. Though the Cleveland-based Nine Inch Nails was initially discounted by metal fans, leader Trent Reznor later moved to Los Angeles and created the crucial blueprint for any band combining angst and samplers. Ministry then took the drum-machine discord of NIN and added synthetic layers of goth rock and hot-rod kitsch. Another Reznor protégé and later Ozzfest headliner, Marilyn Manson brought the shock tactics of Alice Cooper to a supersonic extreme and was consequently for a short while blamed for every teen problem from school shootings to computer espionage.

The next major step toward bringing heavy metal together with machines came from the slick Los Angeles death metal band Fear Factory, who took technology to heart in 1994 and reinvented itself using emerging digital studio techniques. "We recorded *Demanufacture* on tape," reports singer Burton Bell, "but went into computers as well, so everything would be synched up digitally. I sample my voice. I'll just do one chorus as best I can—layer it—and when the chorus comes up again, we just pop my vocals in from the sampler. It saves time, and I just have to sing it once. Even the guitars are done that way. The only thing that's completely live all the way through [is] the drums."

Following several Ozzfest appearances, Fear Factory in 1999 had a Top 40 radio hit for fifteen straight weeks with its remake of Gary Numan's icy "Cars," perhaps the ultimate new wave anthem. Celtic Frost had faced serious criticism for covering a Wall of Voodoo song in 1987, but twelve years later the boundaries of heavy metal were far more abstract. "When we started doing this, we were thinking that the metal crowd wouldn't accept it," says Fear Factory guitarist Dino Cazares. "But they did. First you have to think about what you like and what joy you get out of creating things."

Ultimately even music from the techno underground could embrace the spirit and power of heavy metal music while leaving behind its guitars and other sacred artifacts. By the mid-1990s the digital equivalent of metal was flourishing in three discrete movements from outside the headbanger lineage: DHR, gabber, and tech step. They could scarcely be called heavy metal but were products of an age when the most durable and resilient materials were made of synthetic plastics instead of Birmingham steel. On Berlin's politically inspired Digital Hardcore Recordings, or DHR, the aggressive Atari Teenage Riot, Bomb 20, and Ec8or thrived on a formula of hectic looped drum samples, noise, and guitar layers—topped by activist male/female vocal duos screaming anticorporate agitprop like "Delete Yourself" and "Hunt Down the Nazis!" Atari Teenage Riot, formed by DHR head Alec Empire, gave this routine an imposingly militant visual style—a kind of terrorist chic. "I could see how they might be the Slayer of what they do," says Kerry King, whose guitars Atari Teenage Riot sampled on at least three tracks.

Besides speed metal, DHR borrowed much of its hyperspeed aggression from gabber, an extreme dance style popular in the cheap dance halls of industrial Rotterdam, Holland. In the perpetual blam, blam, blam of that electronic overdrive, tonality and melody were reduced to a 230-beat-per-minute kick drum—often mixed with thrash metal guitar and vocal samples. Gabber was every bit the techno equivalent of extreme metal, attracting Dutch religious protesters and introducing such extravagant personalities as the Headbanger and also Dark Raver—a DJ who wore a cloak and bopped fans on the head with a plastic ax. Not surprisingly, gabber was often the first point of crossover between death metal and techno, as bedroom producers matched suffocating guitar riffs and squawking techno-tronic punch. Earache Records encouraged such blurring of genre lines, even opening its vaults for the *Hellspawn* compilation, in which acts including Morbid Angel were remixed so that their guitar, vocal, and drum tracks fit a techno pattern.

Even gabber's one-dimensional pounding was of fleeting interest in comparison to the twisting, elephantine bass riffs and monster breakbeats of tech step, the heaviest variation of drum and bass. This English music was a baffling, digitally driven gift of the 1990s: a frantic mutation of techno, dub reggae, and hip-hop, based on obvious digital manipulation of a cold, aggressive palette of huge, wobbling, analog synthesizer bass lines, booming bass drums, and snapping snares. Like early Death and Voivod, tech step was propelled by frenetic and awkward rhythms and tinged with ugly postnuclear ambience. The crushing bass riff of Fierce and Nico's "Crystal" in particular recalled Celtic Frost's ugly classic "Visual Aggression." Ex–Napalm Death and Godflesh member Justin Broadrick saw the connection between heavy metal and tech step. During Broadrick's brief tenure as a jungle DJ, his record bag was packed with disks from the No U-turn label—whose album art resembled steroid-laced computer rendering of Judas Priest's *Screaming for Vengeance*. Likewise, the most famous and versatile of British jungle producers, Goldie, named his record company Metalheadz.

After taking hold of Europe in the 1990s, even the heaviest-hitting techno music was slow to cross over to the American metal scene. Ten years earlier metal had looked at hardcore punk and seen an ally, and recently it had done the same with rap music. Metal kept itself vital by accepting new influences while communicating dense, iconoclastic ideals and resisting homogenizing commercial pressures—values shared with the DJ-driven techno underworld. Yet techno music was too loose and subjective. It was repetitive instrumental music meant for dancing. Metal still thrived on stories, with protagonists and high drama.

Though scattered nu metal bands like Static-X, Linkin Park, and System of a Down earned multiple-platinum albums by embracing the techno thump, ultimately the culture clash between the live-band ethic of heavy metal and the DJ-driven culture of club music remained too great for a full-scale transformation. After thirty years of mutation, tossing away guitars remained an upgrade away for the metal massive. Nonetheless, the eventual future transmutation of metal and techno loomed mighty and inevitable—the sound of the future.

As musicians found heavy new electronic sounds, the advent of computers also changed the operating habits of metal fans. While accelerating the speed of communication, the Internet was little different from the system of fanzine and mail-trader relationships used by the metal community for years. Many early heavy metal websites were simply trading lists reformated for Web browsers. Competing on the Internet for heavy metal dollars by 1999 were Relapse, Red Stream, and Blackmetal.com. On any given day the eBay auction site offered tens of thousands of heavy metal collectibles for sale.

The importance of the Internet, along with the superstore trend in American retail, had one unfortunate effect, dimming the niche power of the independently owned mom-and-pop heavy metal record store—a traditional metal meeting place. "Many of them are really struggling," says Matt Jacobson of Relapse Records. "We've had a number of key stores, that I would consider tastemaker stores, that have gone out of business or are close to doing that. I think the ones that are going to survive are the ones that are smart enough to realize they have to cater to the niche. I think there's room. It's definitely sad anytime you see stores like the Heavy Metal Shop or Ace's, places that have been a staple in the American heavy metal scene forever, start to bow out."

Even Napster-style file sharing of MP3 format songs was a high-tech version of tape trading—though that analogy would soon be hotly contested. With Metallica now an insanely lucrative industry,

METALLIC TECHNO

Testing the limits of heavy metal, techno artists like Atari Teenage Riot and Panacea used samplers and drum machines to construct mechanized music every bit as damaging as Slayer's. Without guitars or even vocals, metal-influenced digital musicians pointed the way to a heavy future, constructed via computer. These early electronic acts struggled to overcome their own novelty value, with mixed results. Though they found a respectable niche on the rave scene, the heavy metal world was not yet ready for all-electronic overdrive.

- ❖ Atari Teenage Riot, *Burn Berlin Burn* (1997)
- ❖ Godflesh, *Godflesh* (1988)
- ❖ Goldie, *Incredible Sound of Drum 'n' Bass* (2000)
- ❖ Panacea, *Twisted Disignz* (1997)
- ❖ Scorn, *Evanescence* (1994)
- ❖ Various Artists, *Battlegrounds* (1995)
- ❖ Various Artists, *Hellspawn* (1998)
- ❖ Various Artists, *Renegade Hardware Presents Quantum Mechanics* (1998)
- ❖ Various Artists, *Torque* (1997)

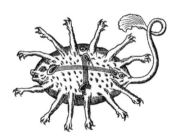

the legal staff of Metallica, Inc., was increasingly active. In 1999 the band's lawyers negotiated settlements with Victoria's Secret to halt sales of "Metallica" lip liner and with Pierre Cardin to bar a "Metallica" tuxedo. They sued Neiman Marcus and the hapless maker of a "Metallica" nail file and won injunctions against a host of radio stations to block unauthorized advance play of "I Disappear," a slightly techno-tinged single from the *Mission: Impossible 2* sound track.

Most notoriously, in April 2000 Metallica took on the Internet music-sharing site Napster and several universities over the issue of unauthorized downloads of MP3-encoded songs from the band's albums. Siding with the RIAA, Lars Ulrich became the music industry's face in the battle to keep tighter control over the distribution of music. This despite Metallica's reputation having been enhanced over the years by cool moves like allowing DAT recorders to tape concerts from a special sweet spot behind the soundboard. Not to mention that the band also streamed free previews from its own website and made new music widely and freely available for download on selected other locations. There was even an overwhelmingly obvious parallel between Napster and Metallica's mechanism for success: tape trading. As the Internet business weekly *Industry Standard* reported, "How much outrage will fans swallow from a band that built its following on bootlegs?"

"Money good. Napster bad." Anti-Metallica animation
(Camp Chaos)

To the Ozzfest audience in particular, who were bred to believe that free MP3s were a God-given right, Metallica was not down with the program. Type O Negative's Peter Steele takes a cynical view of the music industry's attempt to shut down Napster. "I just think it sucks," he says. "There is nothing original. Everything is there just to make a buck. It's not about the music—it's just about making money, which is really sad. I'm glad that this MP3 thing is happening, because it'll put the record companies out of business. Even if it hurts us, I will gladly cut off my nose to spite my face because I hate the record companies so much."

Yet for Lars Ulrich, seeing Napster raise hundreds of millions of dollars from its intended IPO of Napster.com stock was unthinkable. Aside from Napster's file-sharing software, the company's only valuable asset was its user base and name brand—both built on an immense library of free music. There was broad-sighted righteousness in this claim that was lost, however, as Ulrich testified before the U.S. Congress on July 11, 2000, in support of greater industry control of copyrights. Former colleagues stood aghast. Ulrich did not distinguish between the company, Napster, and its millions of users, the Metallica fans. In his unwise protestations about "controlling the music," Lars Ulrich simply appeared to be a greedy rock star piqued at the idea of losing a few dollars after building a multimillion-dollar fortune—in short, a shill for the RIAA.

Pranksters in May 2000 launched an Internet auction for Metallica's integrity—"slightly used"—which reached $10 million before being canceled by eBay.com administrators. Lars Ulrich saw no reason to second-guess his position and did little to dispel negative opinion. He chose to play the lead in facing down Napster, and ultimately he prevailed, as the service was moribund by the end of the year. Even Fred Durst of Limp Bizkit, who had taken $1.8 million from Napster to play a free tour promoting the service, eventually sided with the RIAA. As always, it was difficult to question Lars Ulrich's headstrong assurances. "For the doubters out there, Metallica will carry on for the next twenty years," Ulrich said during an hourlong Internet chat explaining the band's position. "Whether you're around for the ride or not, that's your problem, not ours."

⚜ ✕ ✕ ⚜

Reenthroned Emperors: It's a Headbanging World

➤ **December 4, 1997:** First original Black Sabbath reunion in Birmingham, England

➤ **April 1999:** Metallica joins the San Francisco Symphony Orchestra in Berkeley, California

➤ **August 5, 2000:** Iron Maiden and Halford sell out Madison Square Garden in two hours

➤ **May 2, 2002:** Nielsen reports *The Osbournes* top-rated cable show, with more than 6 million viewers.

"It was back to the beginning last month in Birmingham for the members of Black Sabbath. Where the Reunion tour began December 4, 1997, it ended on a high note December 21 and 22, 1999, with two scintillating shows which proved that, although the legend was being put to rest, its tale will be spun for generations to come. Both nights saw the four legends, energized and emotional, draped in black, the deafening roar of Birmingham's favorite sons washing over fans in the NEC Arena in a tidal wave of history in the making. 'Black Sabbath,' 'Iron Man,' 'Children of the Grave,' 'N.I.B.'—the canon of classics were trumpeted one last time in the company of the hometown Sabbath congregation. Ozzy Osbourne, Geezer Butler, Tony Iommi, Bill Ward—we may never see their like again."
                        —Birmingham, England, news report

As heavy metal was frenzied by new influences and technology, Ozzfest reverted to an undisputedly heavy center when it presented the return of Black Sabbath in 1999. The original quartet had previously played three songs together at the Live Aid benefit concert in July 1985, then briefly reunited in November 1992 for a pair of gigs in Costa Mesa, California, with Rob Halford of Judas Priest handling most of the vocals. This return of the original lineup at the close of the 1990s, however, had a higher, preordained feeling. "It's like putting on old shoes," Ozzy told VH1. "It fits."

Fully thirty years after four lads from Birmingham formed the band and twenty years after parting ways, Ozzy Osbourne, Tony Iommi, Geezer Butler, and Bill Ward were reunited. "I think it's kind of agreed that metal all started with Sabbath, then there was Priest, then Maiden, and so on," says Rob Halford. "By the truest definitions of what we call heavy metal, at least, Sabbath were the godfathers. They were a major inspiration to countless new artists. Even today all the new bands on the block cite this great band Sabbath as a major influence."

Returning with the platinum-selling *Reunion* double CD, recorded on an ecstatic night in Birmingham in 1997, the band headlined Ozzfest in 1999 to gleeful cross-generational crowds. Regaling audiences with "Iron Man," "War Pigs," and "Children of the Grave" for the first time in many fans' lives the band added forgotten gems like "Dirty Women" and "Behind the Wall of Sleep," cloaking three decades of heavy metal in a celebratory mood. Thus marked the return of the solid gravitational core that metal fans had lacked since the mainstreaming of Metallica.

Black Sabbath's Tony Iommi, heavy metal architect
(Deborah Laws/Metalflakes.com)

There were setbacks. Ozzy and the members of Sabbath had been at odds for years over personal rebuffs and unrepaid loans made by Ozzy to the others. Then, when they did get back together, Bill Ward suffered a heart attack. Ward also admitted that after many years of debilitating alcoholism, he could not immediately remember exactly what to do when he sat down at his drums. With these potential hazards in mind, Sabbath kept another former drummer, Vinnie Appice, waiting in the wings in case anything happened to Ward. Nothing did.

For certain, the reinstitution of Ozzy Osbourne to his proper place at the helm of Sabbath revealed the forty-nine-year-old singer's shaky state—antipsychotic medication had transformed him into nearly a virtual rendering of his fiery younger self. Yet the return to form was magical. When reports of Ozzy Osbourne's using an on-stage TelePrompTer called into question the singer's mental condition, radio host Howard Stern defended this natural wonder: "What would you rather have, this Ozzy, who's way out there, or no Ozzy at all?"

After singing for the band during the early 1980s, Ronnie James Dio had briefly rejoined Black Sabbath for the 1992 album *Dehumanizer*. Despite those contributions he respectfully declined to cause friction by joining the reunion and competing with Ozzy. "I had a great time what I consider helping that band get back into reality again and making them successful again," says Dio. "Sabbath was my favorite band to be in, and those are my favorite people to write with. *Heaven and Hell* will always be my favorite album. Tony Iommi is the ultimate riff master; he's got so many of them."

The defiant statements of Sabbath's early albums had become nothing less than modern folklore, and the band on its thirtieth anniversary still defined heavy metal—an incredible feat of longevity. Among other revelations, the reunion confirmed that Black Sabbath had created a new essential repertoire and that Tony Iommi's riffs were the bedrock of heavy metal. "Today it seems like heavy metal replaced what the blues was then," Geezer Butler told *Guitar.* "Everybody gets up and does 'Paranoid'. . . instead of the old blues stuff."

Not surprisingly given the band's vast sphere of influence, the reunion of Black Sabbath's original lineup was the highest-grossing rock tour of 1999. *Billboard* reported that Ozzfest was the top-grossing-per-show summer concert event in both 1997 and 1998, and bringing Black Sabbath aboard only bumped up the festival's bandwidth. For true metal and nu metal alike, Black Sabbath was a shared idol that every phase and flavor of metalhead could honor and adore. The moment augured fertility for the next evolution of heavy metal and promised its permanent survival. As Ozzy flashed peace signs and shouted, "We love you all!" into the night for the four thousandth time, the divisions across generations were mended, and heavy metal once again came surging to the fore.

CΦMEBACKS

Returns to the fold by Dio, Bruce Dickinson, and the mighty Black Sabbath were a welcome surprise to the metal boom of 2001, but Virgin Steele and Necrophagia? Yes, as the twentieth anniversary of *Metal Massacre* came, even the metal underground found room for nostalgia in its perpetual–energy machine. Fortunately for death metal, most of the musicians were so young the first time around that they remain creatively vital—slightly more experienced and just barely reaching into their thirties. In other cases bands like Destruction that were stylistic innovators are able to explore their inventions fully, delivering complex versions of their initial blasts. "When you can make money, you will reform," observes metal lifer Ron Quintana.

The Return

- ❖ Artillery, *B.A.C.K.* (1999)
- ❖ Black Sabbath, *Reunion* (1998)
- ❖ Destruction, *All Hell Breaks Loose* (2000)
- ❖ Dio, *Magica* (2000)
- ❖ Exodus, *Another Lesson in Violence* (1997)
- ❖ Halford, *Live Insurrection* (2001)
- ❖ Necrophagia, *Holocausto de la Morte* (1999)
- ❖ Testament, *First Strike Still Deadly* (2001)

With Black Sabbath crowning a new heavy metal millennium, metal of every conceivable kind soon became again more publicly visible than ever before. In 1999, *Billboard* reported that after a decade of decline, there were more than 500 specialty metal radio shows in the United States, nearly three times more than in 1989, metal's previous heyday. When metal reigned in the 1980s, the audience grew increasingly fractured—at the end of the 1990s it was larger than ever and increasingly unified. Even as they enjoyed changing trends, fans continued to educate themselves in the headbanger classics. "I meet these people who enthusiastically say, 'I still listen to Nuclear Assault's *Game Over* and Anthrax's *Fistful of Metal* and S.O.D.'s *Speak English or Die* every day,'" says Dan Lilker, the bassist on all three albums. "That stuff definitely had an impact. You realize now how many people really got into that stuff and how much it meant to them."

Godfathers like Motörhead and Iron Maiden returned to prominence with a vengeance. Iron Maiden reunited with longtime singer Bruce Dickinson and sold out New York's Madison Square Garden on August 5, 2000, with Queensryche and former Judas Priest singer Halford supporting. "That was mind-blowing," recalls Rob Halford. "It was just amazing, even though it was a blur. It was a thrill to be back in the Garden, simply because it's a landmark venue. Those walls carry so much history. Whenever I play the Garden, it's just one of the most special feelings you can ever get as a musician."

Biff Byford of Saxon reconquers America

Overnight, it seemed every major band from every era of heavy metal was returning for a triumphant curtain call. From the 1970s came Bang, Captain Beyond, and UFO, and from the NWOBHM resurfaced Savage, Sweet Savage, Holocaust, and Raven. From the mid-1980s came a storming torrent of returns to power metal madness by Anvil, Mercyful Fate, Virgin Steele, Exciter, Celtic Frost, Destruction, Hirax, and Whiplash. The fist-shaking glam bands Hanoi Rocks, Ratt, Stryper, and Poison also toured successfully, though wisely without benefit of hair spray.

Some groups re-formed after learning of their enduring popularity via Internet fan sites—a more accurate barometer of public opinion than glossy music magazines. Other musicians driven to disillusionment during earlier pushes for success began playing again for the love of music. After a momentary drought in the mid-1990s, there now seemed to be enough money and enthusiasm for everybody. "I'm not in any position to be retiring, so I do have to think about that," comments John Bush on the subject of Armored Saint's return after an eight-year absence.

Even little-known underground bands reunited, finding that many of their members were no older than thirty. In the case of Necrophagia, which regrouped with Pantera's Phil Anselmo playing guitar under the pseudonym Anton Crowley, the magnificent garage gore of the reunion matched and surpassed what the band had accomplished as a 1980s tape-trader favorite. With no chance of Tom Warrior's ever resurrecting his childishly simplistic Hellhammer, the German trio Warhammer gamely took up the task of emulating the Swiss band's aesthetic on *The Winter of Our Discontent* and *Deathchrist* CDs—like a dark descendant of a *Beatlemania*-style revival.

The new millennium even brought a few blips of recognition to the long-lived doom metal scene, a world so retrograde and entrenched in primitivism that it barely recognized any metal milestones beyond the first Black Sabbath album. Hugely bolstered by the return of Sabbath and heavily in debt to Tony Iommi's mythic riffs, doom metal was a long-lived culture of shadow dwellers that tuned far below even the masters in search of salvation. Beginning with the overlooked Lucifer's Friend and Necromandus in the early 1970s, doom crawled through the 1980s with Trouble, Witchfinder General, the Obsessed, Candlemass, Pentagram, and Saint Vitus, then into the 1990s with Cathedral, Sleep, and Burning Witch. Their plaintive dirges had developed underground from the very dawn of metal, reacting to metallic excess with excursions into deeper, soulful truth.

Swimming against the current—whether that meant the speed of thrash metal or the high technology of nu metal—doom metal searched for the slowest, most emotionally compelling sounds. Throughout every era there were doom metal counterparts to prevailing trends. Chicago's majestic Trouble, for example, were doom preachers whose biblical lyrics served as a counterpoint to Slayer in the 1980s. As doom metal's overlooked figures were finally recognized, they became heroes who had shepherded heavy metal's essence through the meanest environments. Formed in the late 1970s, Saint Vitus was a misfit sludge outfit thrust upon unfriendly Los Angeles punk audiences as an opening act for Black Flag. The members of Saint Vitus were so unpretentious they admitted to writing songs while listening to Iron Maiden on headphones. After several albums the band recruited vocalist Scott Weinrich, aka Wino, to make the brilliantly defiant *Born Too Late* in 1986. From its anthemic title track to "Thirsty and Miserable" (a Black Flag cover twice as long as the original), the album was a victorious tortoise to the misplaced hyperactivity of the frantic Hollywood hair bands.

Doom gods Saint Vitus
(SST Records)

Wino was an authentic throwback with one foot planted deep in the first wave of heavy metal, and his music rang with essential truth. "I saw Sabbath on my twelfth birthday, in 1972," he told *Seconds* magazine. "That was my second concert ever, and I wasn't even really smoking pot yet, but that show made a lifelong impression on me. The power of Sabbath on the *Paranoid* tour in 1972, with all the old gear—the huge walls of Laney—it was just unbelievable. For me, being that young, it was unreal." After the demise of Saint Vitus, Wino reformed his previous outfit, the Obsessed, and released several albums, leading to a deal with Sony/Columbia at the same time as Napalm Death's—again threading through the netherworlds of metal happenings. By the late 1990s he was taking Iommi-style guitar to places even Sabbath could no longer reach.

Formed in the shadows of Trouble and Saint Vitus, a new range of bands arose in the 1990s with members not even born in 1972. The young California quartet Sleep released two albums shamelessly interpolated from between the grooves of the first Black Sabbath album. Coining the sound "stoner rock," Sleep unleashed a fleet of imitators like Orange Goblin and Electric Wizard, who in turn flourished on their own music festivals and "stoner doom" record labels. Finding major backing with London Records in 1995, Sleep meditated on marijuana and the Old Testament to summon *Jerusalem*, a fifty-three-minute single-song slab of career suicide. Apparently not having tested the limits of its major-label benefactors to its own satisfaction, the band promptly announced it would not tour to support this one-song wonder. London dropped the group in 1998, tape traders frantically duplicated rare advance copies of the disc, and Sleep soon broke up—two of its members retreating to monasteries.

Slowed to an extreme atmospheric crawl, pure doom could occasionally transcend the guidelines laid down by Black Sabbath. While he was the bassist of the Melvins, Joe Preston had released a solo album featuring "The Eagle Has Landed," a twenty-minute suite of cascading guitar slabs named after a Saxon live LP.

Joe Preston in the Thrones
(*Vicky Baron*)

Along with Kurt Cobain of Nirvana, Preston also belonged to Earth, a droning, feedback-laden Seattle troupe led by Dylan Carlson. Its *Earth 2 Special Low Frequency Version* in 1993 was a brooding vista of dense, time-stretched bass rumble. With similar intentions Preston later created the Thrones, whose microchip-assisted, low, seeping bass and laser blasts sounded like a bionic version of heaviness. "I want to hear big things that move at weird speeds," says Preston.

Tying together all shreds of doom, gloom, and stoner rock, Cathedral was led by cockeyed cackler Lee Dorrian, yet another former Napalm Death singer. Cathedral defended a citadel of awkward musical exceptions, attacking the unfinished business of Black Sabbath around the time of the threatening denseness of *Sabotage*. Following ten years of releases experimenting with every variation from noise to funk to disco, the band on the *Endtyme* CD in 2001 swayed with charming sleaze while still honoring its original commitment to crushing and suffocating the universe. After a decade-long apprenticeship, Cathedral became castle-crushing masters, enshrining heavy metal with powerful, perpetual poise, in utter defiance of an ephemeral, pitter-patter society.

On the brink of the year 2000 the world of metal paused to admire its own spectacle and saw a metallized planet staring back eagerly. The new millennium found spiked belts, leather pants, and vintage Iron Maiden and Dio shirts once again on the cutting edge of cool. In culture capitals like New York and Los Angeles, designers turned old tour shirts into haute couture, and art galleries were filled with conceptual takes on heavy metal mannerisms by blue-chip artists like Matthew Barney—who made nonlinear films starring former Slayer drummer Tom Lombardo and Morbid Angel singer Steve Tucker.

Although survival during a previous decade of media disrepair was sweet, the victory was not merely financial—the entire culture, beliefs, and interests of heavy metal had infiltrated the mainstream without abandoning heart. There was finally a place for heavy metal in the mainstream—integrity and uncomfortable truths intact. With its emphasis on fan involvement, Metallica had been narrowcasting and viral marketing for a decade before those practices became corporate buzz-

DOOM METAL

The slow-moving antithesis of metal's typically speedy evolution, doom metal began with Black Sabbath and was kept alive through the decades by devoted bands like Witchfinder General, Trouble, and Cathedral—bands whose emotional qualities more than made up for their lack of flash. The resurgence of Black Sabbath at the close of the 1990s was significant enough to shepherd the resurgence of undiscovered greats like the Obsessed. As an earthy counterpoint to nu metal, doom didn't have the commercial clout, but its heavy heart won over more than a few die-hard acolytes. These bell-bottomed throwbacks could be spotted lingering around the periphery of any metal event, tuned in to a slow frequency best described as timeless.

Slow Rides

- Burning Witch, *Crippled Lucifer* (1998)
- Cathedral, *Endtyme* (2001)
- Cathedral, *Hopkins (The Witchfinder General)* (1995)
- Corrupted, *Llenándose de Gusanos* (1999)
- Dream Death, *Journey into Mystery* (1987)
- Earth, *Earth 2 Special Low Frequency Version* (1993)
- Eyehategod, *Take as Needed for Pain* (1993)
- Melvins, *Bullhead* (1991)
- The Obsessed, *The Obsessed* (1990)
- Pentagram, *First Daze Here* (2002)
- Saint Vitus, *Born Too Late* (1986)
- Sleep, *Jerusalem* (1996)
- Trouble, *Psalm 9* (1984)
- Trouble, *The Skull* (1985)

words. Even the gritty realism of . . . *And Justice for All* became standard reality television, as documentary channels and countless hours of dirty laundry urged viewers to judge society for themselves.

Metal storytelling's love of ancient warriors and the demon world turned ratings gold on television shows like *Xena* and *Buffy the Vampire Slayer*. On *Late Night with Conan O'Brien*, sidekick Andy Richter impersonated Ozzy Osbourne, while Craig Kilborn on *Later* fussed over the Scorpions. In one of the weirdest pop-culture moments, Ahmet and Dweezil Zappa—whose father's band, the Mothers of Invention, had influenced Tony Iommi—playfully jammed Sabbath's "The Wizard" on *Late Night with Conan O'Brien*, with schmaltz pianist John Tesh playing strap-on keyboard.

Over at Universal Studios the reins to the annual haunted house were handed over to Rob Zombie, whose creation caused five-mile traffic backups on the Hollywood highways. Metal had prepared a generation for data-drenched information overload. Simultaneously, PlayStation video games borrowed names and plots from metal songs, and pro wrestlers basked in the most macho visual elements borrowed from the heavy metal theater. Deep Purple's "Smoke on the Water," still a bona fide metal anthem, reappeared on HBO as Tony Soprano's favorite driving music. Metal even cracked into the lucrative world of jock rock, as the multiple–World Series–winning New York Yankees' relief pitcher Mariano Rivera put batters to sleep to the thundering tune of Metallica's "Enter Sandman." Megadeth began writing material expressly for use at sporting events. According to Dave Mustaine, "We did 'Crush 'Em' specifically to get rid of Gary Glitter's 'Rock and Roll Part 2.' I hate that song."

Heavy metal was being institutionalized. Following the 1990s success of Nirvana, Starbucks, Nintendo, and Microsoft, a consortium of Seattle high-tech tycoons pooled $600 million to build the Experience Music Project (EMP), designed by architect Frank Gehry and billed as the largest music museum in the world. "Paul Allen, he's one of the owners of the Seattle Seahawks and one of the Microsoft Ten," says Metal Church's former singer, David Wayne. "He located our guitar cross from our first album cover, he bought it, and he's putting an exhibit to Metal Church in the museum." When the EMP opened in July 2000, Metallica performed at the opening festivities, and the Metal Church relic was on display within a Lucite box—along with notes describing how the photographer had first buried the prop in his backyard to get that desired mossy and decaying effect.

Without one single watershed media moment, the United States collectively became a metal nation, as teen metalheads grew up and made room for countless millions more. Thanks to Ronnie James Dio, the devil-horned hand salute became an all-purpose symbol for the little bit of heavy metal in everyone. "My grandmother would always give us the evil eye," he says. "It's called the *malocchio* in Italian, and it's also protection against the evil eye, like a little antenna. When I joined Sabbath, Ozzy had always done the peace signs, like President Richard Nixon. And I was not about to follow

Let there be metal: Ronnie James Dio
striking a Michaelangelo pose
(Deborah Laws/Metalflakes.com)

in his footsteps, so drawing on what my grandmother always did, I started to do it, and it became the symbol. You can probably go to a Backstreet Boys concert these days and they'll probably stick the damn thing up there."

Meanwhile, VH1 reported a 40 percent higher rating on its *Behind the Music* series for the episodes profiling the rise and fall and ultimate rebirth of Quiet Riot, Mötley Crüe, and Poison—all of whom toured again successfully at the close of the 1990s. The channel soon programmed more hard rock and heavy metal music, making frequent studio guests of Rob Halford, Lars Ulrich, Blackie Lawless, and Skid Row's singer, Sebastian Bach. The Metallica episode of *Behind the Music* even benefited from the rare cooperation of former guitarist Dave Mustaine. "When they asked me to do it, I knew I had one chance to tell the truth," he says, "and I did. I said that I deserved to be fired. Truth."

The litany of metal's incursions into pop culture continued, with glam metal parodies surfacing in comedy skits and credit-card ads. Homages to heavy metal by pop bands abounded. Perhaps the ultimate mainstreaming of metal was a Burger King television spot using Judas Priest's "You've Got Another Thing Coming" that promised, "Miss this deal, you'll be banging your head." A Volkswagen commercial played on the camp value of old metal, depicting a soccer mom who relished her days as a Krokus groupie. Reflects Hirax singer Katon W. DePena, "What was cool about all the speed metal and thrash metal, all that heavy shit, is we don't have anything to be ashamed of. Can you imagine if you were in Poison? God, it'd be hard to go to the grocery store!"

>>>>>◉<<<<<

Apart from the spoofs, heavy metal retained its dignity. Without retreating from its simpler efforts of the past several years, Metallica capped off its second decade with a high-minded return to the majesty of early albums like *Ride the Lightning* and *Master of Puppets*. While synthesizers made string sections available to underground musicians, Metallica had access to the real thing. The band adapted twenty songs chosen from its entire career for a classical music collaboration. "You never quite know with us," says Lars Ulrich, still ever the booster. "We have a tendency to make things up as we go along. We never set any barriers or limits or fences around any of the shit we do."

Dubbed *Symphony & Metallica*, the project reunited Metallica with Michael Kamen, the composer who arranged "Nothing Else Matters" with a small string ensemble for the Black Album. This time the full 104-piece San Francisco Symphony Orchestra was in tow for the duration. A frequent pop collaborator, Kamen had orchestrated work for Pink Floyd, Aerosmith, and Bryan Adams as well as the movies *Brazil* and *Die Hard*. He proposed the project to Metallica. "I've been with orchestras that were skeptical to play rock and roll, even rock as relatively gentle and melodic, compared to Metallica, as Eric Clapton or Pink Floyd," the conductor told *BAM*. "But I've seen many times now orchestral players looking on with admiration as they watch Clapton's fingers go up and down the guitar neck just as if they were watching Pinchas Zukerman. There's a great respect among musicians for proficiency and the power of statement."

Ever since the Beatles, rock bands had toyed with classical music with rather mixed results. In fact, early in the career of Deep Purple,

Lars Ulrich's idols had collaborated with the Royal Philharmonic Orchestra on a symphony in three movements written by keyboardist Jon Lord. As part of a fondness for times past, heavy metal musicians in particular romanticized the image of the classical music composer tearing out his hair to find the perfect dramatic chord. In 1993 Metallica colleague Glenn Danzig branched away from his visceral rock formulas to create *Black Aria*, a heavily synthesized orchestral outing with female choral vocals. As was true of his records with the Misfits and Samhain, Danzig played most of the parts himself. "It's easy, but it's hard," says Danzig of his neoclassical work. "You've got to hear it in your head, and you're not just hearing drums, bass, guitar, and vocals. I'm hearing every single little part, this thing and that. It's complex: keyboard, real people backup singers, gongs . . ."

Everyone from Accept and Yngwie Malmsteen to Master's Hammer and Emperor nodded to Western classical music. With the impact of metal on young music students, it was safe to say the transfer went both ways. The thirty years between Black Sabbath and post-black-metal bands Opeth and Dimmu Borgir comprised a legitimate musical tradition of easily recognized standards and innovations—blast beats, original tunings, and vocal techniques—all learned, copied, and bettered by each successive wave of young players. As metal musicians matured and found their way into university music departments, especially in Europe, it was possible that metal would develop into a neoclassical institution, complete with allusions to the Swedish death metal school.

The music of Metallica, with its somber constructions and eye toward the eternal, already possessed the gravitas for symphonic arrangement without sounding pompous or pretentious. At least, that was the idea. Two Metallica classical performances in Berkeley, California, in April 1999 were recorded for posterity and released later in the year as *S&M, Symphony & Metallica*. Reactions wobbled. "I think it should have been a bit more present," says Ronnie Dio. "I think the orchestra was buried behind what they did. If you're going to use an orchestra, go for it!"

Beyond the events themselves, however, there was an immense majesty to the orchestral undertaking that vindicated two decades of trials. Certainly the arrangements were not equally inspired for every song, but the movement of downward-cascading strings falling onto the machine-gun double-bass drums at the beginning of "For Whom the Bell Tolls" brought old fans to tears. After all, Lars Ulrich and James Hetfield—once lost and lonely children who hurried to finish "Hit the Lights" for the first *Metal Massacre* album—were now grown men commanding a sea of musicians successfully through their terrain.

Kirk Hammett and peers
(Filip Malinowski)

The vast differences between the naïvely intrepid spirit that created the *Master of Puppets* instrumental "Orion" and the mature hand that orchestrated that song for a symphony were sobering. At long last here was a soothing gesture, a requiem for the obscurity of the struggle, the nobility of the garage days, and of the many leather-jacketed scientists who defined the metal experience. Over its career Metallica had encouraged its audience to embrace life with vigor, to express anger at injustice, and to relax and savor due rewards. Now it endeavored to bring home powerful beauty—and was awarded a sixth Grammy, for a sweeping symphonic rendition of Cliff Burton's "The Call of Ktulu."

A congratulatory move by an increasingly self-gratifying band, *S&M* brought Metallica into a serious mode lacking over the prior playful half decade. "My attitude with Metallica over the last eight years is simple," says the band's old friend John Bush. "They should do whatever they want. I think if this is what they want to do, then God love them. They experiment with all this different stuff, maybe because they're bored or maybe because they just don't know what to do anymore, because they've done everything. You've got to have the utmost respect for Metallica. They're important. We all need them, because they've been there for metal, and they will always represent that. Whether it's Motörhead or Kid Rock, it doesn't matter—everybody needs Metallica."

DEATH
IN METAL

The popular resurgence of heavy metal underscored the absence of many faces. Metallers, forever obsessed with morbid subjects, were growing old enough to face death. Aside from the martyrs Randy Rhoads and Cliff Burton, the sacrifices of Dead and Euronymous of Mayhem, and even the suicide of Kurt Cobain, metal at the turn of the century faced its mortality. "There were so many bands when we first came to the States," notes Celtic Frost's Tom Warrior, "and I always wonder what happened to those musicians. I know lots of them were already in severe financial problems at that time. Who knows who recovered and who didn't? Are they dead? Are they flipping burgers somewhere? There's AIDS and drugs— it's not too absurd to wonder if they're still alive."

Sadly, a number of headbangers turned in their denim and leather prematurely:

❖ One of the earliest thrash metal casualties was **DAVE HOLO-CAUST** of the gusto-laden Ohio band Destructor, who was stabbed by a stranger in January 1988 at the band's practice space, just after the release of the metal-psyched *Maximum Destruction* LP.

❖ Bassist **ROB STERZEL** of Deceased was struck and killed by a passing van while fixing a flat tire on his car by the side of the road in 1988.

❖ The technically adept death metal band Atheist lost its ultra-proficient bassist, **ROGER PATTERSON**, in a car accident in Louisiana on February 12, 1990, as the band returned from a triumphant tour supporting Candlemass.

❖ Talented Savatage guitarist **CRISS OLIVA** was killed by a drunk driver near his home in Clearwater, Florida, on October 17, 1993.

❖ **DAVE PRICHARD** of Armored Saint was felled by leukemia in 1990, after struggling with the disease during the creation of *Symbol of Salvation.* "He was a pillar of strength," says singer John Bush. "He never made it an issue. Hardly anybody really knew, and I think he wanted it that way. He was adopted, and he had to find somebody with a match to give him a bone-marrow transplant. When you have a bone-marrow transplant, either it takes or it doesn't, and if it doesn't, you're done. That's what happened, and that was pretty brutal."

❖ Founder **PAUL SAMSON** of the NWOBHM stalwarts Samson died at home in England at age forty-nine during the afternoon of Friday, August 9, 2002, following a protracted fight against cancer. He had recently completed work on a new Samson album.

❖ Former Riot vocalist **RHETT FORRESTER** was shot through the heart and killed in January 1994, at age thirty-seven, the victim of an apparent carjacking at an Atlanta traffic intersection. He was stopping only briefly in Georgia to visit his mother, La Fortune Forrester.

❖ After a half dozen unsuccessful stints in rehab, **STEVE CLARK** of Def Leppard died of an overdose of alcohol, antidepressants, and painkillers in 1992, during the recording of *Adrenalize.*

❖ According to Blaine Cook of the Accused, **CHIBON BATTERMAN**, aka Chewy, the former bass player, died a drug-related death in the late 1990s.

❖ **DAWN CROSBY** sang and wrote politically charged lyrics for the hardcore-influenced thrash metal bands Detente and Fear of God and once shared a house in Los Angeles with Dave Mustaine. She also shared his affection for alcohol: Crosby died of acute liver failure in December 1996.

❖ In July 1999 a rough lifestyle caught up with forty-one-year-old original Megadeth drummer **GAR SAMUELSON**, credited with expanding the band's lyrical scope beyond witchcraft and headbanging. "The press release said that it was complications to the liver that were undiagnosed," says Dave Mustaine ruefully. "It could have been cirrhosis, it could have been hepatitis, it could have been HIV or even full-blown AIDS. There's only so many things that can happen to a liver."

❖ **ROBBIN CROSBY** of Ratt was entirely debilitated by full-blown AIDS and spent the latter half of the 1990s convalescing. He blamed the infection on his rampant heroin use during the heyday of the Hollywood glam era. He died of AIDS-related complications in June 2002, at age forty-two, and friends and former bandmates paddled into the waves on surfboards to spread his ashes off the San Diego coast.

❖ In April 1998 **WENDY O. WILLIAMS** shot herself at home in Storrs, Connecticut. A rarely acknowledged influence, her band, the Plasmatics, was the most visible punk nightmare of the early 1980s—their public nudity, onstage use of chain saws and shotguns, and ethos of destruction was unrivaled before Marilyn Manson. "I can only say the best about Wendy," says Plasmatics guitarist Richie Stotts. "I learned how to make hummus from her, and she was really a sweetheart. I never saw her drink or smoke pot. She always encouraged me in whatever I wanted to do." A lighthearted 1982 collaboration with Lemmy on Tammy Wynette's "Stand by Your Man" may have hurt Motörhead, but it earned Williams a place in the hearts of metal fans.

❖ Wendy O. was not alone among metal suicides. **TOTTSUAN** of the groundbreaking Japanese grindcore band S.O.B. also took his own life in 1994, reputedly throwing himself in front of a subway train in despondency after several drug arrests. Corrupted performed its hundred-minute epic *Llenándose de Gusanos* live in his memory. Norwegian drummer **GRIM**, of Immortal and later of

Borknagar, committed suicide by ingesting a quantity of pills on October 4, 1999.

There were also plenty of close calls, such as Voivod guitarist Denis D'Amour's recurring problems with thyroid cancer and Testament vocalist Chuck Billy's battle with germ cell seminoma, a rare form of cancer. Testament guitarist James Murphy also battled a brain tumor.

In January 2000 Chuck Schuldiner of Death underwent experimental brain surgery after spending a year fighting pontine glioma, a rare form of brain tumor. He had earlier put to rest the name of his band, Death, returning with a new singer in the optimistic but defiant Control Denied, which titled its debut *Fragile Art of Existence*. According to Schuldiner's sister, the $100,000 brain operation was financed partially through a deal that signed away "Evil" Chuck's royalties to NYU Medical Center's Tisch Hospital—a strange twist of fate considering the lyrical nature of *Scream Bloody Gore, Leprosy, Spiritual Healing*, and the four other Death albums covered by the agreement. Schuldiner finally succumbed to the disease on December 13, 2001, at the age of thirty-four.

Shockingly and sadly, just as Exodus began work on a new album with original singer Paul Baloff, the Bay Area metal fixture suffered a stroke on February 2, 2002, and died during the night at the age of forty-one. Friends and former bandmates, including Kirk Hammett, lionized Baloff, a man whose mirth-filled but unrelenting war with the world embodied the heavy metal attitude. "He was my idol," said S.O.D. singer and loudmouth Billy Milano. "Every time I was in a room with him, I was invisible."

The healthy found themselves acting increasingly in a guidance capacity, an interesting role considering metal's aversion to authority figures. "I've gone from being the voice of the youth of America to being an elder statesman," says Dave Mustaine. "I've watched a lot of things come and go in my career, and I see a lot of people right now doing things that, if they asked me what I thought about what they were doing—if—I would say they're going about it wrong. But people have to learn the hard way."

In 2001 *Forbes* magazine ranked Metallica as a unit the eighteenth most powerful celebrity in the world, citing $28 million in profits in 2000 without the aid of a single major magazine cover story. (Among musicians in the ratings, the band was bested only by the long money earned by the Beatles and the short money of teen trilogy Britney Spears, N'Sync, and the Backstreet Boys.) Courting the final frontier of celebrity-face recognition, Lars Ulrich guested on *Who Wants to Be a Millionaire* and appeared frequently on *The Charlie Rose Show* and VH1 specials, arguing his anti-Napster views and reveling in tales of dirty deeds Metallica had done.

Still reaping the rewards, Metallica's 2000 tour was second in total ticket sales only to Barbra Streisand—famous for her $450 ticket prices. The band estimated the figure for worldwide sales of its albums at more than 60 million. Thus it came as a great shock after a nine-and-a-half-hour band meeting when Jason Newsted left Metallica in January 2001 after fourteen years with the band, citing "private and personal reasons and the damage I have done to myself over the years." The last to come was the first to leave. Newsted soon surfaced in three new bands, including the revered Montreal thrash metal giant Voivod. Hetfield and Ulrich, meanwhile, were absorbed with parenthood, as their toddlers, born seven weeks apart in the summer of 1998, undoubtedly changed priorities for the fathers of thrash metal.

Among further surprises, James Hetfield—formerly a one-man marketing campaign for Smirnoff vodka—checked into a rehab clinic for treatment for alcoholism and a period of forced self-evaluation. With Metallica the longtime pacesetters for the music, there remained new standards to be set and hope for more surprises, worlds to be turned upside down in the forthcoming epoch. After all, Lars Ulrich's tennis-star father, Torben Ulrich, set a record as the oldest player to ever play in the Davis Cup, competing just one month before his forty-ninth birthday,

Though it grips by the neck in adolescence, heavy metal certainly does not dry up and blow away as each generation reaches maturity. Says Rob Halford, who turned fifty in 2001, "I've been lucky that I've been around to experience so many different styles of metal, from the early traditional stuff that I was a part of to seeing how it's changed into Slipknot and all over the place. It's great. I've experimented, I've had my fun, but out of all that experimentation I've had the realization that what I love the most, and what I do best, is heavy metal music. I think that all the things I get out of it are still intact. Here I am in 2002, working on my twenty-sixth release, and I have to scream my lungs out and turn my vocal cords to shreds. I just can't let that go."

As the world now faces great uncertainty, heavy metal leads the way with huge ideas and unblinking eyes, coursing through new mediums with vigor as it attacks convention with songs too long for radio, visions too twisted for television, and unpopular topical critiques in advance of mainstream social sensibilities. The entire experience, gleefully absurd to observers, continues to lay down impossible standards, meet them, then tear all expectations apart and begin anew. "We need to stay rebellious now more than ever in a world that tries to make us conform to a base set of typical values," urges Jeff Becerra of Possessed.

Of course, heavy metal will surface in forms that many metallers of today will barely recognize and may be loath to embrace. What approaches next is left to the loudly bawling infants of this minute. They will take what they wish from the long-raging legacy of heavy metal and leave the rest to the dust. Though metal is larger than life, it ultimately comes from life: inflaming the intellect, shaking the senses, and stroking the soul more completely than any sound before. More than ever, humanity needs these risks and contradictions.

As we stare into infinity, the void beckons, and heavy metal tempts its edges.

2001: Iron Man Lives Again

In the meantime, Ozzy Osbourne and Black Sabbath enjoyed the limelight. A stupefying thirty years after the song's original release, Black Sabbath won a Grammy for Best Metal Performance on February 28, 2000, for its rendition of "Iron Man" on the live *Reunion* CD. Bill Ward accepted on behalf of the band, although Ozzy Osbourne and Geezer Butler and their families were also in attendance. Oddly enough, after being nominated for the Rock and Roll Hall of Fame in 1998 and 1999, Sabbath asked to be taken off the list for consideration in 2000 and 2001. "As it stands now, what's the point?" said Ozzy Osbourne in his official statement. "It's a joke. It's about glad-handing and grandstanding and I don't want any part of it."

Instead Ozzy opened his house and family to MTV for the documentary/improvised situation-comedy series *The Osbournes*. Consisting of little more than footage of the foible-ridden figure of Ozzy Osbourne haunting his California mansion, the program drew more than 6 million viewers a week in the summer of 2002, becoming the top-rated program on cable television—and the most popular show by a great magnitude ever to air on MTV. In the wake of this sudden discovery of the universal appeal of Ozzy, he was awarded a star on the Hollywood Walk of Fame. Ozzy soon stole the spotlight at the 2002 White House Correspondents Dinner in Washington, D.C.—taking tremendous applause from the political elite as President George W. Bush sang the praises of "Sabbath Bloody Sabbath," oblivious to the fact that Ozzy was once arrested for urinating on the Alamo.

In June 2002, Ozzy and Tony Iommi performed "Paranoid" at Buckingham Palace for the Queen Elizabeth II Jubilee celebration. Both the monarch herself and Prince Charles were present, earthly rulers playing host to otherworldly regents. "This means more to me than anything," said Ozzy about being an invited guest of the crown. Only knighthood would be a greater honor for a poor son of Birmingham.

Oddly, a fierce unexplained blaze broke out in the upper floors during rehearsals as Ozzy was finishing his sound check, forcing the first evacuation of the palace since World War II.

The Best 25 Heavy Metal Albums of All Time

AC/DC ⟷ *Back in Black*

ANGEL WITCH ⟷ *Angel Witch*

BATHORY ⟷ *Under the Sign of the Black Mark*

BLACK SABBATH ⟷ *Black Sabbath*

CARCASS ⟷ *Heartwork*

CELTIC FROST ⟷ *To Mega Therion*

DESTRUCTION ⟷ *Infernal Overkill*

DREAM DEATH ⟷ *Journey into Mystery*

EMPEROR ⟷ *In the Nightside Eclipse*

EXODUS ⟷ *Bonded by Blood*

HOLY TERROR ⟷ *Terror and Submission*

IMMORTAL ⟷ *Battles in the North*

IRON MAIDEN ⟷ *Killers*

JUDAS PRIEST ⟷ *Unleashed in the East*

KREATOR ⟷ *Terrible Certainty*

MERCYFUL FATE ❀ *Melissa*

METALLICA ❀ *Ride the Lightning*

MORBID ANGEL ❀ *Formulas Fatal to the Flesh*

MÖTLEY CRÜE ❀ *Shout at the Devil*

MOTÖRHEAD ❀ *Overkill*

NAPALM DEATH ❀ *Fear, Emptiness, Despair*

RAINBOW ❀ *Rising*

SAXON ❀ *The Eagle Has Landed*

SLAYER ❀ *Hell Awaits*

VOIVOD ❀ *Dimension Hatross*

❧ APPENDIX B ❦

Index of Genre Boxes

The Fine Print—Metal Lists

Greatest Fist-Pumping True Metal Anthems
1. "Denim and Leather," Saxon
2. "Gloves of Metal," Manowar
3. "Metal Health," Quiet Riot

Dreaming On: Greatest Metal Power Ballads
1. "Bringin' on the Heartbreak," Def Leppard
2. "Home Sweet Home," Mötley Crüe
3. "In the End," Linkin Park

Greatest Power Ballads Disguised as True Metal
1. "Fade to Black," Metallica
2. "Hallowed Be Thy Name," Iron Maiden
3. "Cemetary Gates," Pantera

Shamelessly Weak False Metal Anthems
1. "When the Children Cry," White Lion
2. "Every Rose Has Its Thorn," Poison
3. "Only God Knows Why," Kid Rock
4. "The Final Countdown," Europe

Best Live Records
1. *No Sleep 'Til Hammersmith*, Motörhead
2. *If You Want Blood . . .*, AC/DC
3. *Live and Dangerous*, Thin Lizzy

Best Concert Film
Live Intrusion, Slayer

Best Faked Live Records

1. *Unleashed in the East*, Judas Priest
2. *Live ?!*@ Like a Suicide*, Guns N' Roses
3. *Jump in the Fire* EP, Metallica

Short Cuts: The Best of Blipcore

1. "Micro-E!," Wehrmacht, 0.1 secs
2. "You Suffer," Napalm Death, 0.7 secs.
3. "Mutually Assured Destruction," Electro Hippies, 1.0 secs

Vidcore

"Collateral Damage" video, Brutal Truth, 2.5 secs

Epicus Metallicus in Extremo

1. "Llenandose de Gusanos," Corrupted, 100 mins
2. "Jerusalem," Sleep, 53 mins
3. "At War with Satan," Venom, 23 mins

Most Likely to Mention
Their Own Band Name in Song

1. Hanoi Rocks
2. Manowar
3. Suicidal Tendencies

Couldn't help it: Death

Strangest Album Titles

1. *Pink Bubbles Go Ape*, Helloween
2. *Rather Death than False of Faith*, Hydra Vein
3. *The Music of Erich Zahn*, Mekong Delta

What Would Ozzy Do? Headbanging
Born-Agains

1. P.O.D.
2. Trouble
3. High on Fire

Songbirds of the Stool: Singing Drummers

1. Dan Beehler, Exciter
2. Barry Stern, Zoetrope
3. King Fowley, Deceased

Heavy Selassie: Dreadlock Pioneers

1. Tommy Niemeyer (guitarist), The Accused
2. Mike "Puffy" Bordin (drummer), Faith No More
3. Max Cavalera (singer/guitarist), Sepultura

Heavy Metal Medical Students

1. Jeff Walker (bassist/vocalist), Carcass (entirely self-taught)
2. Chris Lykins (guitarist), Atrophy (Yale Medical School)
3. King Diamond (laboratory research chemist, Denmark)

Weirdest Metal Stage Tricks

1. Inflating thick rubber hot water bottle by mouth—
   Thor (bodybuilder/vocalist)
2. Scraping bloody knuckles on cheese grater attached to
   guitar—Don Costa (M-80/Ozzy Osbourne bassist)
3. Wearing inverted KFC chicken tub over head—Buckethead
   (Guns N' Roses guitarist)

Numerals of the Beast

Official members of Black Sabbath from 1970–2002: **29**

Members of Slipknot by the end of 2002: **9 and slipping**

Members of Guns N' Roses by the end of 2002: **9 and rising**

Recording acts featuring members of Napalm Death: **34**

Bands named Mayhem (*not including Tommy Lee's Methods of Mayhem*): **4**

Totally different self-titled LPs by Accept: **2**

Record companies that signed Motörhead: **16 and counting**

Number of times the words "heavy metal" appear in this book: **555**

Lists advisory committee: Jem Aswad, Rob Dyrenforth, Kevin Sharp, Phil Vera, Pat Delaney, Bret Witter

⊰ ᗋLL HᗋIL TO THEE ⊱

THE INNER CIRCLE: Peter McGuigan, Bret Witter, and Josh Behar for their long-standing bravery, patience, and cleverness.

ADVANCE TERROR SQUAD: Patrick Delaney, Anne Kugler, Kerri Culhane, Jaime Eldredge, Jeff Wagner, Thomas Fischer, Margaret Hallisey, Stephen O'Malley, Omid Yamini, and Aaron Cantor for their eyes.

IMAGES OF THE BEAST: Dan Sokol, Tim Falke, Roy Dressel, Harry Maat, Jonathan Munro, Vidar Sandnes, Lucifera Elena Leon, Scott Colburn, Christy Davis, Samantha Nickerson, Austin Majors, Filip Malinowski, Morten Anderson, Dean Sternberg, Charles Peterson, Jean-François "Big" Lavallée, John Michaels, Raimo Autio, Jeanne Mitchell, King Django, Vicky Baron, Stew Milne—and especially Todd Nakamine and Deborah Lynn Laws.

MOUTHS OF THE PIT: Dan Lilker, Tom Warrior, Lars Ulrich, Monte Conner, King Diamond, Peter Steele, John Gallagher, Ritchie Stotts, Glenn Danzig, Tom Niemeyer, Blaine Cook, Rob Halford, Ronnie James Dio, Jess Cox, Dee Snider, Chuck D, Jeff Krulik, John Heyn, Shawn Crahan, Quorthon, Ihsahn, Samoth, Trym, Tim "Ripper" Owens, Joe Berlinger, Bruce Sinofsky, Chuck Billy, Alex Skolnick, Eric Peterson, Trey Azagthoth, Gary Holt, Kirk Hammett, Glen Benton, Michael D. Williams, Alicia Morgan, Max Cavalera, Katon W. DePena, Joey DeMaio, Bill Lindsey, Dan Clements, Nasty Ronnie, Dave Mustaine, Michael Sweet, Rob Zombie, Yamatsuka Eye, Nick Bullen, Dino Cazares, Burton Bell, Shane Embury, Barney Greenway, Mitch Harris, Mick Harrris, Jesse Pintado, Jeff Becerra, Larry Lalonde, Treponem Pal, King Fowley, Mike Smail, Cliff Burton, James Hetfield, Scott Ian, John Bush, Tommy Victor, Ian MacKaye, Tommy Stewart, Steve Albini, Gene Simmons, Paul Stanley, Carmine Appice, Tom Araya, Kerry King, Jeff Hanneman, Away, Snake, Brian Slagel, Monte Conner, Kevin Sharp, Les Claypool, Blackie Lawless, Ben Liemer, Katherine Ludwig, Billy Milano, Trey Spruance, Joe Preston, Ron Quintana, Derek Riggs, Wino, and Bob Muldowney, MIA.

AGENTS OF DISEASE: "Metal" Maria Ferraro, Chip Ruggieri, Mark Morton, Michael Mazur, Debbie Sellnow, Jamie Roberts, Jon Paris, Curran Reynolds, Steve Joh, Jocelyn Labelle, Veronique Cordier, Felice Ecker, Deborah Orr, Janet Billig, Steve Martin, Rayshele Tiege, Jonny Hart, and special thanks to Jeff Stone at *Pollstar*.

INFERNAL LEGIONS: Christes far and wide, Greg Fiering, Rob Dyrenforth, Portia Jane Cook, Kris Durso, David Sprague, Martin Popoff, Ben Ratliff, Jem Aswad, Vern Key, Don Weeks, Mark Vincent, Duff Kobrock, Shawn McCullough, Peter Paulson, Tom Russ, Chris and Scott Badger, Karin and Sandra Tidwell, Sheenah Van Spec, Simon Timony, Eric O'Brien, Mike Nicoletti, Tom Alessio, Tony Scialdone, Mary Ann Bella, Bob Apell, Anania O'Leary, Steve Peck, Rudo Anvilmeister, Frank "Killjoy" Pucci, "Terror" Ken McIntyre, Edward Field, Thurston Moore, Jake Vandervloed, Ky Anderson, Mike Anderson, Emmett Williams, Rob "The Saint" Francis, Phil Wilhelm, Michael Pebworth, John Race, Harvey Bennett Stafford, Chas Nielson, Brian Hageman, Ted Atherton, Christine Shields, Fritz Welch, Paige Martin, Nondor Nevai, Windy Chien, AQ thrashers, Tinuviel, Chew, Chris Orloski, Andy TerHaar, Shayne Stacy, Janice Steinschneider, Curtiss Pernice, Lily Samille Sickles, Carter Strickland, Nicole Gueron, Rich Hosey, Bob Plante, Jonathan Spottiswoode, Greg Brooks, Bill Stier, Pat Nyffler, Mason Williams, James Plotkin, John Zeps, Jason Pettigrew, Scott Helig, Richard Karsmakers, Karin Kessels, Elizabeth Butler, Amy Miller, Phil Franklin, Steve Hurley, Mr. Snuggles, Nicole Noselli, Daphne Gutierrez, Beth Coleman, Greg Anderson, Rattlehead and Captain Anthrax, Warren Appleby, Gary Chechak, Pat Nyffeler, Gibbs Chapman, Brently Pusser, Mark Driver, Mike Peters, Sandra Gordon, Bill Landis, Nate Peone, Rich McMillan, Ben Siegal, Kei Katsunuma, Lita and Javier, Alain Tello-Christe, Nelvin Chee, Johnny Blue Eyes and the Navajo Nation, and Mike the freak.

SPECIAL THANKS to true believers Christopher Anderson, Joe Banks, Kevin Imamura, Mark Woodlief, John Alderman, James Lo,

Rob Cherry, Ira Robbins, Mike McGonigal, Joey Anuff, Scott Frampton, Melissa Weiner, Brian Monnin, Steven Daly, and Harmony Korine.

AND VERY SPECIAL THANKS to Jessica, Gary, Greg Prevost, Armand Schaubroeck, and the great House of Guitars of Rochester, New York, for raw insane inspiration and the juice.

APOLOGIES to the ones who got away!

Number of the Beast * (212) 69-666-83

www.SOUNDOFTHEBEAST.com

READ AT MAXIMUM VOLUME!!!

✳ INDEX ✤

GIT (Guitar Institute of Technology), 160–61

Godflesh, 189, 248, 249, 332–33, 335, 337

Goldie, 335, 337

Goo Goo Dolls, 256, 302

Gore, Sen. Al, 119, 121, 221, 303

Gore, Tipper, 118, 119, 120, 123. *See also* PMRC

Graham, Bill (promoter), 144

Grammy Awards, 213, 214, 221, 234, 258, 268, 315–16, 354, 361

Grand Funk Railroad, 12, 230

Grandmaster Flash (DJ), 205, 207

Grant, Lloyd (guitarist), 60, 61, 206. *See also* Metallica

Grateful Dead, the, 180, 213

Green Day, 305

Greenway, Barney (singer), 250, 259, 260; *See also* Napalm Death

Grohl, Dave (drummer), 232. *See also* Nirvana

grunge, 159, 230–32, 236, 242, 247, 322

Guns N' Roses, 159, 164–65, 194, 206, 213, 228, 234–36, 318

Gwar, 247, 301

Hagar, Sammy (singer), 195. *See also* Van Halen

Halford, Rob (singer), 9, 29, 69, 74, 155, 221, 227, 229–30, 239, 319, 340–41, 351, 359–60; in Judas Priest, 20, 22, 36, 40, 46, 58, 76–77, 79, 297, 317; music of, after Judas Priest, 309–10, 332, 343, 344, 351. *See also* Judas Priest

Hammerfall, 319

Hammersmith Odeon (club), 33

Hammett, Kirk (guitarist), 75, 87–88, 89, 90, 127, 130, 134, 179, 192, 216, 233, 311, 315, 358. *See also* Metallica

Hanneman, Jeff (guitarist), 64, 103, 104, 108, 110, 150, 304–05. *See also* Slayer

Hanoi Rocks, 156–57, 159, 164, 318, 344

Harris, Mick (drummer), 187, 189, 246, 252, 333. *See also* Napalm Death; Painkiller; Scorn

Harris, Mitch (guitarist), 246, 261, 266. *See also* Napalm Death

Harris, Steve (bassist), 34, 45, 72. *See also* Iron Maiden

Hawkwind, 16, 29

Headbangers Ball, 165, 168, 170, 200, 305. *See also* MTV

Heavy Metal Parking Lot, 170–71

Hellhammer (band), 61, 102, 105–06, 107, 109, 110, 111, 114, 198; demise of, 111–12, 197; legacy of, 238, 262, 270, 272, 275, 281, 345. *See also* Celtic Frost

Hellhammer (drummer), 275, 276, 281, 286, 287. *See also* Mayhem

Hellion, 100

Helmet, 225

Hendrix, Jimi (guitarist), 7, 10, 16, 29, 50, 51, 177, 206

Hetfield, James (singer/guitarist), 52, 62, 65, 87, 120, 128, 149, 150, 208, 233, 235, 311, 354, 359; before Metallica, 44, 54–55, 57, 59, 60, 61, 78, 170; guitar style, 75, 89, 90, 98, 130; personal image, 97, 104, 149, 203, 217, 281, 308, 312; songwriting, 127, 196, 215–16, 309; vocal development, 63, 91, 136, 216, 219, 239, 192, 217, 234; *See also* Metallica; Spastik Children

Hirax, 90, 98, 168, 173, 181, 185, 206, 254, 266, 318, 344

Hit Parader, 80–83, 85, 162, 195

Hoglan, Gene (drummer), 242. *See also* Dark Angel; Death

Holmes, Chris (guitarist), 158. *See also* W.A.S.P.

Holocaust (UK), 44, 193, 316, 344

Holt, Gary (guitarist), 135, 169, 182, 226. *See also* Exodus

Holy Terror, 137, 197

horror films, 4, 35, 158, 177, 199, 241, 224, 241, 280

Ian, Scott (guitarist), 87, 175, 177. *See also* Anthrax, S.O.D.

Ice Cube (rapper), 207

Iced Earth, 319

Ice-T (rapper), 205, 207, 300–01, 302. *See also* Body Count

Ihsahn (singer/guitarist), 275, 276, 278, 280, 286, 288. *See also* Emperor

Immolation, 247

Immortal, 271, 272, 274, 283–84, 286, 357

The beautifully rendered book jacket on *Sound of the Beast* deserves special attention for all heavy metal fans. The painting by metal priestess Madeline von Foerster is based on a section from the massively illustrated underceiling to the sacred Baptistery of San Giovanni—St. John the Baptist—in Florence, Italy. It is part of a huge mosaic that took more than 200 years to construct and was completed in the thirteenth century.

The most prominent monument in its distinguished home city, the Baptistery was owned for centuries by the Merchant's Guild. Its exterior espouses a grand yet plain geometric workaday presence. Inside is contained a most awe-inspiring sight—a lavish gold-paneled tile ceiling depicting hundreds of images of Christ, the Apostles, holy angels, and other religious scenes installed by faithful artisans during a thousand years of devoted labor.

Obscured beside a large rendering of Christ is the most striking element in the fray—a single frieze, the inspiration for the jacket of *Sound of the Beast*. Completely distinct from all the other panels, this segment depicts a hellish and disturbing landscape of the last judgment, where a horned beast has been damned to devour and dispose of sinners while commanding a sea of winged demons, faceless vermin, and all-devouring serpents.

This tableau has already profoundly influenced civilization. Dante himself was baptized in the Baptistery, and was later inspired to write several Cantos of the *Inferno* when he returned and discovered our demonic panel between the more obvious heavenly angels and golden light. When we first saw the frame, we instantly began banging our heads, flipping the devil horns, and turning up the heaviest metal we could find in tribute. We searched for other images beforehand, but this was the only one that did *Sound of the Beast* justice.